W9-AGE-034

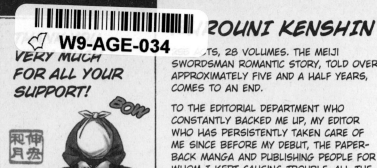

THANK YOU
VERY MUCH
FOR ALL YOUR
SUPPORT!

BOW

和月伸宏

NOBUHIRO WATSUKI

ROUNI KENSHIN

...TS, 28 VOLUMES. THE MEIJI SWORDSMAN ROMANTIC STORY, TOLD OVER APPROXIMATELY FIVE AND A HALF YEARS, COMES TO AN END.

TO THE EDITORIAL DEPARTMENT WHO CONSTANTLY BACKED ME UP, MY EDITOR WHO HAS PERSISTENTLY TAKEN CARE OF ME SINCE BEFORE MY DEBUT, THE PAPER-BACK MANGA AND PUBLISHING PEOPLE FOR WHOM I KEPT CAUSING TROUBLE, ALL THE ASSISTANTS WHO STAYED BY MY SIDE THROUGH THE HARD TIMES, AND THE READERS WHO HAVE THIS BOOK IN HAND NOW...

THANK YOU ALL SO VERY MUCH!!

Rurouni Kenshin, which has found fans not only in Japan but around the world, first made its appearance in 1992, as an original short story in **Weekly Shonen Jump Special**. Later rewritten and published as a regular, continuing **Jump** series in 1994, **Rurouni Kenshin** ended serialization in 1999 but continued in popularity, as evidenced by the 2000 publication of **Yahiko no Sakabatô** ("Yahiko's Reversed-Edge Sword") in **Weekly Shonen Jump**. His most current work, **Buso Renkin** ("Armored Alchemist"), began publication in June 2003, also in **Jump**.

RUROUNI KENSHIN
VOL. 28: TOWARD A NEW ERA
The SHONEN JUMP Manga Edition

STORY AND ART BY
NOBUHIRO WATSUKI

English Adaptation/Pancha Diaz
Translation/Kenichiro Yagi
Touch-Up Art & Lettering/Steve Dutro
Design/Matt Hinrichs
Editor/Kit Fox

Managing Editor/Frances E. Wall
Editorial Director/Elizabeth Kawasaki
VP & Editor in Chief/Yumi Hoashi
Sr. Director of Acquisitions/Rika Inouye
Sr. VP of Marketing/Liza Coppola
Exec. VP of Sales & Marketing/John Easum
Publisher/Hyoe Narita

RUROUNI KENSHIN © 1994 by Nobuhiro Watsuki. All rights reserved. First published in Japan in 1994 by SHUEISHA Inc., Tokyo. English translation rights in the United States of America and Canada arranged by SHUEISHA Inc. The stories, characters and incidents mentioned in this publication are entirely fictional.

No portion of this book may be reproduced or transmitted in any form or by any means without written permission from the copyright holders.

Printed in the U.S.A.

Published by VIZ Media, LLC
P.O. Box 77010
San Francisco, CA 94107

SHONEN JUMP Manga Edition
10 9 8 7 6 5 4 3 2
First printing, July 2006
Second printing, July 2006

T 251694

www.viz.com

PARENTAL ADVISORY
RUROUNI KENSHIN is rated T+ for Older Teen and is recommended for ages 16 and up. This volume contains realistic violence and alcohol and tobacco use.

THE WORLD'S
MOST POPULAR MANGA
www.shonenjump.com

SHONEN JUMP MANGA

Rurouni Kenshin™

STORY & ART BY NOBUHIRO WATSUKI

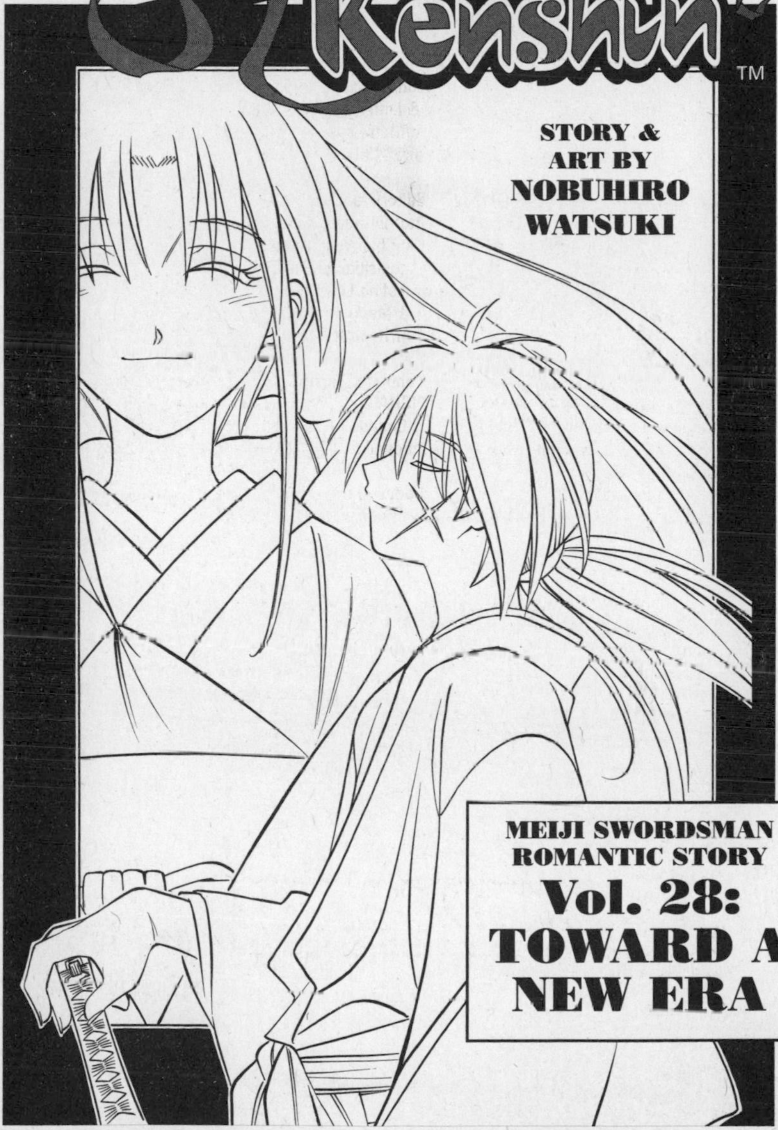

MEIJI SWORDSMAN ROMANTIC STORY

Vol. 28: TOWARD A NEW ERA

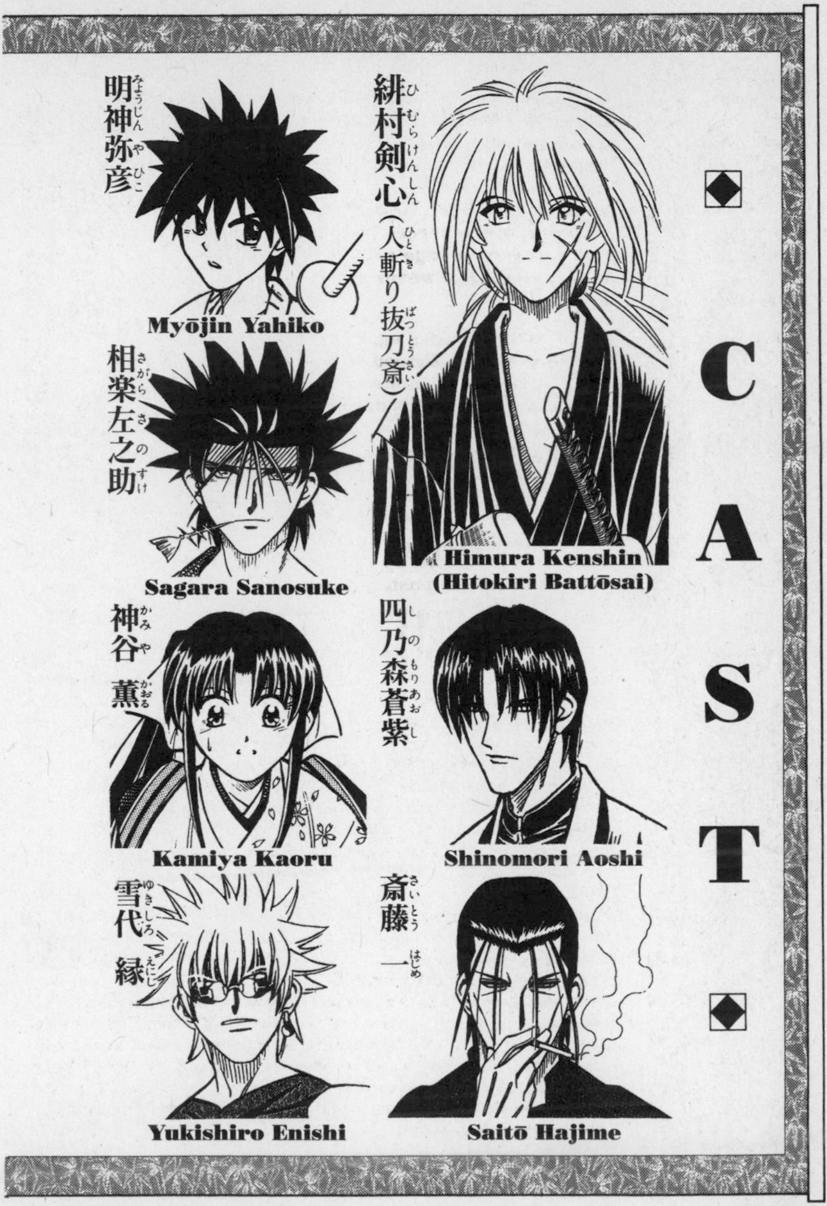
CAST
緋村剣心（人斬り抜刀斎）
Himura Kenshin
(Hitokiri Battōsai)
明神弥彦
Myōjin Yahiko
相楽左之助
Sagara Sanosuke
四乃森蒼紫
Shinomori Aoshi
神谷薫
Kamiya Kaoru
斎藤一
Saitō Hajime
雪代縁
Yukishiro Enishi

Once he was *hitokiri*, an assassin, called Battōsai. His name was legend among the pro-Imperialist or "patriot" warriors who launched the Meiji Era. Now, Himura Kenshin is *rurouni*, a wanderer, and carries a reversed-edge *sakabatō* blade, vowing to never kill another soul.

Those with grudges against Battōsai have gathered to take their revenge. To make matters worse, Kenshin finds out that the mastermind of this new attack is Enishi, the brother of Kenshin's deceased wife Tomoe—who died at Kenshin's own hand. And yet Kenshin decides to fight in order to protect the present, and begins by telling his friends of his past.

高荷恵 (たかに めぐみ)

Takani Megumi

巻町操 (まきまち みさお)

Makimachi Misao

THUS FAR

Enishi and his crew appear midair above the Kamiya dojo in hot air balloons. In the midst of the battle that follows, Enishi murders Kaoru. Overwhelmed by the guilt of not saving Kaoru, Kenshin exiles himself to the "Fallen Village." However, the others discover that Kaoru's body is actually one of the "corpse dolls" created by Gein. Kaoru has been spirited away to the island in Tokyo bay that Enishi's organization uses as a relay point. When a friend must beg Kenshin for help, he is finally able to realize the truth he holds within himself, a truth he cannot abandon. Kenshin sets out with his six comrades to rescue Kaoru, but upon reaching the island, Woo Heishin and his *Sū-shin* bodyguards are waiting to challenge them. Four battles commence—Saitō vs. Seiryū, Aoshi vs. Suzaku, Sanosuke vs. Byakko and Yahiko vs. Genbu—and are won by Kenshin's allies. Then Kaoru appears, and in front of the now-complete audience, the duel between Enishi and Kenshin begins. Enishi's strength has increased since his attack on the dojo, but Kenshin is fortified by the power of the truth he has discovered. Unwavering, Kenshin faces Enishi's *Kyōkeimyaku* (Frenzied Nerves) with his own *Ryūmeisen* (Dragon Howl Strike)...

CONTENTS

RUROUNI KENSHIN
Meiji Swordsman Romantic Story
BOOK TWENTY-EIGHT: TOWARD A NEW ERA

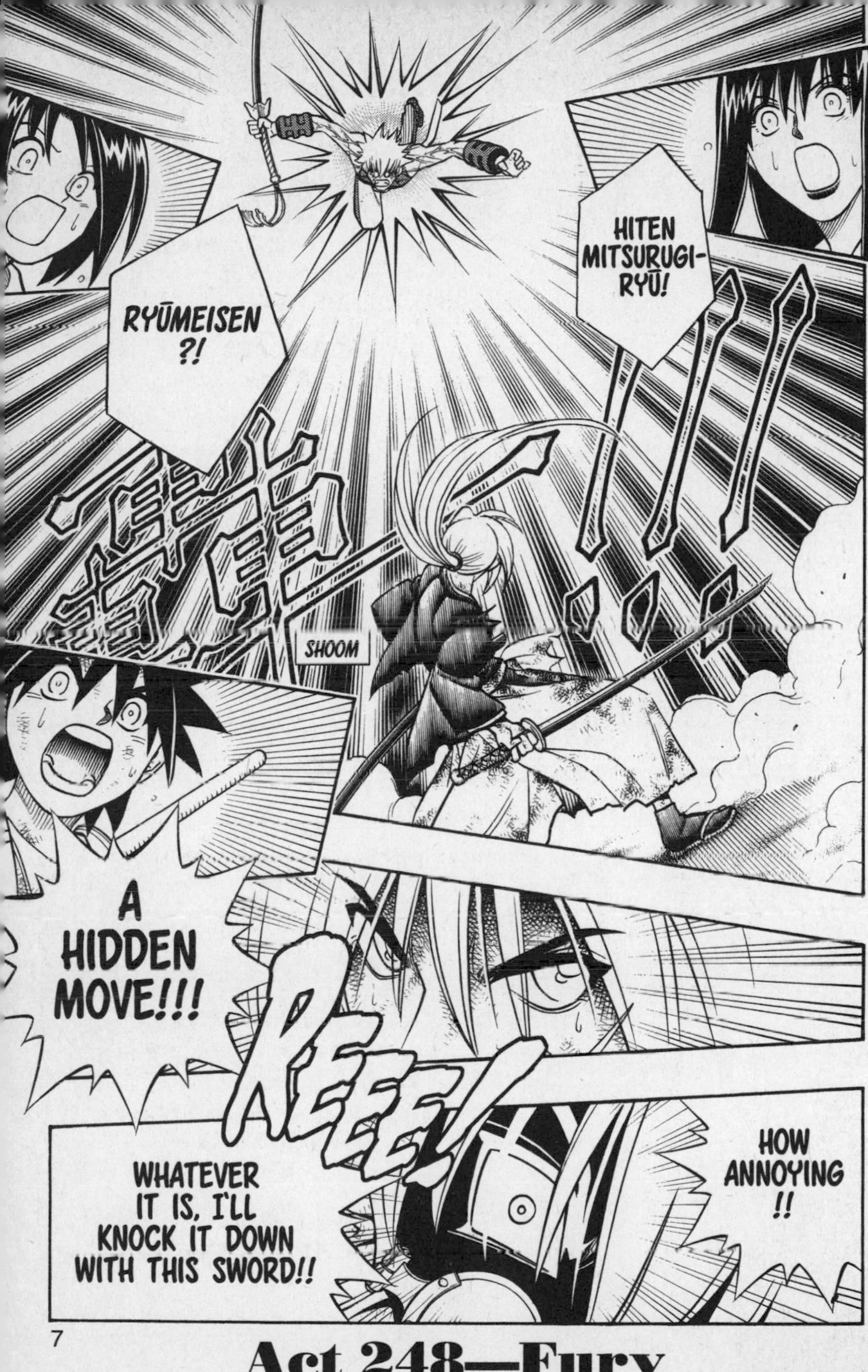
HITEN MITSURUGI-RYŪ!
RYŪMEISEN ?!
SHOOM
A HIDDEN MOVE!!!
REEE!
HOW ANNOYING !!
WHATEVER IT IS, I'LL KNOCK IT DOWN WITH THIS SWORD!!

Act 248—Fury

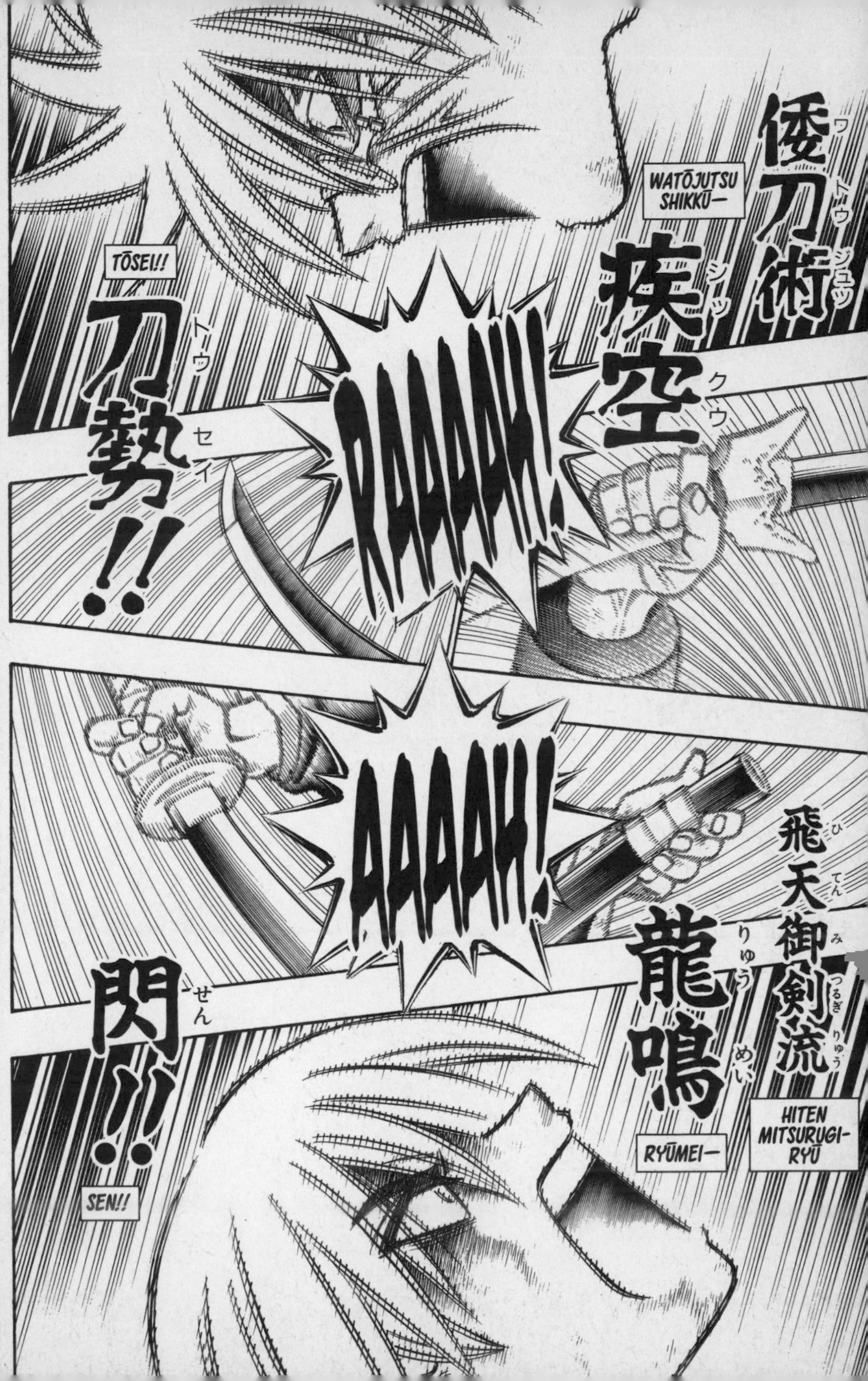
倭刀術
WATŌJUTSU SHIKKŪ—
疾空
刀勢!!
TŌSEI!!
RAAAAH!
飛天御剣流
HITEN MITSURUGI-RYŪ
龍鳴
RYŪMEI—
AAAAH!
閃!!
SEN!!

Act 248—Fury

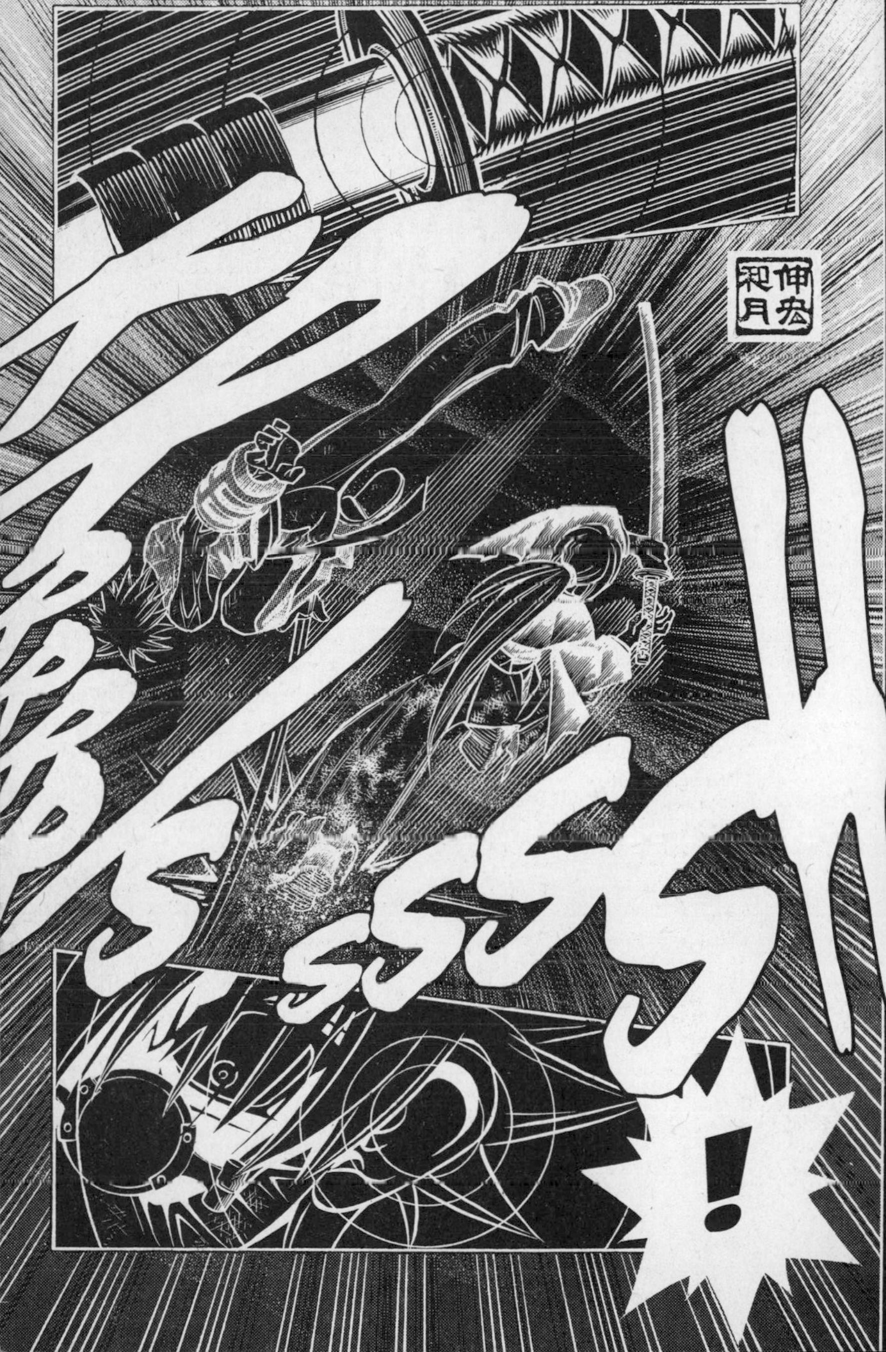
伸宏和月

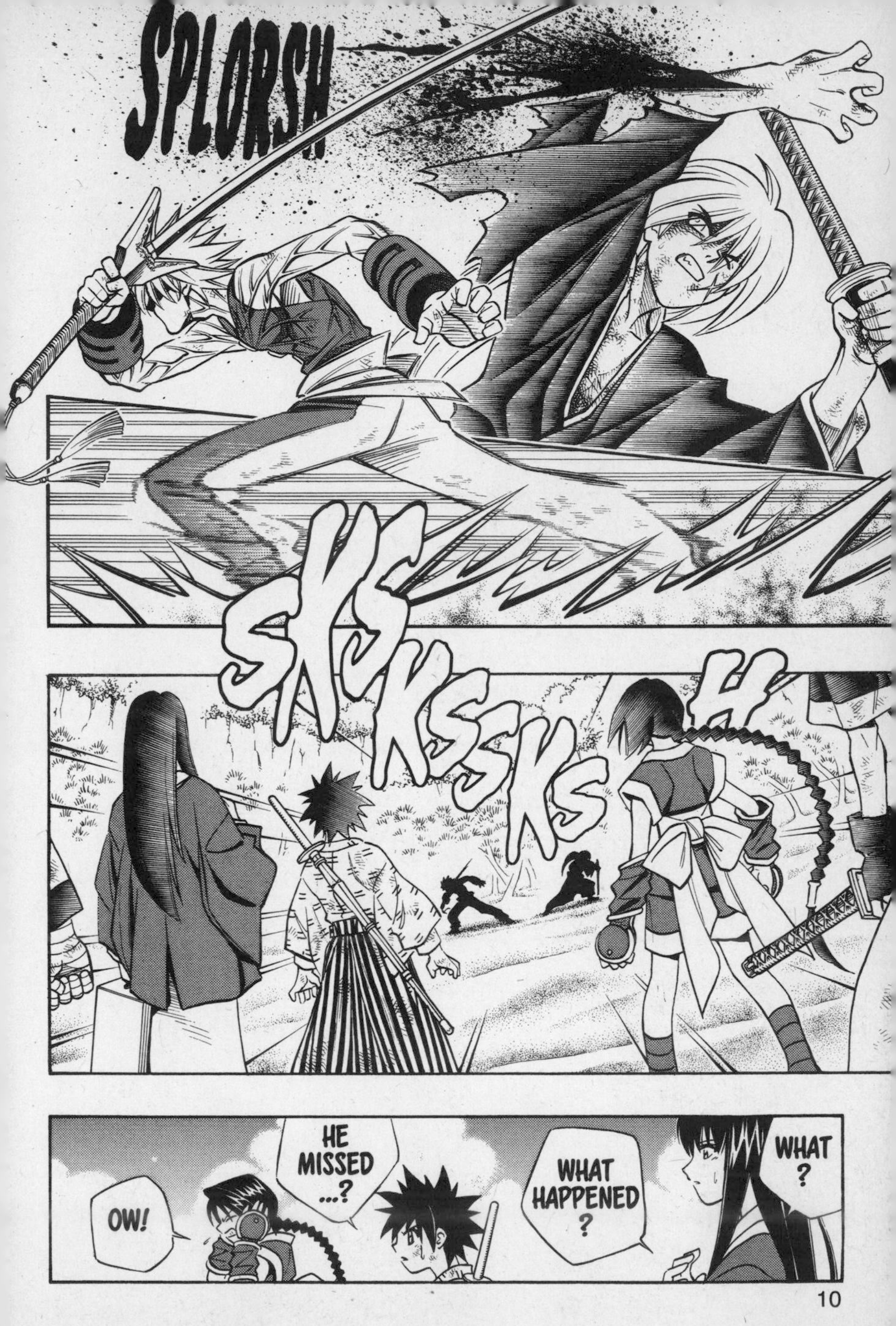
SPLORSH
WHAT?
WHAT HAPPENED?
HE MISSED...?
OW!

READ THIS WAY

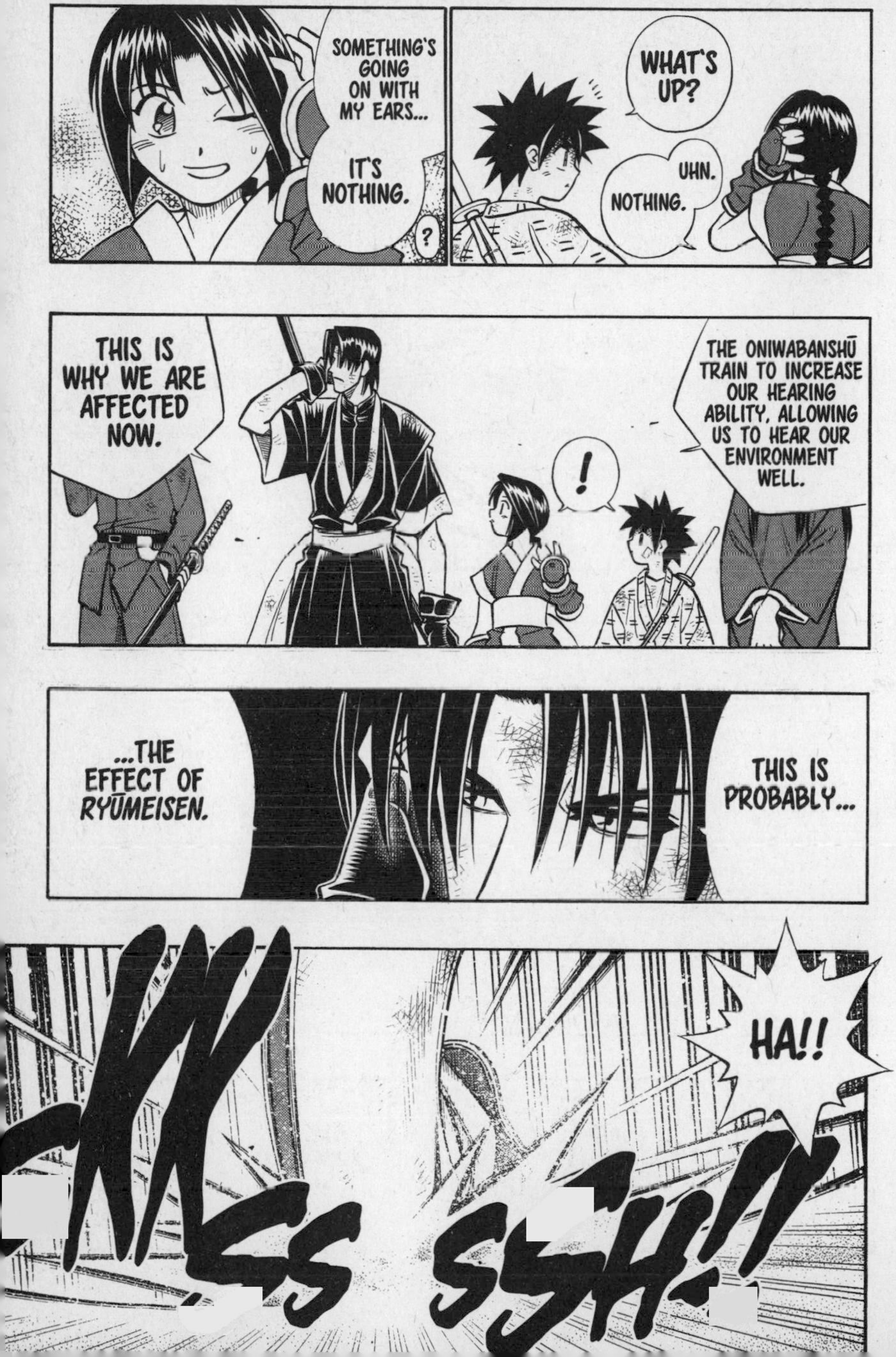
WHAT'S UP?
UHN. NOTHING.
SOMETHING'S GOING ON WITH MY EARS...
IT'S NOTHING.
?
THE ONIWABANSHŪ TRAIN TO INCREASE OUR HEARING ABILITY, ALLOWING US TO HEAR OUR ENVIRONMENT WELL.
!
THIS IS WHY WE ARE AFFECTED NOW.
THIS IS PROBABLY...
...THE EFFECT OF RYŪMEISEN.
HA!!

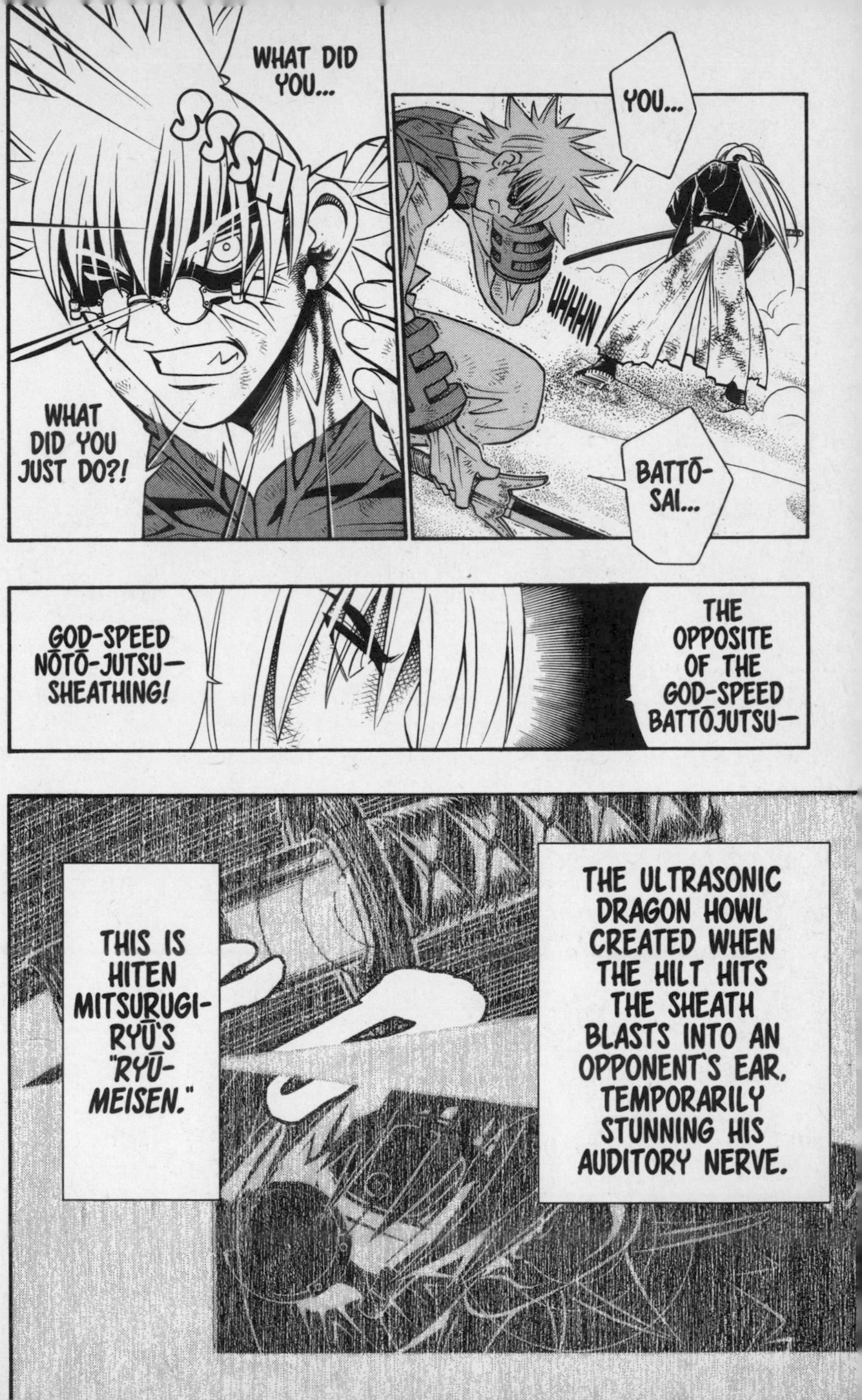
YOU...
UHHHN
BATTŌ-SAI...
WHAT DID YOU...
SSSH
WHAT DID YOU JUST DO?!
THE OPPOSITE OF THE GOD-SPEED BATTŌJUTSU—
GOD-SPEED NŌTŌ-JUTSU— SHEATHING!
THE ULTRASONIC DRAGON HOWL CREATED WHEN THE HILT HITS THE SHEATH BLASTS INTO AN OPPONENT'S EAR, TEMPORARILY STUNNING HIS AUDITORY NERVE.
THIS IS HITEN MITSURUGI-RYŪ'S "RYŪ-MEISEN."

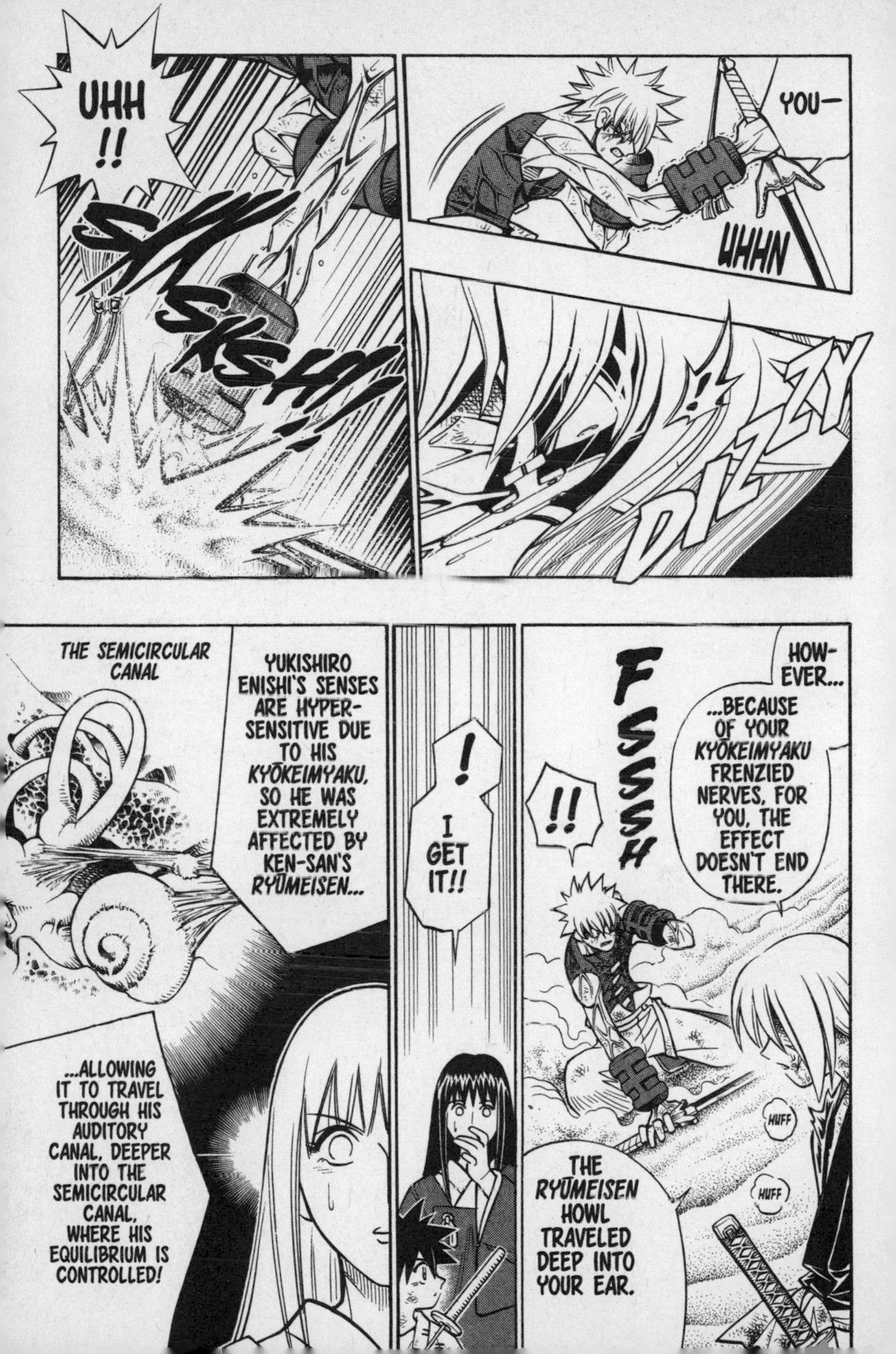
YOU—
UHHN
!
DIZZY
UHH!!
SHKSHH!!
HOW-EVER...
...BECAUSE OF YOUR KYŌKEIMYAKU FRENZIED NERVES, FOR YOU, THE EFFECT DOESN'T END THERE.
FSSSH
!!
THE RYŪMEISEN HOWL TRAVELED DEEP INTO YOUR EAR.
HUFF
HUFF
!
I GET IT!!
YUKISHIRO ENISHI'S SENSES ARE HYPER-SENSITIVE DUE TO HIS KYŌKEIMYAKU, SO HE WAS EXTREMELY AFFECTED BY KEN-SAN'S RYŪMEISEN...
THE SEMICIRCULAR CANAL
...ALLOWING IT TO TRAVEL THROUGH HIS AUDITORY CANAL, DEEPER INTO THE SEMICIRCULAR CANAL, WHERE HIS EQUILIBRIUM IS CONTROLLED!

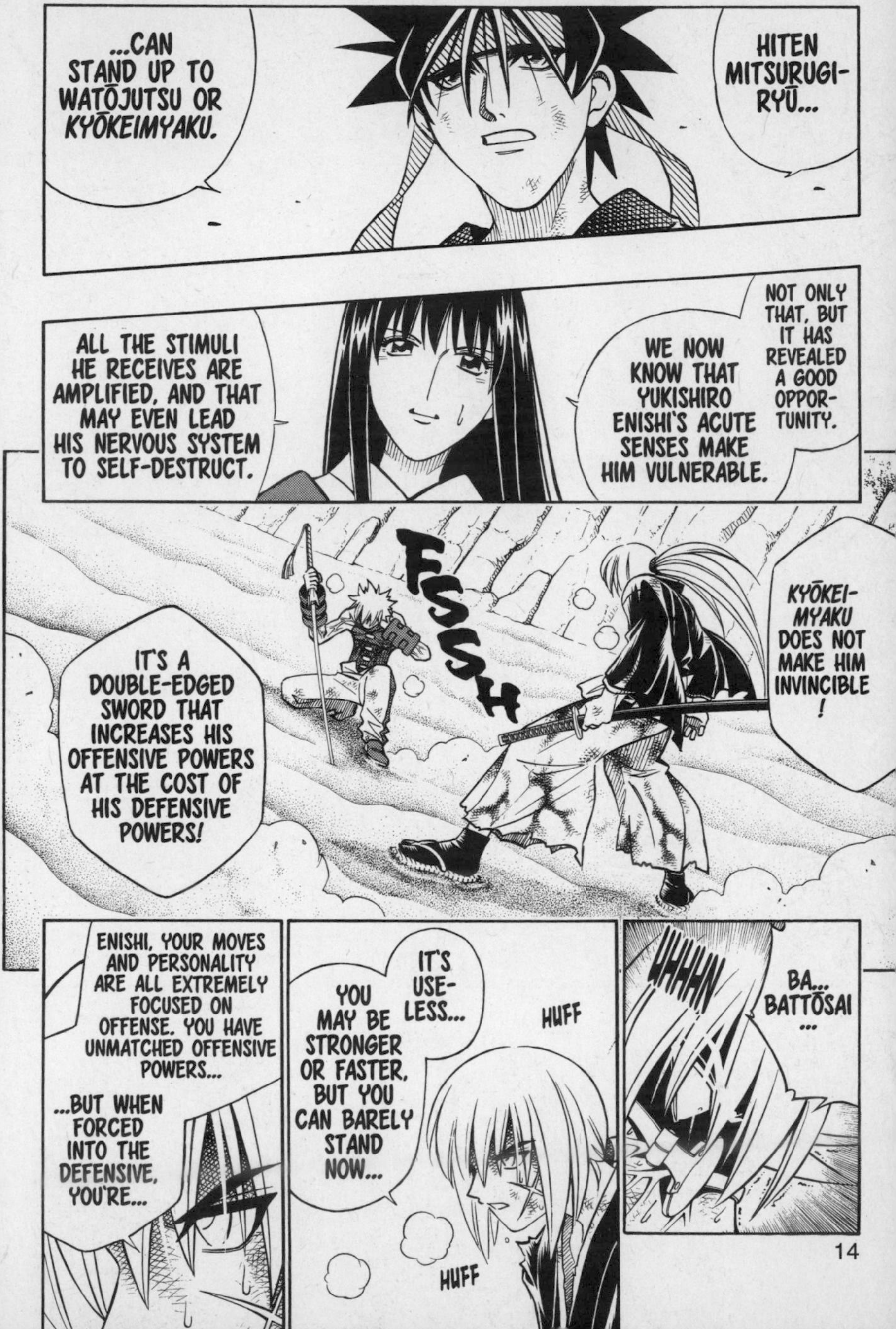
HITEN MITSURUGI-RYŪ...
...CAN STAND UP TO WATŌJUTSU OR KYŌKEIMYAKU.
NOT ONLY THAT, BUT IT HAS REVEALED A GOOD OPPORTUNITY.
WE NOW KNOW THAT YUKISHIRO ENISHI'S ACUTE SENSES MAKE HIM VULNERABLE.
ALL THE STIMULI HE RECEIVES ARE AMPLIFIED, AND THAT MAY EVEN LEAD HIS NERVOUS SYSTEM TO SELF-DESTRUCT.
KYŌKEIMYAKU DOES NOT MAKE HIM INVINCIBLE!
FSSSH
IT'S A DOUBLE-EDGED SWORD THAT INCREASES HIS OFFENSIVE POWERS AT THE COST OF HIS DEFENSIVE POWERS!
UHHHN
BA... BATTŌSAI...
HUFF
IT'S USELESS...
YOU MAY BE STRONGER OR FASTER, BUT YOU CAN BARELY STAND NOW...
HUFF
ENISHI, YOUR MOVES AND PERSONALITY ARE ALL EXTREMELY FOCUSED ON OFFENSE. YOU HAVE UNMATCHED OFFENSIVE POWERS...
...BUT WHEN FORCED INTO THE DEFENSIVE, YOU'RE...

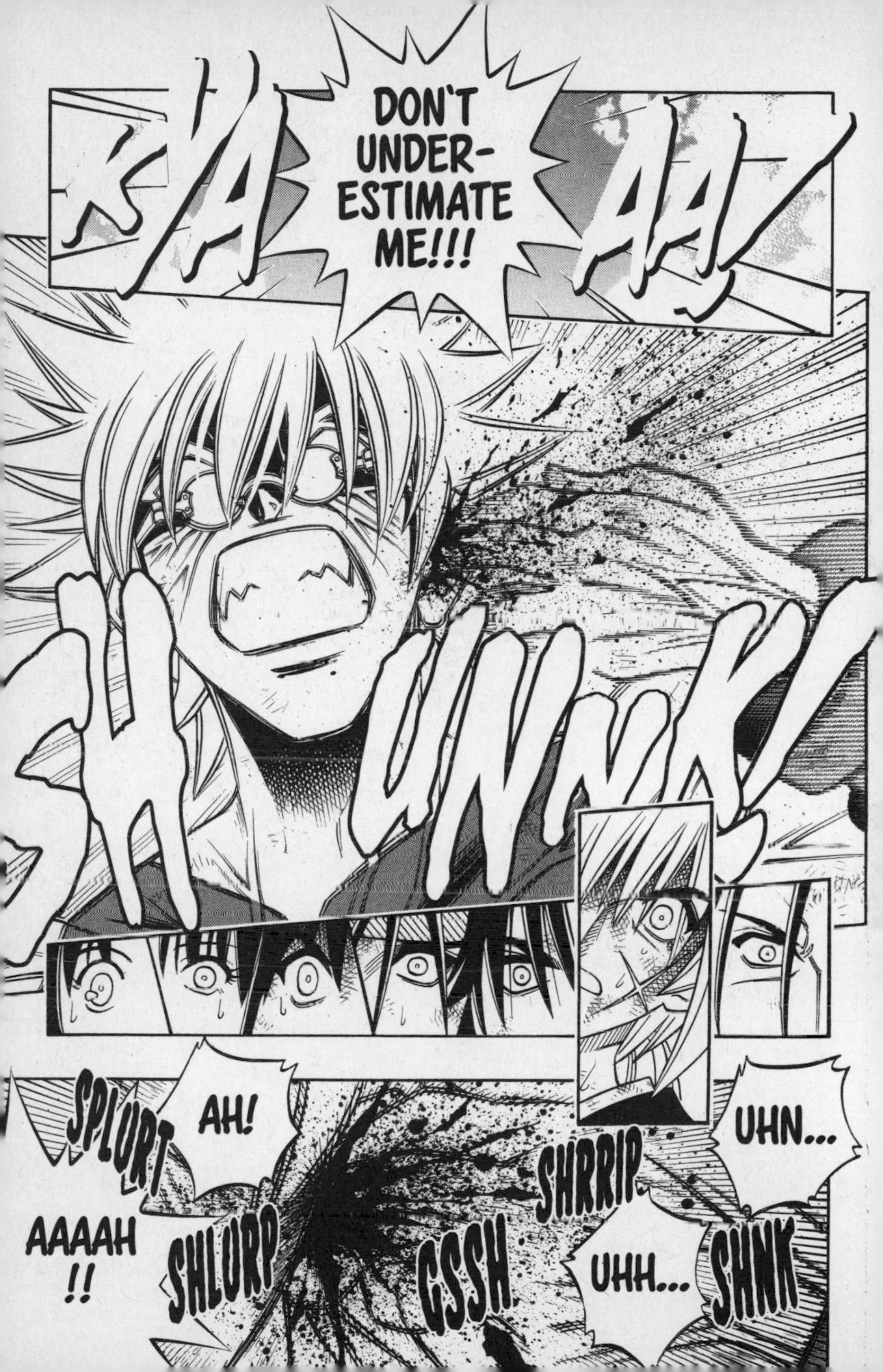
KA
DON'T UNDER-ESTIMATE ME!!!
AA!
SHUNK!
UHN...
SHRRIP
SHNK
UHH...
GSSH
SHLURP
AH!
SPLURT
AAAAH !!

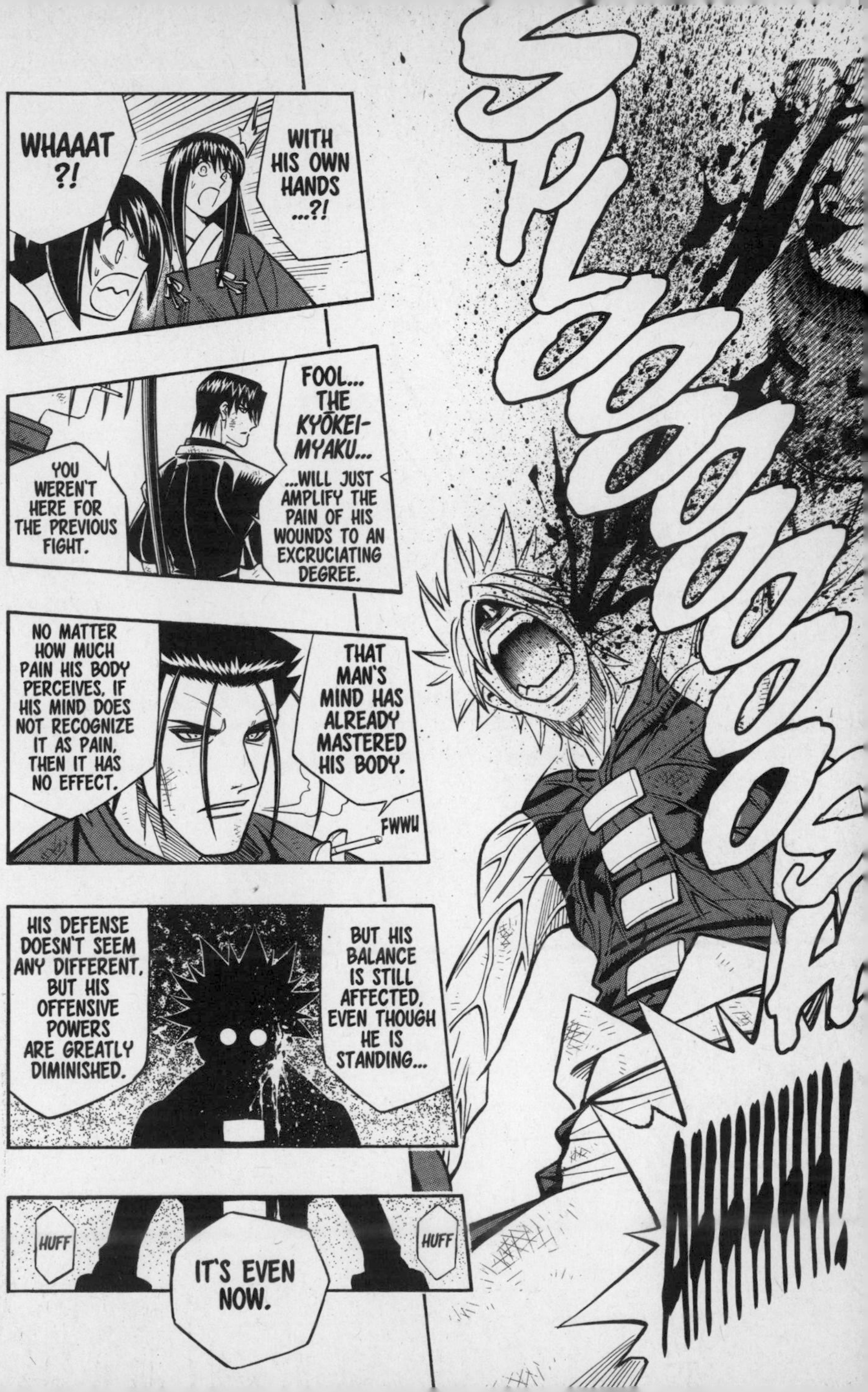
SPLOOOOOOOSH
AHHHHHH!
WITH HIS OWN HANDS ...?!
WHAAAT ?!
FOOL... THE KYŌKEI-MYAKU... ...WILL JUST AMPLIFY THE PAIN OF HIS WOUNDS TO AN EXCRUCIATING DEGREE.
YOU WEREN'T HERE FOR THE PREVIOUS FIGHT.
THAT MAN'S MIND HAS ALREADY MASTERED HIS BODY.
FWWU
NO MATTER HOW MUCH PAIN HIS BODY PERCEIVES, IF HIS MIND DOES NOT RECOGNIZE IT AS PAIN, THEN IT HAS NO EFFECT.
BUT HIS BALANCE IS STILL AFFECTED, EVEN THOUGH HE IS STANDING...
HIS DEFENSE DOESN'T SEEM ANY DIFFERENT, BUT HIS OFFENSIVE POWERS ARE GREATLY DIMINISHED.
HUFF
IT'S EVEN NOW.
HUFF

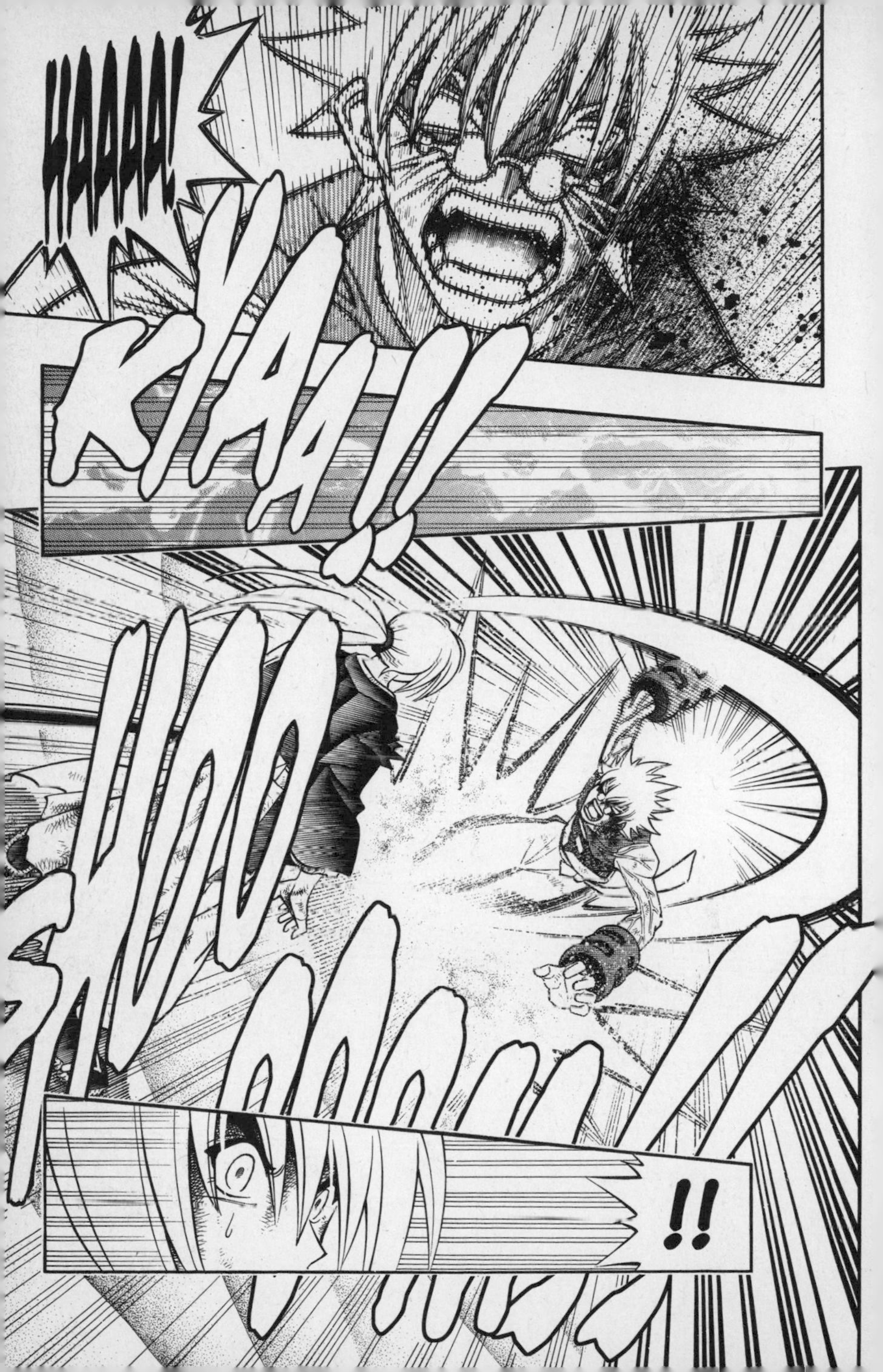
HAAAA!
KIYAA!!
!!

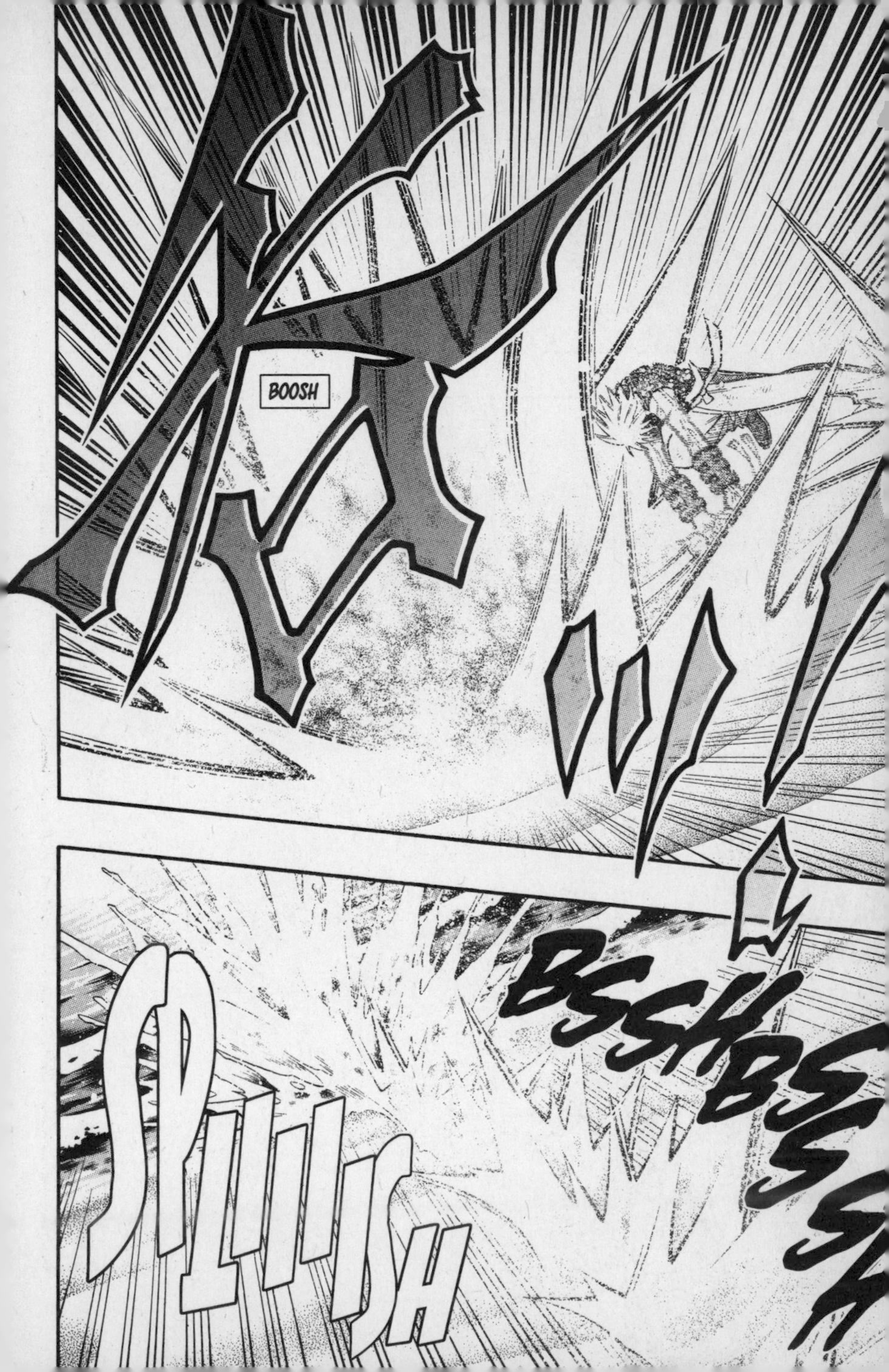
BOOSH

READ THIS WAY

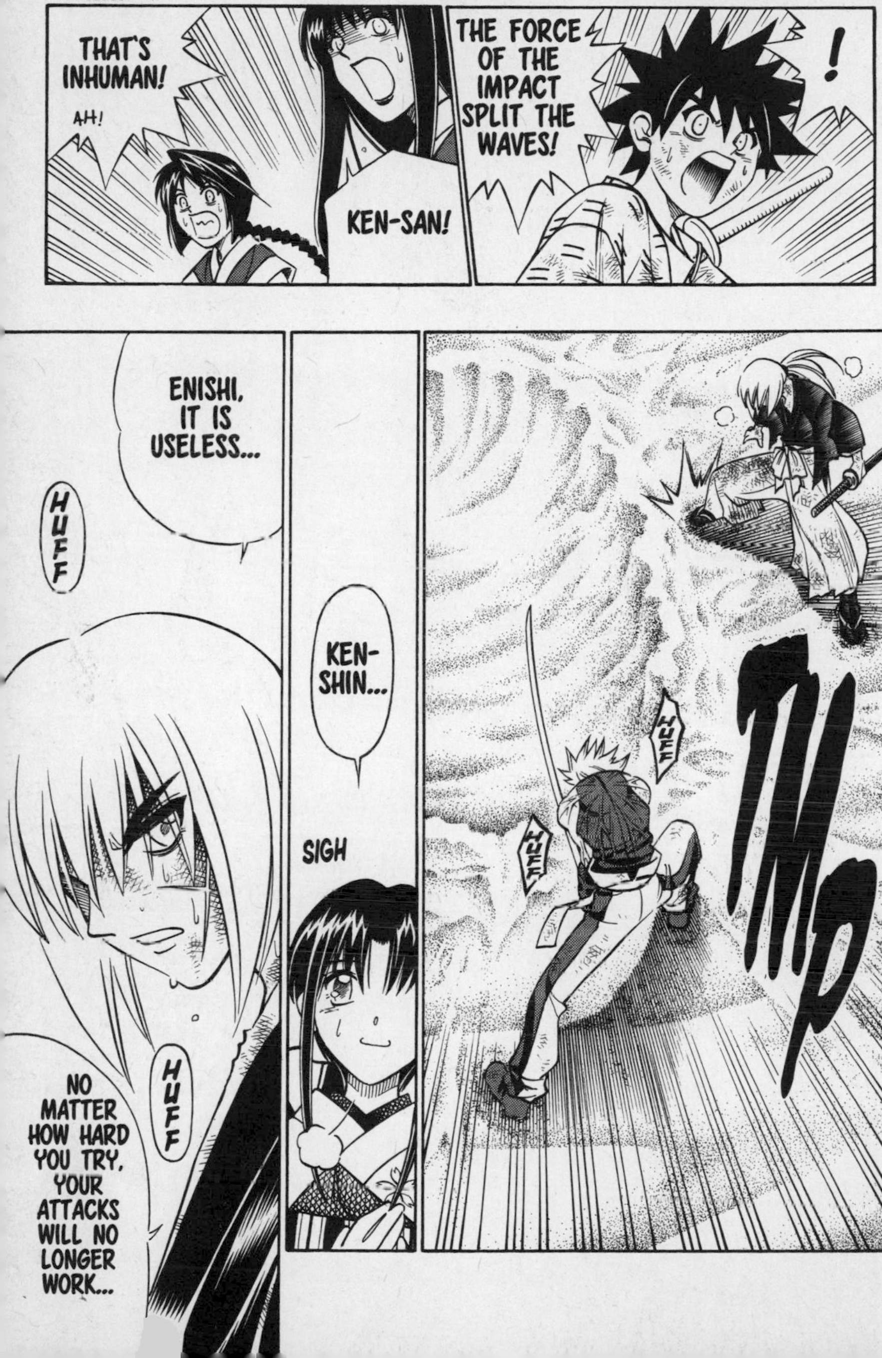
THE FORCE OF THE IMPACT SPLIT THE WAVES!
!
THAT'S INHUMAN!
AH!
KEN-SAN!
HUFF
HUFF
TMP
KEN-SHIN...
SIGH
ENISHI, IT IS USELESS...
HUFF
HUFF
NO MATTER HOW HARD YOU TRY, YOUR ATTACKS WILL NO LONGER WORK...

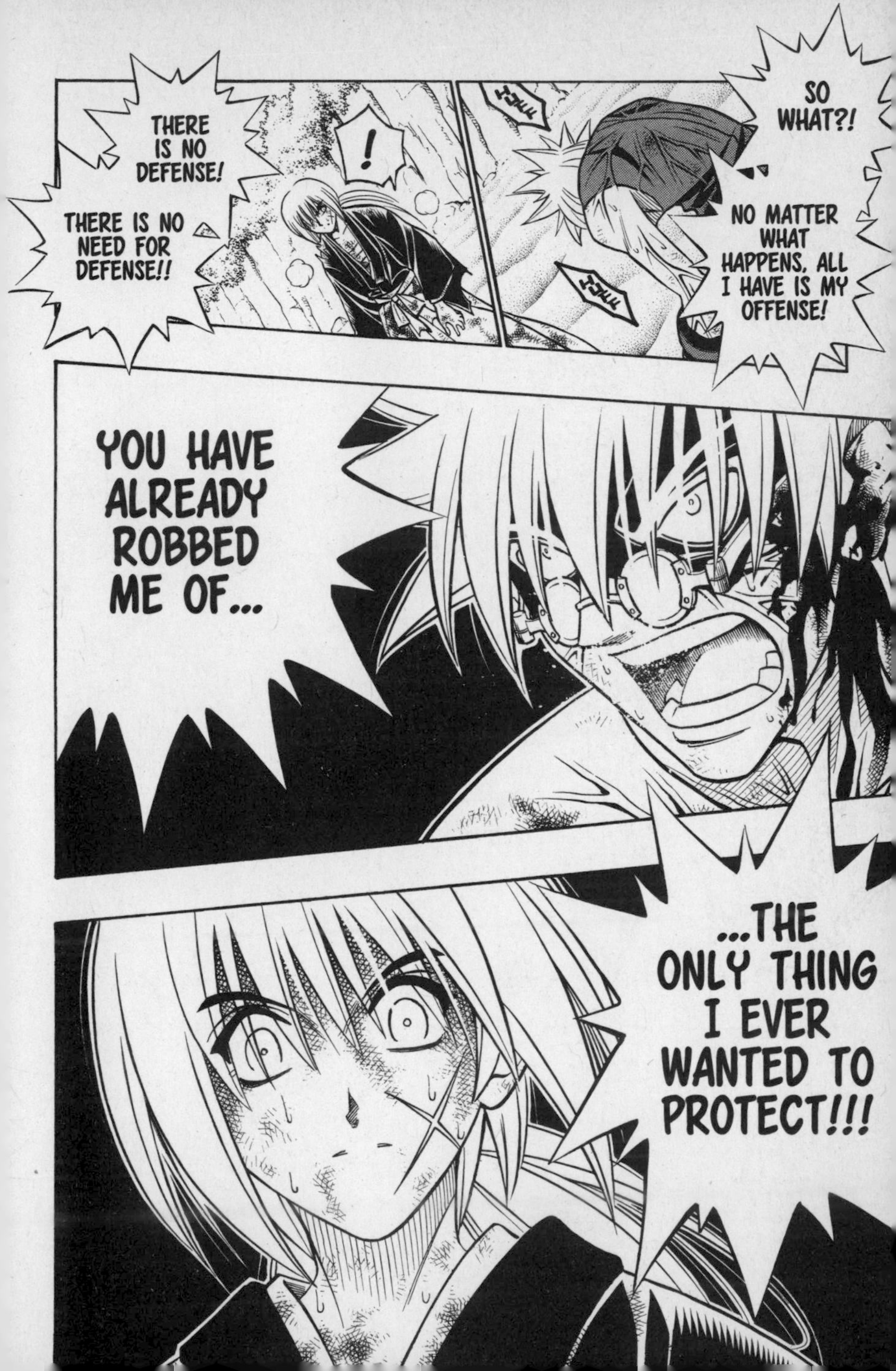
THERE IS NO DEFENSE!
THERE IS NO NEED FOR DEFENSE!!
!
SO WHAT?!
NO MATTER WHAT HAPPENS, ALL I HAVE IS MY OFFENSE!
YOU HAVE ALREADY ROBBED ME OF...
...THE ONLY THING I EVER WANTED TO PROTECT!!!

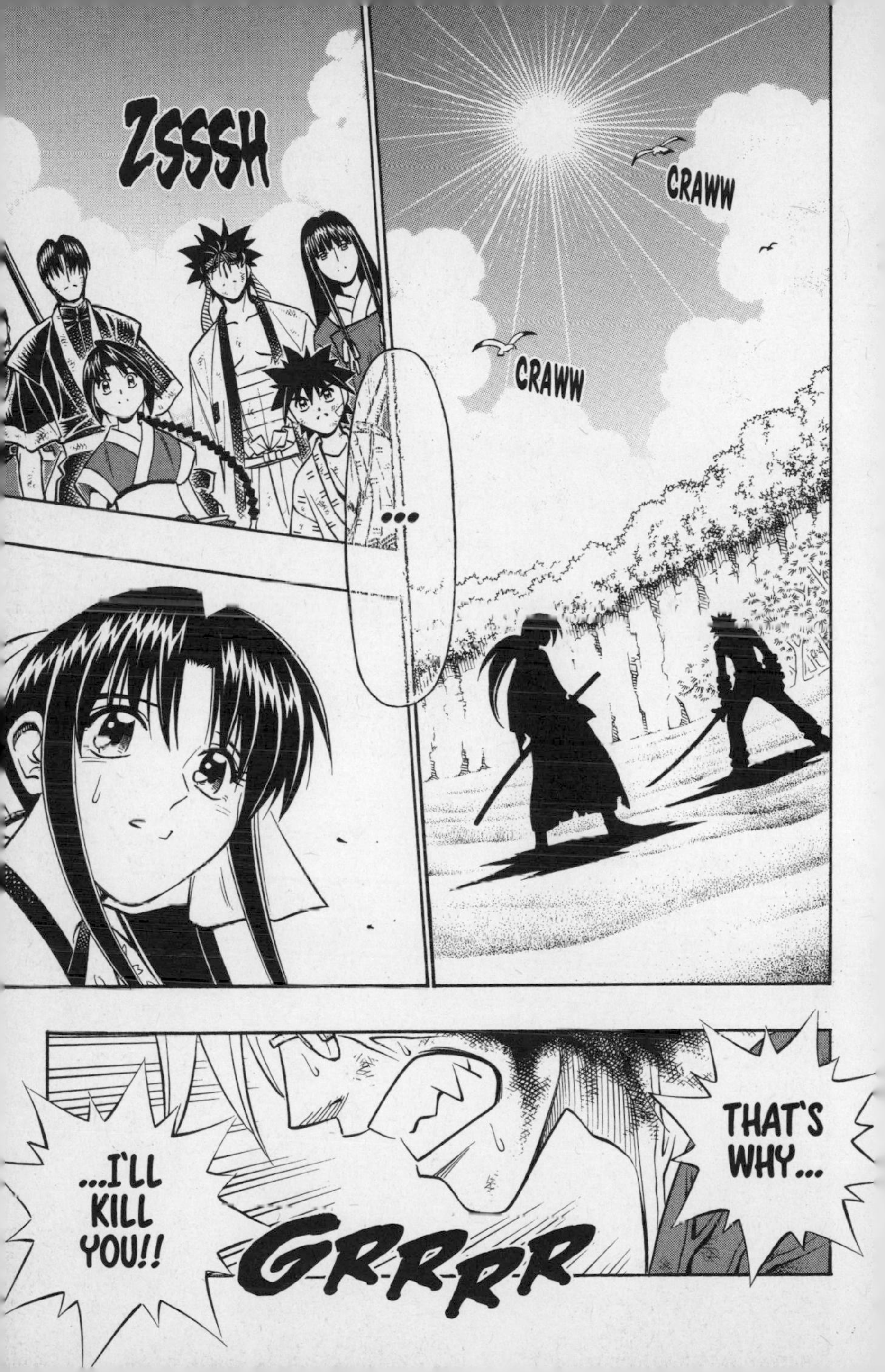
CRAWW
CRAWW
ZSSSH
...
THAT'S WHY...
GRRRR
...I'LL KILL YOU!!

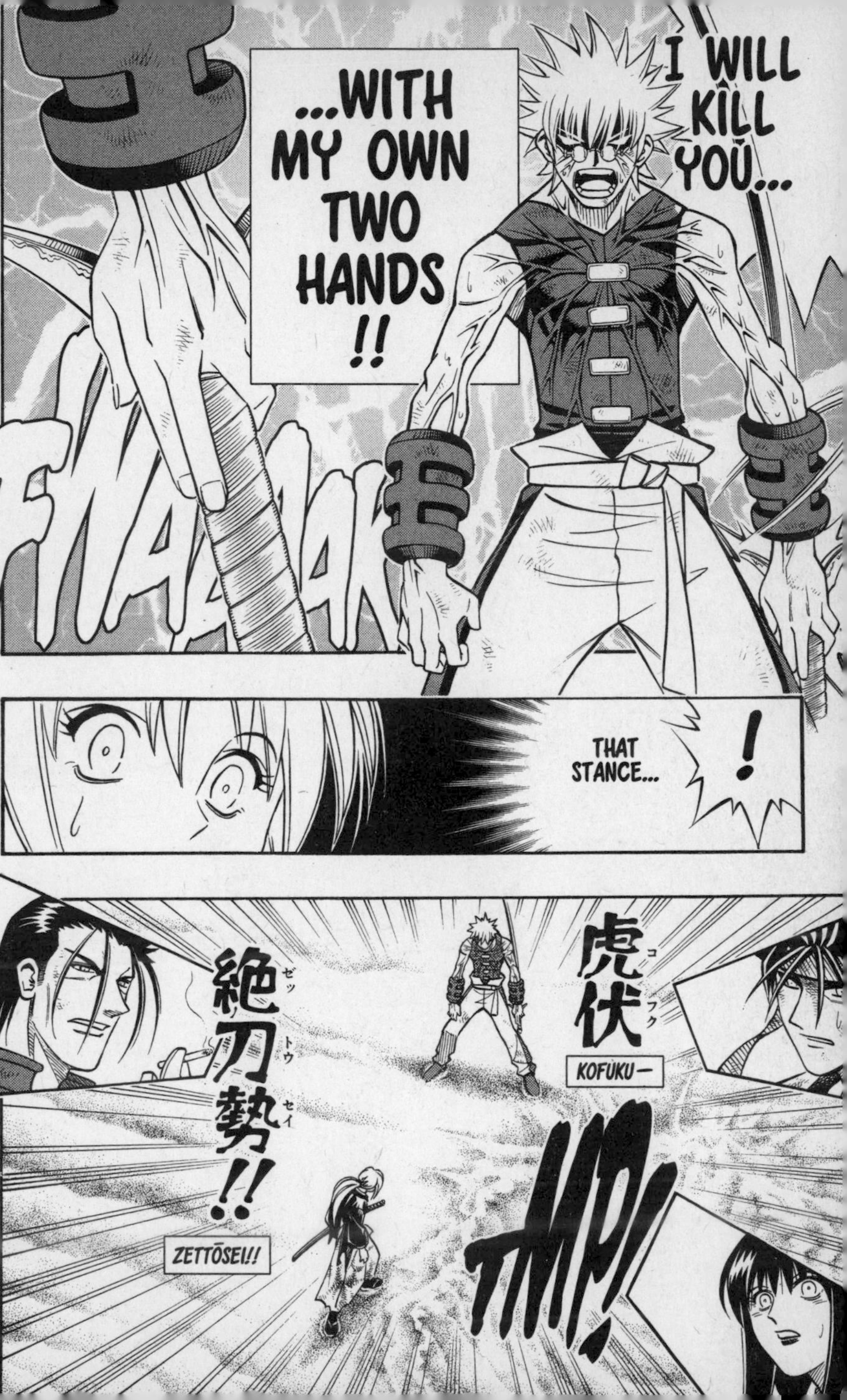
I WILL KILL YOU...
...WITH MY OWN TWO HANDS!!
!
THAT STANCE...
虎伏
KOFUKU—
THMP!
絶刀勢!!
ZETTŌSEI!!

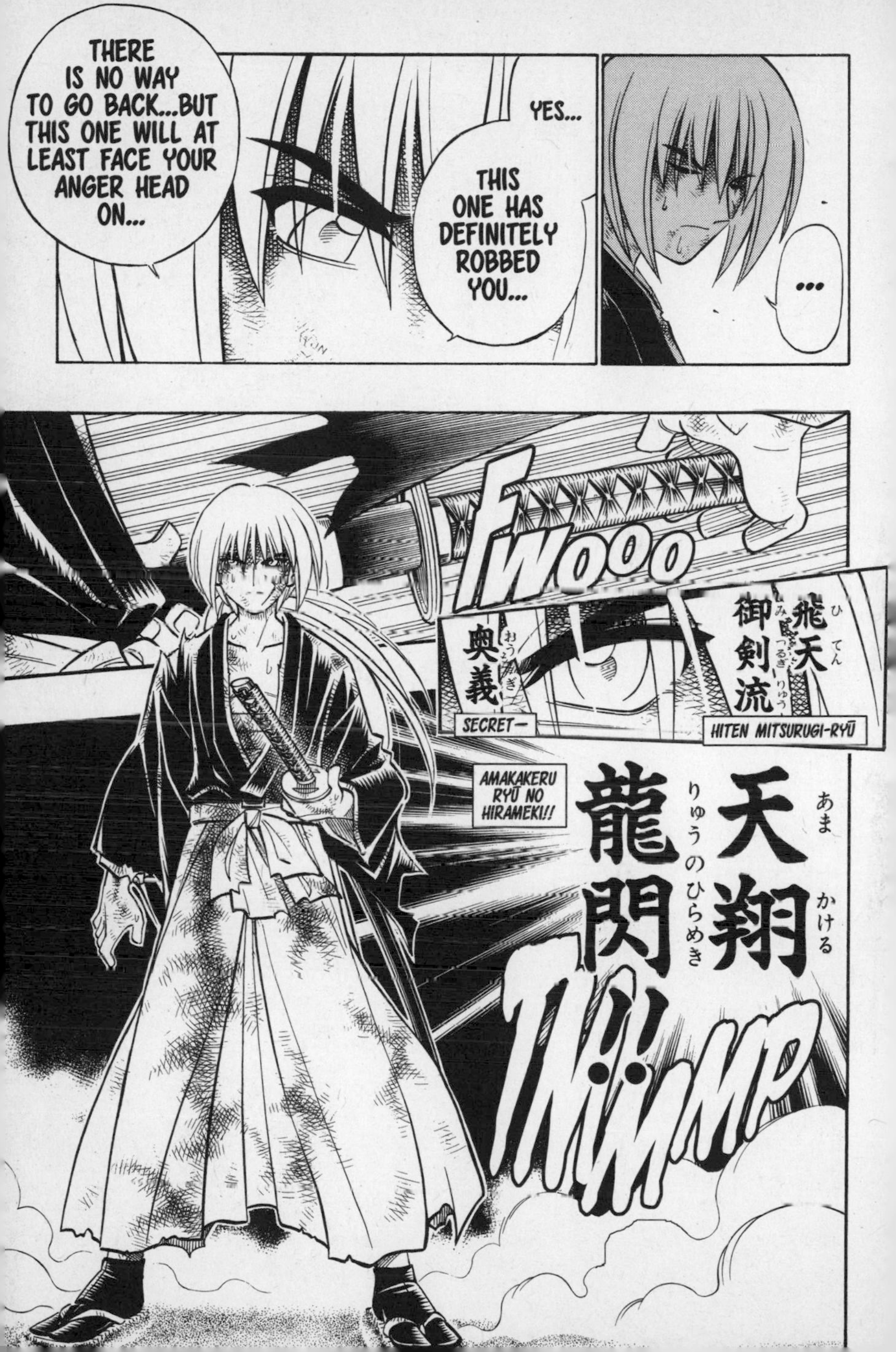
...
YES...
THIS ONE HAS DEFINITELY ROBBED YOU...
THERE IS NO WAY TO GO BACK...BUT THIS ONE WILL AT LEAST FACE YOUR ANGER HEAD ON...
FWOOO
飛天御剣流
HITEN MITSURUGI-RYŪ
奥義
SECRET—
天翔龍閃
AMAKAKERU RYŪ NO HIRAMEKI!!
THWUMP

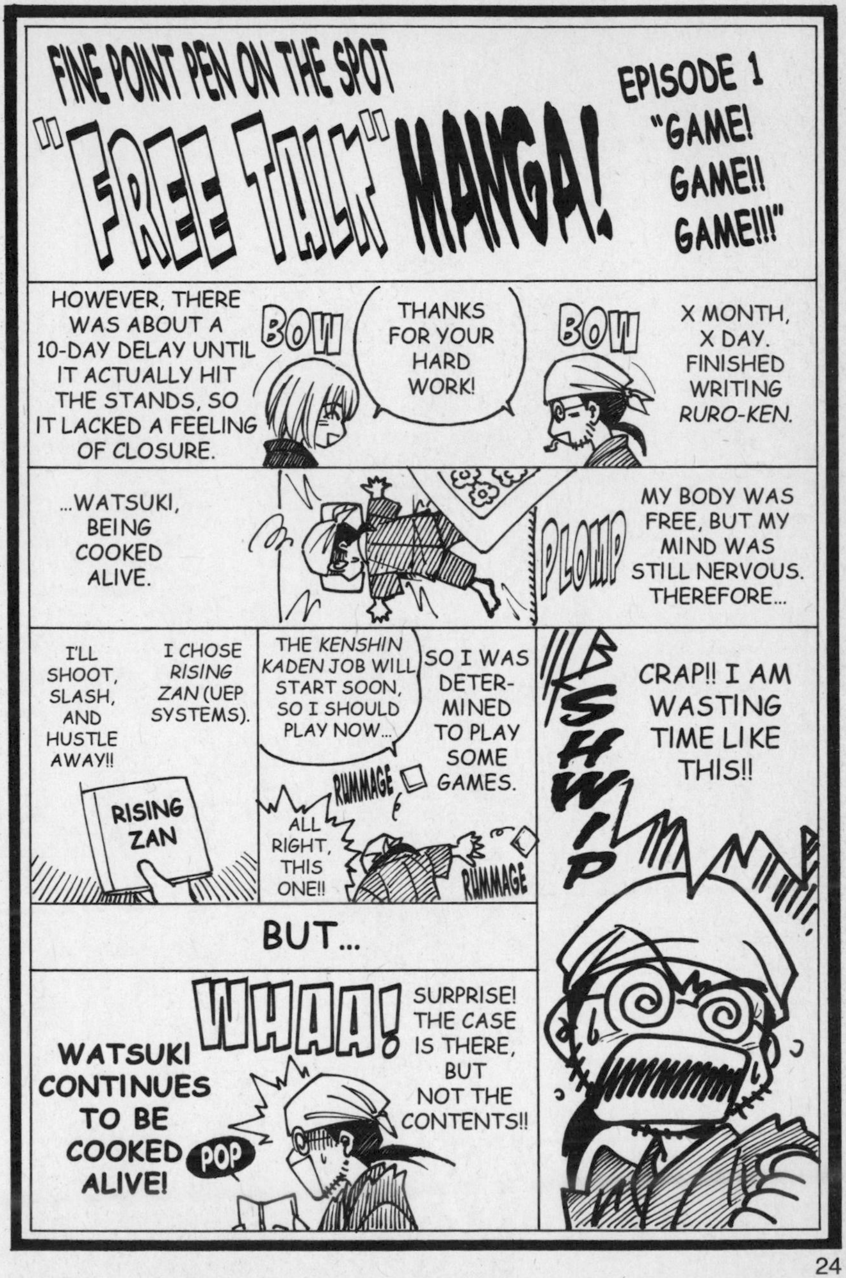
FINE POINT PEN ON THE SPOT
"FREE TALK" MANGA!
EPISODE 1
"GAME! GAME!! GAME!!!"
X MONTH, X DAY. FINISHED WRITING *RURO-KEN*.
BOW
THANKS FOR YOUR HARD WORK!
BOW
HOWEVER, THERE WAS ABOUT A 10-DAY DELAY UNTIL IT ACTUALLY HIT THE STANDS, SO IT LACKED A FEELING OF CLOSURE.
MY BODY WAS FREE, BUT MY MIND WAS STILL NERVOUS. THEREFORE...
PLOMP
...WATSUKI, BEING COOKED ALIVE.
CRAP!! I AM WASTING TIME LIKE THIS!!
SHWIP
SO I WAS DETERMINED TO PLAY SOME GAMES.
THE *KENSHIN KADEN* JOB WILL START SOON, SO I SHOULD PLAY NOW...
RUMMAGE
ALL RIGHT, THIS ONE!!
RUMMAGE
I CHOSE *RISING ZAN* (UEP SYSTEMS).
I'LL SHOOT, SLASH, AND HUSTLE AWAY!!
RISING ZAN
BUT...
SURPRISE! THE CASE IS THERE, BUT NOT THE CONTENTS!!
WHAA!
POP
WATSUKI CONTINUES TO BE COOKED ALIVE!

Act 249—A New Step

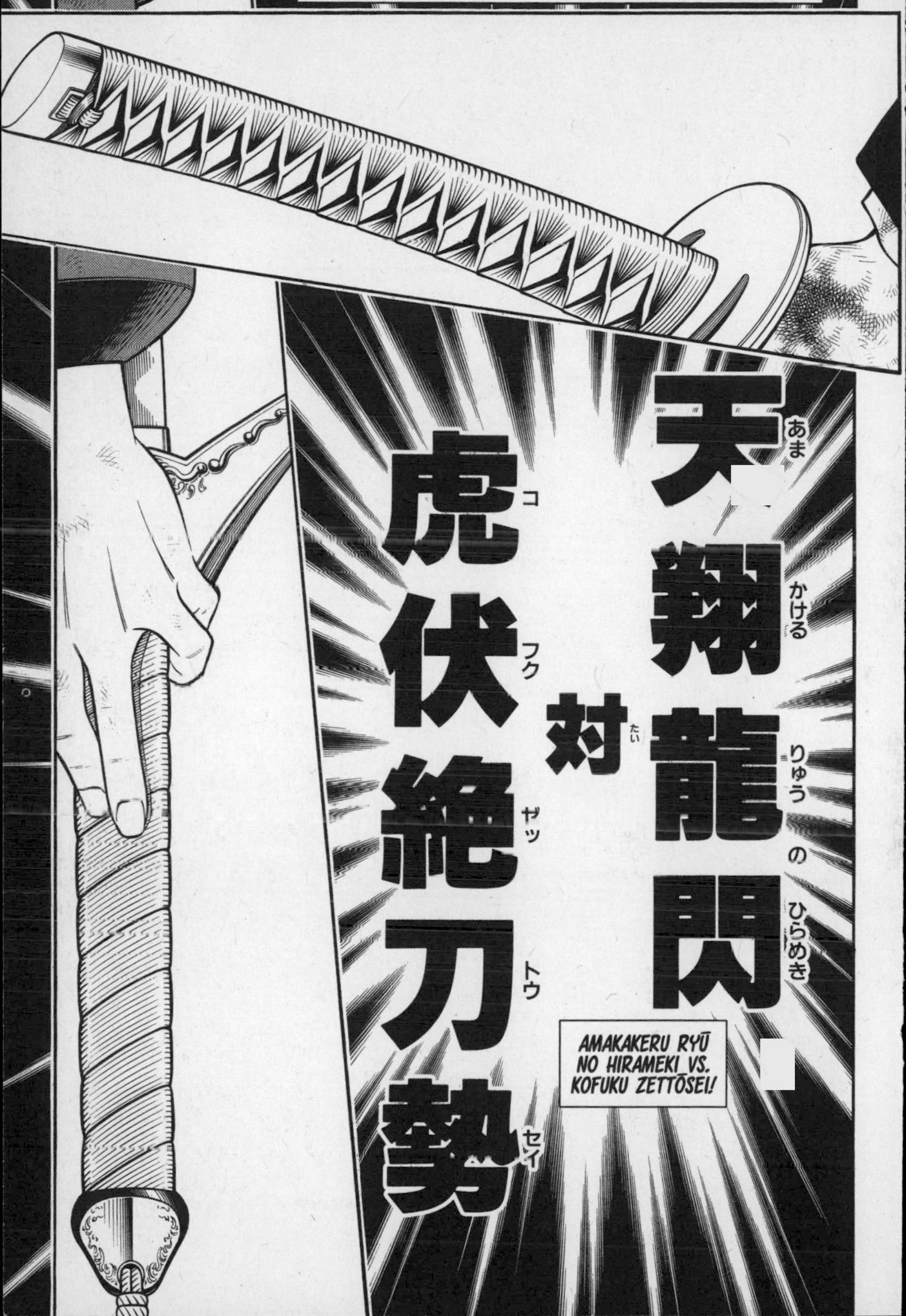
天翔龍閃
対
虎伏絶刀勢
AMAKAKERU RYŪ NO HIRAMEKI VS. KOFUKU ZETTŌSEI!

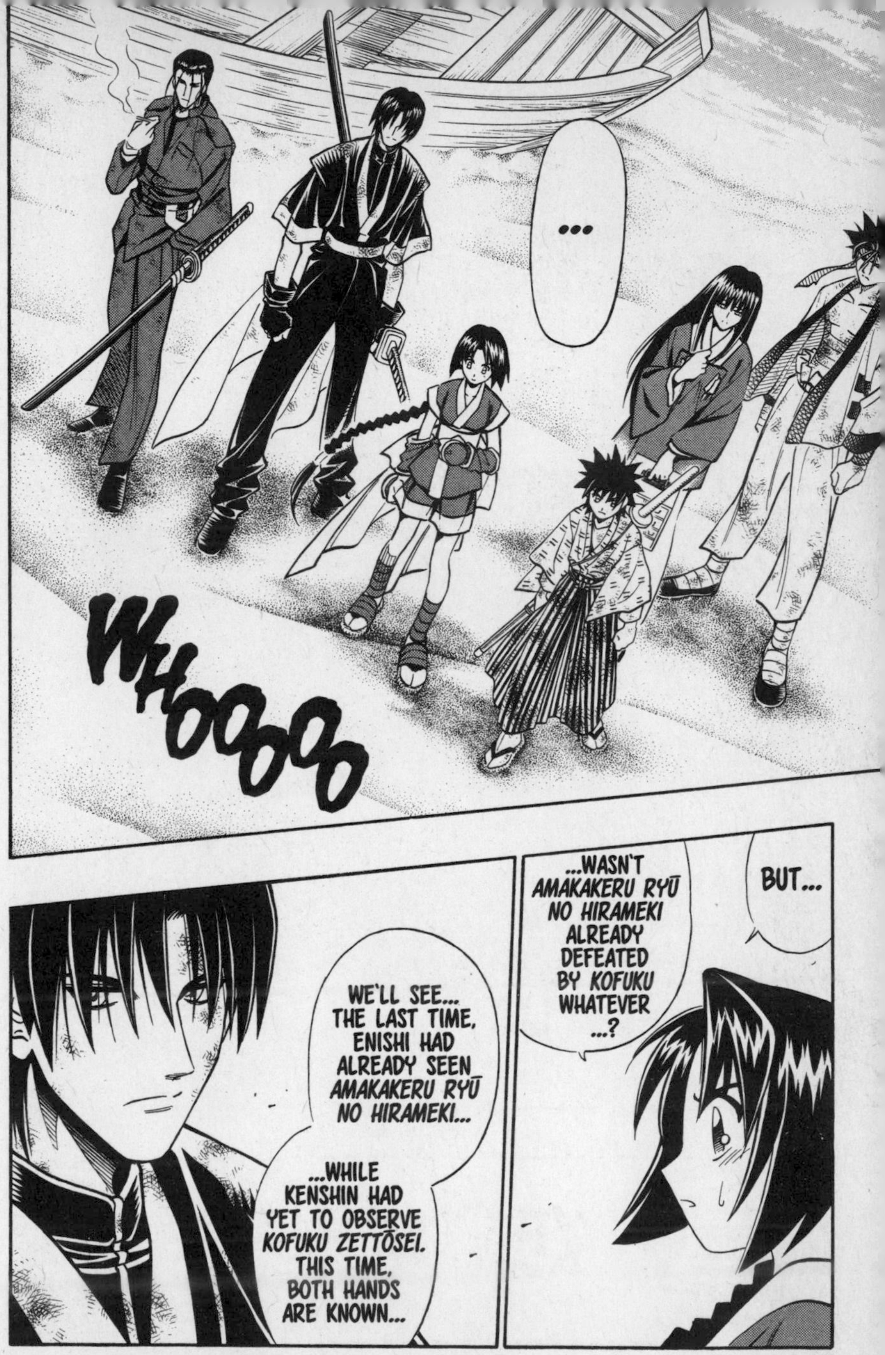
...
WHOOOOO
BUT...
...WASN'T AMAKAKERU RYŪ NO HIRAMEKI ALREADY DEFEATED BY KOFUKU WHATEVER ...?
WE'LL SEE... THE LAST TIME, ENISHI HAD ALREADY SEEN AMAKAKERU RYŪ NO HIRAMEKI...
...WHILE KENSHIN HAD YET TO OBSERVE KOFUKU ZETTŌSEI. THIS TIME, BOTH HANDS ARE KNOWN...

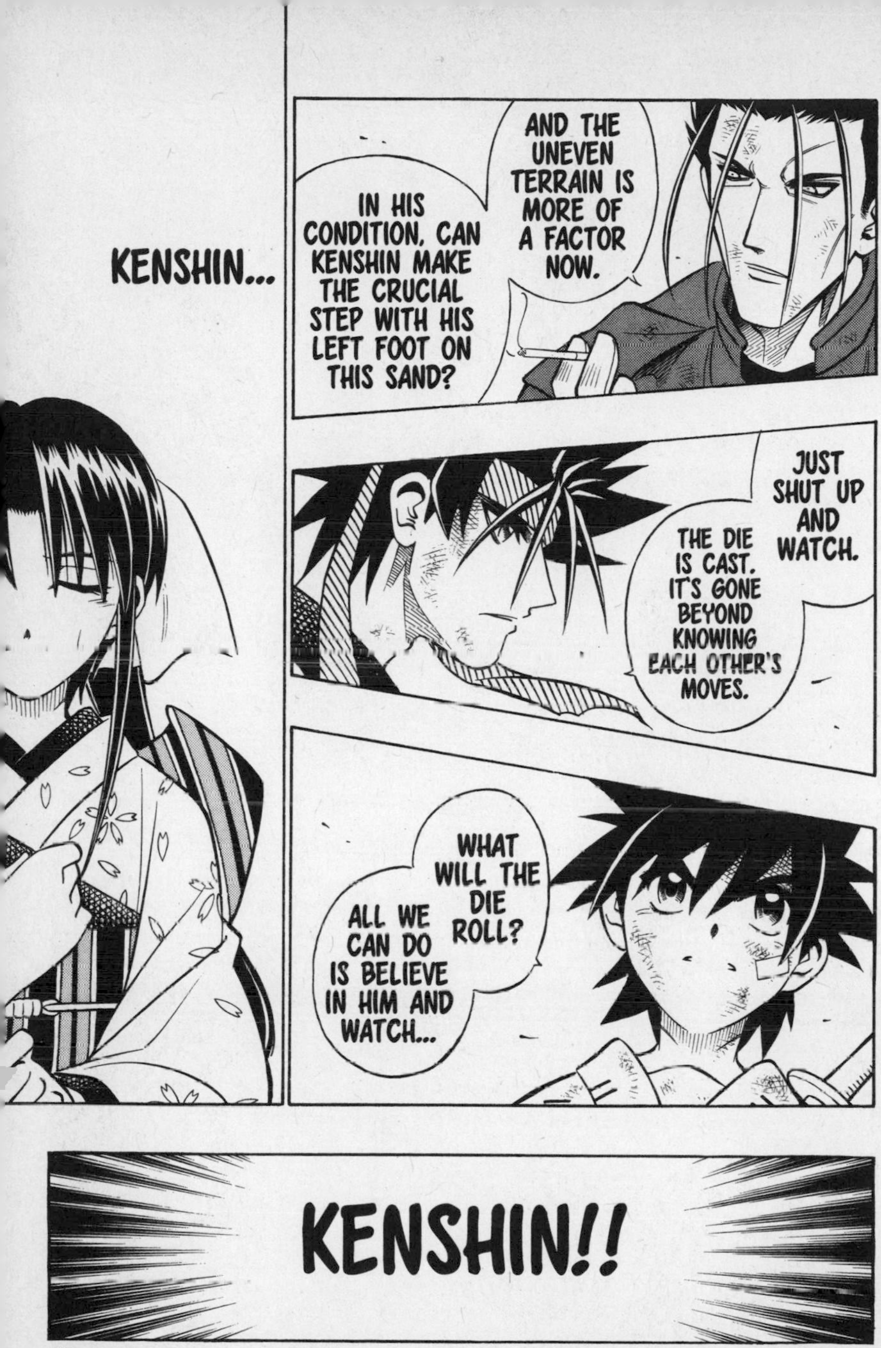
AND THE UNEVEN TERRAIN IS MORE OF A FACTOR NOW.
IN HIS CONDITION, CAN KENSHIN MAKE THE CRUCIAL STEP WITH HIS LEFT FOOT ON THIS SAND?
JUST SHUT UP AND WATCH.
THE DIE IS CAST. IT'S GONE BEYOND KNOWING EACH OTHER'S MOVES.
WHAT WILL THE DIE ROLL?
ALL WE CAN DO IS BELIEVE IN HIM AND WATCH...
KENSHIN...
KENSHIN!!

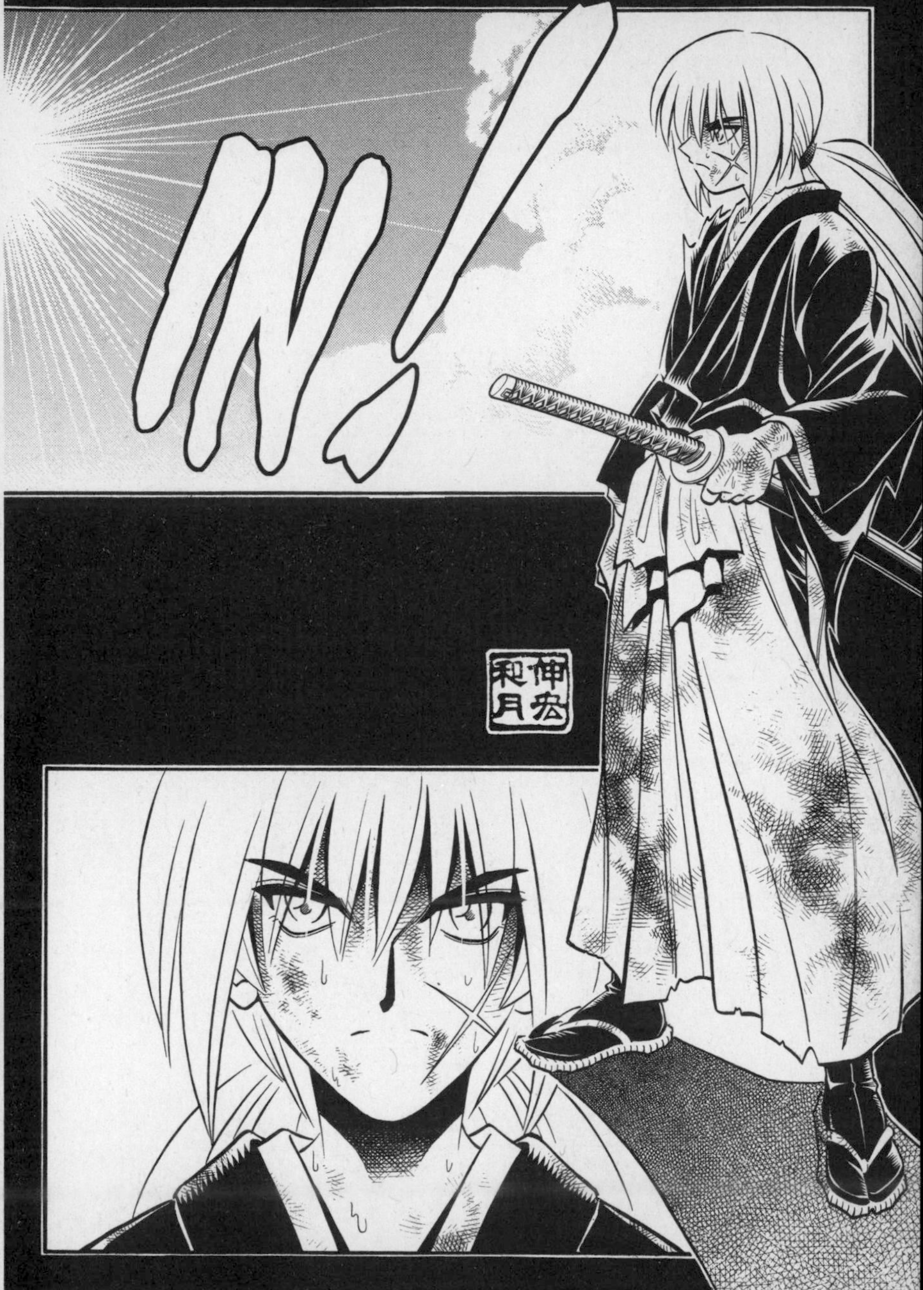
N!
伸宏和月

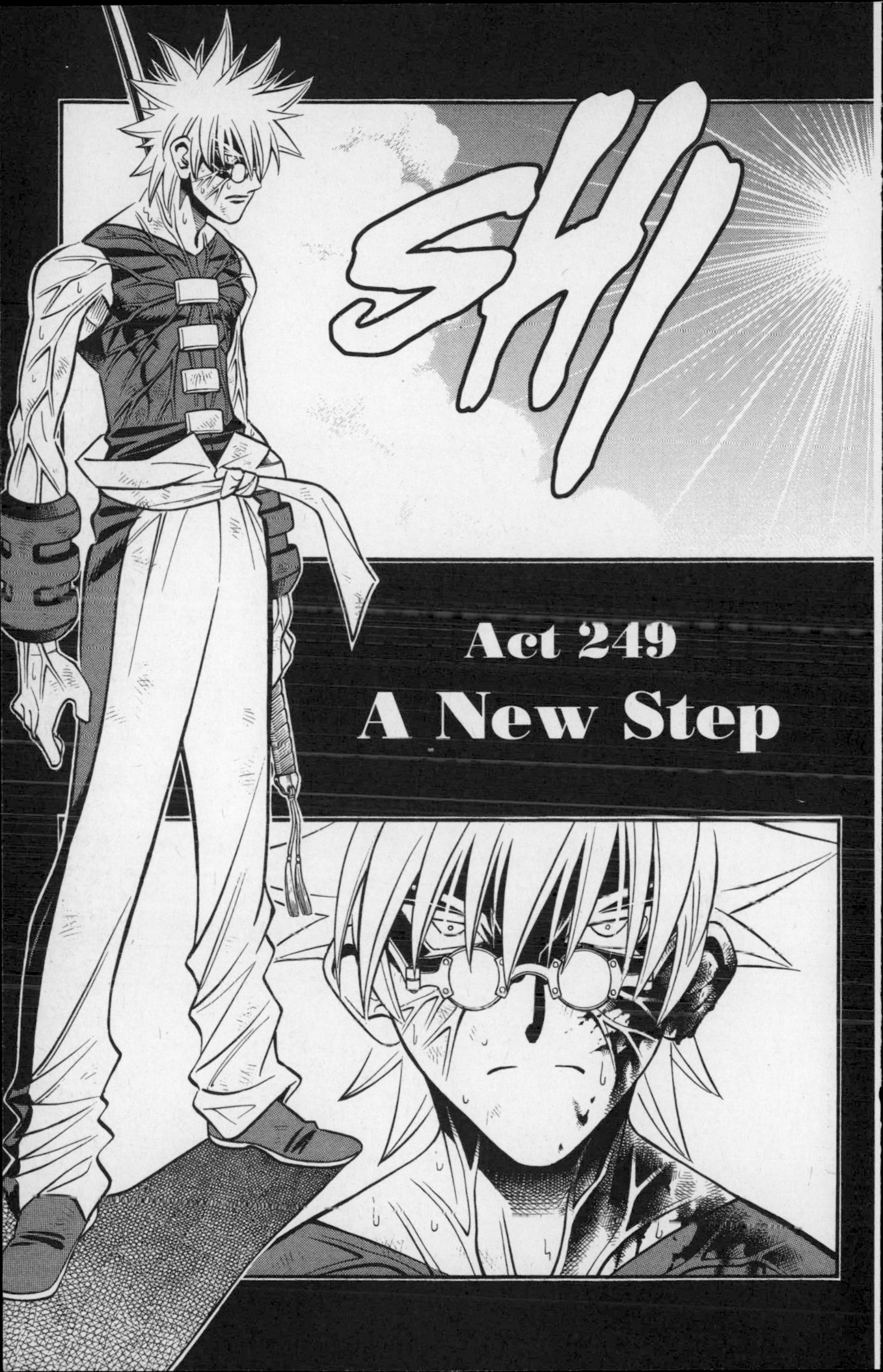
SHI
Act 249
A New Step

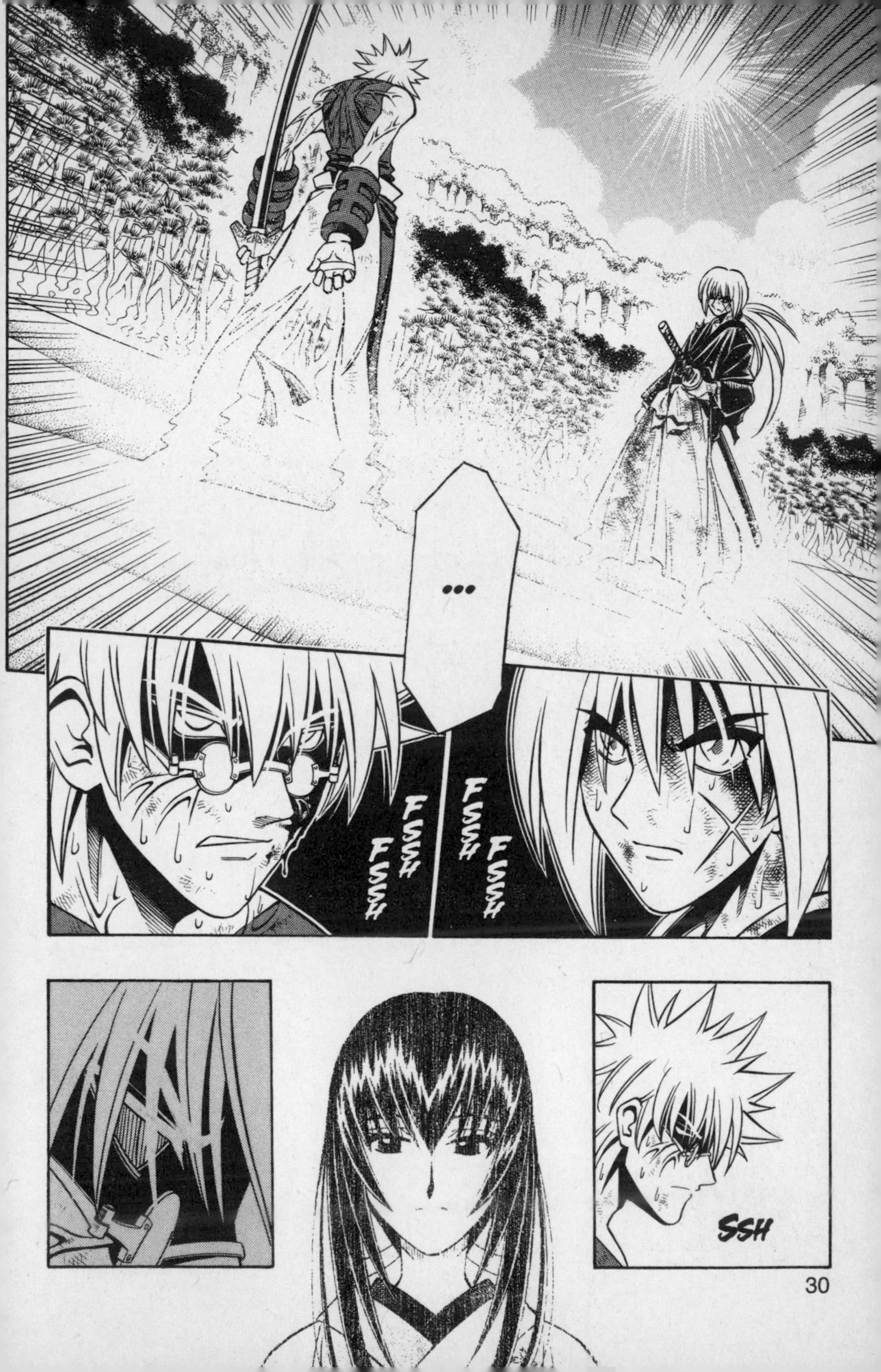
...
FSSH
FSSH
FSSH
FSSH
SSH

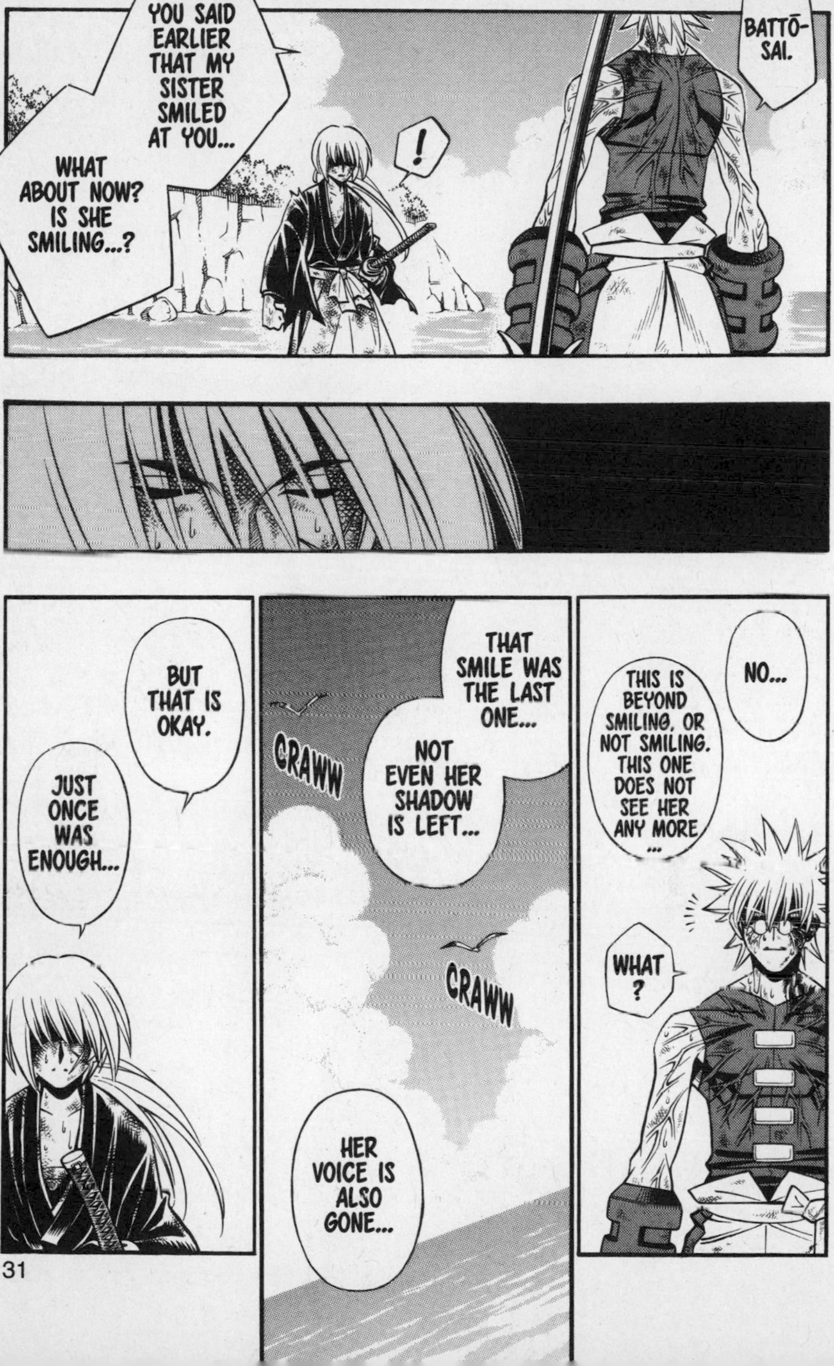
BATTŌ-SAI.
YOU SAID EARLIER THAT MY SISTER SMILED AT YOU...
WHAT ABOUT NOW? IS SHE SMILING...?
!
NO...
THIS IS BEYOND SMILING, OR NOT SMILING. THIS ONE DOES NOT SEE HER ANY MORE ...
WHAT ?
THAT SMILE WAS THE LAST ONE...
NOT EVEN HER SHADOW IS LEFT...
CRAWW
CRAWW
HER VOICE IS ALSO GONE...
BUT THAT IS OKAY.
JUST ONCE WAS ENOUGH...

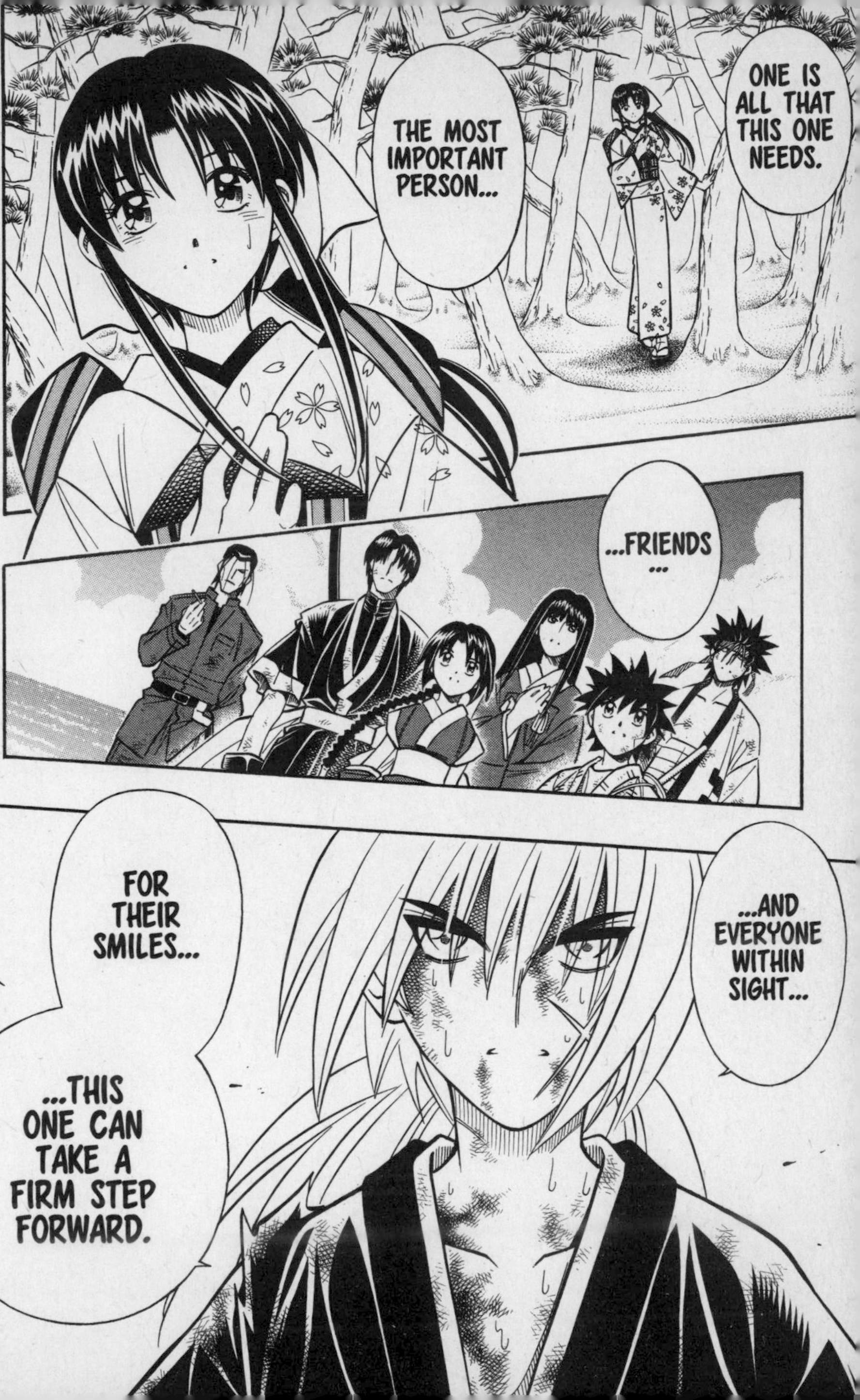

ONE IS ALL THAT THIS ONE NEEDS.
THE MOST IMPORTANT PERSON...
...FRIENDS ...
...AND EVERYONE WITHIN SIGHT...
FOR THEIR SMILES...
...THIS ONE CAN TAKE A FIRM STEP FORWARD.

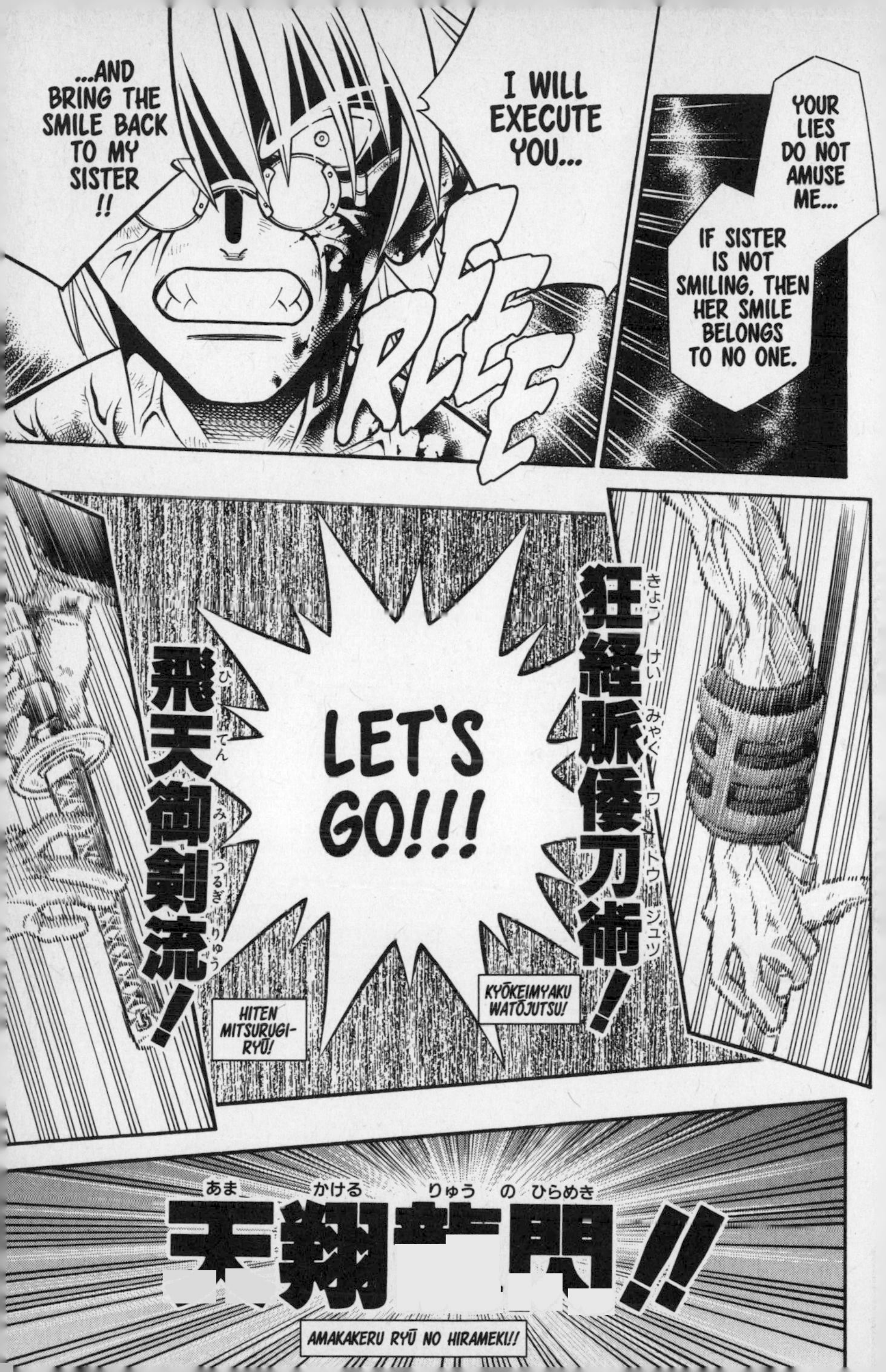
YOUR LIES DO NOT AMUSE ME...
IF SISTER IS NOT SMILING, THEN HER SMILE BELONGS TO NO ONE.
I WILL EXECUTE YOU...
...AND BRING THE SMILE BACK TO MY SISTER !!
狂経脈倭刀術！
KYŌKEIMYAKU WATŌJUTSU!
LET'S GO!!!
飛天御剣流！
HITEN MITSURUGI-RYŪ!
天翔龍閃!!
AMAKAKERU RYŪ NO HIRAMEKI!!

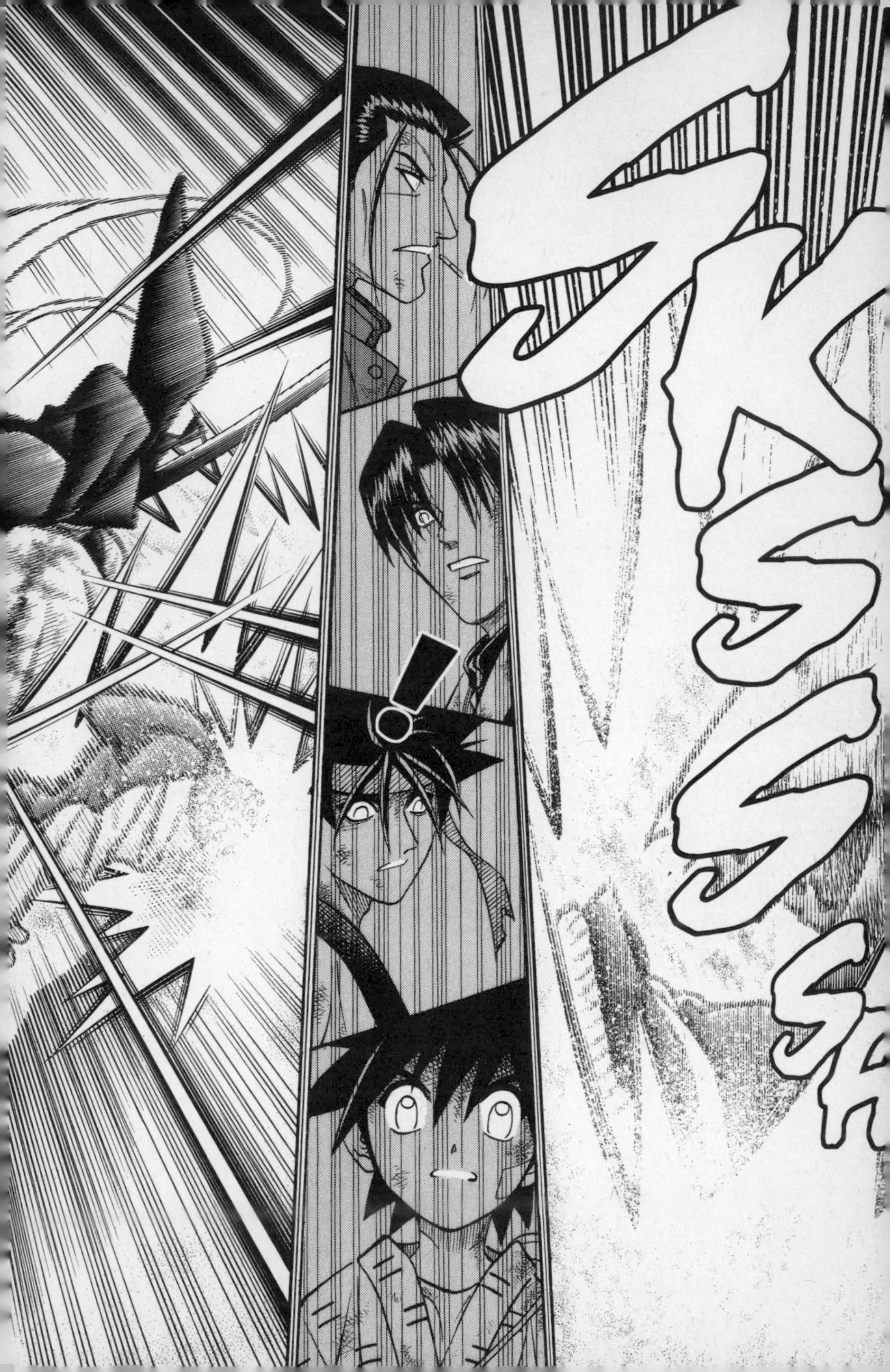
SKSSSH

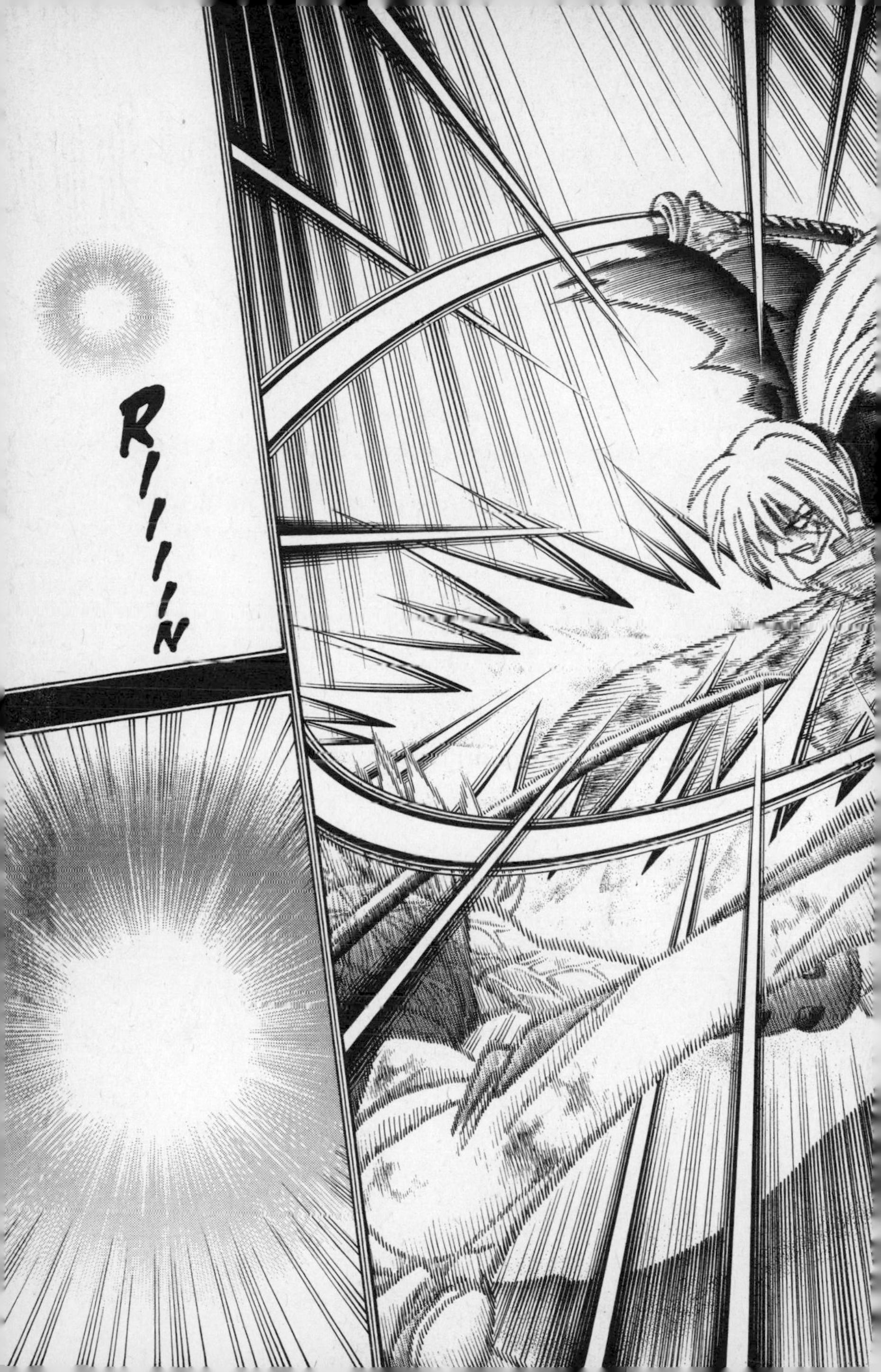
RIIIIN

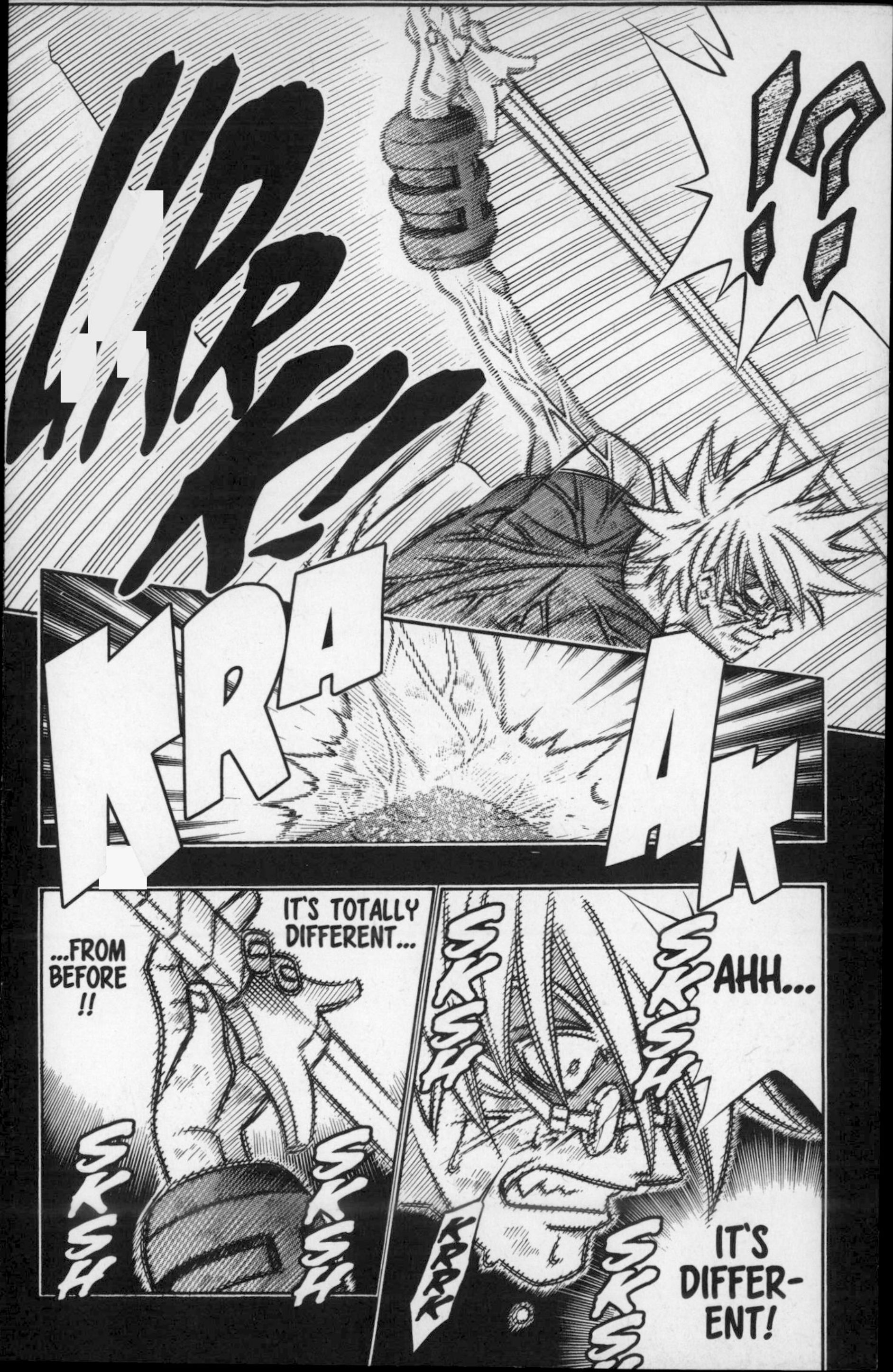
!?
KRAAK
AHH...
SKSH
SKSH
KRRK
IT'S DIFFERENT!
IT'S TOTALLY DIFFERENT...
...FROM BEFORE !!
SKSH
SKSH

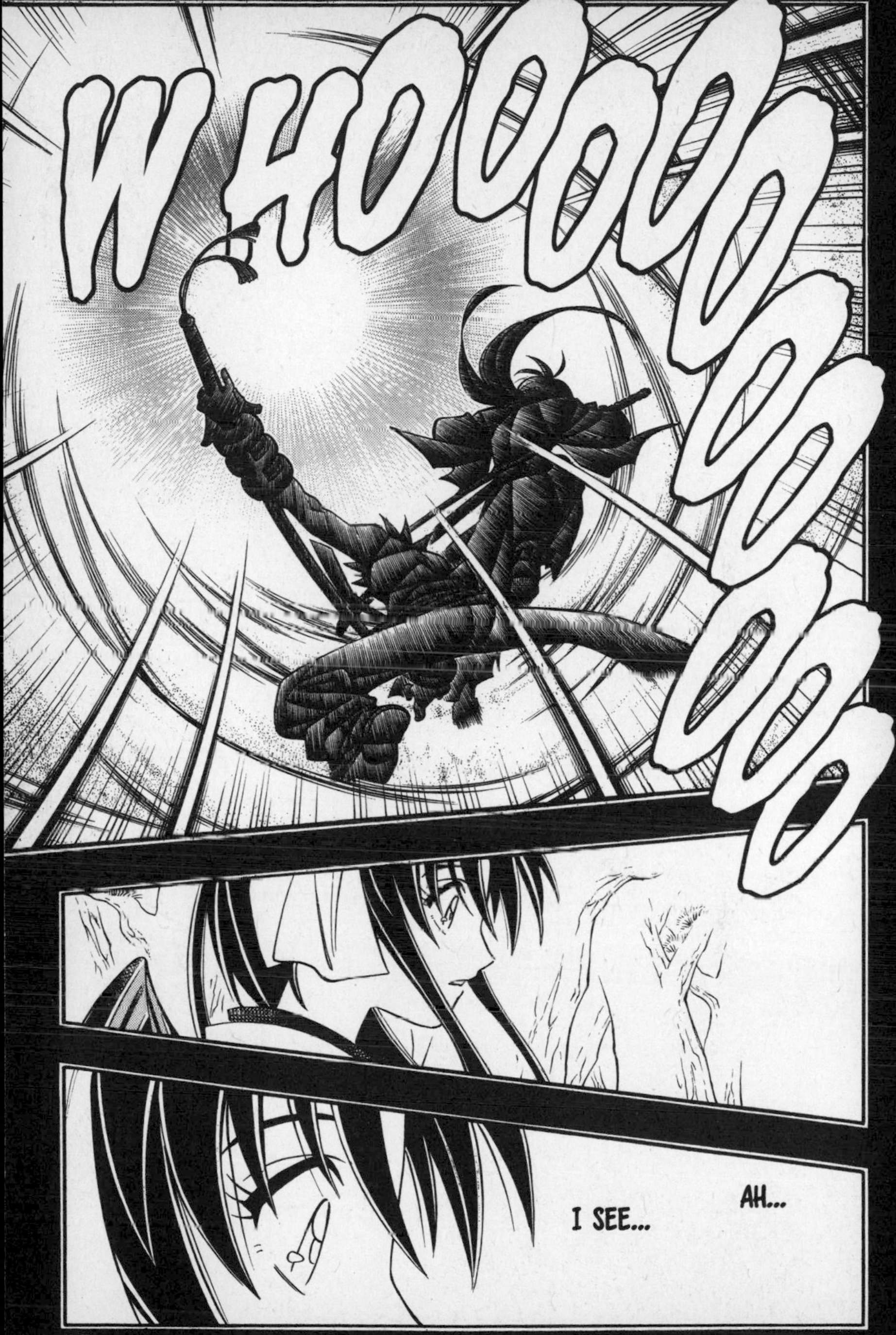
WHOOOOOOOOOOOO
AH...
I SEE...

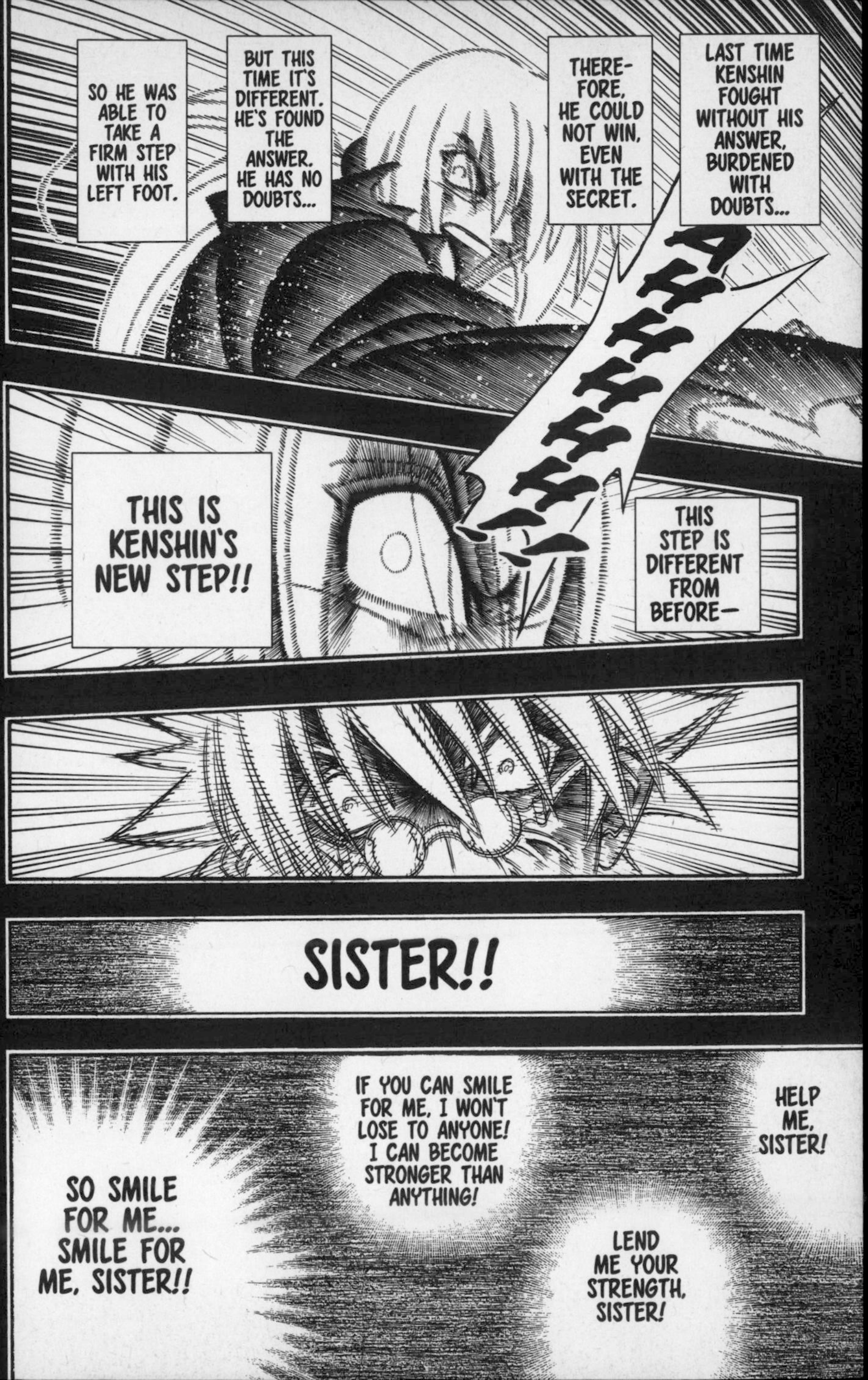
LAST TIME KENSHIN FOUGHT WITHOUT HIS ANSWER, BURDENED WITH DOUBTS...
THERE-FORE, HE COULD NOT WIN, EVEN WITH THE SECRET.
BUT THIS TIME IT'S DIFFERENT. HE'S FOUND THE ANSWER. HE HAS NO DOUBTS...
SO HE WAS ABLE TO TAKE A FIRM STEP WITH HIS LEFT FOOT.
AHHHHHH!!
THIS STEP IS DIFFERENT FROM BEFORE—
THIS IS KENSHIN'S NEW STEP!!
SISTER!!
HELP ME, SISTER!
IF YOU CAN SMILE FOR ME, I WON'T LOSE TO ANYONE! I CAN BECOME STRONGER THAN ANYTHING!
LEND ME YOUR STRENGTH, SISTER!
SO SMILE FOR ME... SMILE FOR ME, SISTER!!

READ THIS WAY

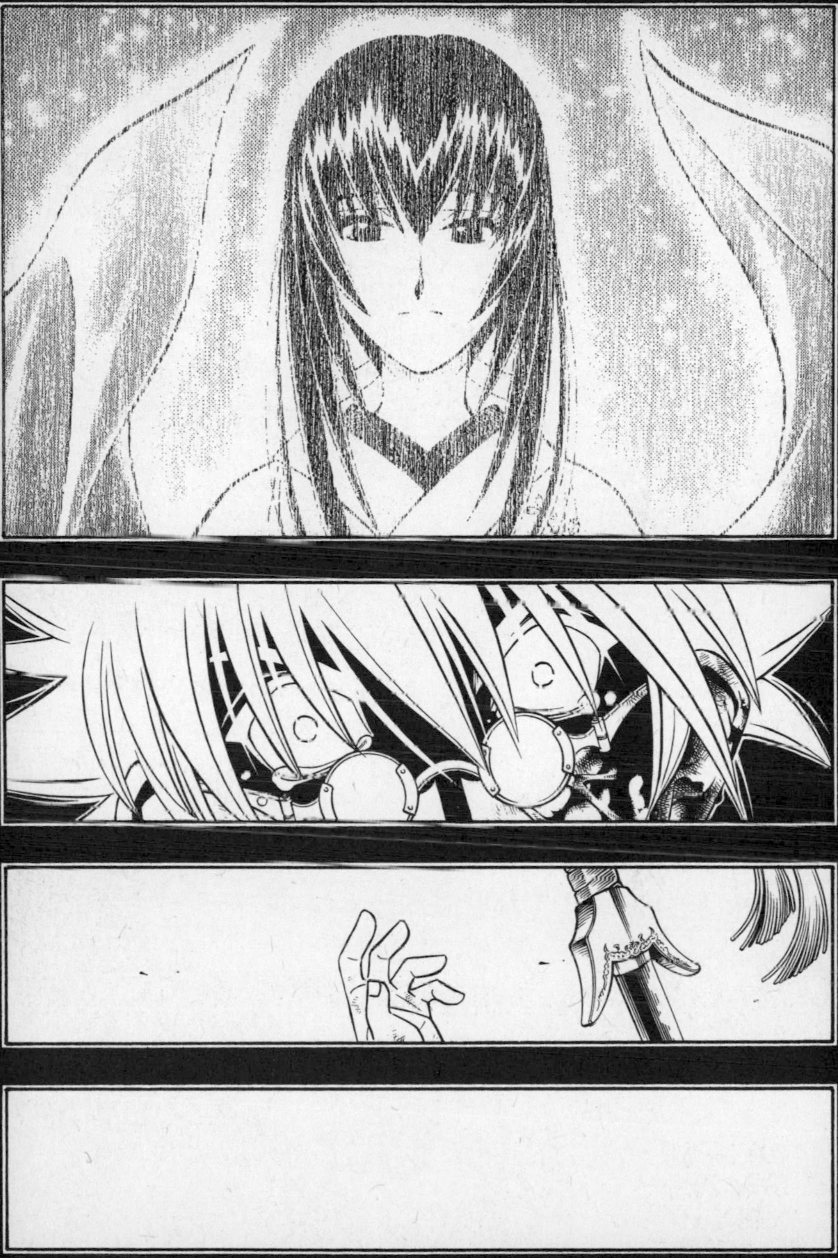

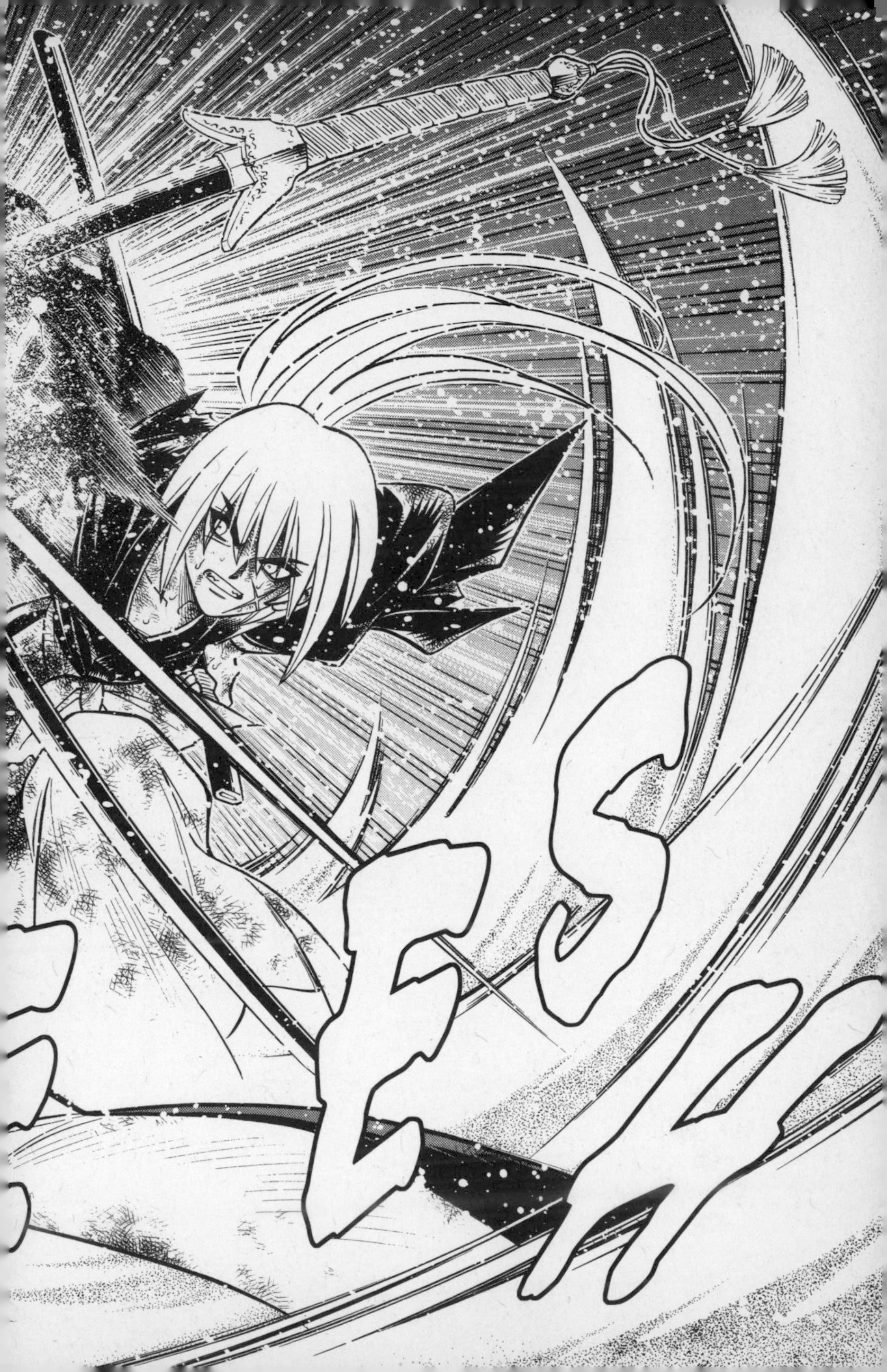

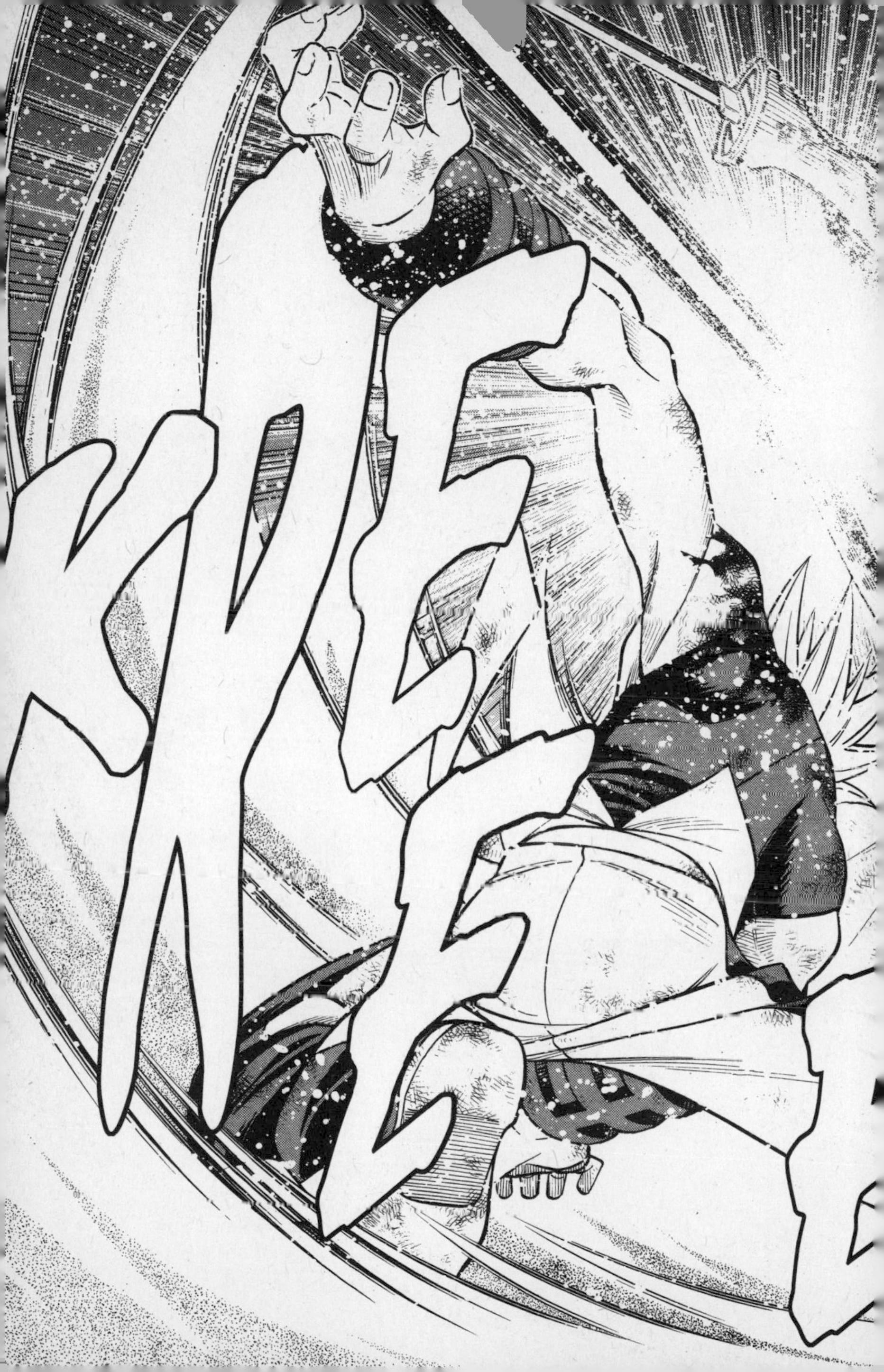

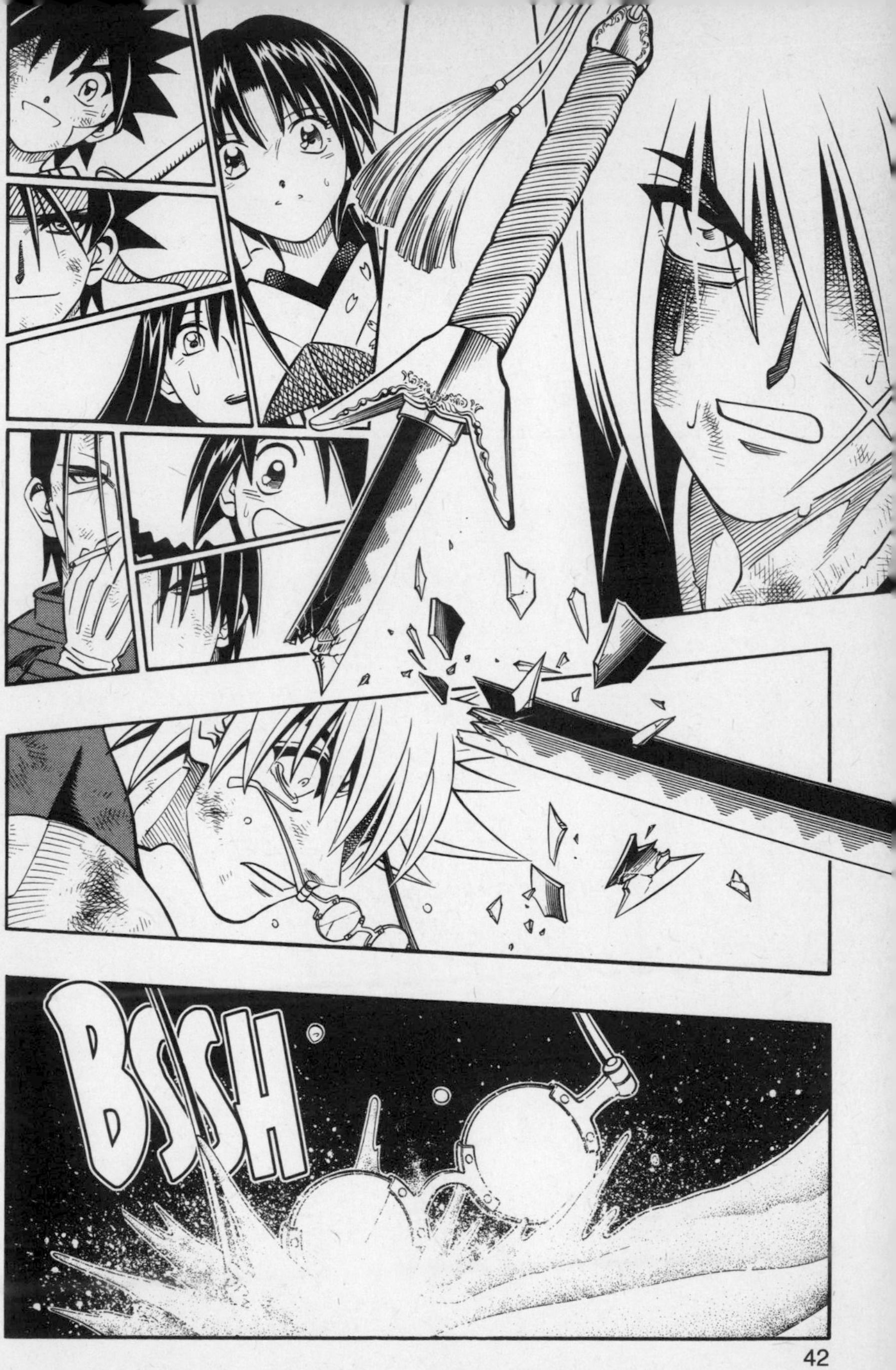
BSSH

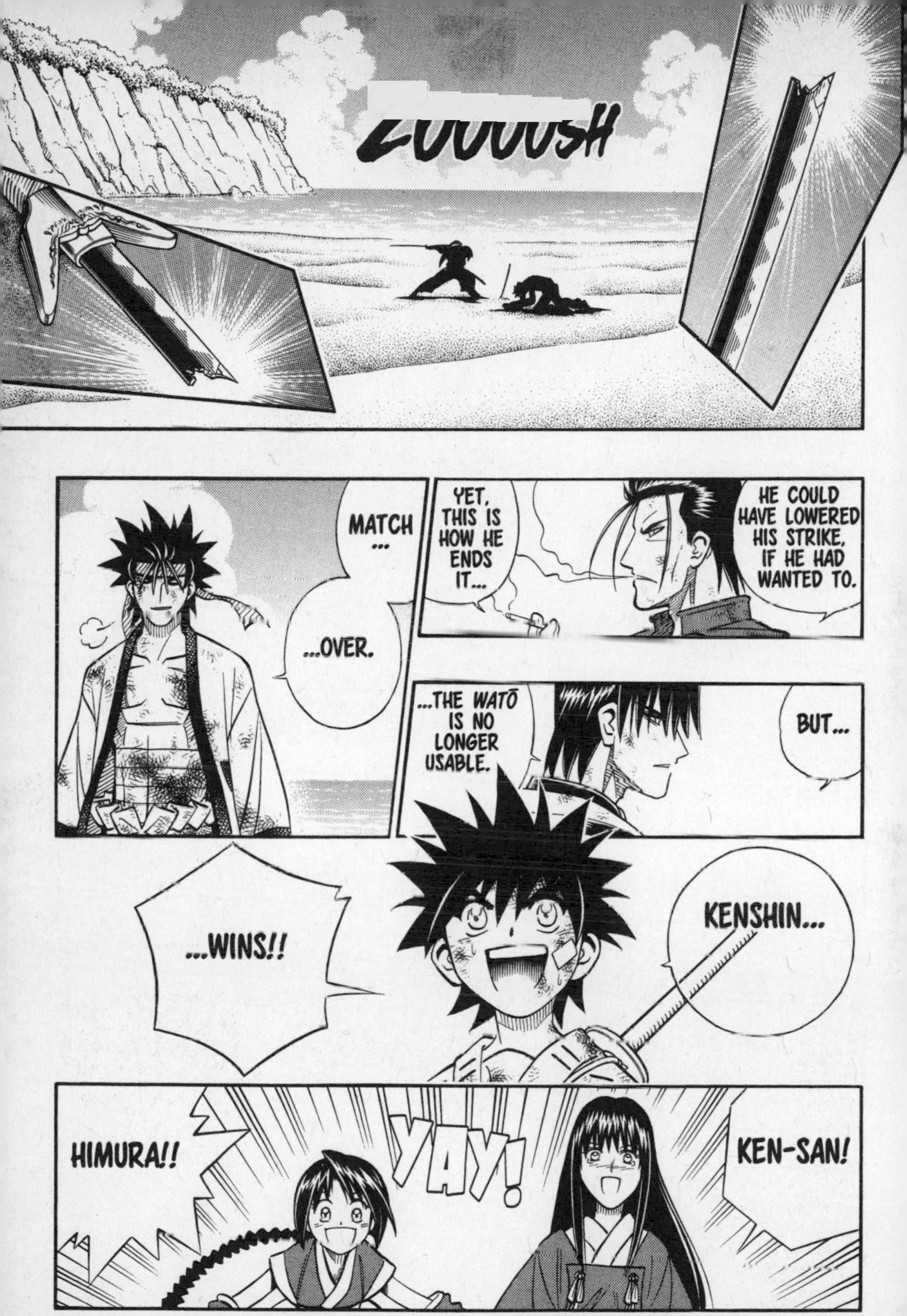
ZOOOOOSH
HE COULD HAVE LOWERED HIS STRIKE, IF HE HAD WANTED TO.
YET, THIS IS HOW HE ENDS IT...
BUT...
...THE WATŌ IS NO LONGER USABLE.
MATCH...
...OVER.
KENSHIN...
...WINS!!
KEN-SAN!
YAY!
HIMURA!!

Act 250—Smile Once More

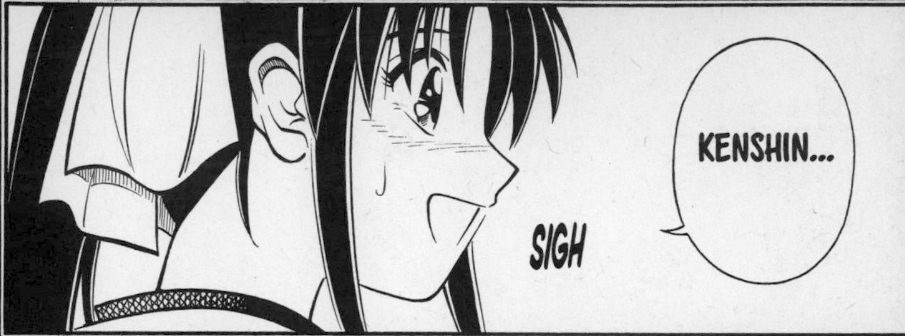
KENSHIN...
SIGH

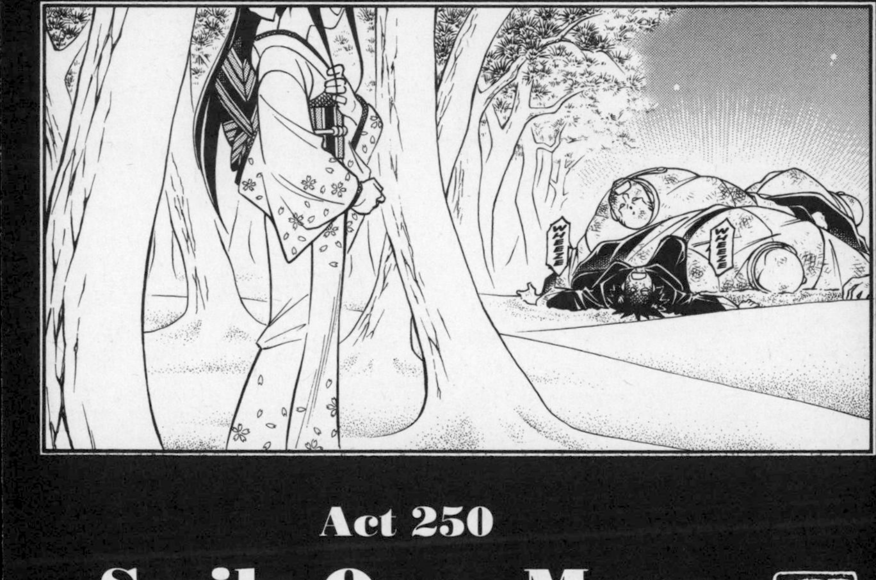
WHEEZE
WHEEZE

Act 250

Smile Once More

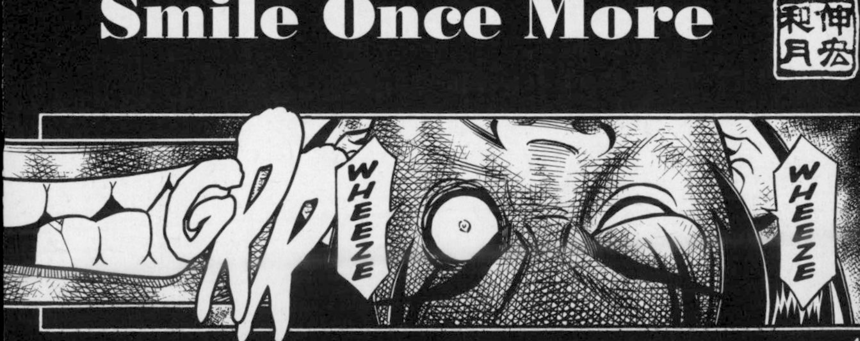
WHEEZE
WHEEZE

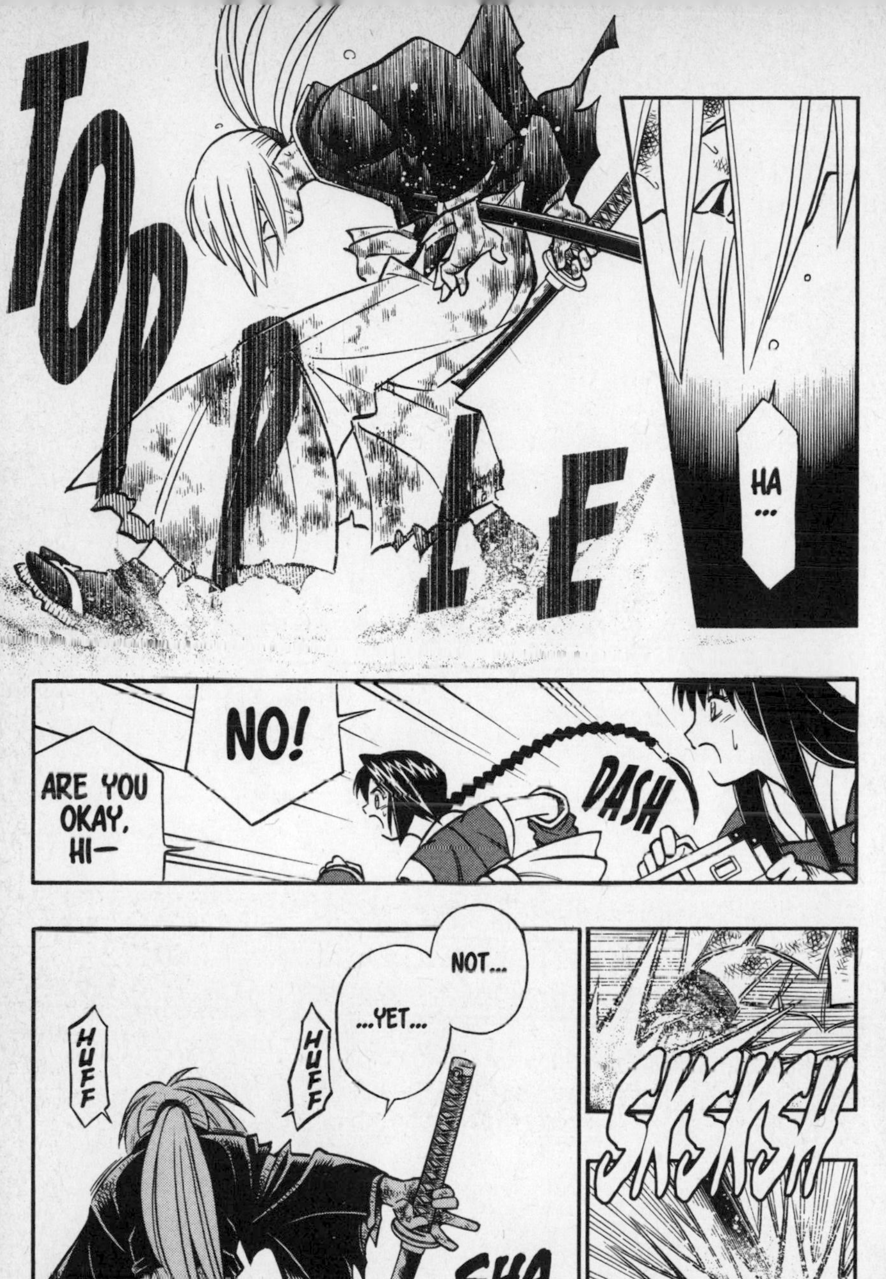
HA...
TOPPLE
NO!
DASH
ARE YOU OKAY, HI—
SKSKSH
NOT...
...YET...
HUFF
HUFF
SHA

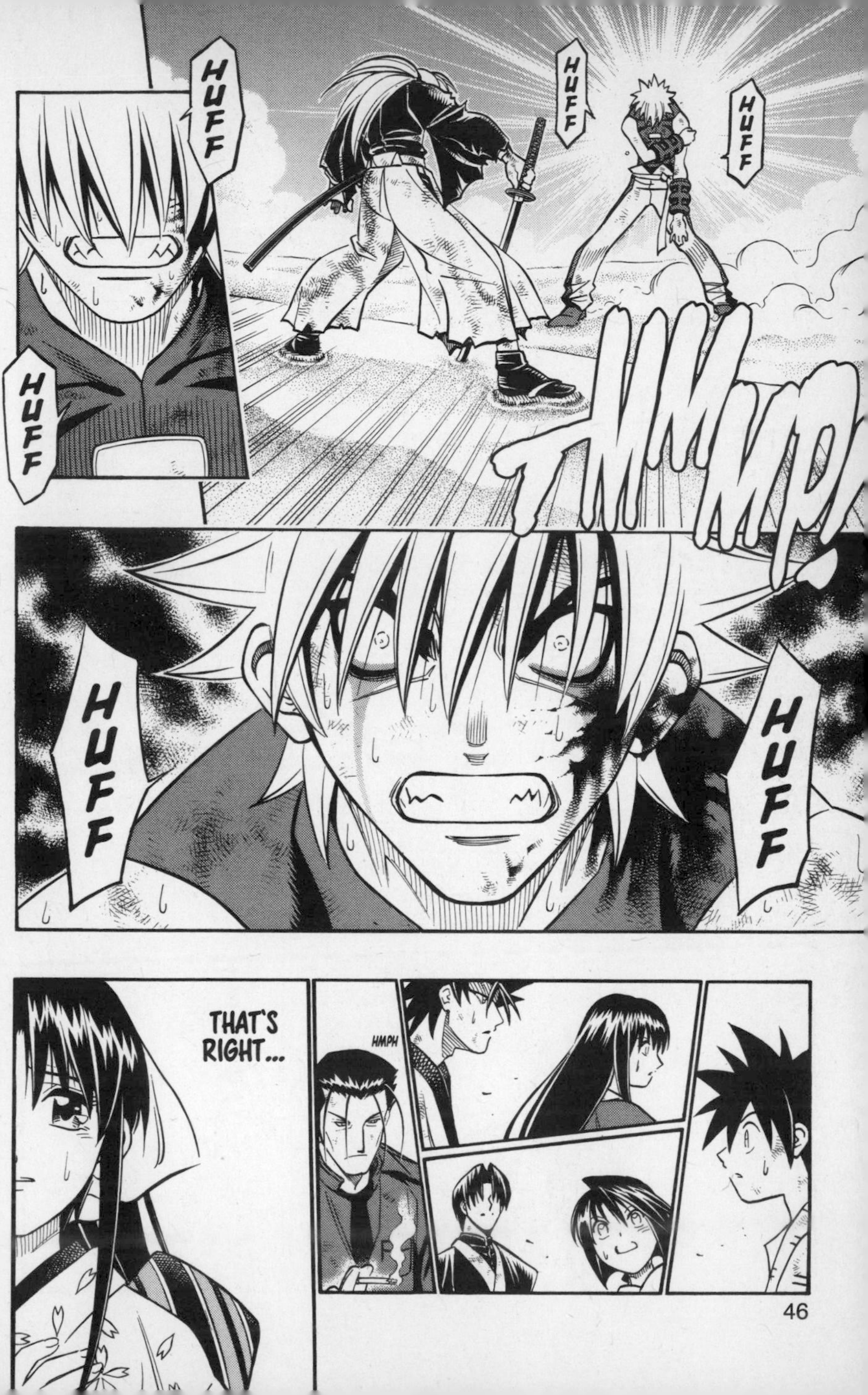
HUFF
HUFF
HUFF
HUFF
THWMP!
HUFF
HUFF
HUFF
HUFF
HMPH
THAT'S RIGHT...

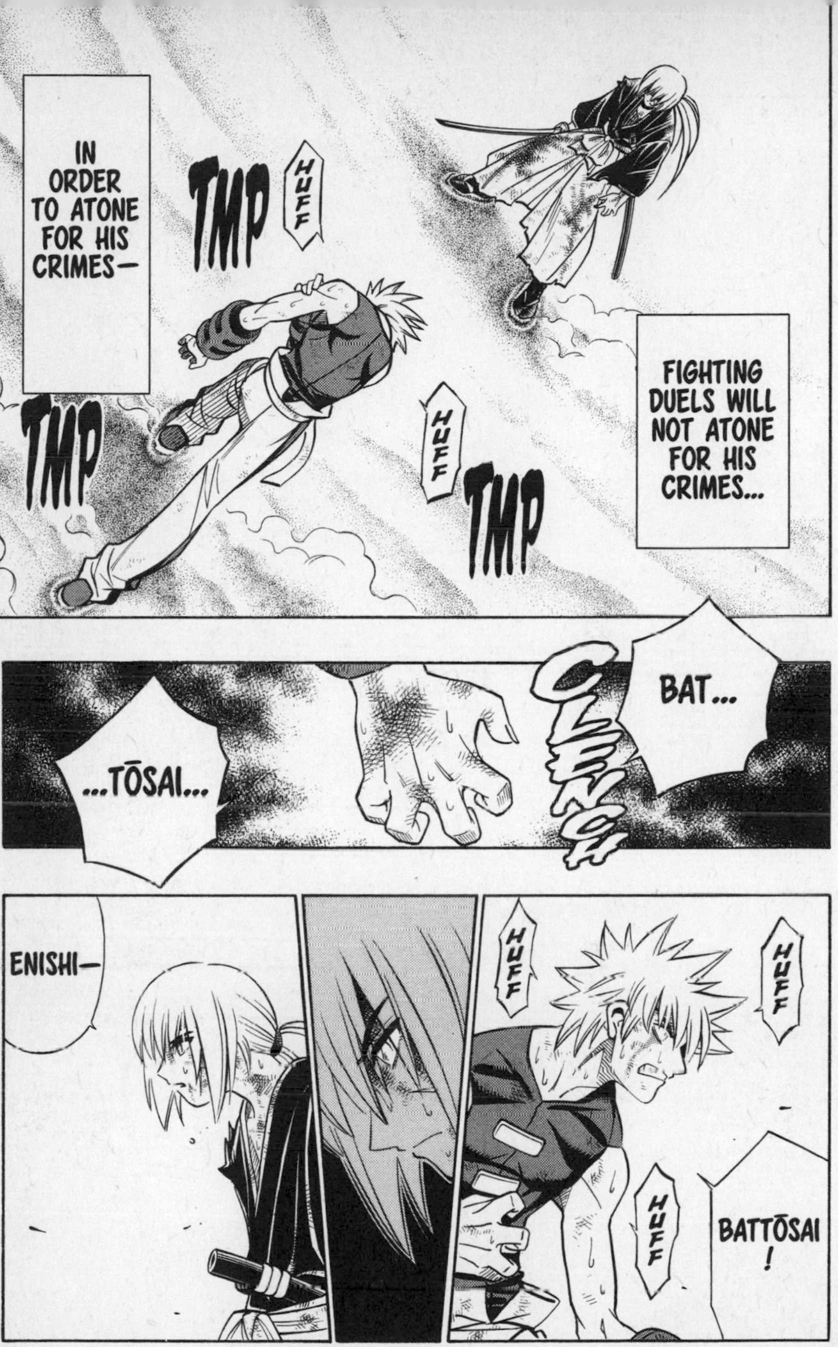
IN ORDER TO ATONE FOR HIS CRIMES—
HUFF
TMP
HUFF
TMP
TMP
FIGHTING DUELS WILL NOT ATONE FOR HIS CRIMES...
BAT...
CLENCH
...TŌSAI...
HUFF
HUFF
HUFF
BATTŌSAI!
ENISHI—

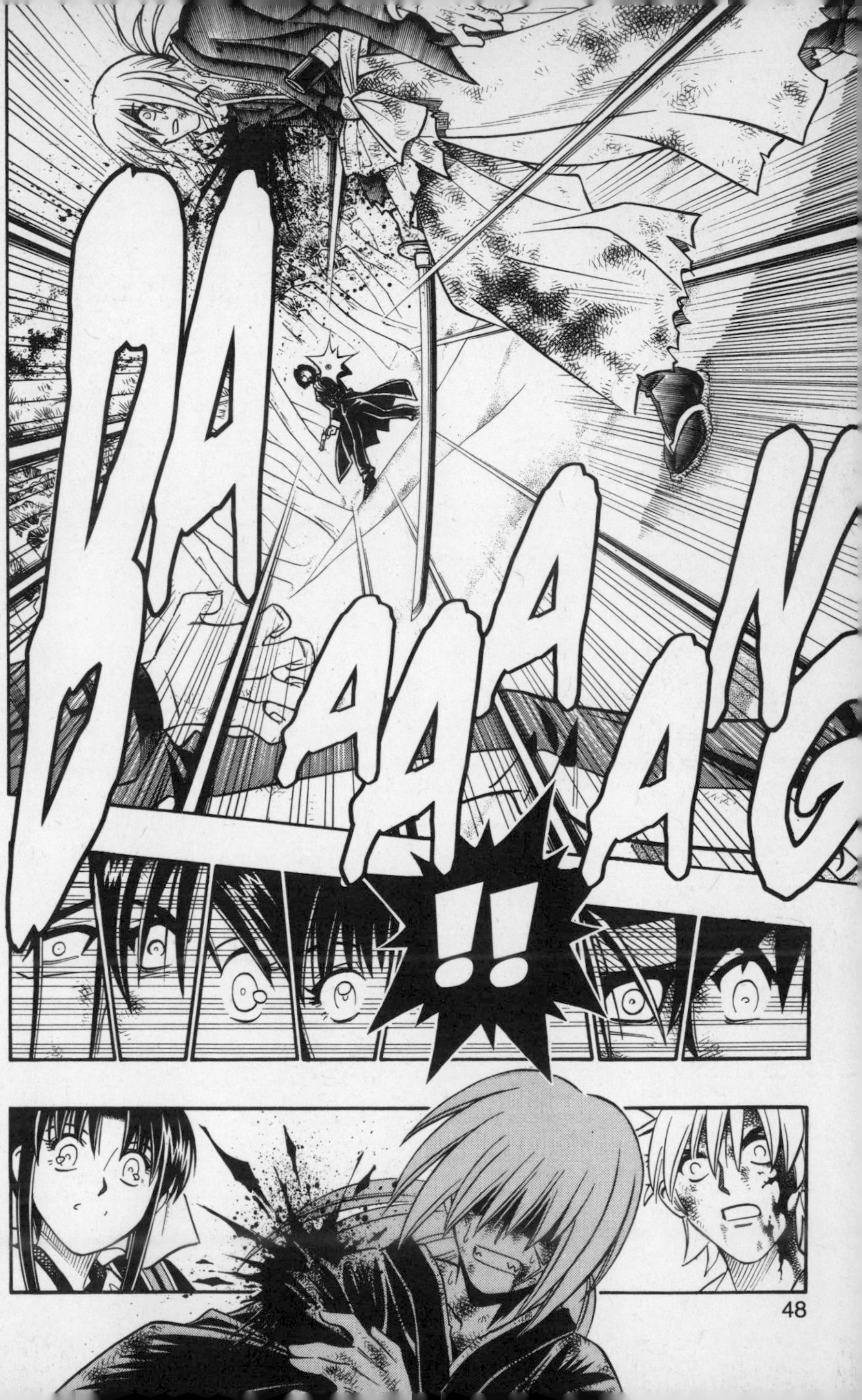
DAAAANG!!

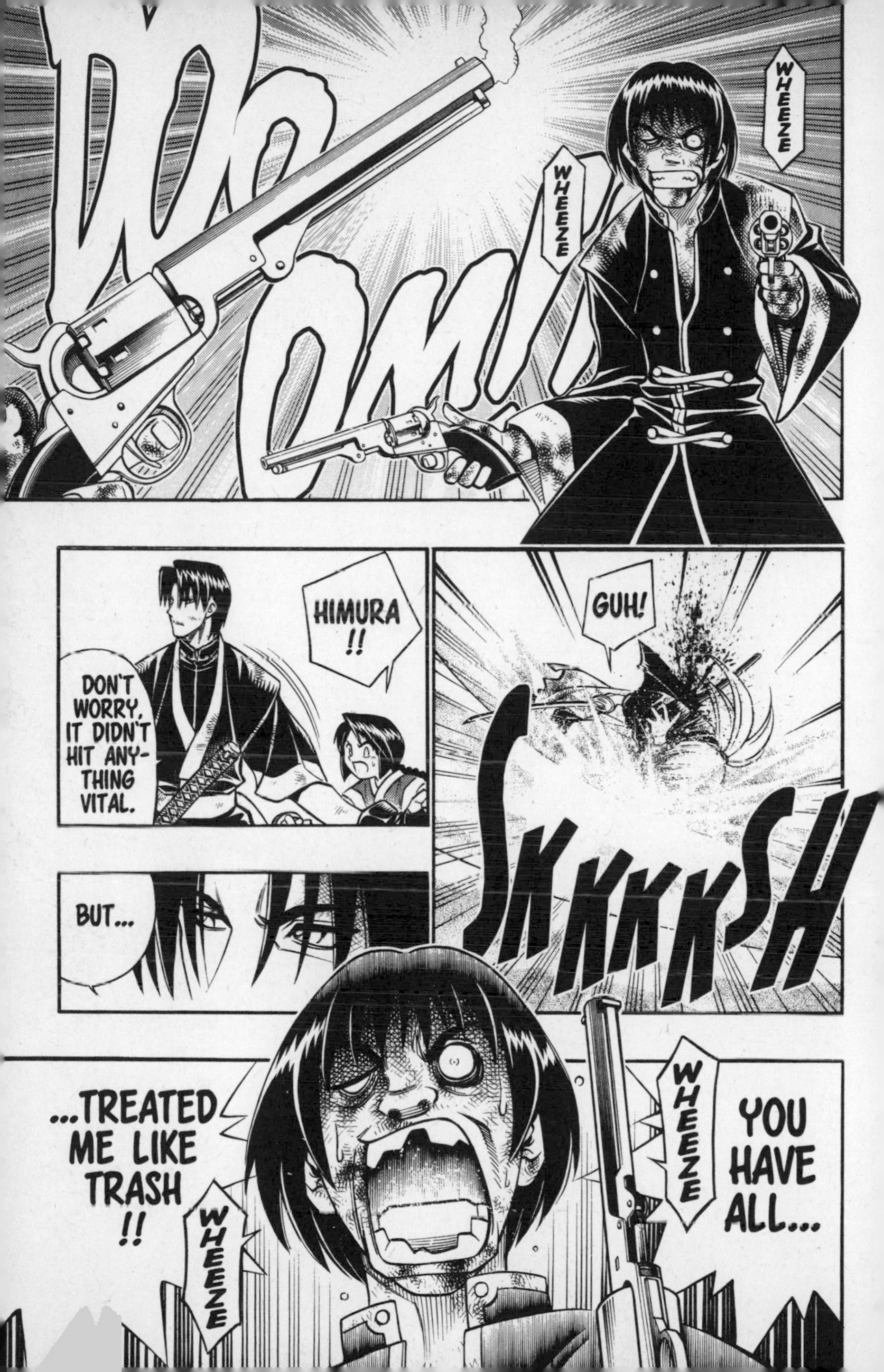
WHEEZE
WHEEZE
GUH!
SKKKKSH
HIMURA!!
DON'T WORRY, IT DIDN'T HIT ANYTHING VITAL.
BUT...
YOU HAVE ALL...
WHEEZE
...TREATED ME LIKE TRASH!!
WHEEZE

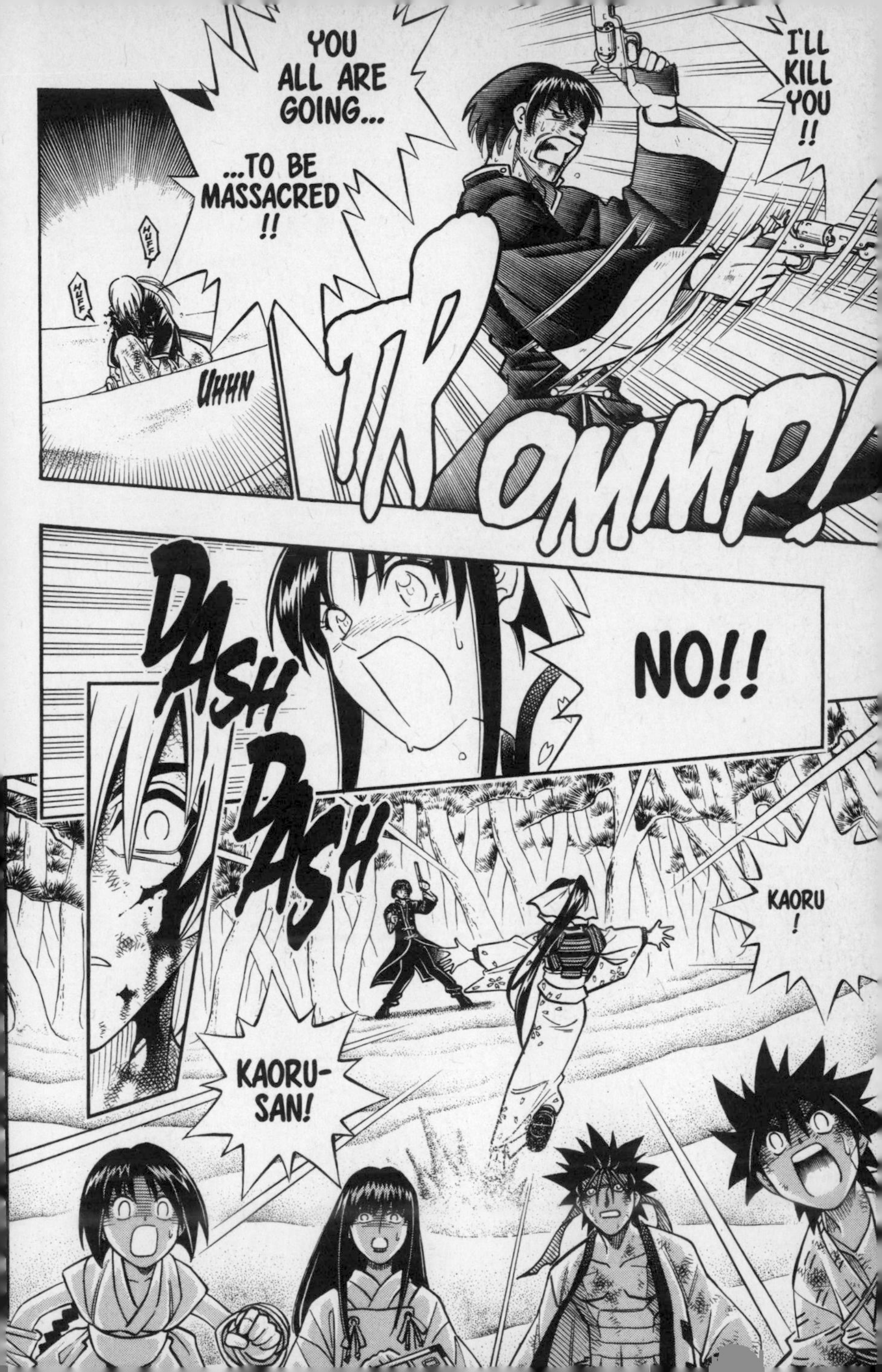
I'LL KILL YOU!!
YOU ALL ARE GOING...
...TO BE MASSACRED!!
HUFF
HUFF
UHHN
THOMMP!
NO!!
DASH
DASH
KAORU!
KAORU-SAN!

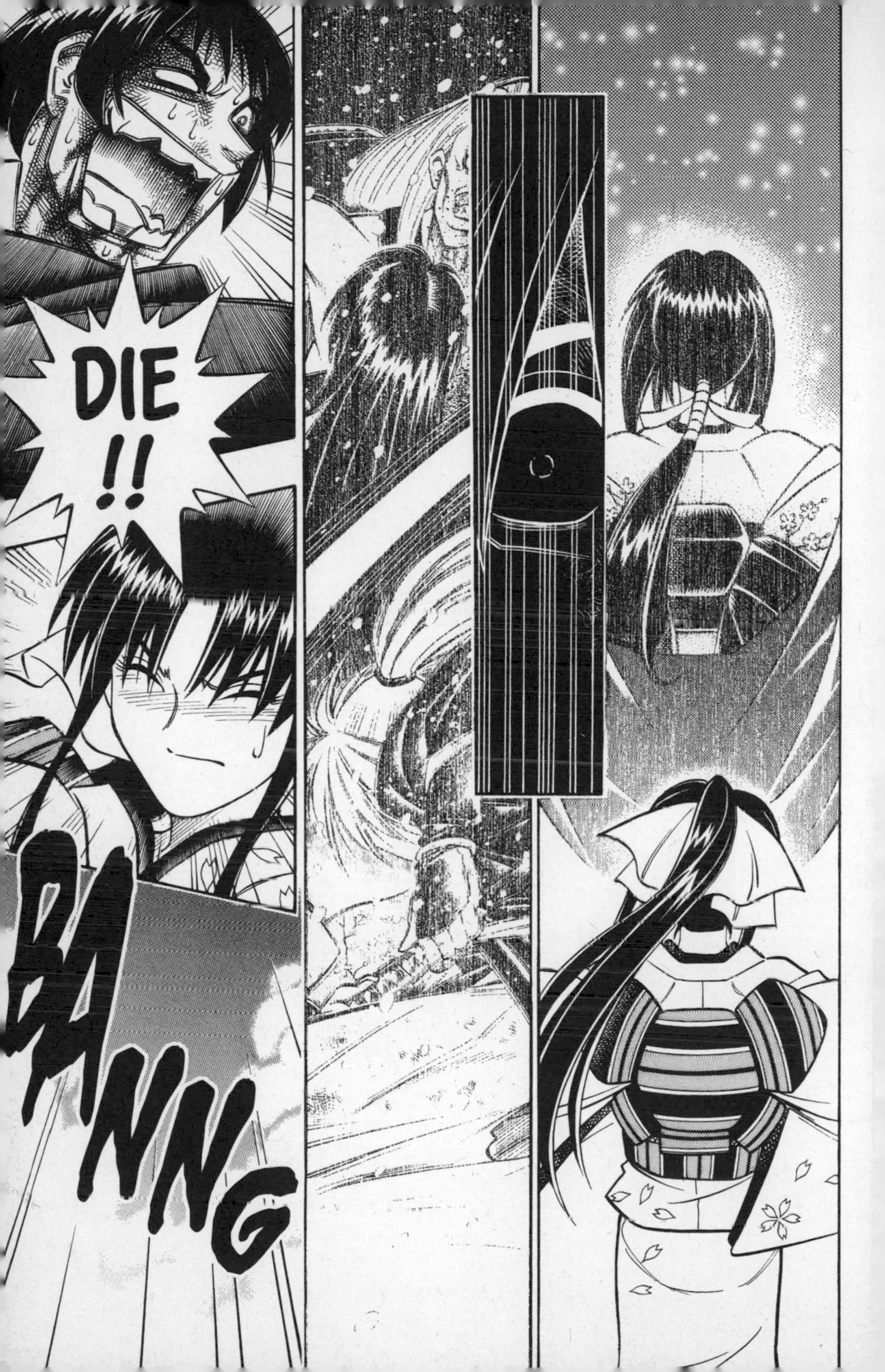
DIE !!
BAMNNG

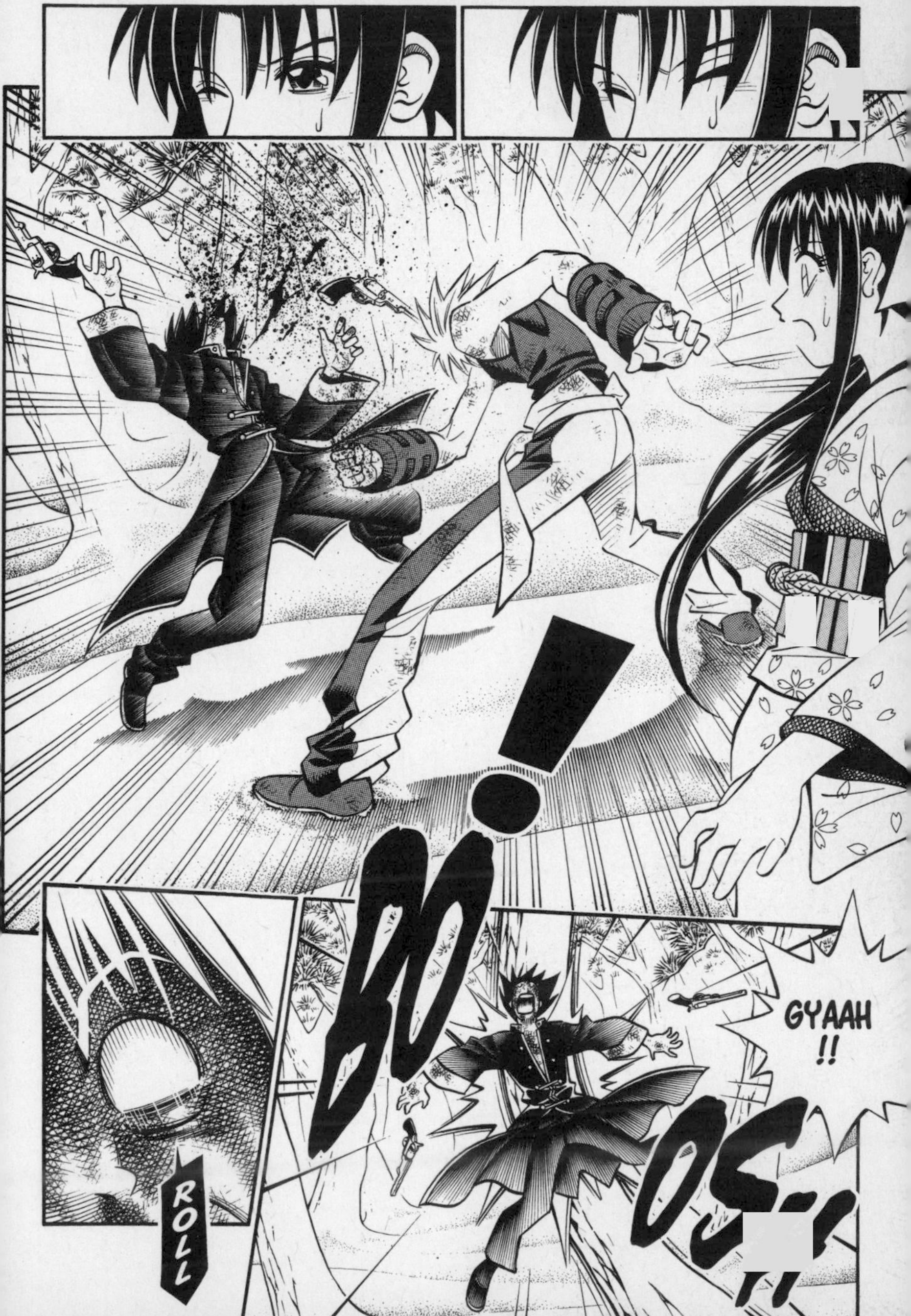
!
GYAAH !!
BO
OS!!
ROLL

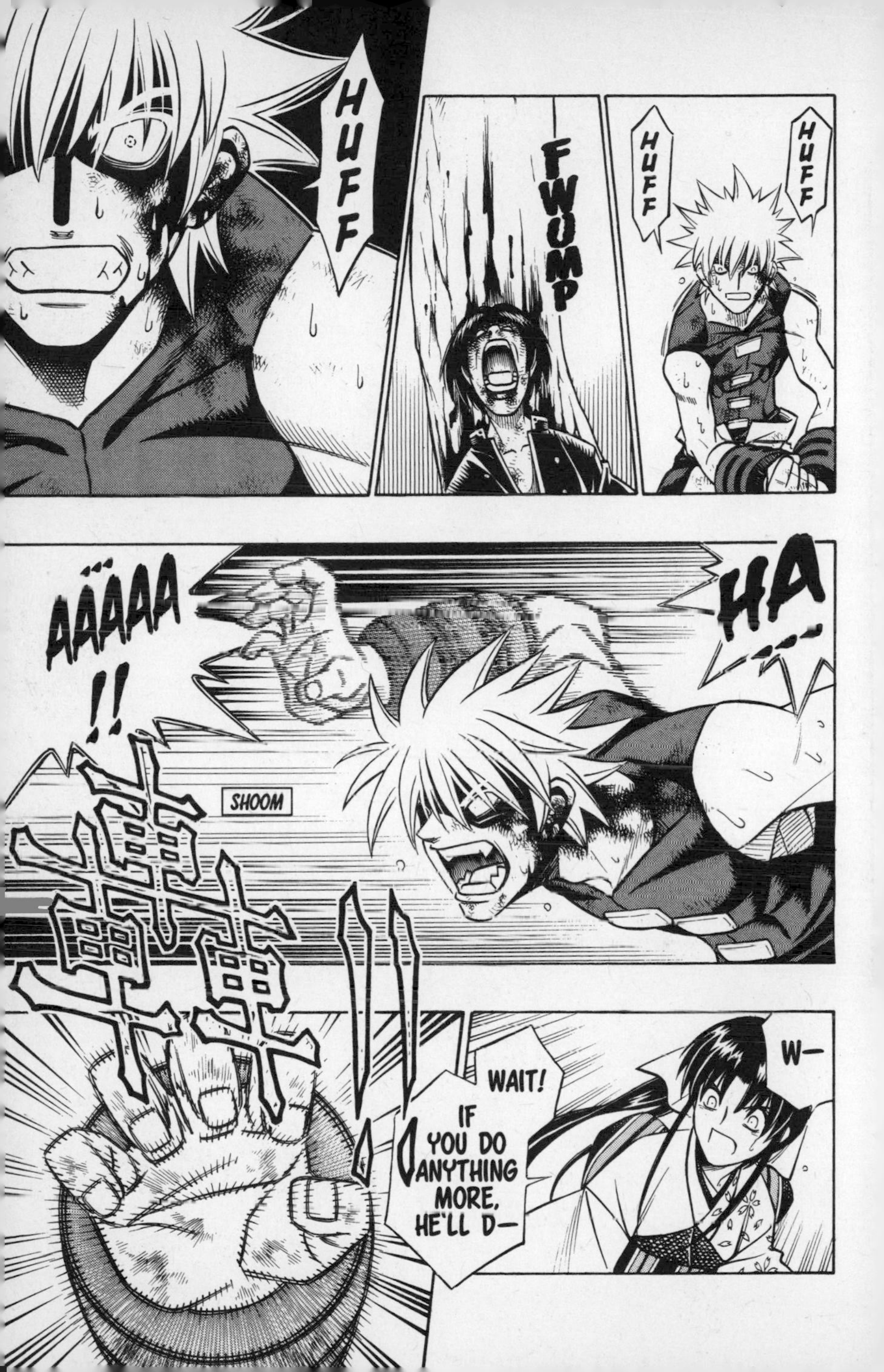
HUFF
HUFF
FWUMP
HUFF
HA
SHOOM
AAAAA!!
W—
WAIT!
IF YOU DO ANYTHING MORE, HE'LL D—

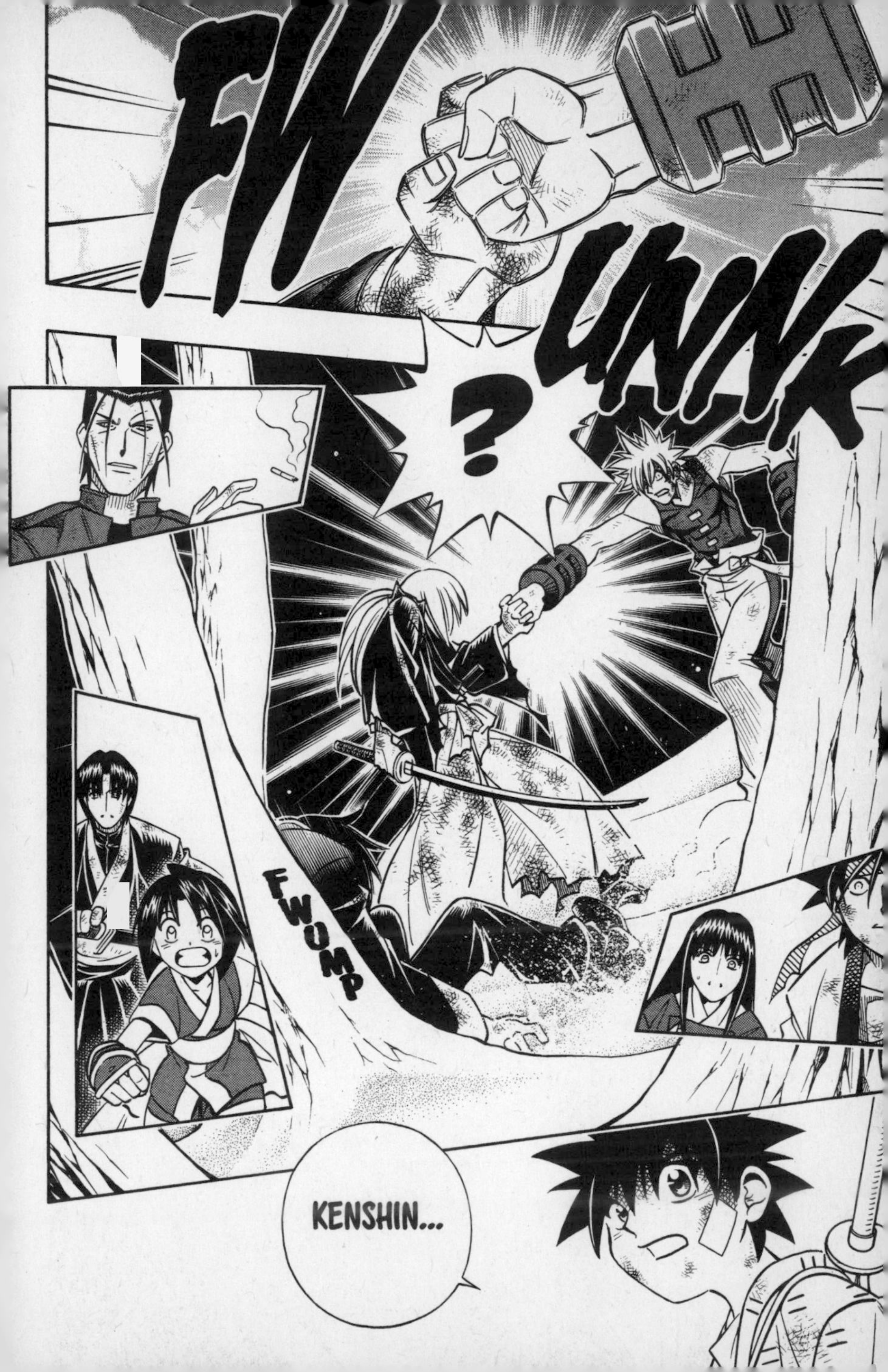
FWUNK
?
FWUMP
KENSHIN...

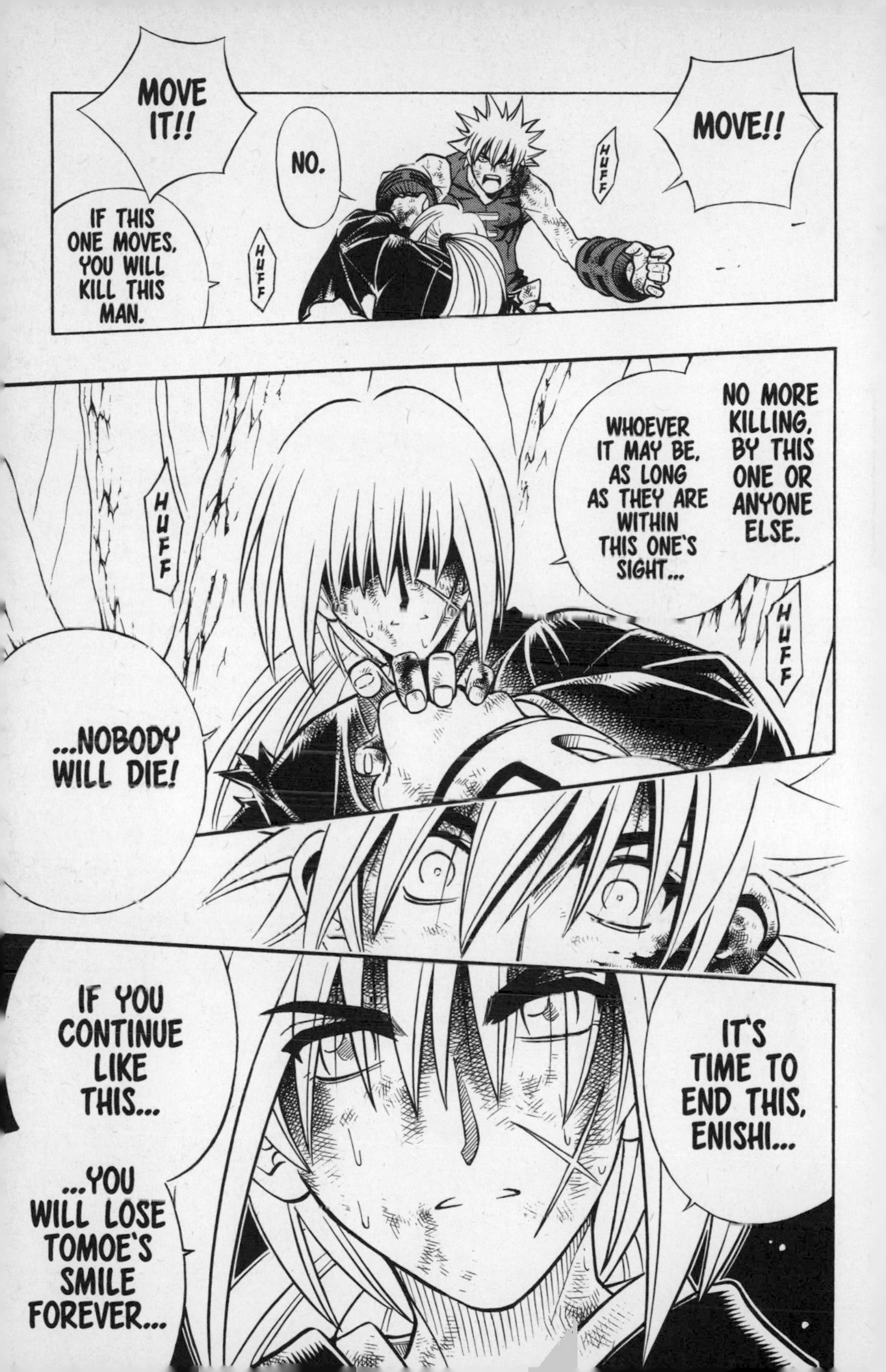

MOVE!!
HUFF
MOVE IT!!
NO.
HUFF
IF THIS ONE MOVES, YOU WILL KILL THIS MAN.
NO MORE KILLING, BY THIS ONE OR ANYONE ELSE.
WHOEVER IT MAY BE, AS LONG AS THEY ARE WITHIN THIS ONE'S SIGHT...
HUFF
HUFF
...NOBODY WILL DIE!
IT'S TIME TO END THIS, ENISHI...
IF YOU CONTINUE LIKE THIS...
...YOU WILL LOSE TOMOE'S SMILE FOREVER...

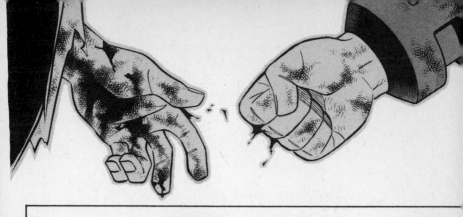

...KAORU-DONO...

THANK YOU...

...FOR PROTECT-ING...

TMP

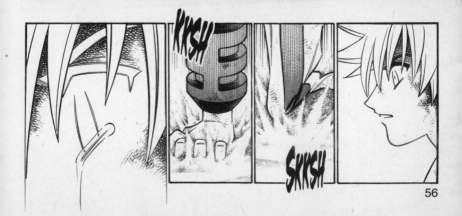

KKSH

SKKSH

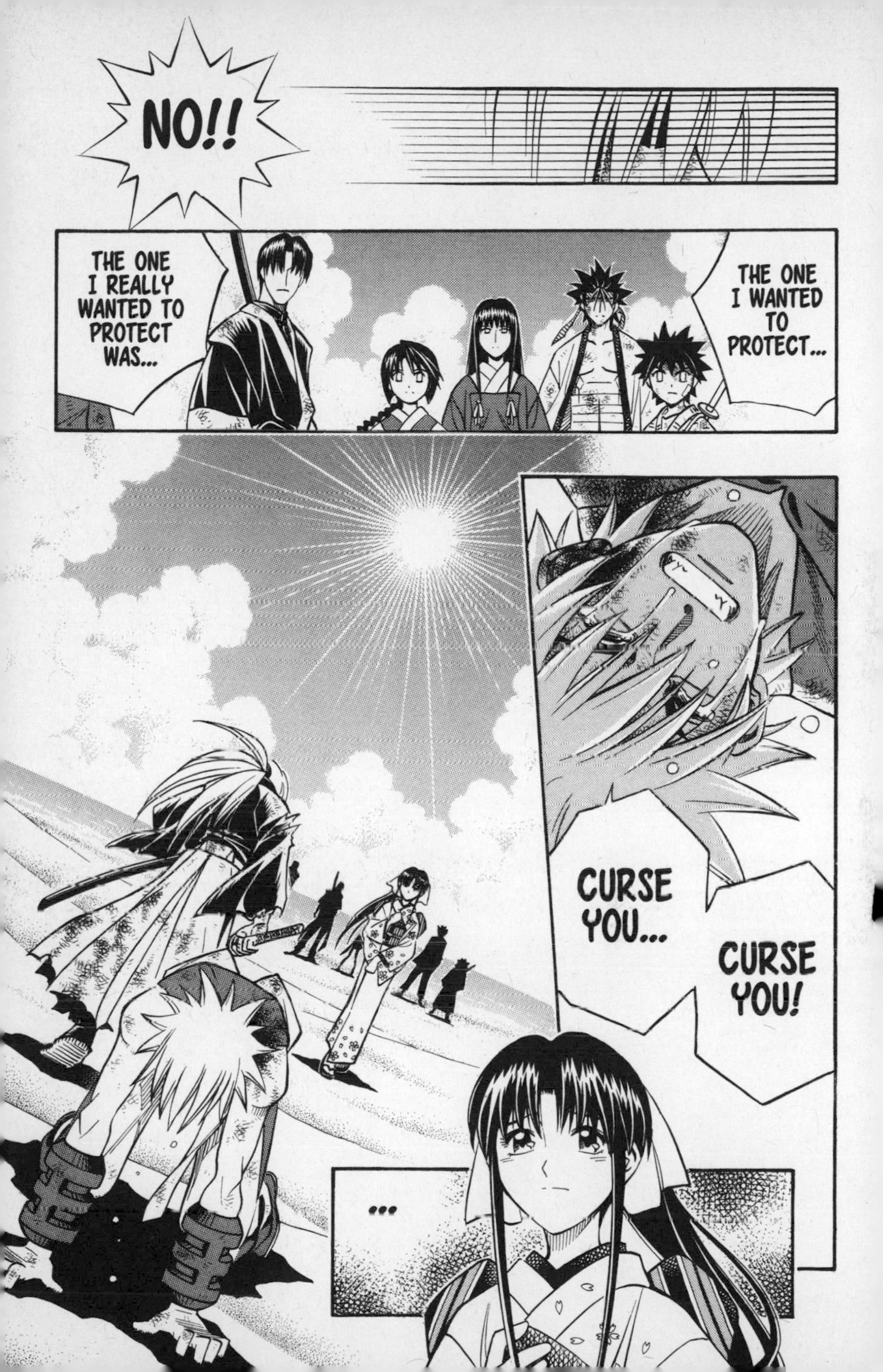
NO!!
THE ONE I WANTED TO PROTECT...
THE ONE I REALLY WANTED TO PROTECT WAS...
CURSE YOU...
CURSE YOU!
...

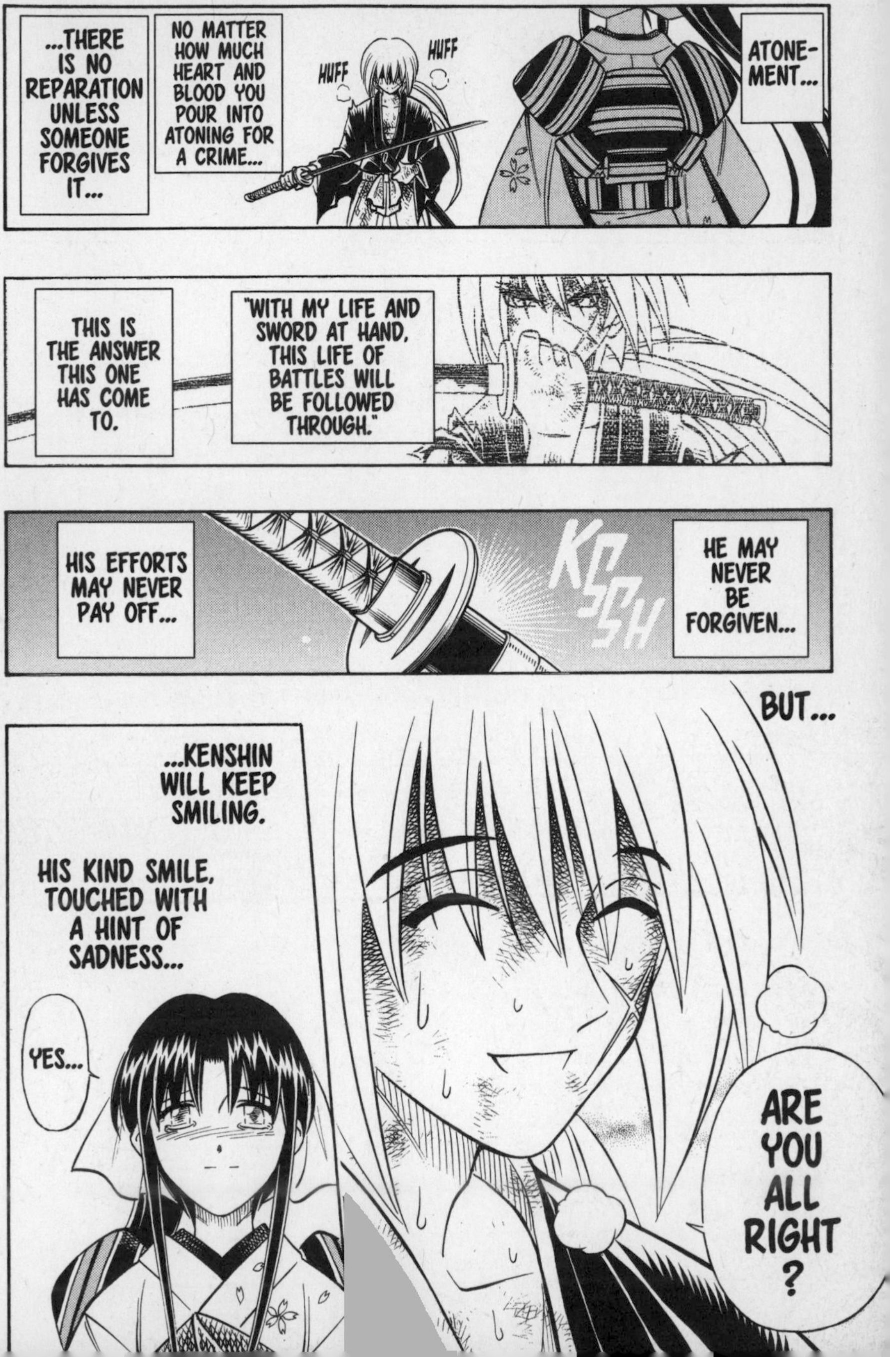

ATONEMENT...
HUFF
HUFF
NO MATTER HOW MUCH HEART AND BLOOD YOU POUR INTO ATONING FOR A CRIME...
...THERE IS NO REPARATION UNLESS SOMEONE FORGIVES IT...
"WITH MY LIFE AND SWORD AT HAND, THIS LIFE OF BATTLES WILL BE FOLLOWED THROUGH."
THIS IS THE ANSWER THIS ONE HAS COME TO.
HE MAY NEVER BE FORGIVEN...
KSSH
HIS EFFORTS MAY NEVER PAY OFF...
BUT...
...KENSHIN WILL KEEP SMILING.
HIS KIND SMILE, TOUCHED WITH A HINT OF SADNESS...
ARE YOU ALL RIGHT?
YES...

READ THIS WAY

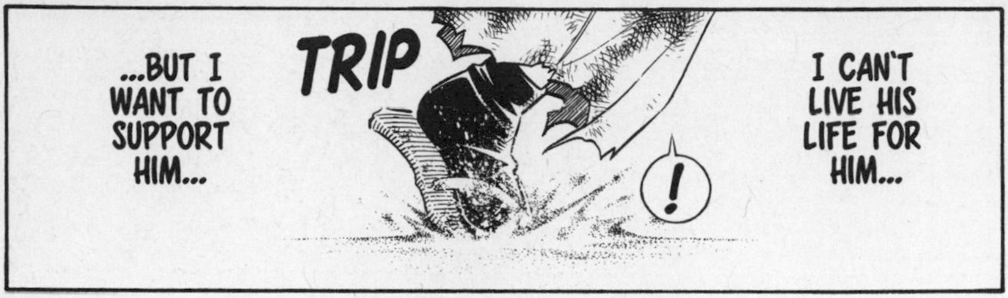

I CAN'T LIVE HIS LIFE FOR HIM...
TRIP
...BUT I WANT TO SUPPORT HIM...
!

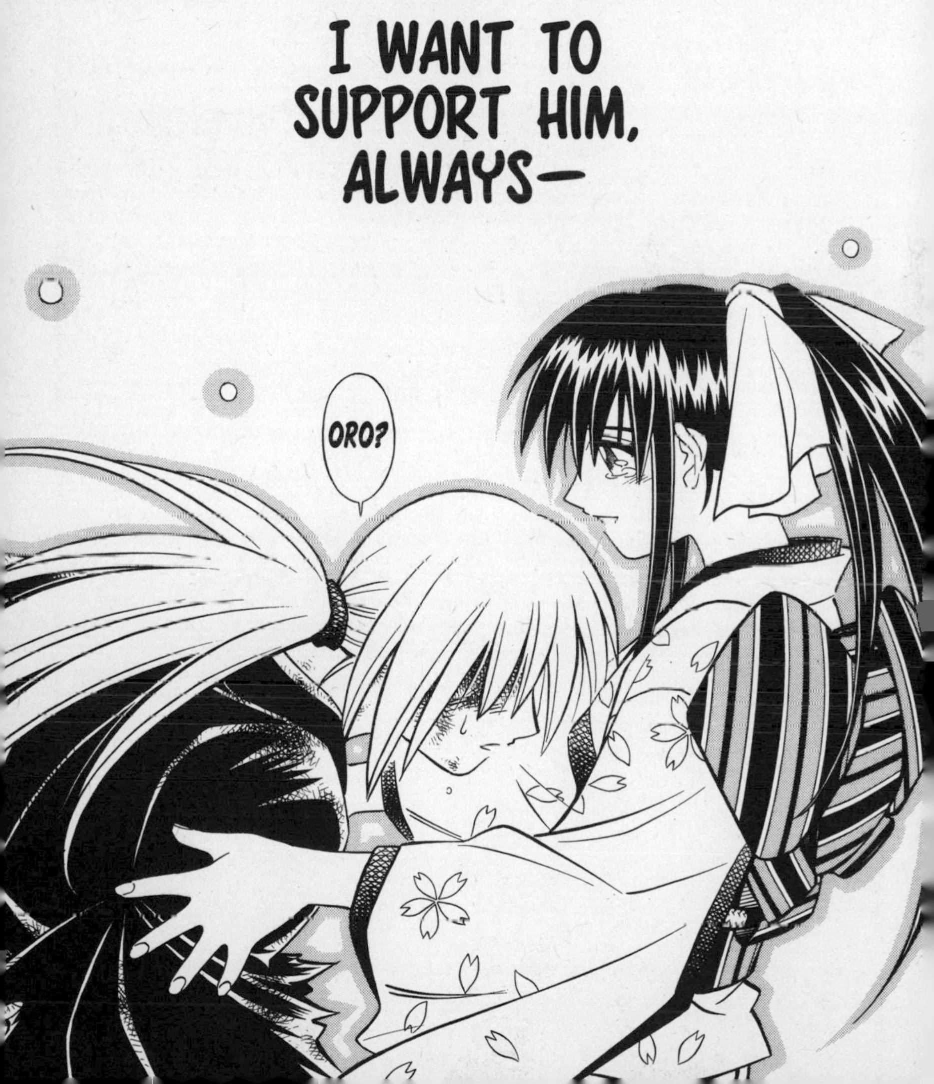

I WANT TO SUPPORT HIM, ALWAYS—
ORO?

The Secret Life of Characters (53)

—Yukishiro Enishi—

His model or concept is "revenge."

Shishio, the last boss from the Kyoto episodes, was the manic-type who kept going higher and higher and higher. So I wanted to make Enishi the depressive type, who kept falling deeper and deeper and deeper. But Shishio's influence remained, and so Enishi was sort of wishy-washy. Now I can see that Enishi has "obsession" in his heart, fit for the Terminator-like character Watsuki has wanted to depict. If instead of the Six Comrades *vs.* Kenshin and friends it had been Enishi *vs.* Kenshin and friends, and he fought against Aoshi, Saitō, Saonsuke, Yahiko and then got to Kenshin even after being seriously injured, Enishi would have been a more attractive character. But that is all hindsight. Crap. Enishi's obsessive personality, his admiration of Tomoe and grudge against Kenshin, is actually a reflection of Watsuki's dark side. (However, Watsuki does not have an older sister, and no one to take revenge on). This aspect was also designed to be the opposite of Shishio. Shishio has qualities Watsuki likes about himself, so Enishi in contrast is a projection of qualities Watsuki hates about himself...

While drawing Enishi, I fell into bouts of self-disgust. However, Enishi is a character I have some attachment to. Like Tomoe, I would like to have him reborn in another work. When that time comes, he will be the best Terminator-type character ever!

People often guess Basara from *Macross 7* as the design model for Enishi. Sometimes I hear Vash from *Trigun* by Naitow Yasuhiro-*sensei*, but both are incorrect. If I say it in one breath, it is, "A slightly deviant, white-haired, pointy-haired, handsome young man, appearing in a fancy Kamijō Atushi-*sensei*-like manga." (So there is no specific model). Of course, Watsuki's inadequate art skill was unable to draw this correctly. Models are strictly models. He has been converted to my style, and had sunglasses added since he's in the mafia, shady Chinese clothing since he's from the continent, and the half cape from Gambit in *X-Men A.O.A.*, completing Enishi. I think this is actually one of the better designs, but he was a bit too handsome for a final boss, in my honest opinion. I am a bit tired of drawing the handsome types.

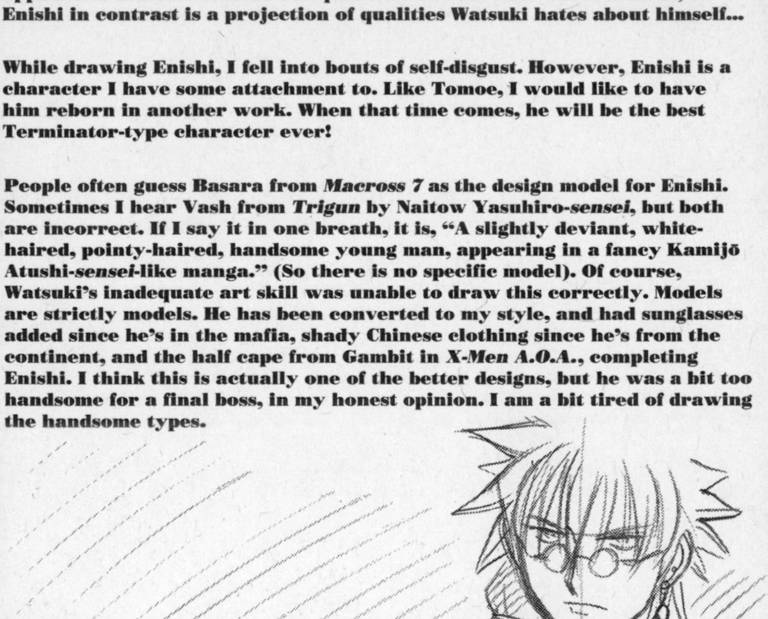
伸宏
和月

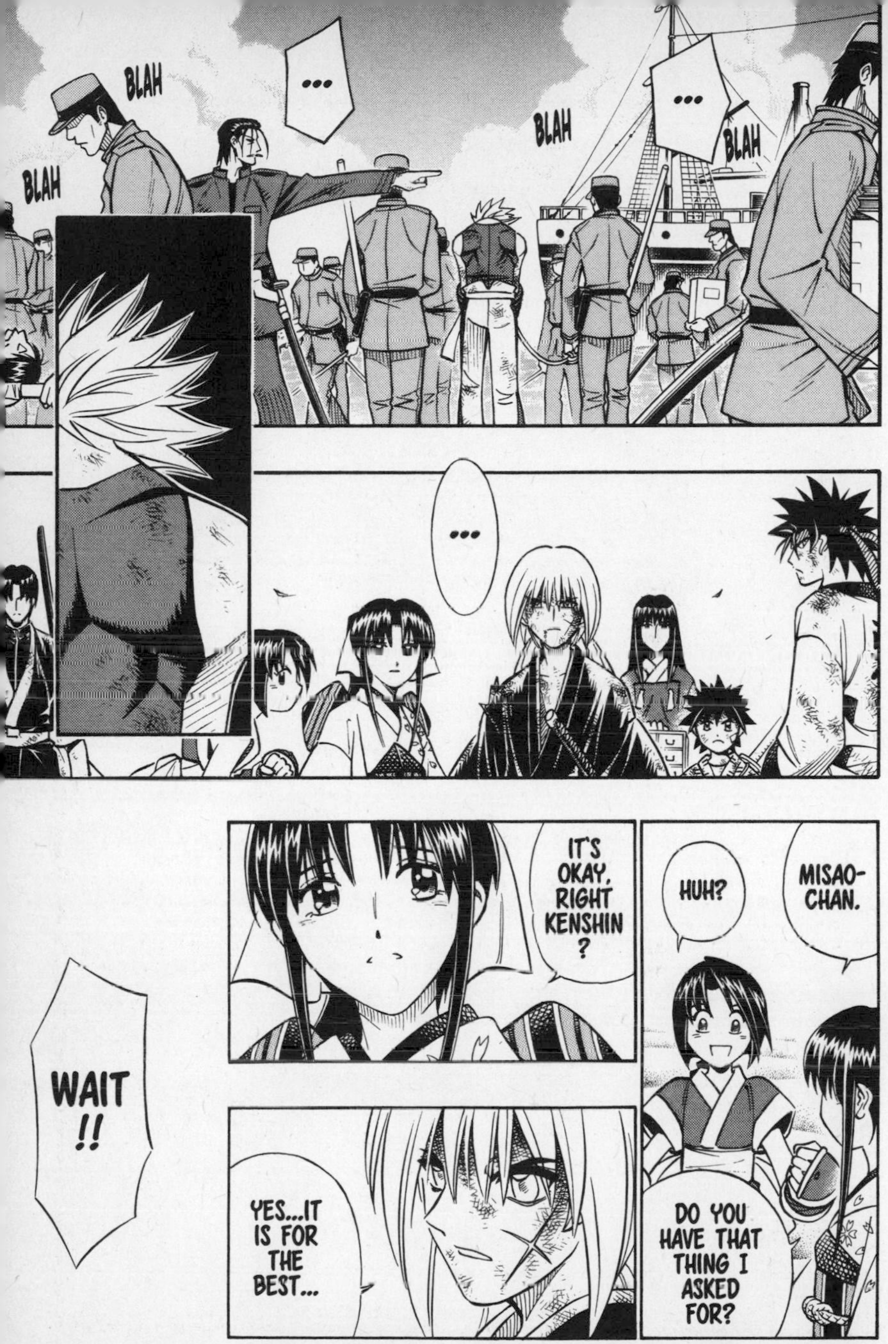
...
BLAH
BLAH
...
BLAH
BLAH
...
MISAO-CHAN.
HUH?
DO YOU HAVE THAT THING I ASKED FOR?
IT'S OKAY, RIGHT KENSHIN?
YES...IT IS FOR THE BEST...
WAIT!!

Act 251—Hurry Go Round

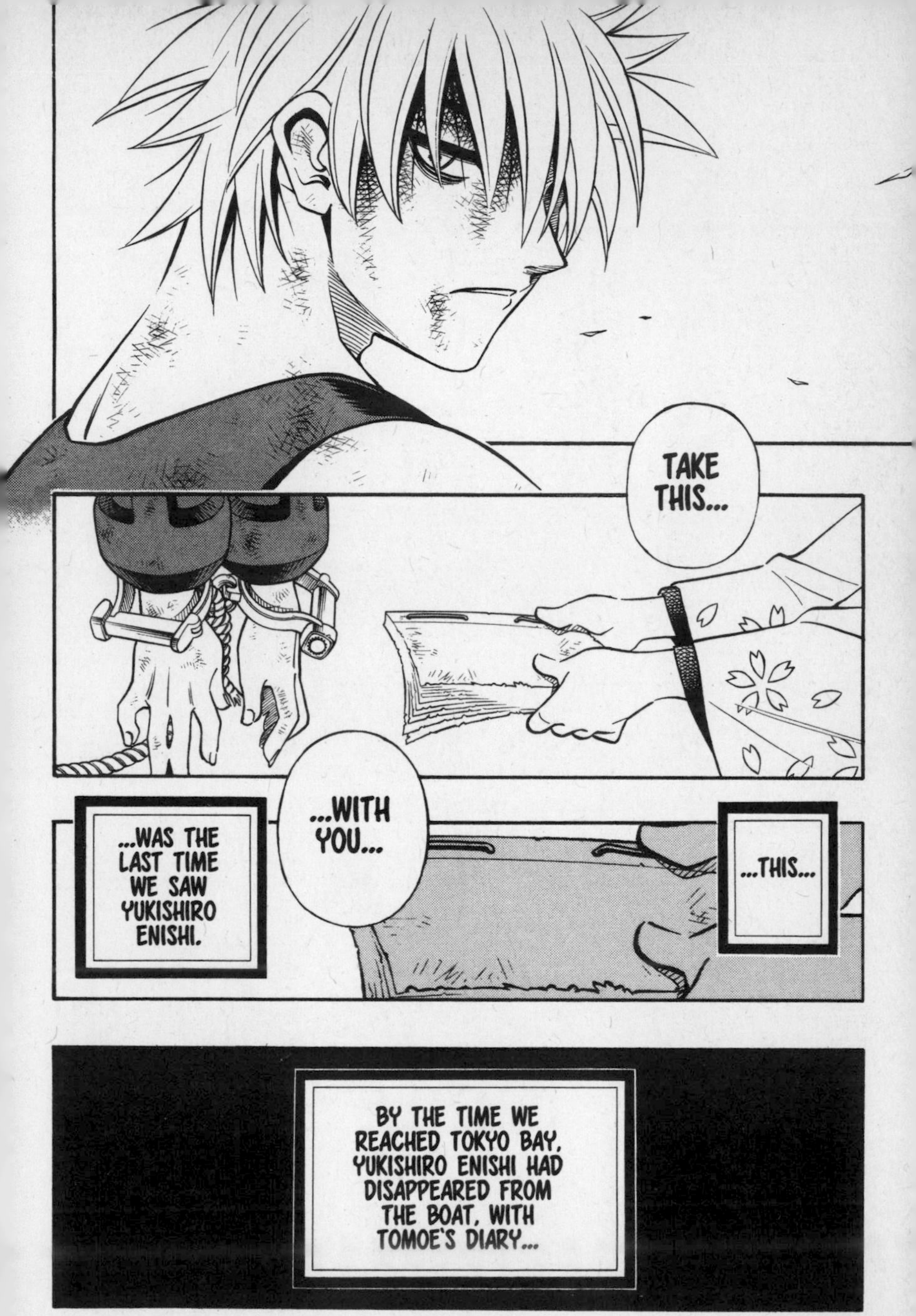
TAKE THIS...
...WITH YOU...
...THIS...
...WAS THE LAST TIME WE SAW YUKISHIRO ENISHI.
BY THE TIME WE REACHED TOKYO BAY, YUKISHIRO ENISHI HAD DISAPPEARED FROM THE BOAT, WITH TOMOE'S DIARY...

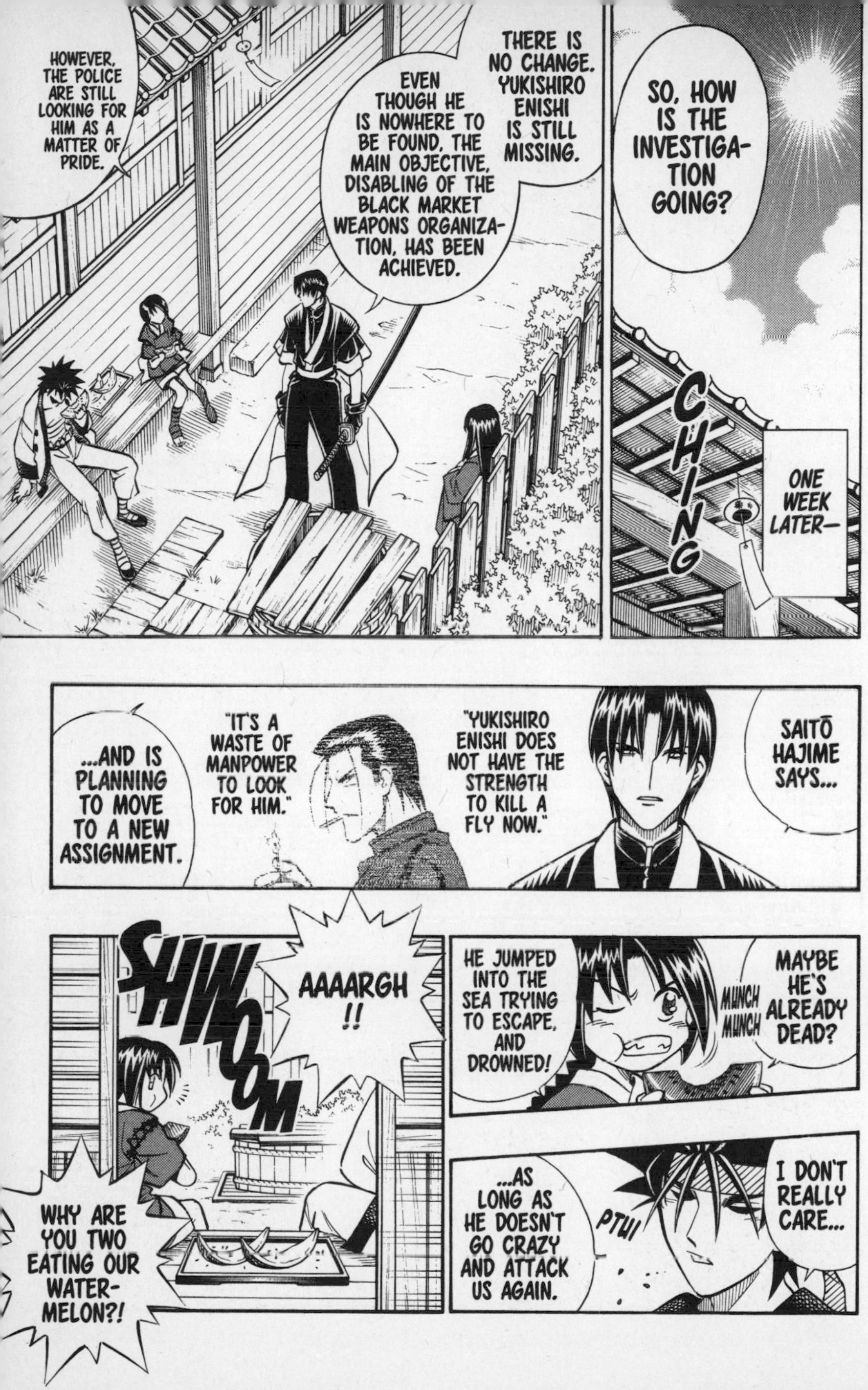

SO, HOW IS THE INVESTIGATION GOING?
CHING
ONE WEEK LATER—
THERE IS NO CHANGE. YUKISHIRO ENISHI IS STILL MISSING.
EVEN THOUGH HE IS NOWHERE TO BE FOUND, THE MAIN OBJECTIVE, DISABLING OF THE BLACK MARKET WEAPONS ORGANIZATION, HAS BEEN ACHIEVED.
HOWEVER, THE POLICE ARE STILL LOOKING FOR HIM AS A MATTER OF PRIDE.
SAITŌ HAJIME SAYS...
"YUKISHIRO ENISHI DOES NOT HAVE THE STRENGTH TO KILL A FLY NOW."
"IT'S A WASTE OF MANPOWER TO LOOK FOR HIM."
...AND IS PLANNING TO MOVE TO A NEW ASSIGNMENT.
MAYBE HE'S ALREADY DEAD?
MUNCH MUNCH
HE JUMPED INTO THE SEA TRYING TO ESCAPE, AND DROWNED!
I DON'T REALLY CARE...
PTUI
...AS LONG AS HE DOESN'T GO CRAZY AND ATTACK US AGAIN.
AAAARGH !!
SHWOOM
WHY ARE YOU TWO EATING OUR WATER-MELON?!

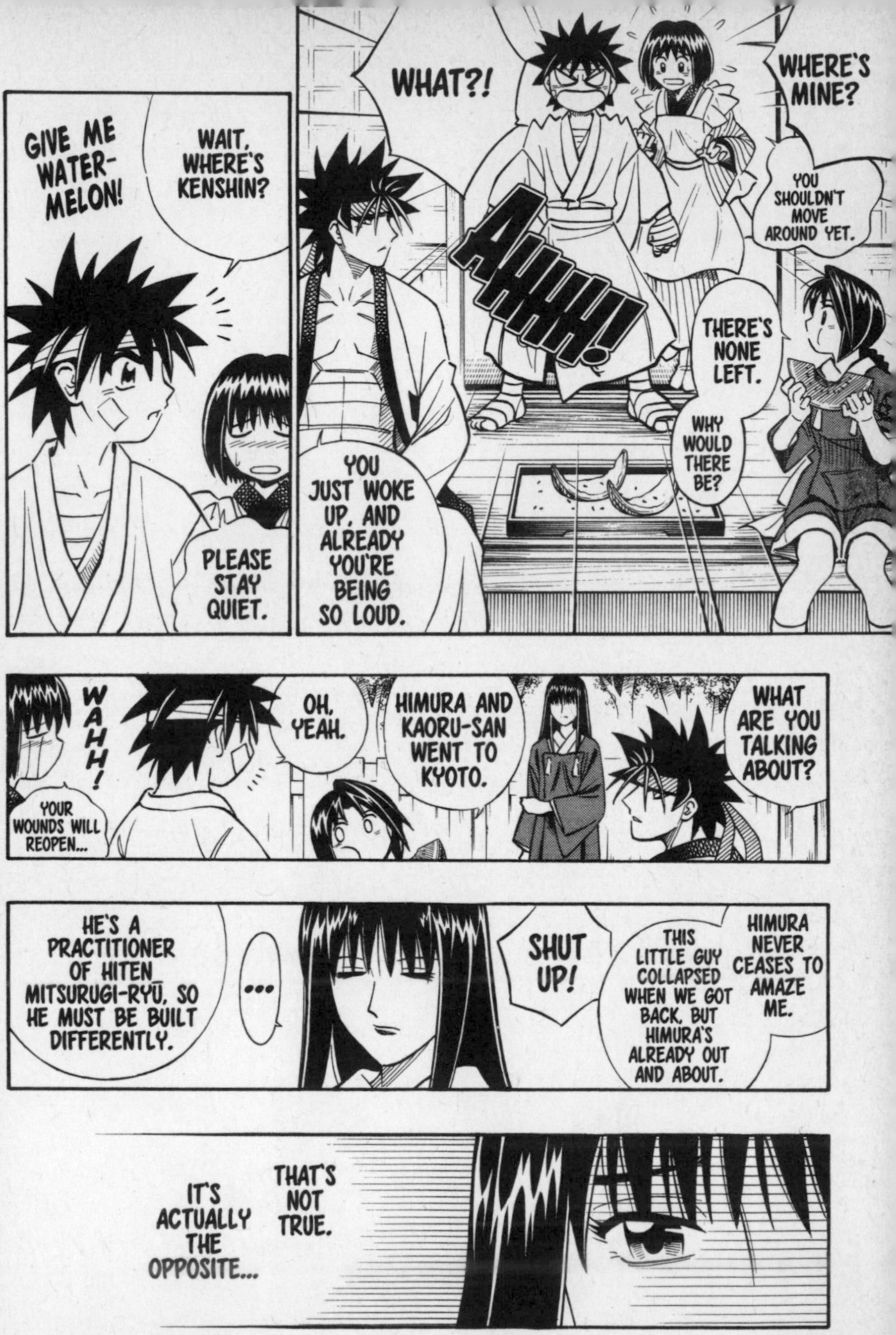
WHERE'S MINE?
YOU SHOULDN'T MOVE AROUND YET.
WHAT?!
AHHH!
THERE'S NONE LEFT.
WHY WOULD THERE BE?
YOU JUST WOKE UP, AND ALREADY YOU'RE BEING SO LOUD.
WAIT, WHERE'S KENSHIN?
GIVE ME WATER-MELON!
PLEASE STAY QUIET.
WHAT ARE YOU TALKING ABOUT?
HIMURA AND KAORU-SAN WENT TO KYOTO.
OH, YEAH.
WAHH!
YOUR WOUNDS WILL REOPEN...
HIMURA NEVER CEASES TO AMAZE ME.
THIS LITTLE GUY COLLAPSED WHEN WE GOT BACK, BUT HIMURA'S ALREADY OUT AND ABOUT.
SHUT UP!
...
HE'S A PRACTITIONER OF HITEN MITSURUGI-RYŪ, SO HE MUST BE BUILT DIFFERENTLY.
THAT'S NOT TRUE.
IT'S ACTUALLY THE OPPOSITE...

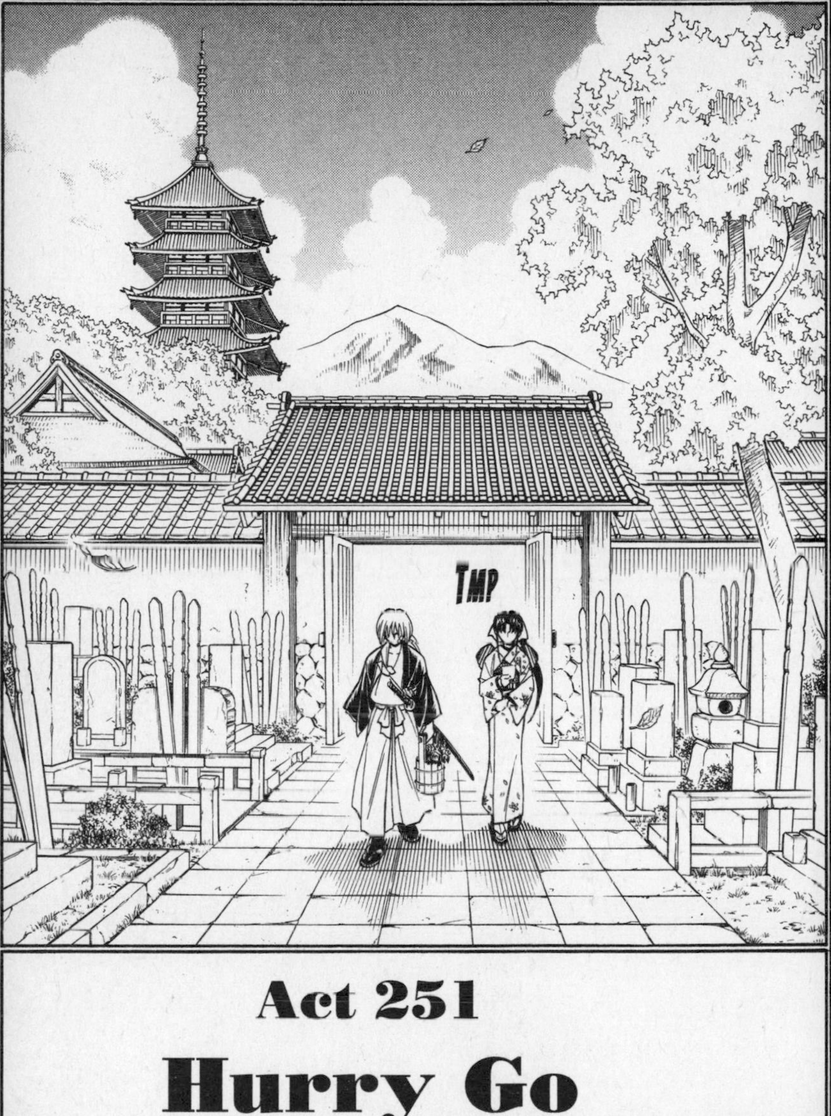
TMP

Act 251
Hurry Go Round

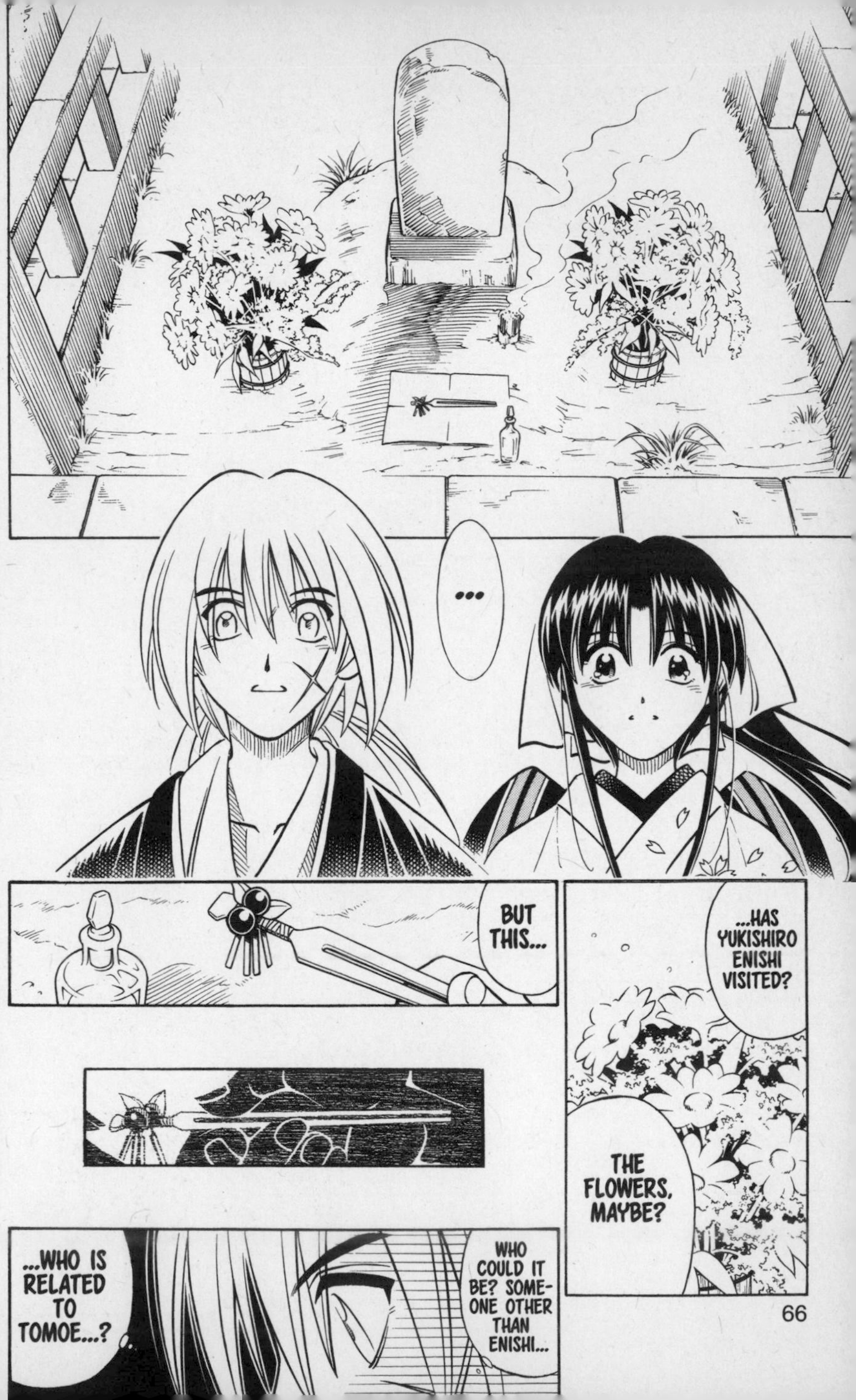
...
...HAS YUKISHIRO ENISHI VISITED?
THE FLOWERS, MAYBE?
BUT THIS...
WHO COULD IT BE? SOME-ONE OTHER THAN ENISHI...
...WHO IS RELATED TO TOMOE...?

READ THIS WAY

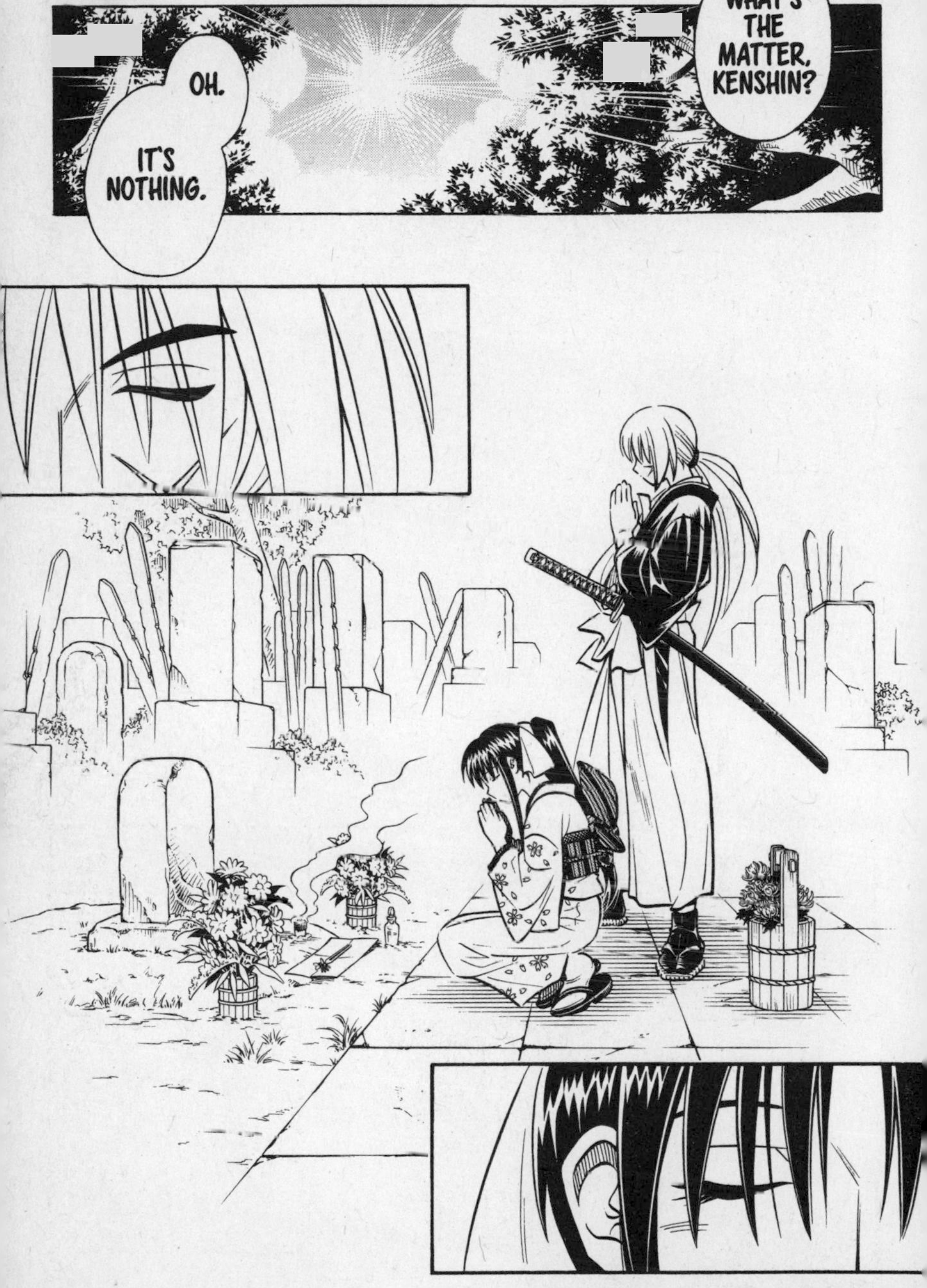
WHAT'S THE MATTER, KENSHIN?
OH.
IT'S NOTHING.

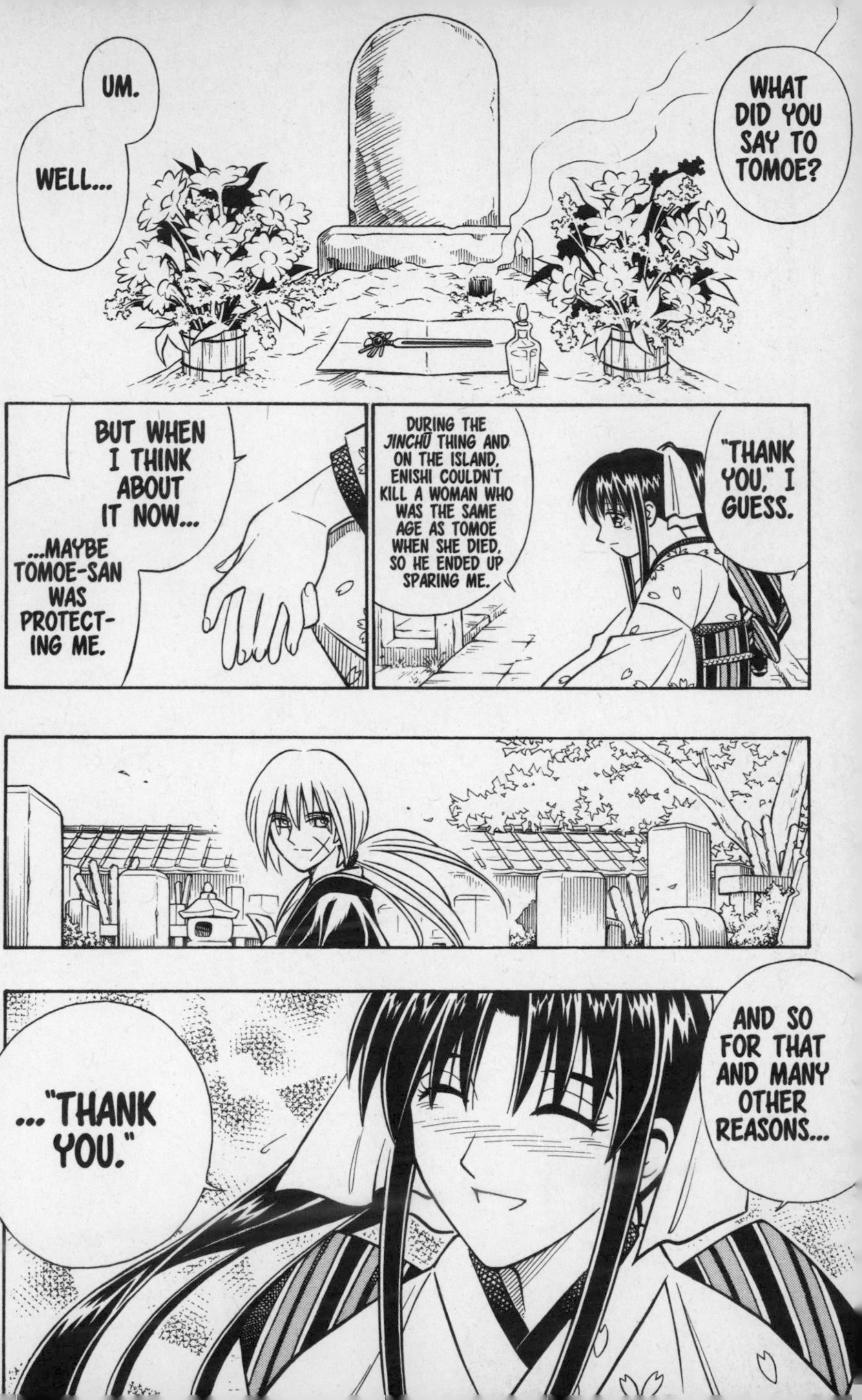
WHAT DID YOU SAY TO TOMOE?
UM.
WELL...
"THANK YOU," I GUESS.
DURING THE JINCHŪ THING AND ON THE ISLAND, ENISHI COULDN'T KILL A WOMAN WHO WAS THE SAME AGE AS TOMOE WHEN SHE DIED, SO HE ENDED UP SPARING ME.
BUT WHEN I THINK ABOUT IT NOW...
...MAYBE TOMOE-SAN WAS PROTECTING ME.
AND SO FOR THAT AND MANY OTHER REASONS...
..."THANK YOU."

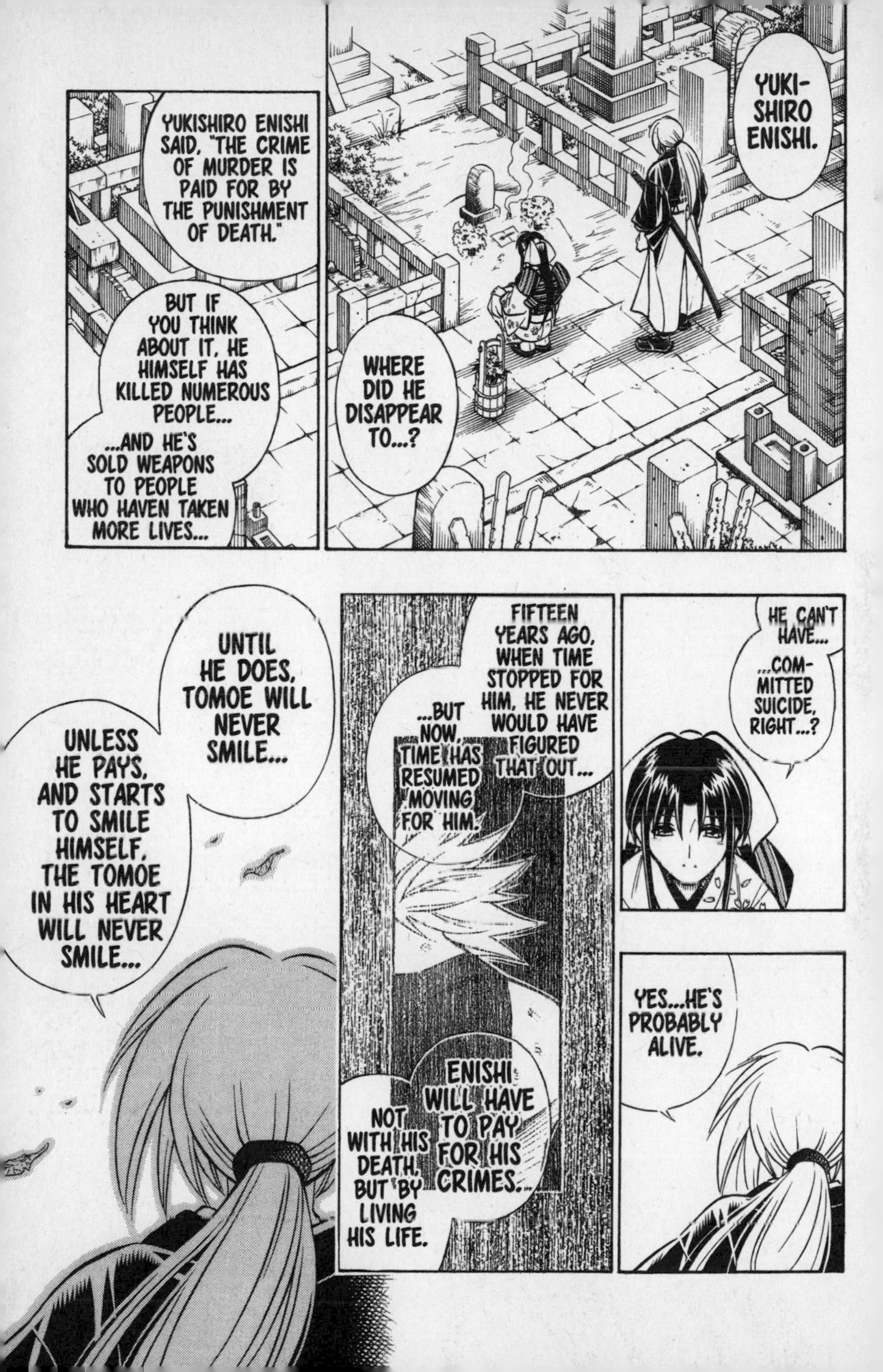
YUKI-SHIRO ENISHI.
WHERE DID HE DISAPPEAR TO...?
YUKISHIRO ENISHI SAID, "THE CRIME OF MURDER IS PAID FOR BY THE PUNISHMENT OF DEATH."
BUT IF YOU THINK ABOUT IT, HE HIMSELF HAS KILLED NUMEROUS PEOPLE...
...AND HE'S SOLD WEAPONS TO PEOPLE WHO HAVEN TAKEN MORE LIVES...
HE CAN'T HAVE...
...COM-MITTED SUICIDE, RIGHT...?
YES...HE'S PROBABLY ALIVE.
FIFTEEN YEARS AGO, WHEN TIME STOPPED FOR HIM, HE NEVER WOULD HAVE FIGURED THAT OUT...
...BUT NOW, TIME HAS RESUMED MOVING FOR HIM.
ENISHI WILL HAVE TO PAY FOR HIS CRIMES...
NOT WITH HIS DEATH, BUT BY LIVING HIS LIFE.
UNTIL HE DOES, TOMOE WILL NEVER SMILE...
UNLESS HE PAYS, AND STARTS TO SMILE HIMSELF, THE TOMOE IN HIS HEART WILL NEVER SMILE...

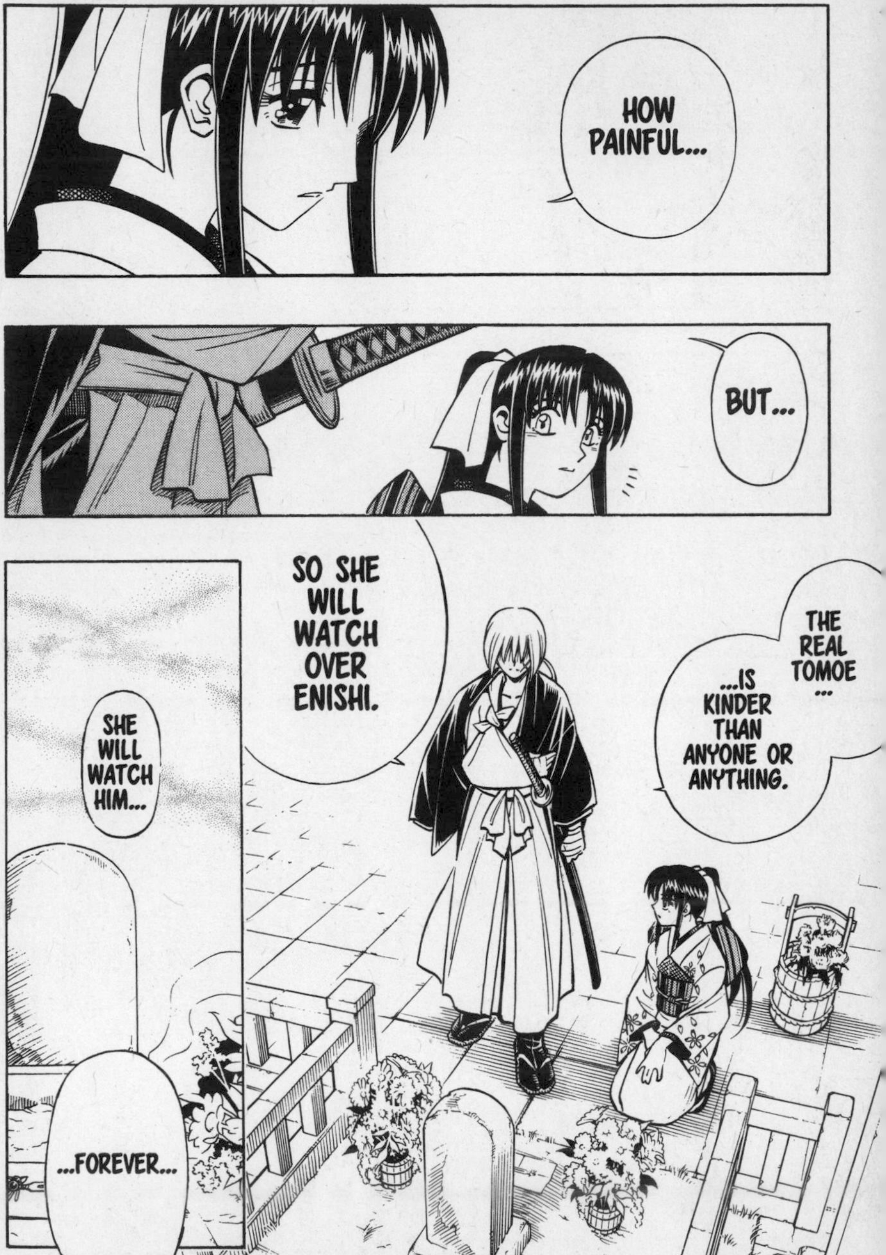
HOW PAINFUL...
BUT...
THE REAL TOMOE ...
...IS KINDER THAN ANYONE OR ANYTHING.
SO SHE WILL WATCH OVER ENISHI.
SHE WILL WATCH HIM...
...FOREVER...

READ THIS WAY

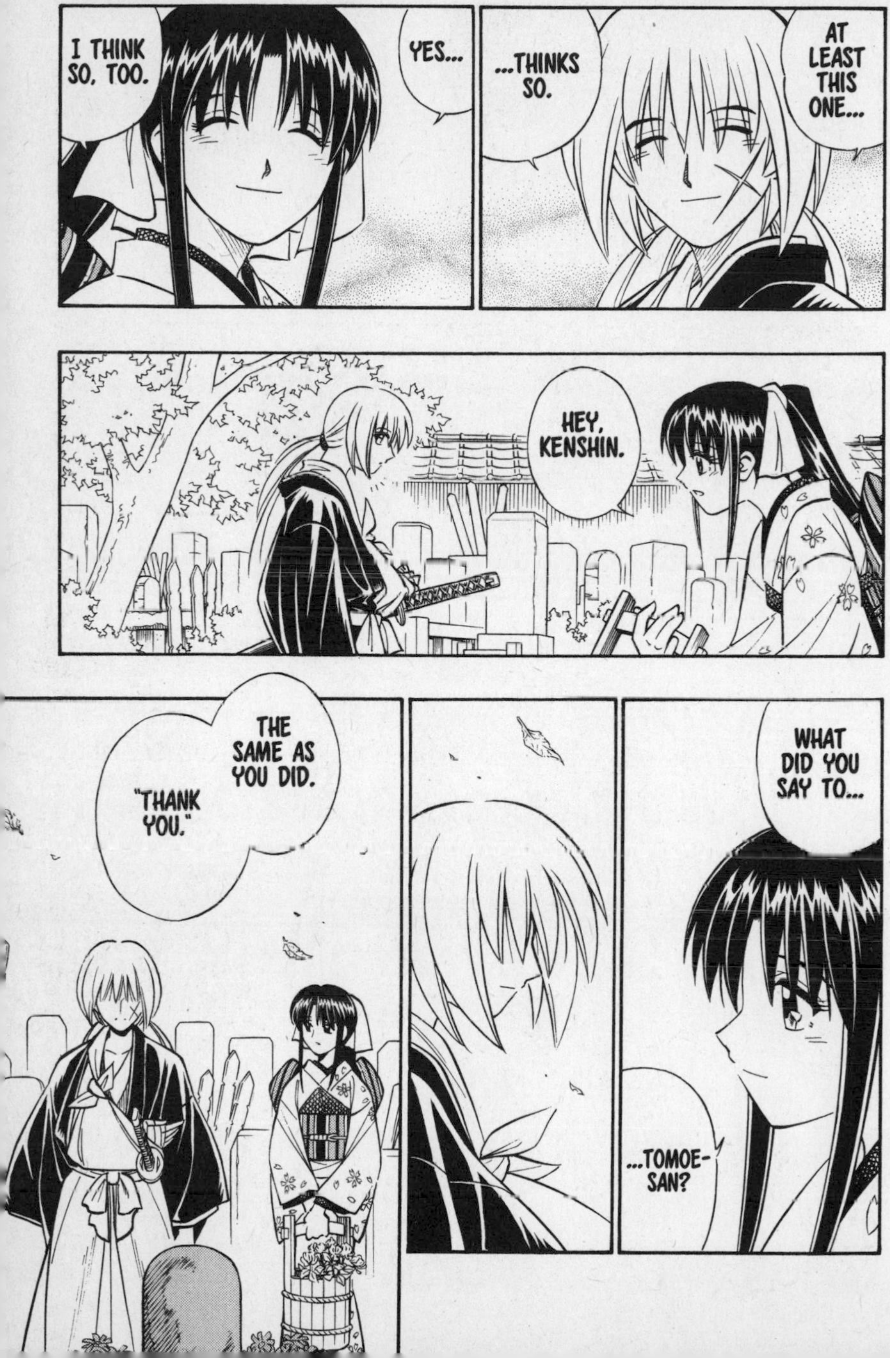
AT LEAST THIS ONE...
...THINKS SO.
YES...
I THINK SO, TOO.
HEY, KENSHIN.
WHAT DID YOU SAY TO...
...TOMOE-SAN?
THE SAME AS YOU DID.
"THANK YOU."

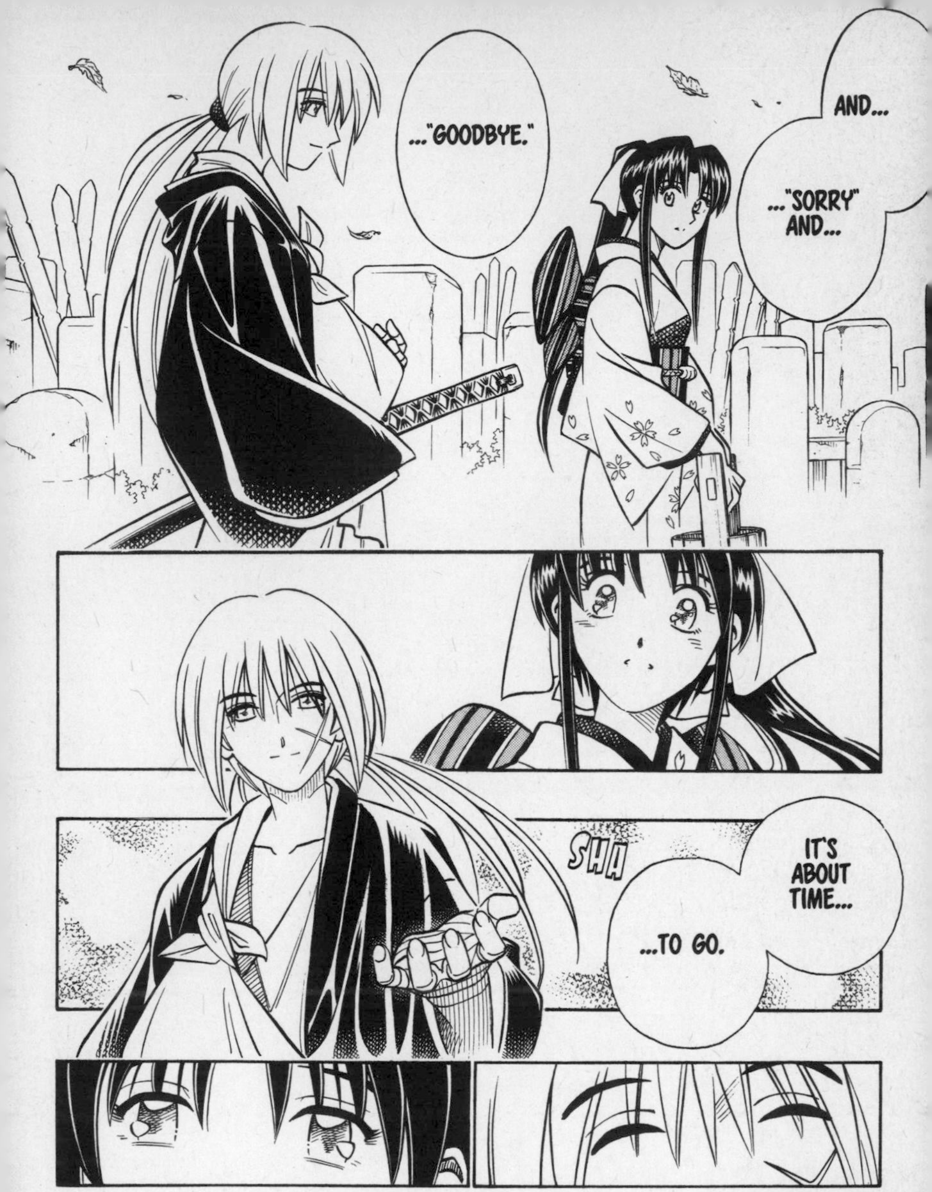
AND...
..."SORRY" AND...
..."GOODBYE."
IT'S ABOUT TIME...
...TO GO.
SHA
RUSTLE

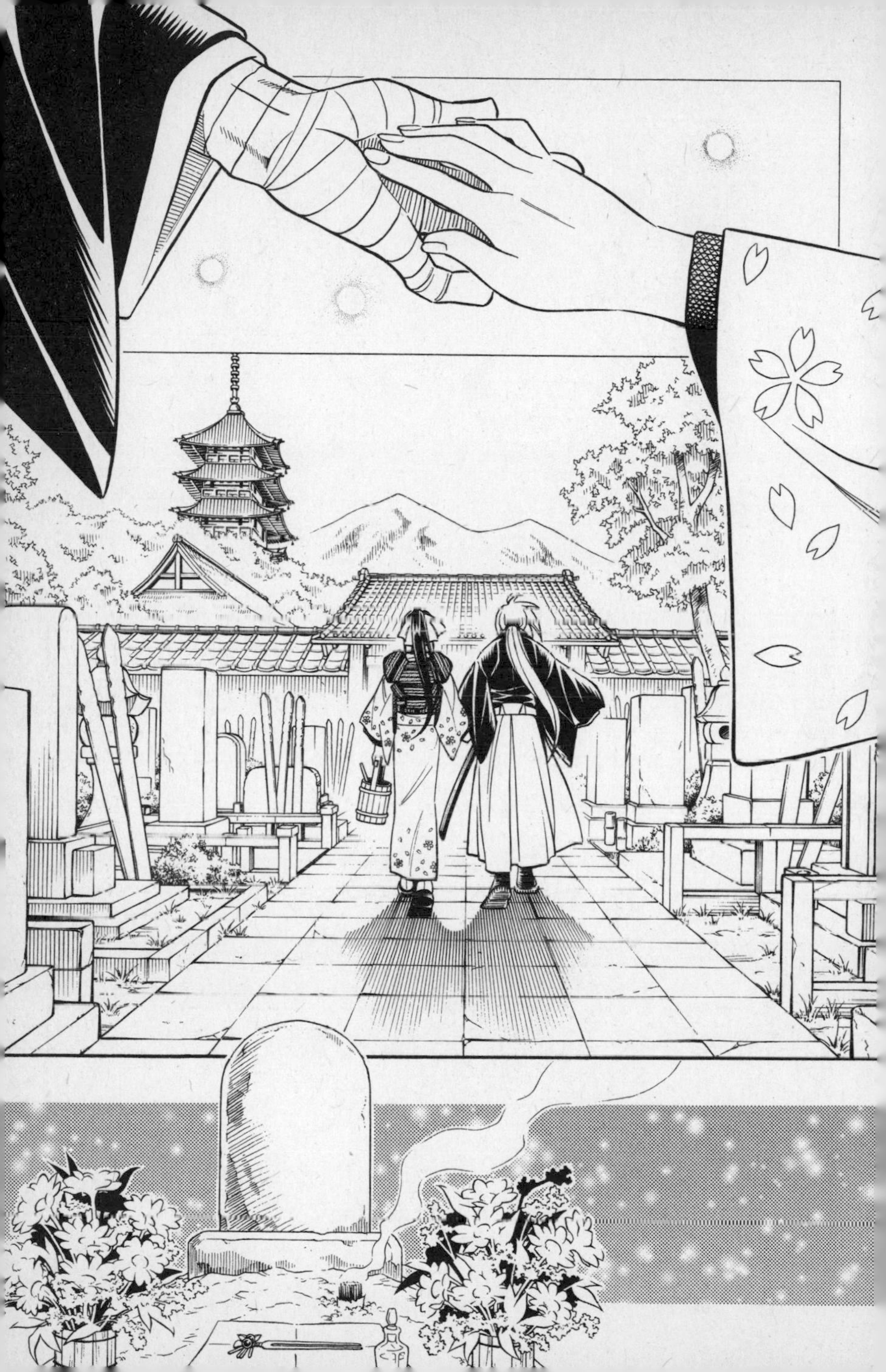

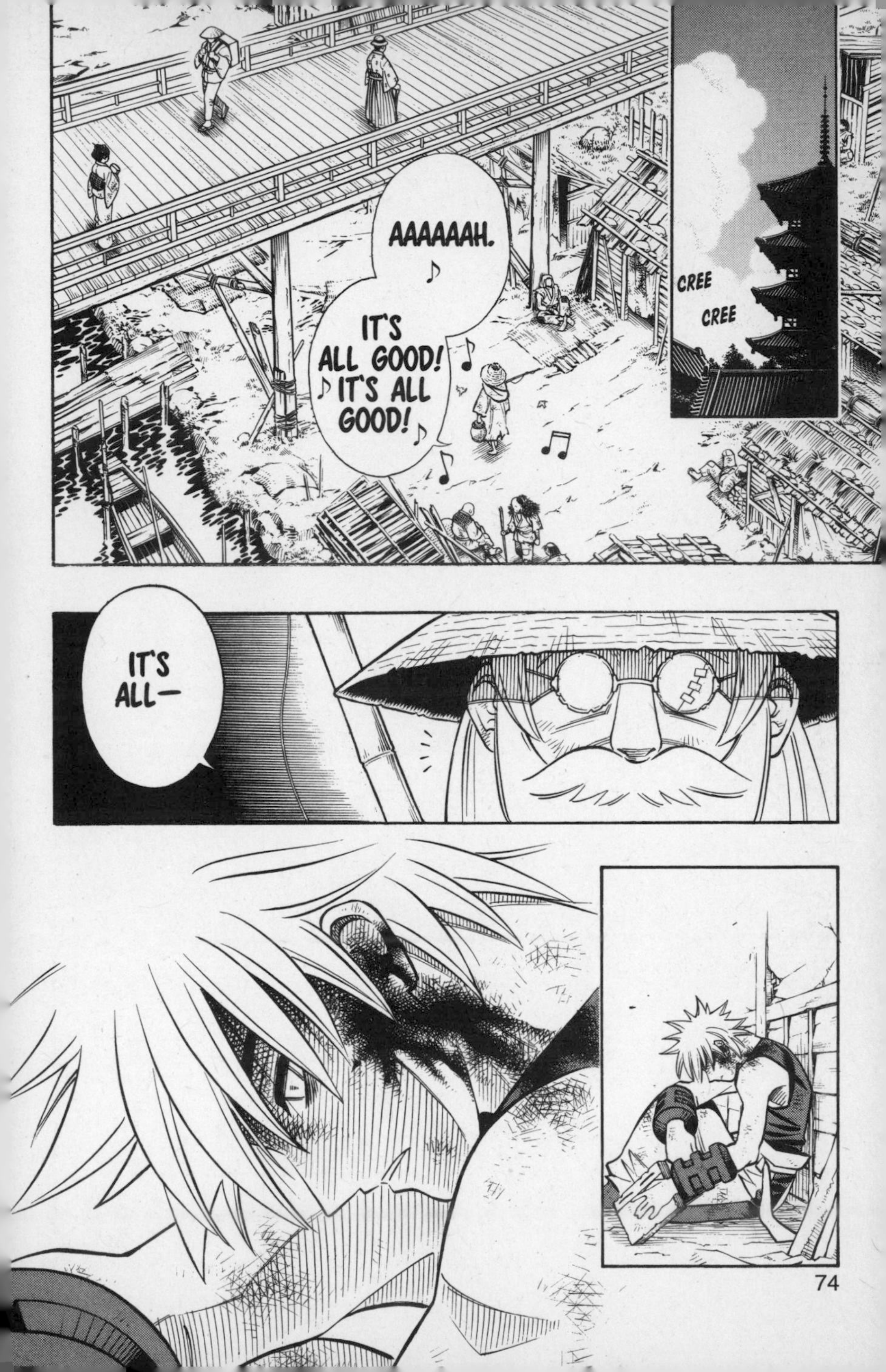
CREE
CREE
AAAAAAH. ♪
IT'S ALL GOOD! ♪ IT'S ALL GOOD! ♪
IT'S ALL—

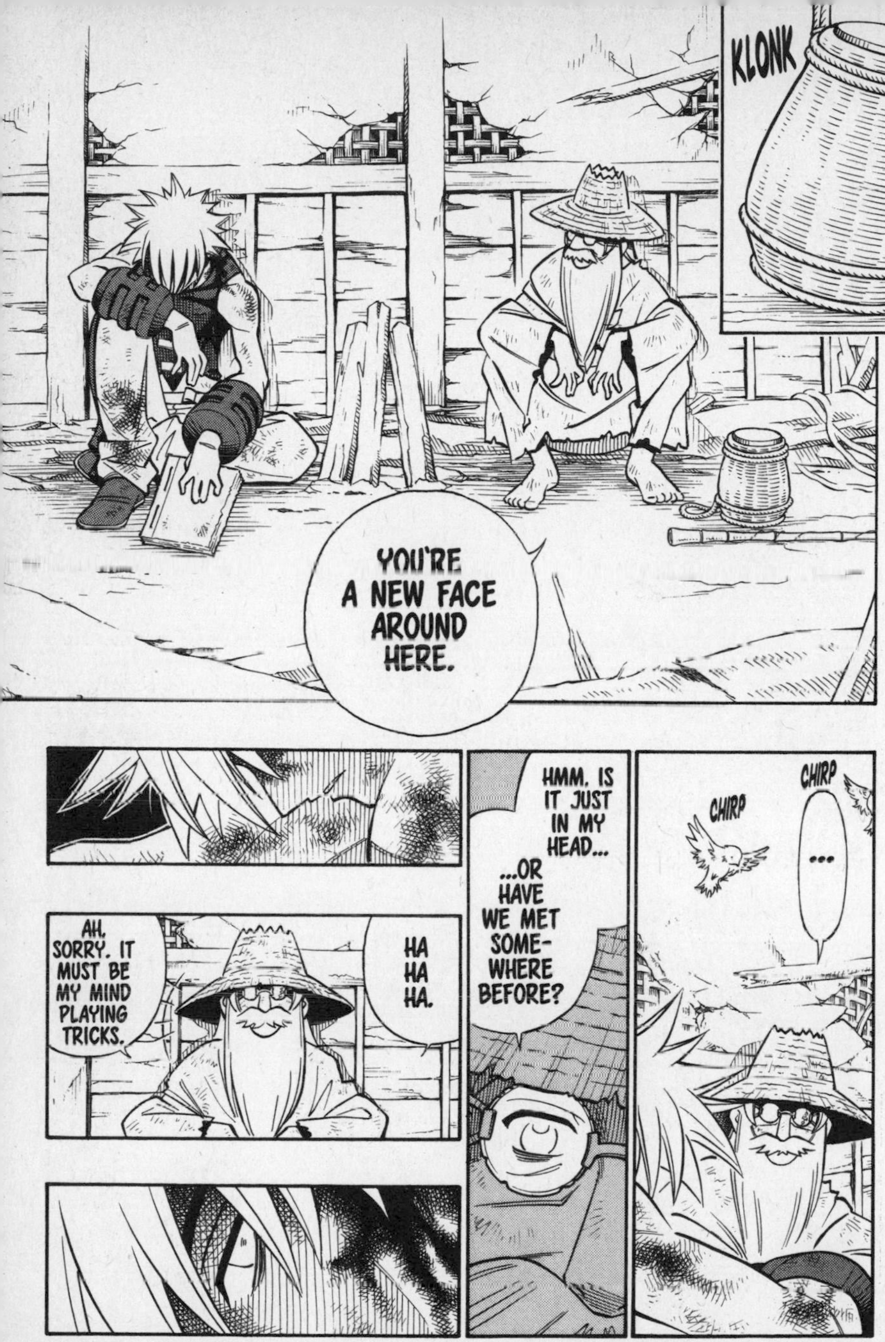
KLONK
YOU'RE A NEW FACE AROUND HERE.
CHIRP
CHIRP
...
HMM. IS IT JUST IN MY HEAD...
...OR HAVE WE MET SOME-WHERE BEFORE?
HA HA HA.
AH, SORRY. IT MUST BE MY MIND PLAYING TRICKS.

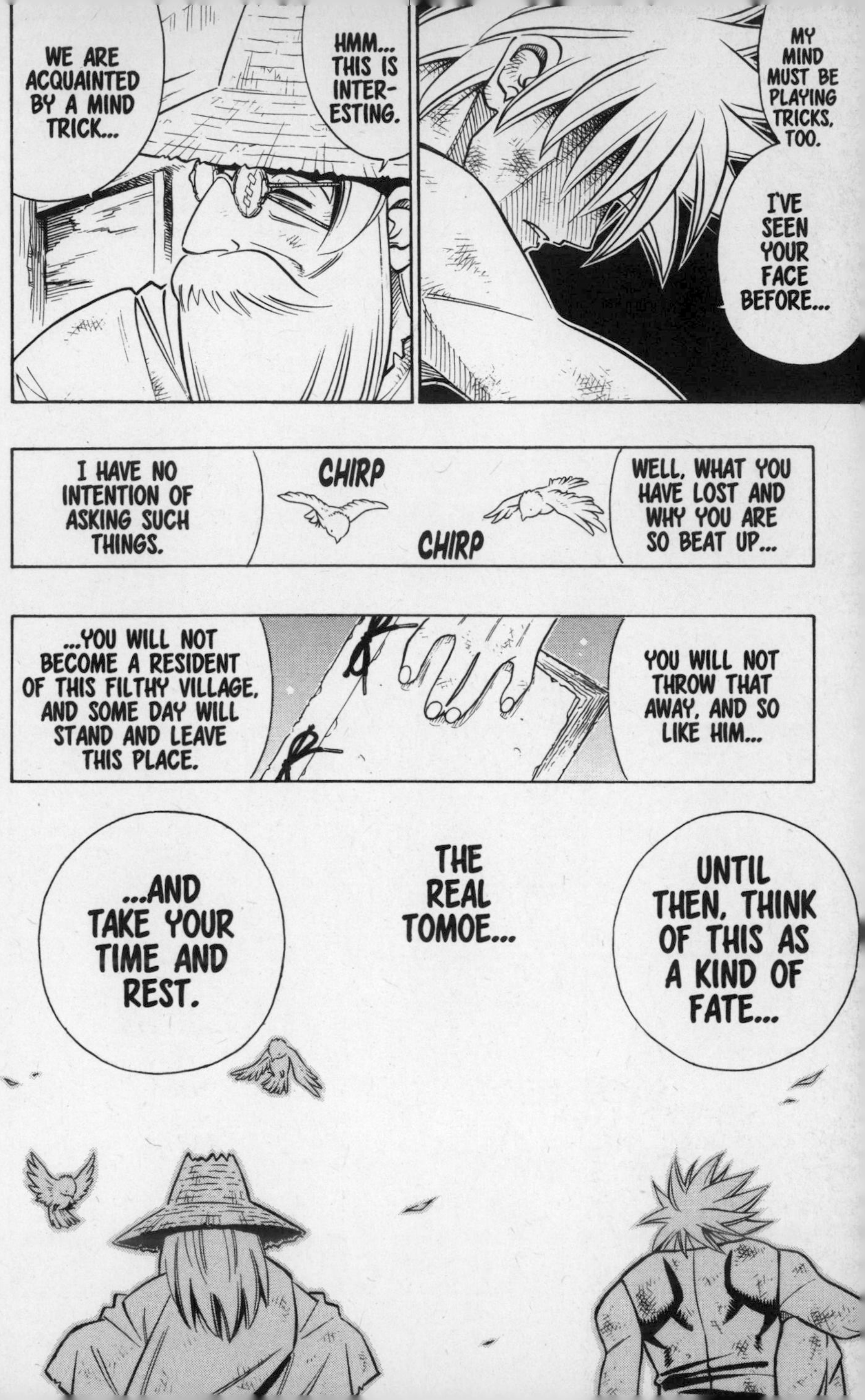
MY MIND MUST BE PLAYING TRICKS, TOO.
I'VE SEEN YOUR FACE BEFORE...
HMM... THIS IS INTER-ESTING.
WE ARE ACQUAINTED BY A MIND TRICK...
WELL, WHAT YOU HAVE LOST AND WHY YOU ARE SO BEAT UP...
CHIRP
CHIRP
I HAVE NO INTENTION OF ASKING SUCH THINGS.
YOU WILL NOT THROW THAT AWAY, AND SO LIKE HIM...
...YOU WILL NOT BECOME A RESIDENT OF THIS FILTHY VILLAGE, AND SOME DAY WILL STAND AND LEAVE THIS PLACE.
UNTIL THEN, THINK OF THIS AS A KIND OF FATE...
THE REAL TOMOE...
...AND TAKE YOUR TIME AND REST.

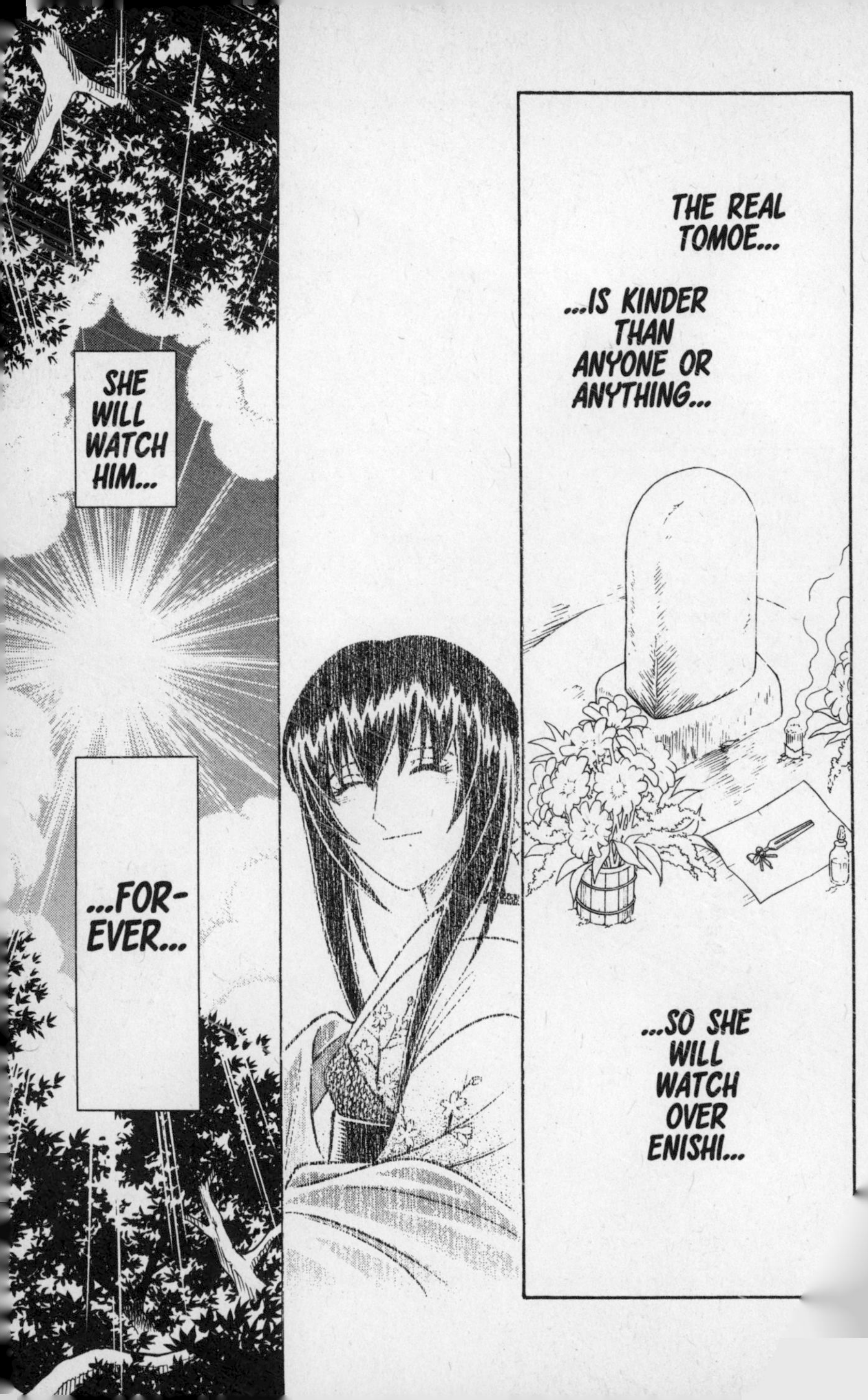
THE REAL TOMOE...
...IS KINDER THAN ANYONE OR ANYTHING...
...SO SHE WILL WATCH OVER ENISHI...
SHE WILL WATCH HIM...
...FOR-EVER...

"FREE TALK"

The last episode of the *Jinchū* arc is "Hurry Go Round." This title was borrowed from a song in hide's album, *Ja, Zoo*. I originally acquired this CD in order to listen to a TV anime theme song, and it also has this song on it. After listening to it, it seemed to fit well with Enishi and Battōsai (not Kenshin), so I made it the *Jinchū* arc theme song without permission. Towards the end, I was listening to it frequently. hide passed away soon after I discovered him, so I am very disappointed.

So, the *Jinchū* are... I have finally been able to row my way to the end. If anyone asks if it was good, I won't have a clear alswer, but I do feel good about having written it.

I wrote the *Jinchū* episodes in a different mode than the Kyoto episodes, which were aimed at entertaining boys. Actually, the Kyoto episodes were in a mode that was suggested by my editor in the middle of production. The original *Rurouni Kenshin* was supposed to be along the lines of the *Jinchū* episodes. But after the Kyoto episodes, Watsuki realized the pleasure he gets from writing a shonen manga. As a result, my mind and senses clashed in the *Jinchū* episode, resulting in some incomplete areas.

One of the joys of a manga artist is writing what he thinks is entertaining, but the sense of what is entertaining changes as a work progresses. Yet I was unable to adapt the work to this change in perception. It's been five and a half years, but I am still very immature.

Rurouni Kenshin will conclude here. There were ideas for a Hokkaido episode, a sequel. But I wanted to start a new series and have the fans read it, and thought that would be best, rather than continuing on with this work. The editors allowed me this wise decision, and so that's how things went.

This is very close to selfishness on Watsuki's part, so I shouldn't talk too much, but please give me your support.

I will work hard on my next series.

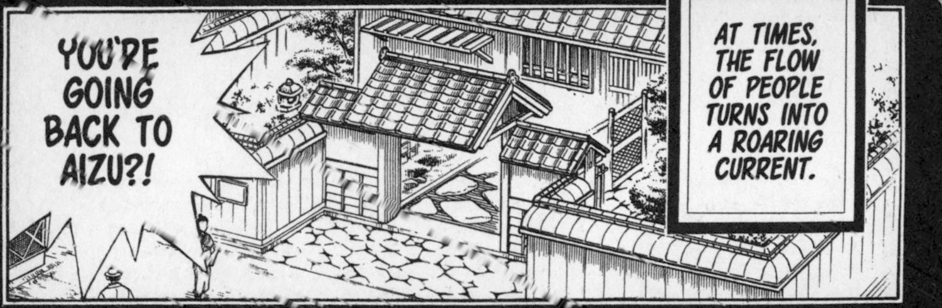
AT TIMES, THE FLOW OF PEOPLE TURNS INTO A ROARING CURRENT.
YOU'RE GOING BACK TO AIZU?!

Act 252
Autumn Wind

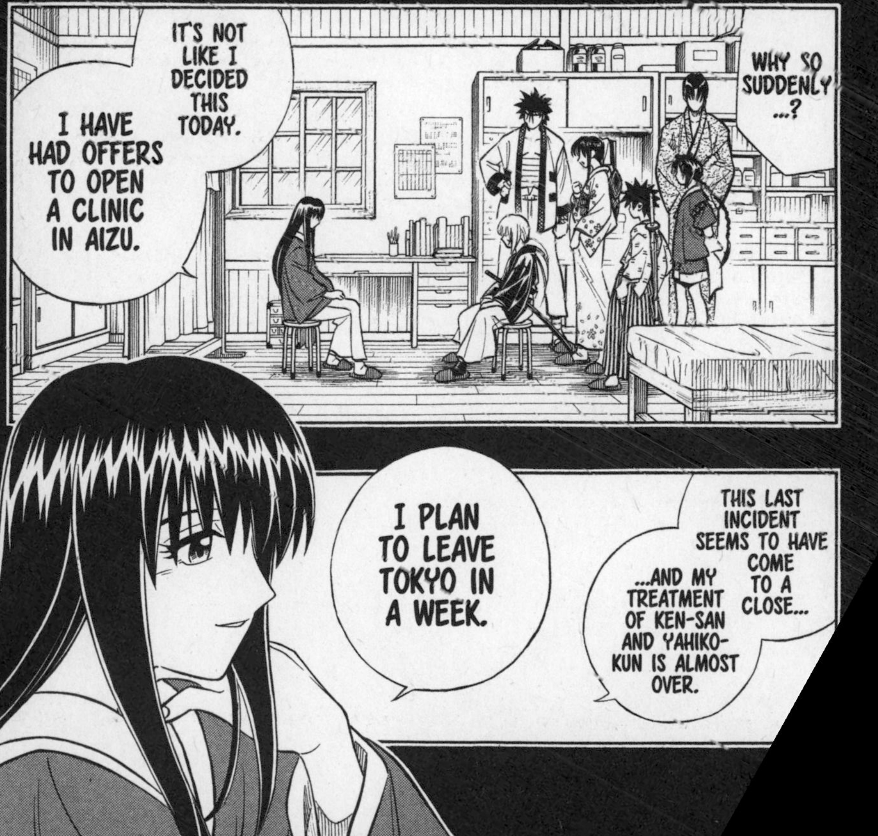
WHY SO SUDDENLY ...?
IT'S NOT LIKE I DECIDED THIS TODAY.
I HAVE HAD OFFERS TO OPEN A CLINIC IN AIZU.
THIS LAST INCIDENT SEEMS TO HAVE COME TO A CLOSE...
...AND MY TREATMENT OF KEN-SAN AND YAHIKO-KUN IS ALMOST OVER.
I PLAN TO LEAVE TOKYO IN A WEEK.

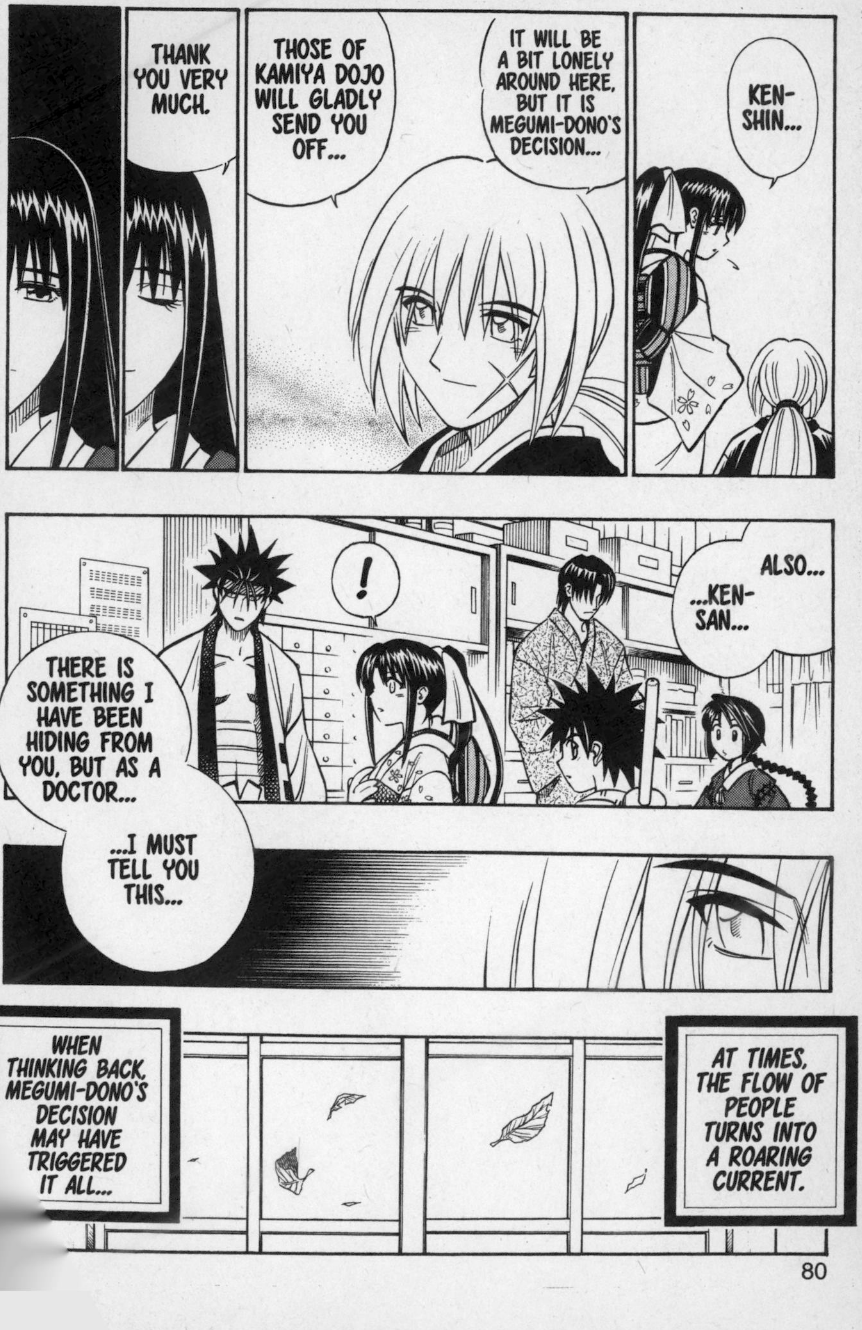
KEN-SHIN...
IT WILL BE A BIT LONELY AROUND HERE, BUT IT IS MEGUMI-DONO'S DECISION...
THOSE OF KAMIYA DOJO WILL GLADLY SEND YOU OFF...
THANK YOU VERY MUCH.
ALSO... ...KEN-SAN...
!
THERE IS SOMETHING I HAVE BEEN HIDING FROM YOU, BUT AS A DOCTOR...
...I MUST TELL YOU THIS...
AT TIMES, THE FLOW OF PEOPLE TURNS INTO A ROARING CURRENT.
WHEN THINKING BACK, MEGUMI-DONO'S DECISION MAY HAVE TRIGGERED IT ALL...

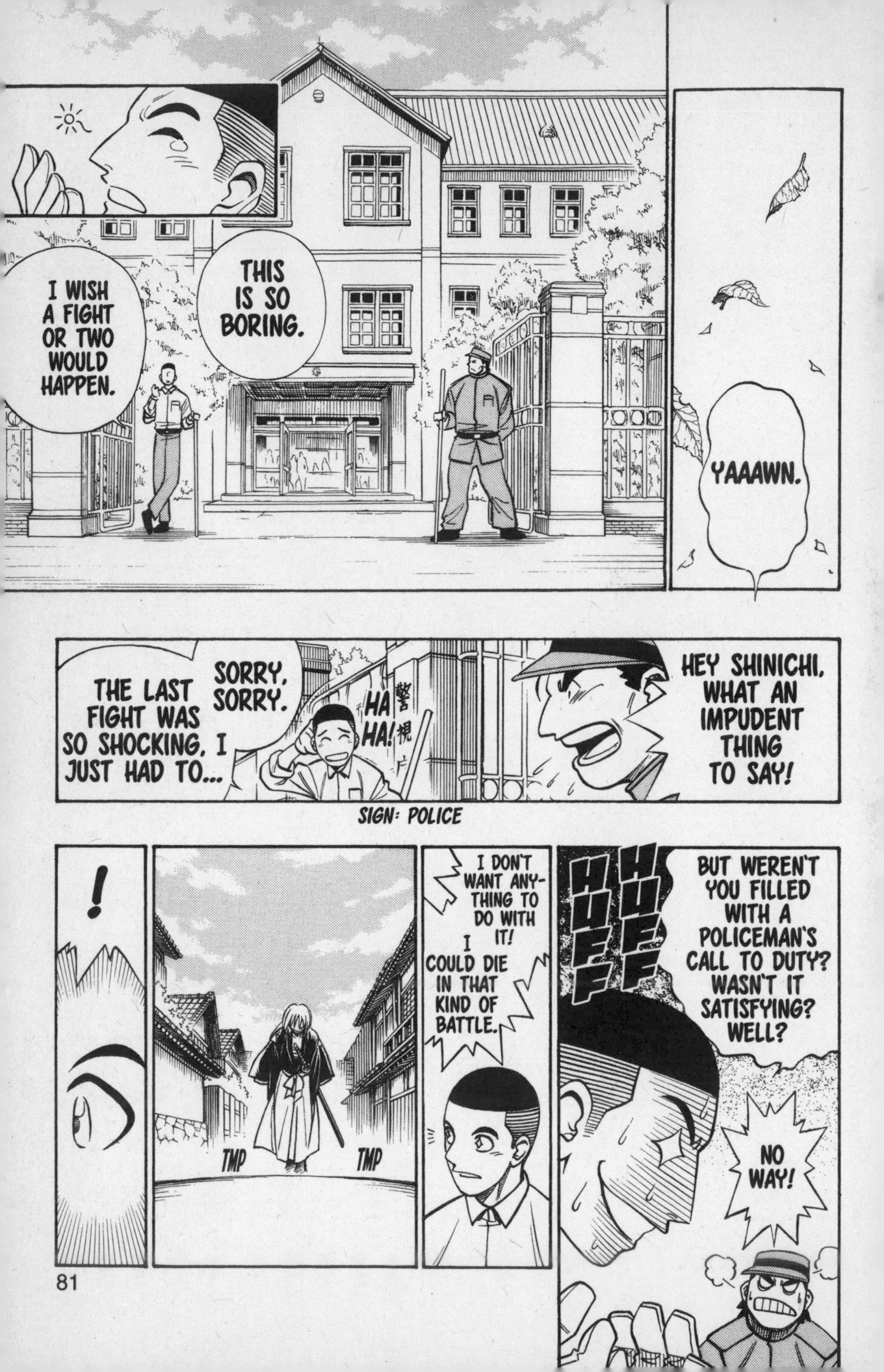
YAAAWN.
THIS IS SO BORING.
I WISH A FIGHT OR TWO WOULD HAPPEN.
HEY SHINICHI, WHAT AN IMPUDENT THING TO SAY!
警視庁
HA HA!
SORRY, SORRY.
THE LAST FIGHT WAS SO SHOCKING, I JUST HAD TO...
SIGN: POLICE
HUFF HUFF
BUT WEREN'T YOU FILLED WITH A POLICEMAN'S CALL TO DUTY? WASN'T IT SATISFYING? WELL?
NO WAY!
I DON'T WANT ANY-THING TO DO WITH IT!
I COULD DIE IN THAT KIND OF BATTLE.
TMP
TMP
!

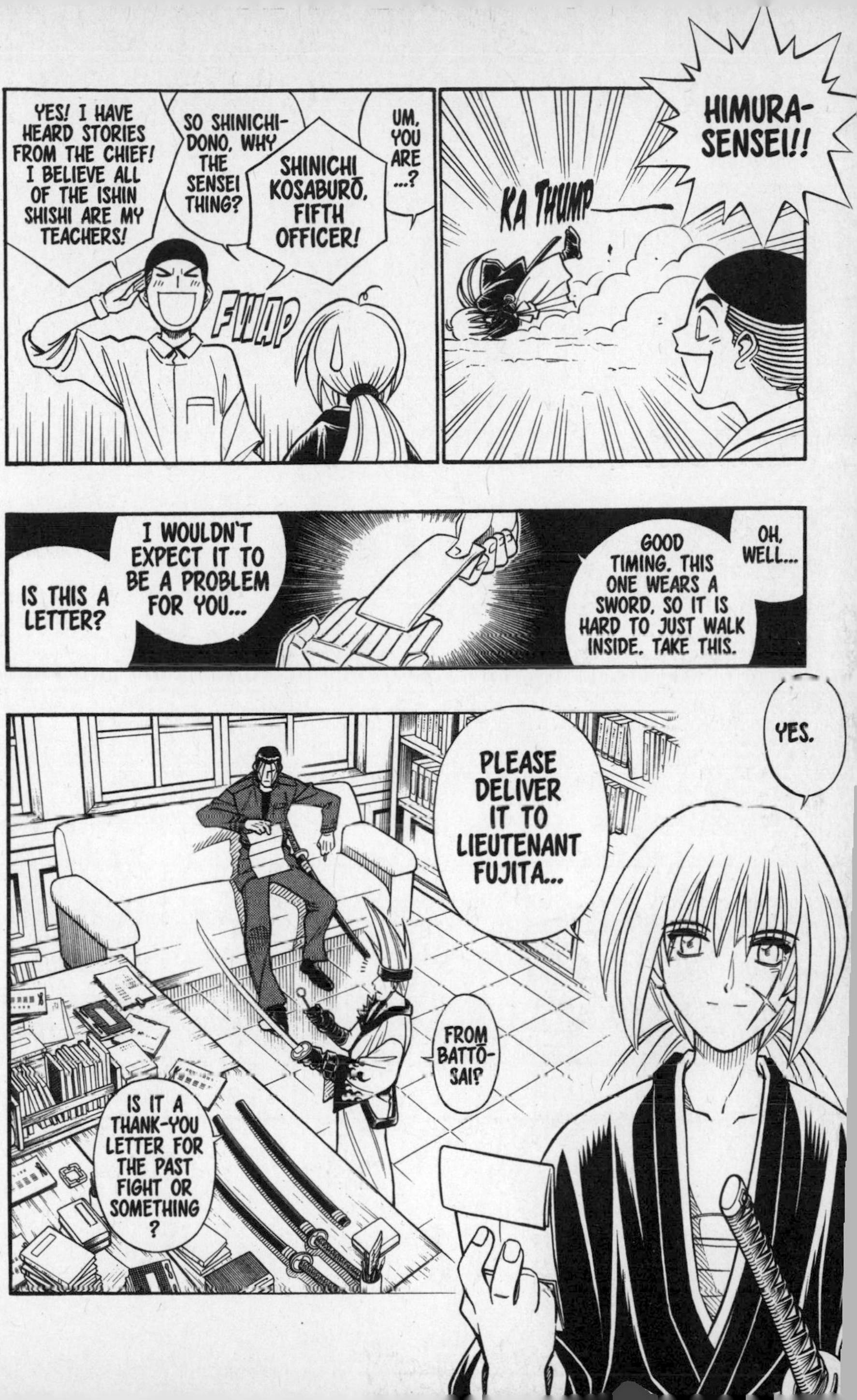
HIMURA-SENSEI!!
KA THUMP
UM, YOU ARE ...?
SHINICHI KOSABURŌ, FIFTH OFFICER!
FWAP
SO SHINICHI-DONO, WHY THE SENSEI THING?
YES! I HAVE HEARD STORIES FROM THE CHIEF! I BELIEVE ALL OF THE ISHIN SHISHI ARE MY TEACHERS!
OH, WELL...
GOOD TIMING. THIS ONE WEARS A SWORD, SO IT IS HARD TO JUST WALK INSIDE. TAKE THIS.
I WOULDN'T EXPECT IT TO BE A PROBLEM FOR YOU...
IS THIS A LETTER?
YES.
PLEASE DELIVER IT TO LIEUTENANT FUJITA...
FROM BATTŌSAI?
IS IT A THANK-YOU LETTER FOR THE PAST FIGHT OR SOMETHING?

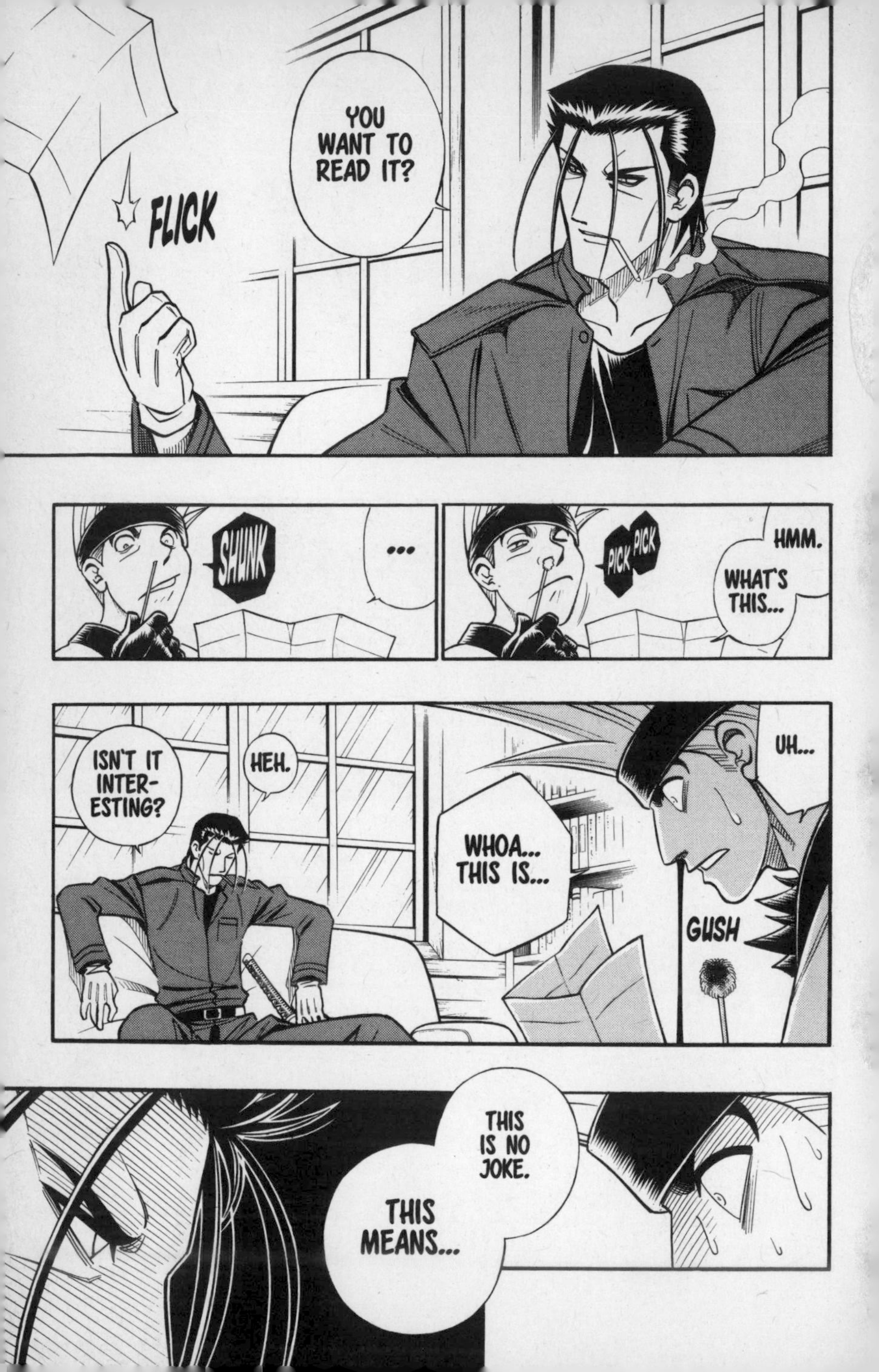
YOU WANT TO READ IT?
FLICK
HMM.
WHAT'S THIS...
PICK PICK
...
SHUNK
UH...
WHOA... THIS IS...
GUSH
HEH.
ISN'T IT INTER-ESTING?
THIS IS NO JOKE.
THIS MEANS...

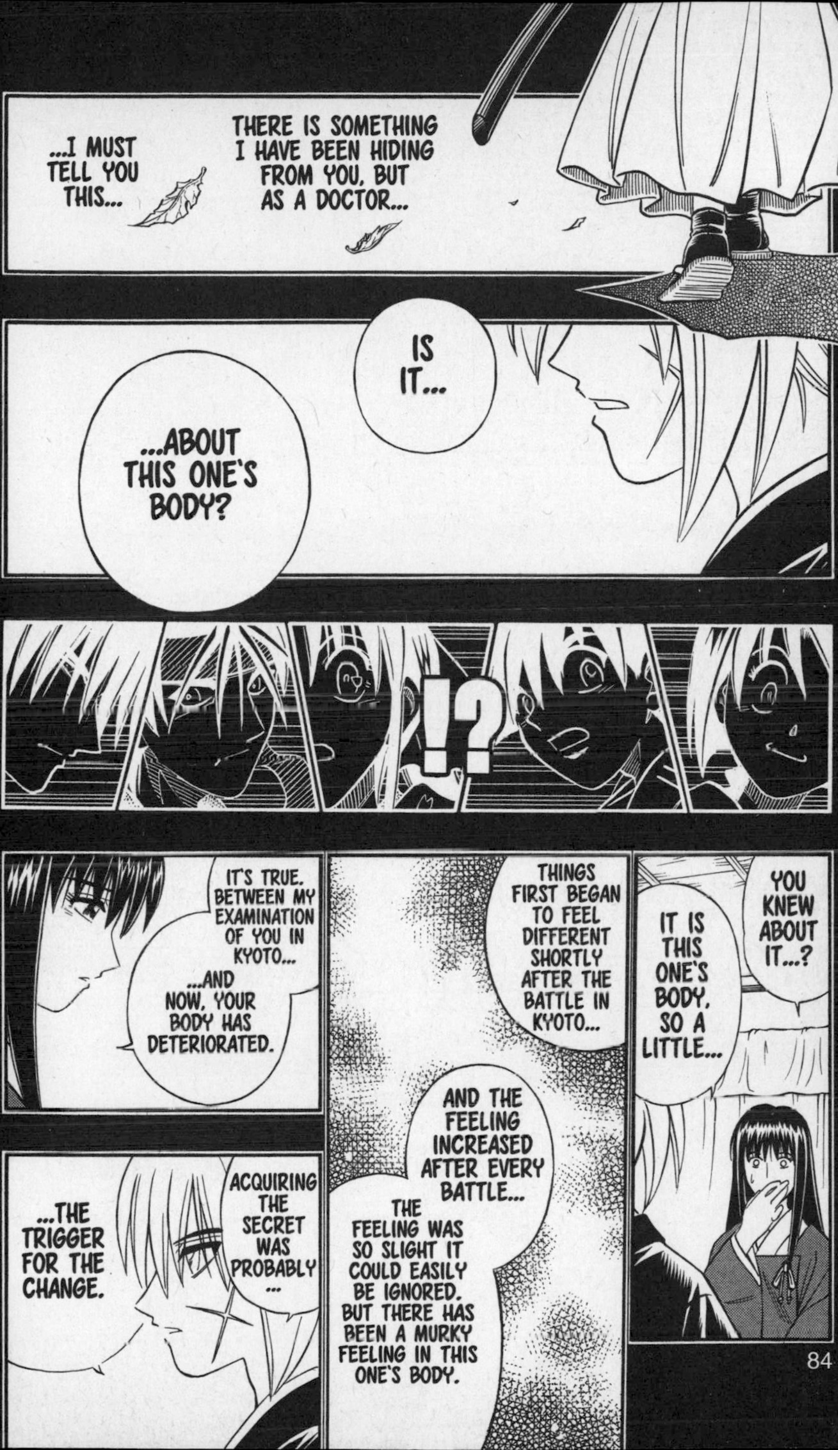
THERE IS SOMETHING I HAVE BEEN HIDING FROM YOU, BUT AS A DOCTOR...
...I MUST TELL YOU THIS...
IS IT...
...ABOUT THIS ONE'S BODY?
!?
YOU KNEW ABOUT IT...?
IT IS THIS ONE'S BODY, SO A LITTLE...
THINGS FIRST BEGAN TO FEEL DIFFERENT SHORTLY AFTER THE BATTLE IN KYOTO...
AND THE FEELING INCREASED AFTER EVERY BATTLE...
THE FEELING WAS SO SLIGHT IT COULD EASILY BE IGNORED. BUT THERE HAS BEEN A MURKY FEELING IN THIS ONE'S BODY.
IT'S TRUE. BETWEEN MY EXAMINATION OF YOU IN KYOTO...
...AND NOW, YOUR BODY HAS DETERIORATED.
ACQUIRING THE SECRET WAS PROBABLY...
...THE TRIGGER FOR THE CHANGE.

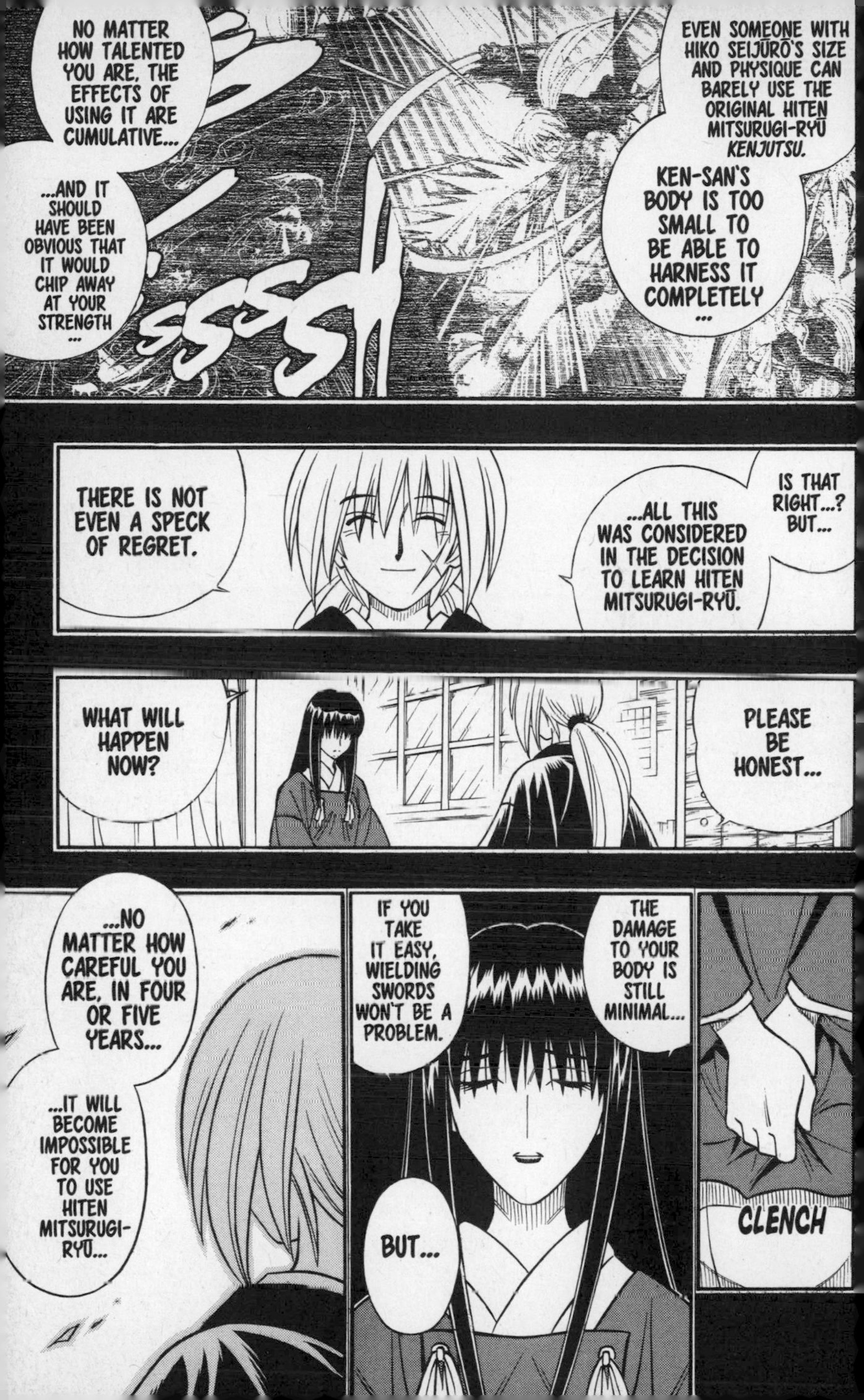
EVEN SOMEONE WITH HIKO SEIJŪRŌ'S SIZE AND PHYSIQUE CAN BARELY USE THE ORIGINAL HITEN MITSURUGI-RYŪ *KENJUTSU.*
KEN-SAN'S BODY IS TOO SMALL TO BE ABLE TO HARNESS IT COMPLETELY...
NO MATTER HOW TALENTED YOU ARE, THE EFFECTS OF USING IT ARE CUMULATIVE...
...AND IT SHOULD HAVE BEEN OBVIOUS THAT IT WOULD CHIP AWAY AT YOUR STRENGTH...
SSSSH
IS THAT RIGHT...? BUT...
...ALL THIS WAS CONSIDERED IN THE DECISION TO LEARN HITEN MITSURUGI-RYŪ.
THERE IS NOT EVEN A SPECK OF REGRET.
PLEASE BE HONEST...
WHAT WILL HAPPEN NOW?
CLENCH
THE DAMAGE TO YOUR BODY IS STILL MINIMAL...
IF YOU TAKE IT EASY, WIELDING SWORDS WON'T BE A PROBLEM.
BUT...
...NO MATTER HOW CAREFUL YOU ARE, IN FOUR OR FIVE YEARS...
...IT WILL BECOME IMPOSSIBLE FOR YOU TO USE HITEN MITSURUGI-RYŪ...

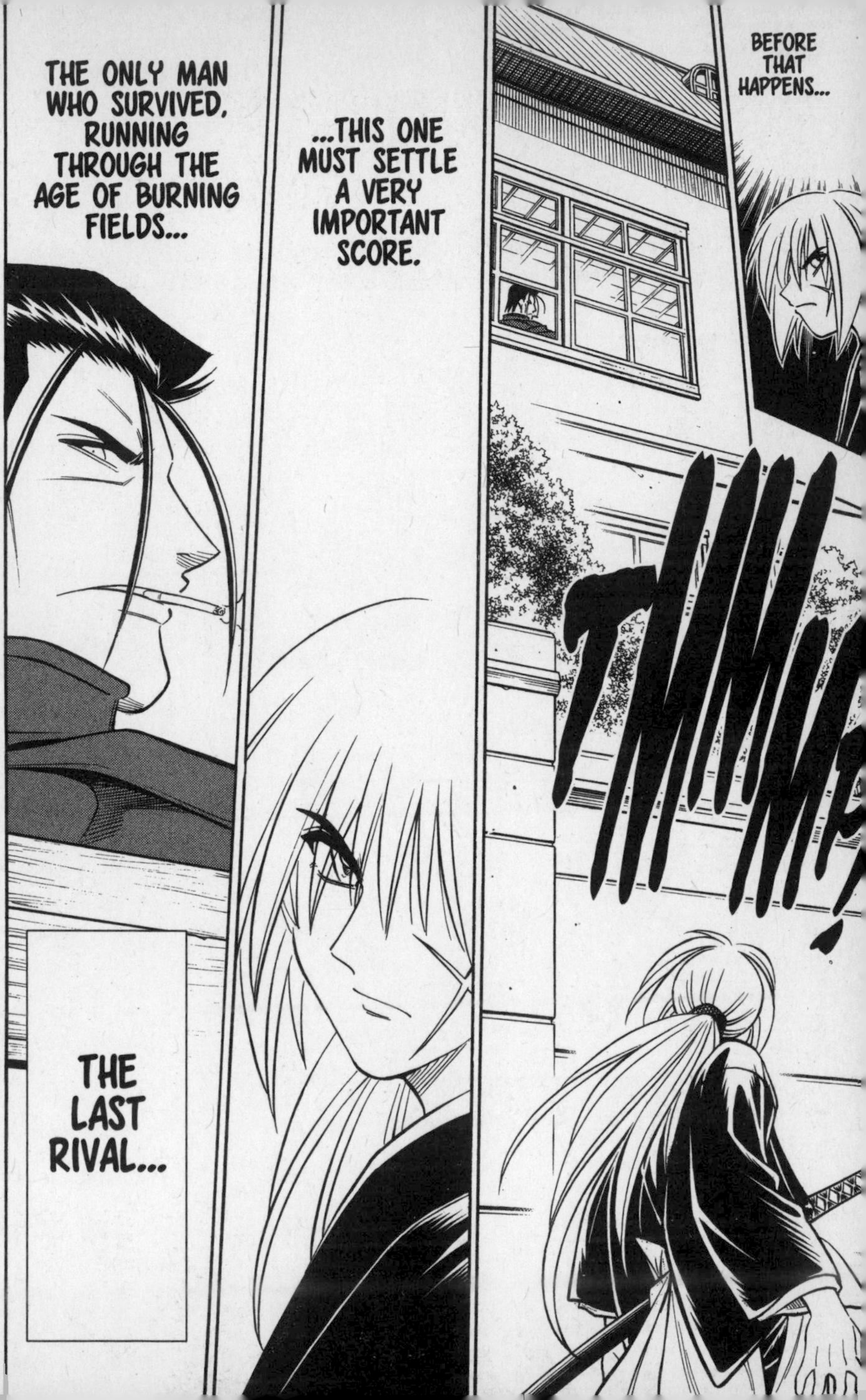
BEFORE THAT HAPPENS...
...THIS ONE MUST SETTLE A VERY IMPORTANT SCORE.
THE ONLY MAN WHO SURVIVED, RUNNING THROUGH THE AGE OF BURNING FIELDS...
THE LAST RIVAL...

READ THIS WAY

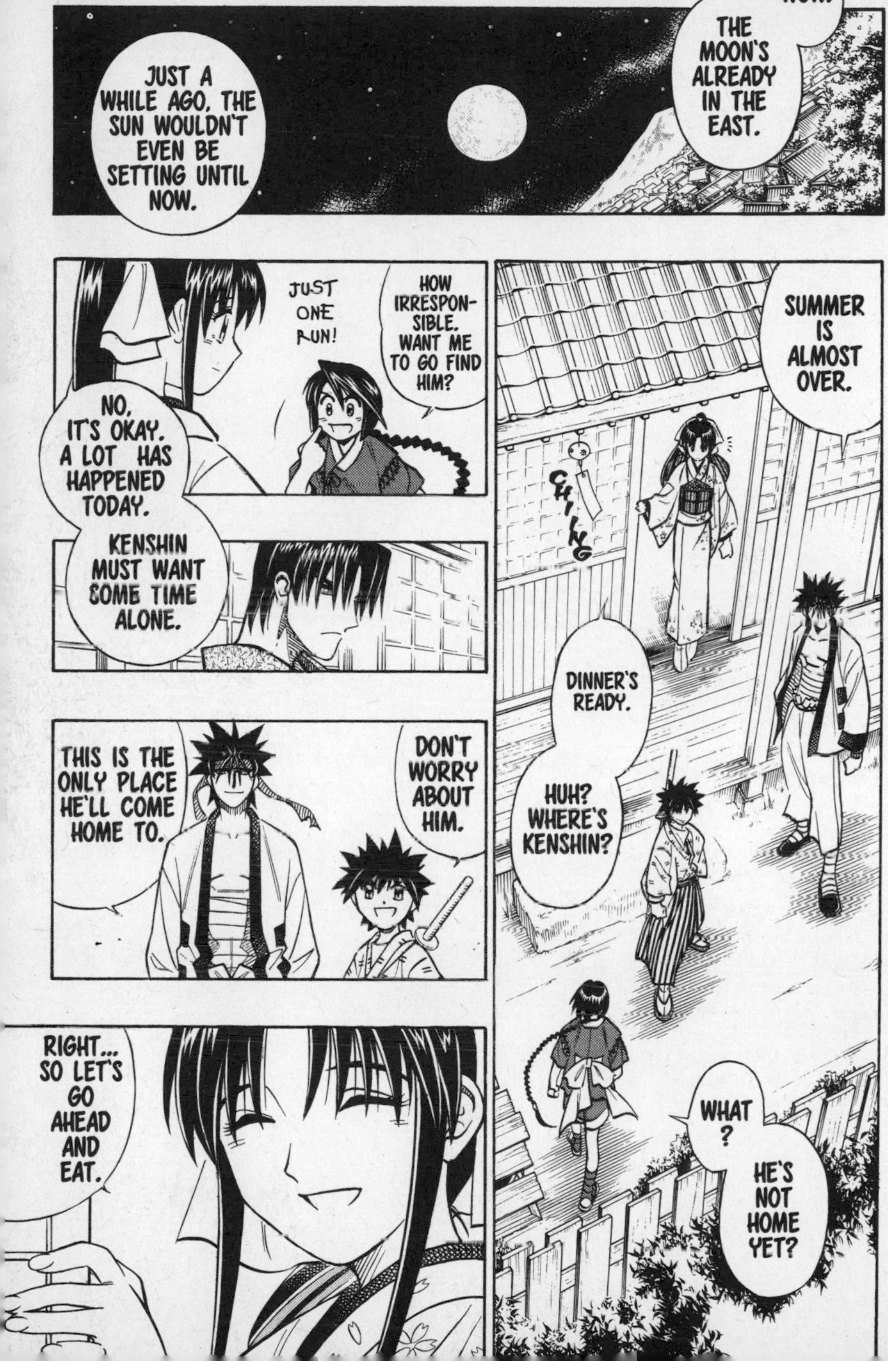
WOW.
THE MOON'S ALREADY IN THE EAST.
JUST A WHILE AGO, THE SUN WOULDN'T EVEN BE SETTING UNTIL NOW.
SUMMER IS ALMOST OVER.
CHING
DINNER'S READY.
HUH? WHERE'S KENSHIN?
WHAT? HE'S NOT HOME YET?
HOW IRRESPONSIBLE. WANT ME TO GO FIND HIM?
JUST ONE RUN!
NO, IT'S OKAY. A LOT HAS HAPPENED TODAY.
KENSHIN MUST WANT SOME TIME ALONE.
DON'T WORRY ABOUT HIM.
THIS IS THE ONLY PLACE HE'LL COME HOME TO.
RIGHT... SO LET'S GO AHEAD AND EAT.

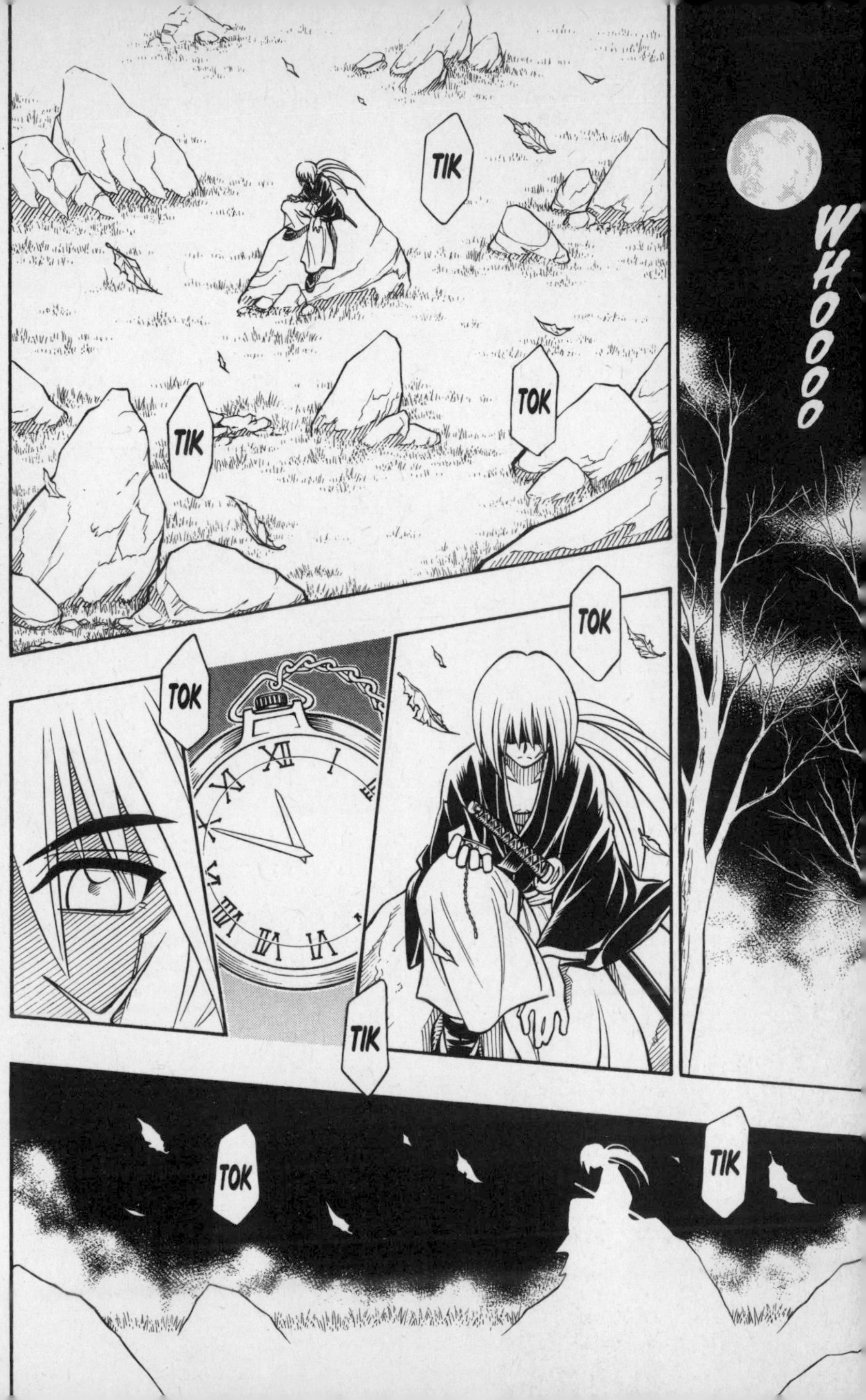
WHOOOOO
TIK
TOK
TIK
TOK
TIK
TOK
TIK
TOK

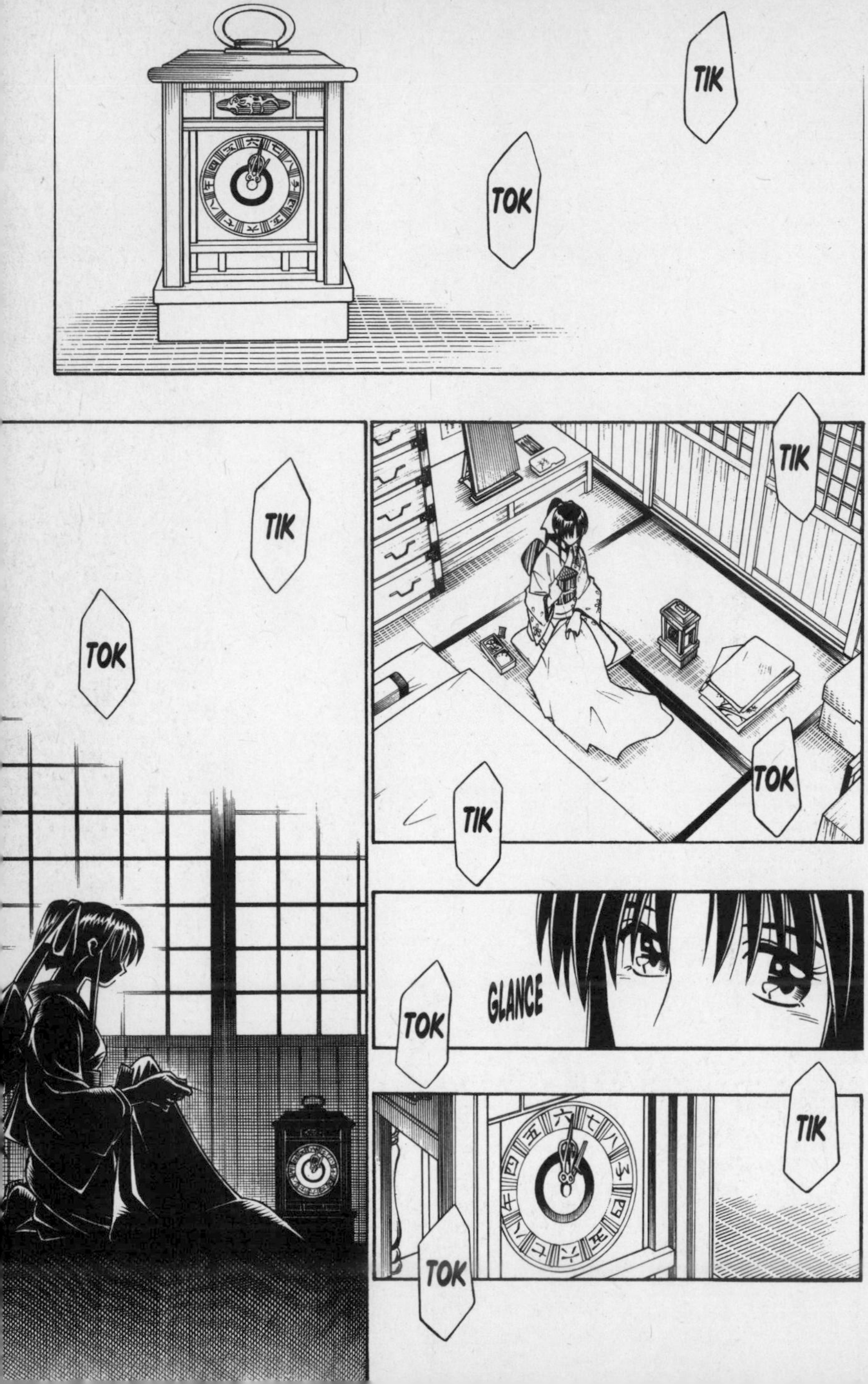
TIK
TOK
TIK
TOK
TIK
GLANCE
TOK
TIK
TOK
TIK
TOK

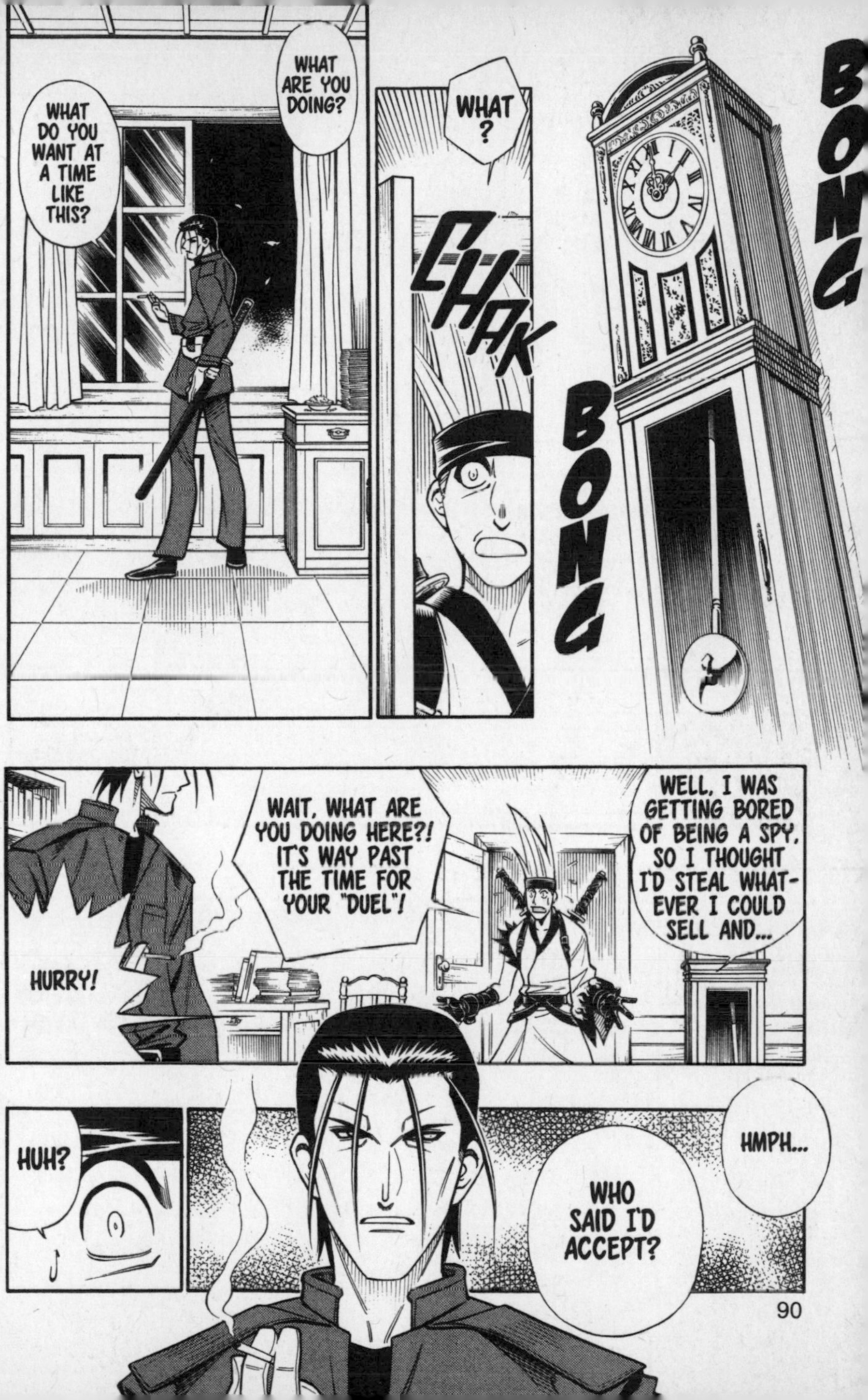
BONG
BONG
BONG
WHAT?
CHAK
WHAT ARE YOU DOING?
WHAT DO YOU WANT AT A TIME LIKE THIS?
WELL, I WAS GETTING BORED OF BEING A SPY, SO I THOUGHT I'D STEAL WHAT-EVER I COULD SELL AND...
WAIT, WHAT ARE YOU DOING HERE?! IT'S WAY PAST THE TIME FOR YOUR "DUEL"!
HURRY!
HMPH...
WHO SAID I'D ACCEPT?
HUH?

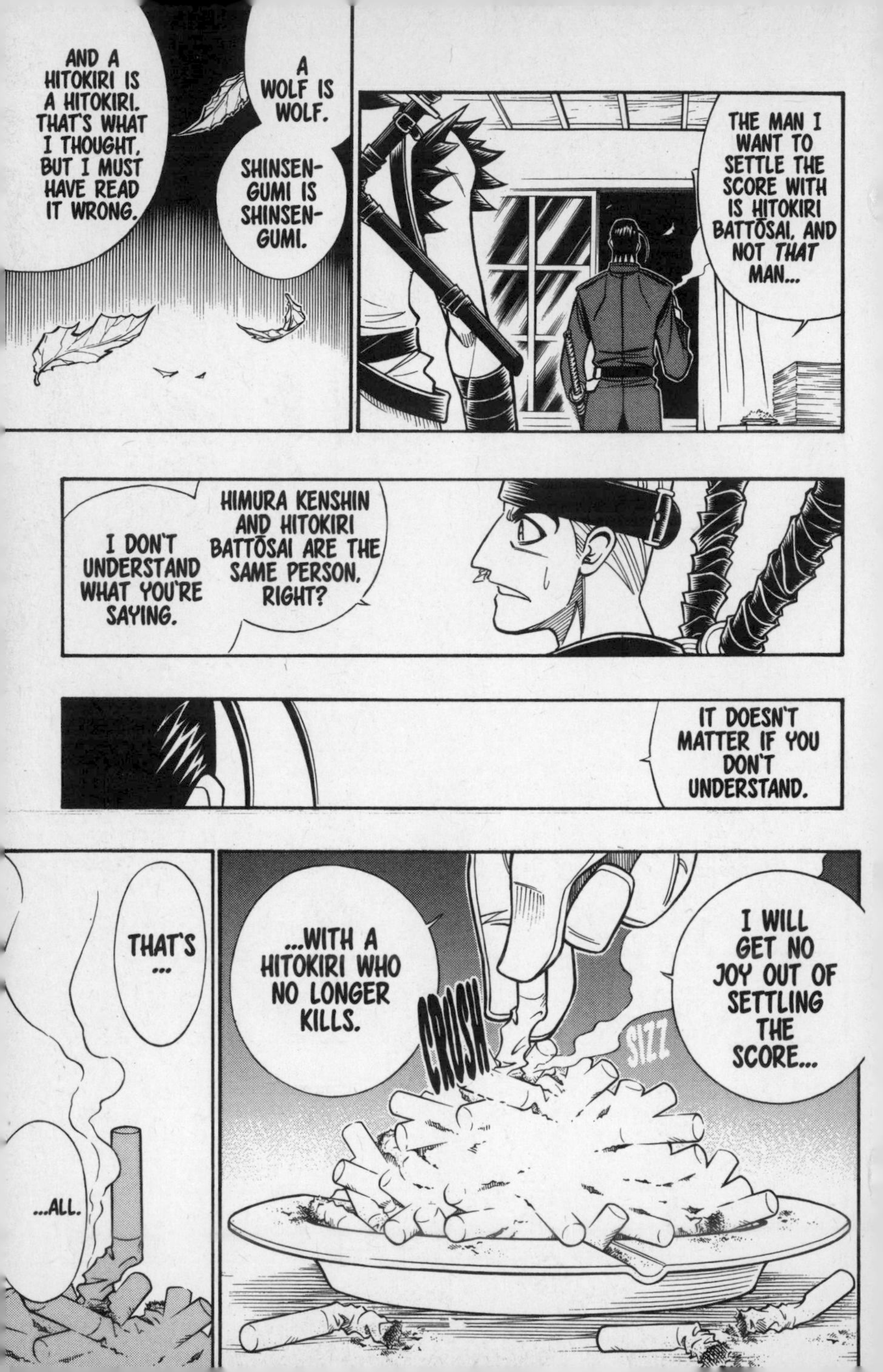
THE MAN I WANT TO SETTLE THE SCORE WITH IS HITOKIRI BATTŌSAI, AND NOT *THAT* MAN...
A WOLF IS WOLF.
SHINSEN-GUMI IS SHINSEN-GUMI.
AND A HITOKIRI IS A HITOKIRI. THAT'S WHAT I THOUGHT, BUT I MUST HAVE READ IT WRONG.
HIMURA KENSHIN AND HITOKIRI BATTŌSAI ARE THE SAME PERSON, RIGHT?
I DON'T UNDERSTAND WHAT YOU'RE SAYING.
IT DOESN'T MATTER IF YOU DON'T UNDERSTAND.
I WILL GET NO JOY OUT OF SETTLING THE SCORE...
SIZZ
CRUSH
...WITH A HITOKIRI WHO NO LONGER KILLS.
THAT'S...
...ALL.

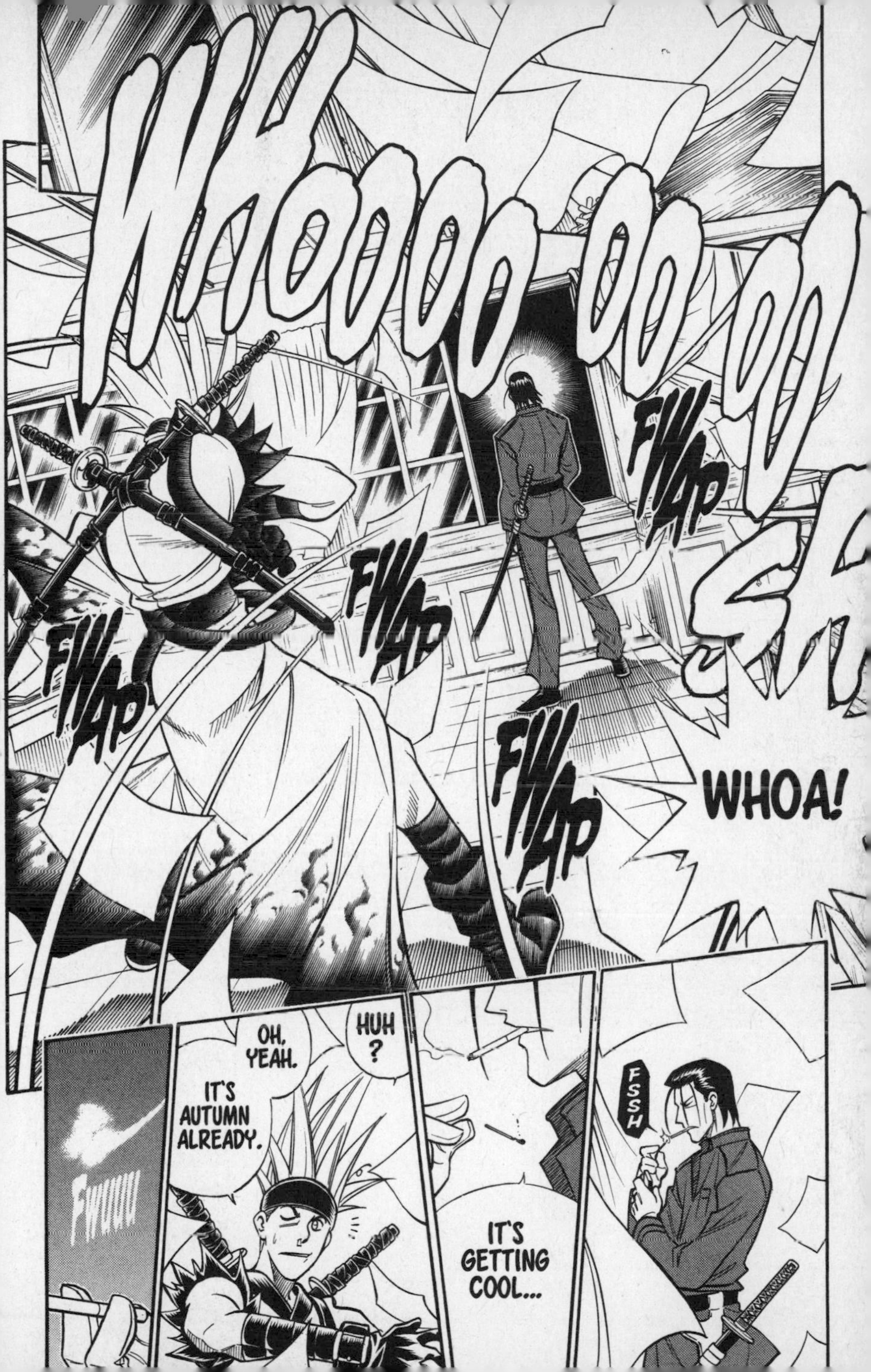
Whoooo oo oo sh
FWAP
FWAP
FWAP
FWAP
WHOA!
FSSH
IT'S GETTING COOL...
HUH?
OH, YEAH.
IT'S AUTUMN ALREADY.
Fwuuu

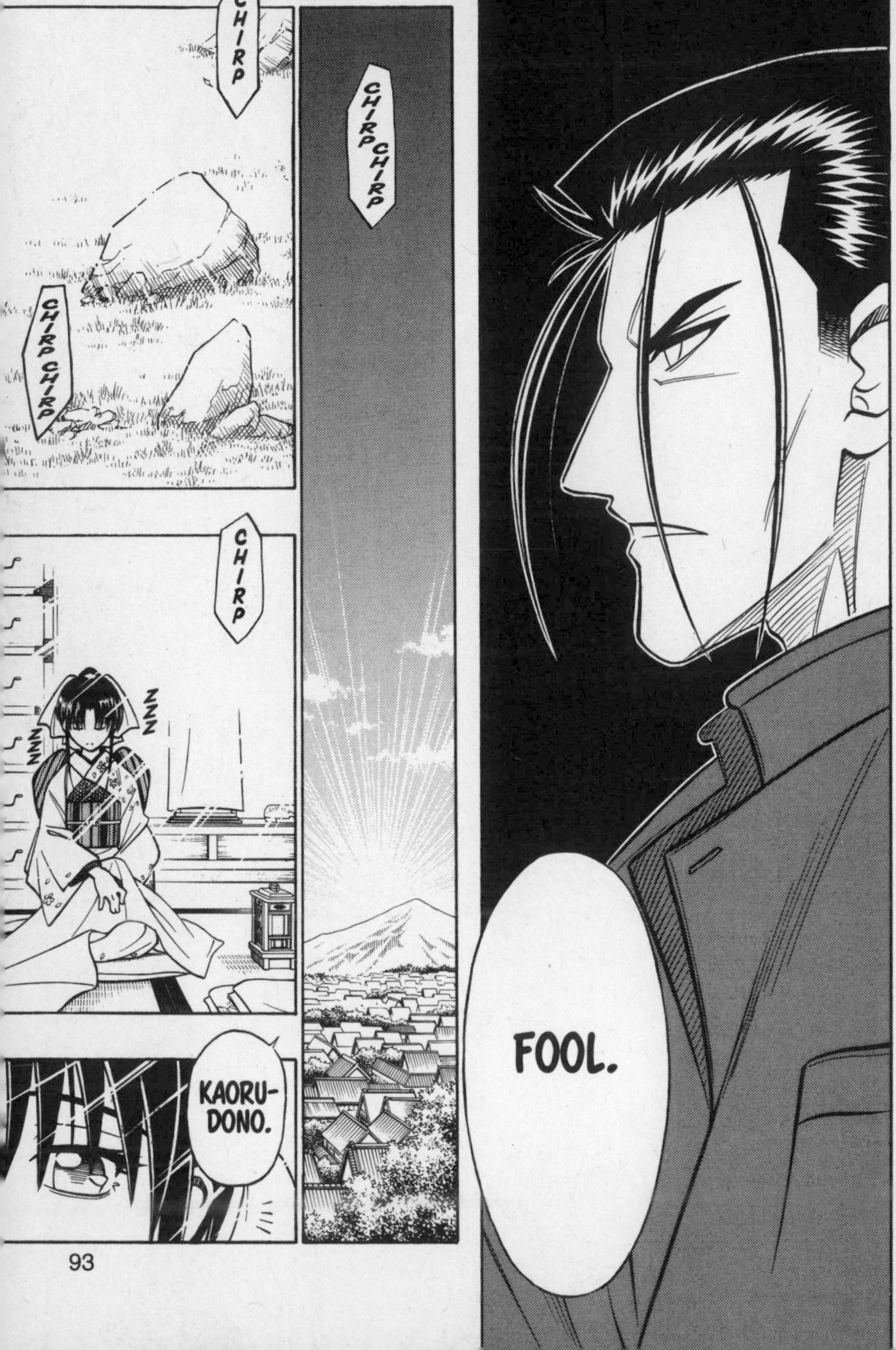
FOOL.
CHIRP CHIRP
CHIRP
CHIRP CHIRP
CHIRP
ZZZ
ZZZ
KAORU-DONO.

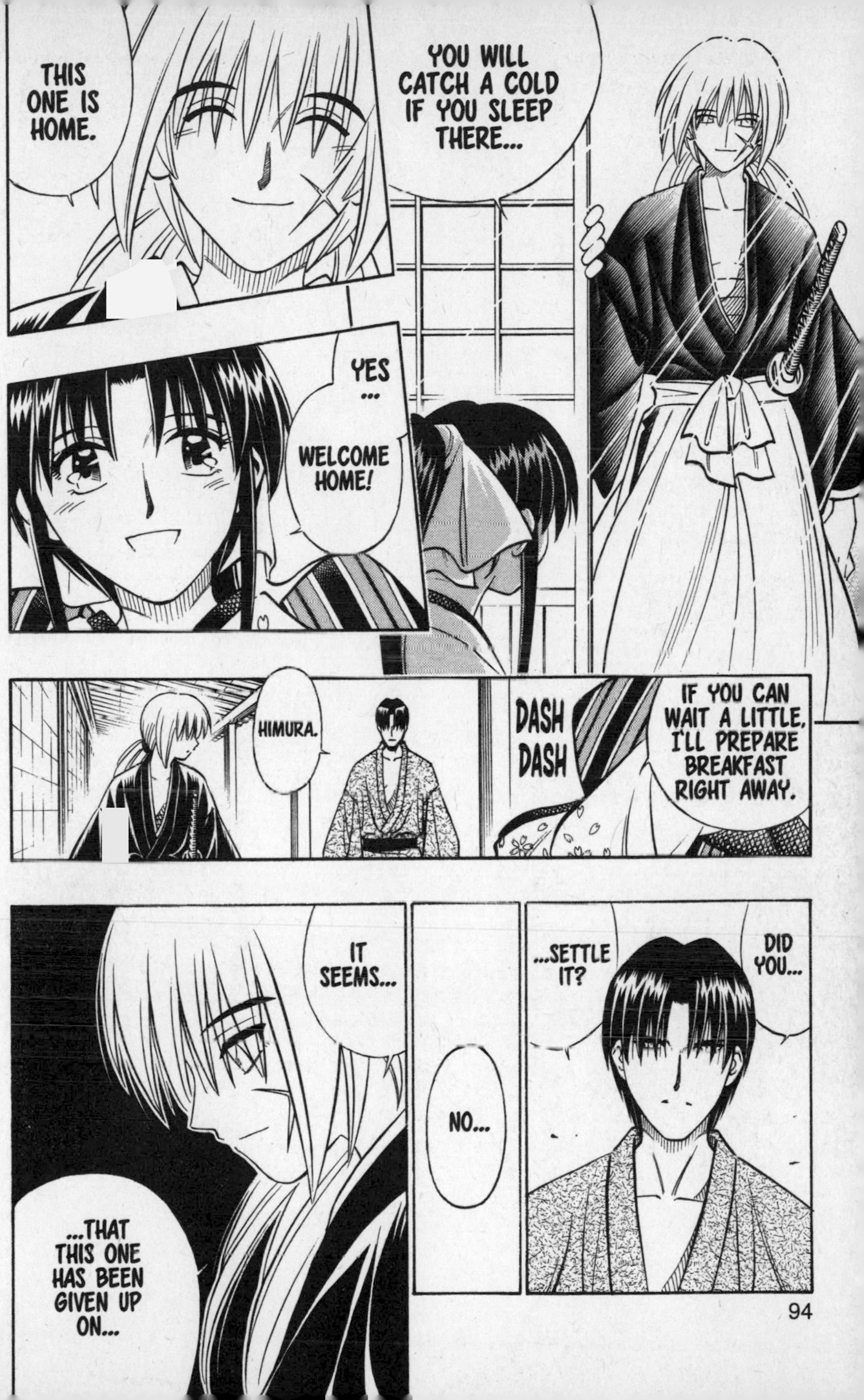
YOU WILL CATCH A COLD IF YOU SLEEP THERE...
THIS ONE IS HOME.
YES ...
WELCOME HOME!
IF YOU CAN WAIT A LITTLE, I'LL PREPARE BREAKFAST RIGHT AWAY.
DASH DASH
HIMURA.
DID YOU...
...SETTLE IT?
NO...
IT SEEMS...
...THAT THIS ONE HAS BEEN GIVEN UP ON...

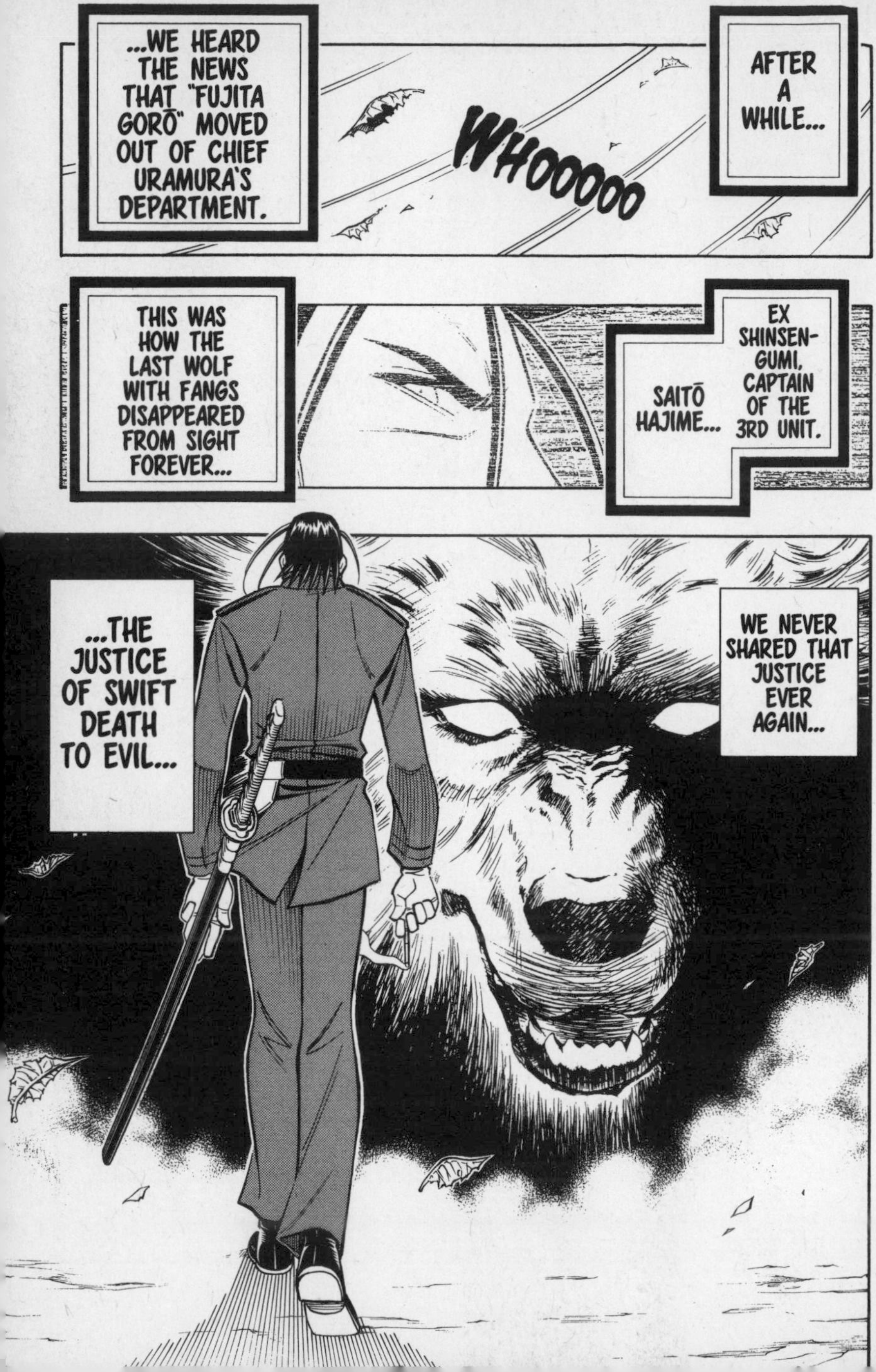
AFTER A WHILE...
WHOOOOOO
...WE HEARD THE NEWS THAT "FUJITA GORŌ" MOVED OUT OF CHIEF URAMURA'S DEPARTMENT.
EX SHINSEN-GUMI, CAPTAIN OF THE 3RD UNIT.
SAITŌ HAJIME...
THIS WAS HOW THE LAST WOLF WITH FANGS DISAPPEARED FROM SIGHT FOREVER...
WE NEVER SHARED THAT JUSTICE EVER AGAIN...
...THE JUSTICE OF SWIFT DEATH TO EVIL...

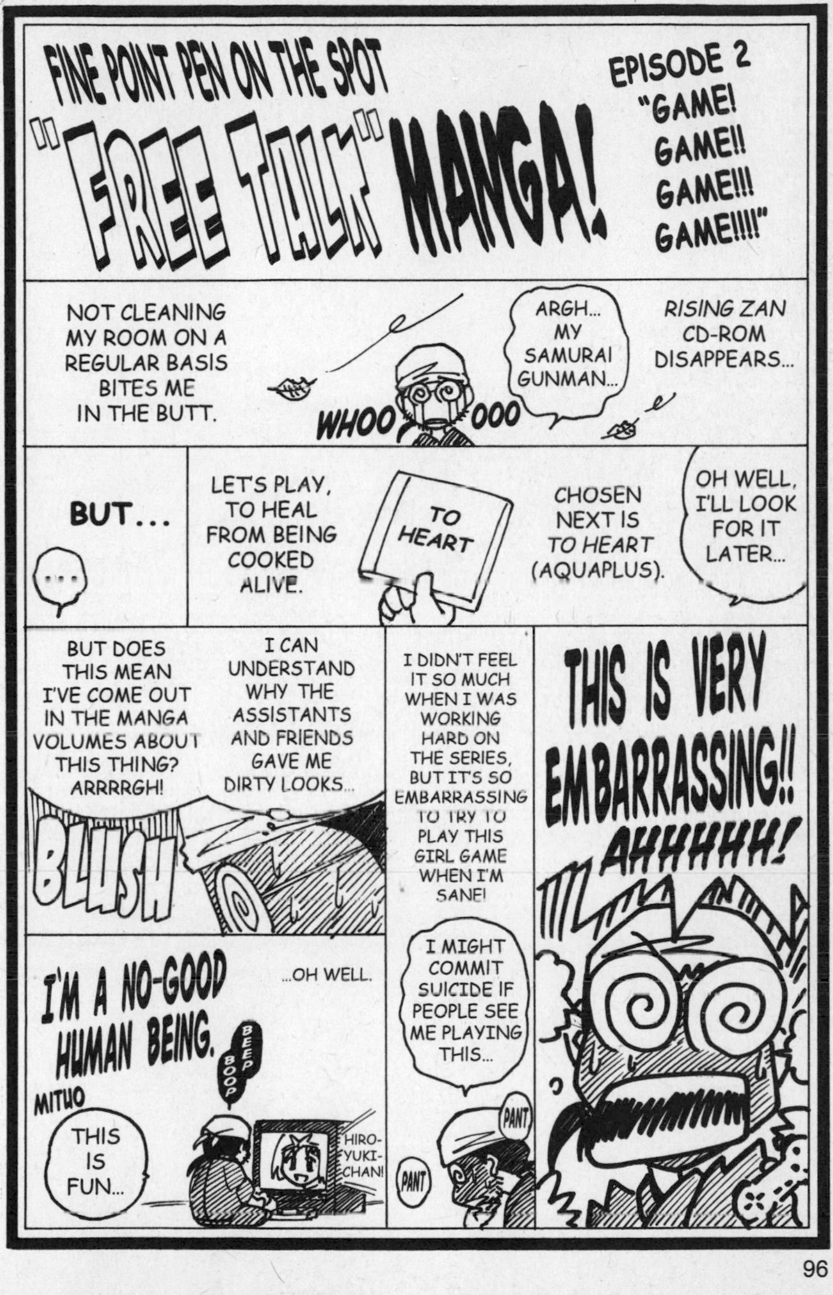
FINE POINT PEN ON THE SPOT
"FREE TALK" MANGA!
EPISODE 2
"GAME! GAME!! GAME!!! GAME!!!!"
RISING ZAN CD-ROM DISAPPEARS...
ARGH... MY SAMURAI GUNMAN...
WHOOOOO
NOT CLEANING MY ROOM ON A REGULAR BASIS BITES ME IN THE BUTT.
OH WELL, I'LL LOOK FOR IT LATER...
CHOSEN NEXT IS TO HEART (AQUAPLUS).
TO HEART
LET'S PLAY, TO HEAL FROM BEING COOKED ALIVE.
BUT...
...
THIS IS VERY EMBARRASSING!!
AHHHHH!
I DIDN'T FEEL IT SO MUCH WHEN I WAS WORKING HARD ON THE SERIES, BUT IT'S SO EMBARRASSING TO TRY TO PLAY THIS GIRL GAME WHEN I'M SANE!
I MIGHT COMMIT SUICIDE IF PEOPLE SEE ME PLAYING THIS...
PANT
PANT
I CAN UNDERSTAND WHY THE ASSISTANTS AND FRIENDS GAVE ME DIRTY LOOKS...
BUT DOES THIS MEAN I'VE COME OUT IN THE MANGA VOLUMES ABOUT THIS THING? ARRRRGH!
BLUSH
...OH WELL.
I'M A NO-GOOD HUMAN BEING.
BEEP BOOP
HIRO-YUKI-CHAN!
MITUO
THIS IS FUN...

Act 253—Early Spring Sunshine

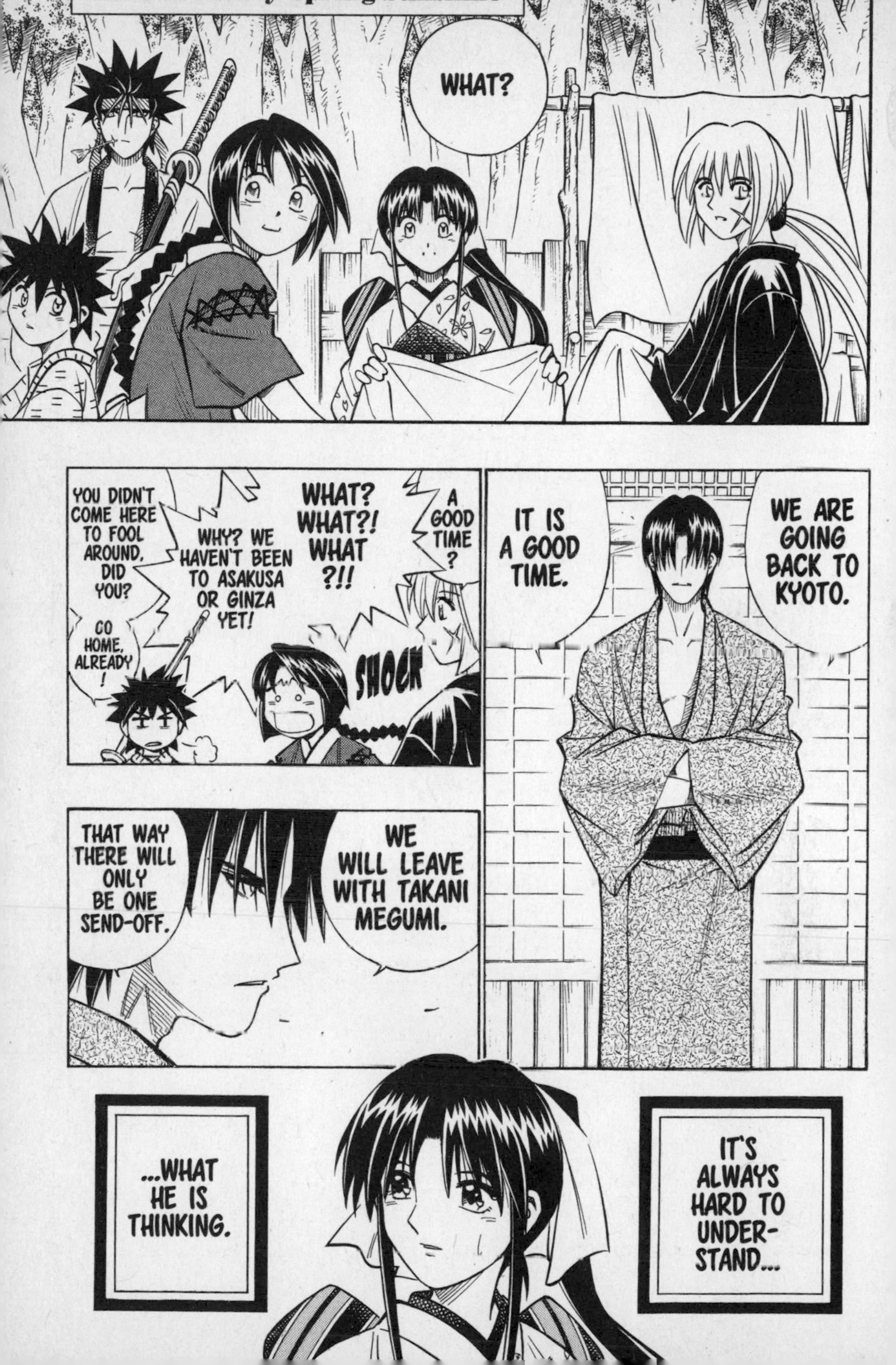
WHAT?
WE ARE GOING BACK TO KYOTO.
IT IS A GOOD TIME.
A GOOD TIME?
WHAT? WHAT?! WHAT?!!
SHOCK
WHY? WE HAVEN'T BEEN TO ASAKUSA OR GINZA YET!
YOU DIDN'T COME HERE TO FOOL AROUND, DID YOU?
CO HOME, ALREADY!
WE WILL LEAVE WITH TAKANI MEGUMI.
THAT WAY THERE WILL ONLY BE ONE SEND-OFF.
IT'S ALWAYS HARD TO UNDER-STAND...
...WHAT HE IS THINKING.

Sunshine

Act 253
Early Spring

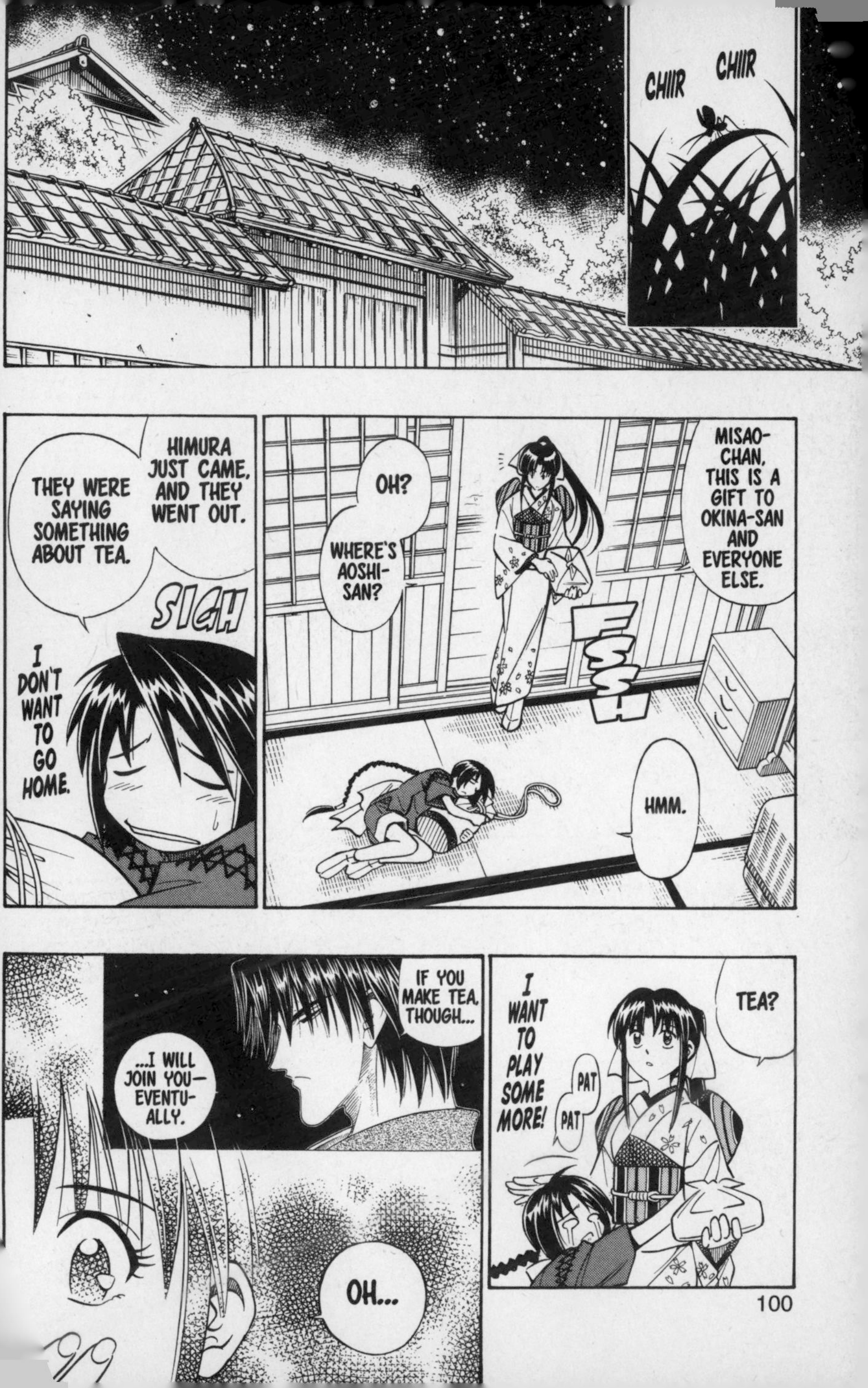
CHIIR
CHIIR
MISAO-CHAN, THIS IS A GIFT TO OKINA-SAN AND EVERYONE ELSE.
FSSH
OH?
WHERE'S AOSHI-SAN?
HMM.
HIMURA JUST CAME, AND THEY WENT OUT.
THEY WERE SAYING SOMETHING ABOUT TEA.
SIGH
I DON'T WANT TO GO HOME.
TEA?
I WANT TO PLAY SOME MORE!
PAT
PAT
IF YOU MAKE TEA, THOUGH...
...I WILL JOIN YOU—EVENTUALLY.
OH...

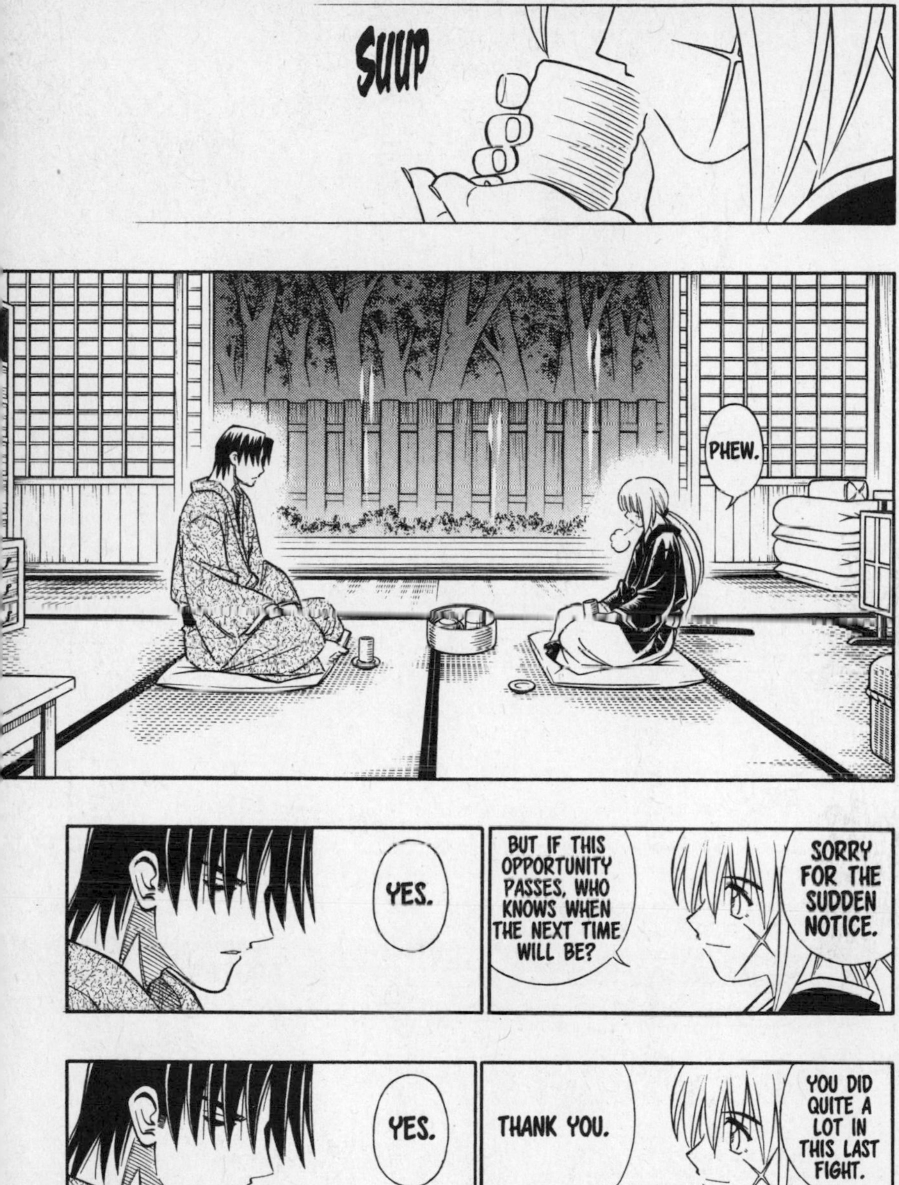
SUUP
PHEW.
SORRY FOR THE SUDDEN NOTICE.
BUT IF THIS OPPORTUNITY PASSES, WHO KNOWS WHEN THE NEXT TIME WILL BE?
YES.
YOU DID QUITE A LOT IN THIS LAST FIGHT.
THANK YOU.
YES.

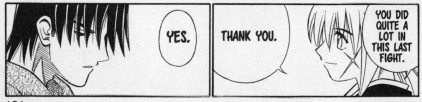

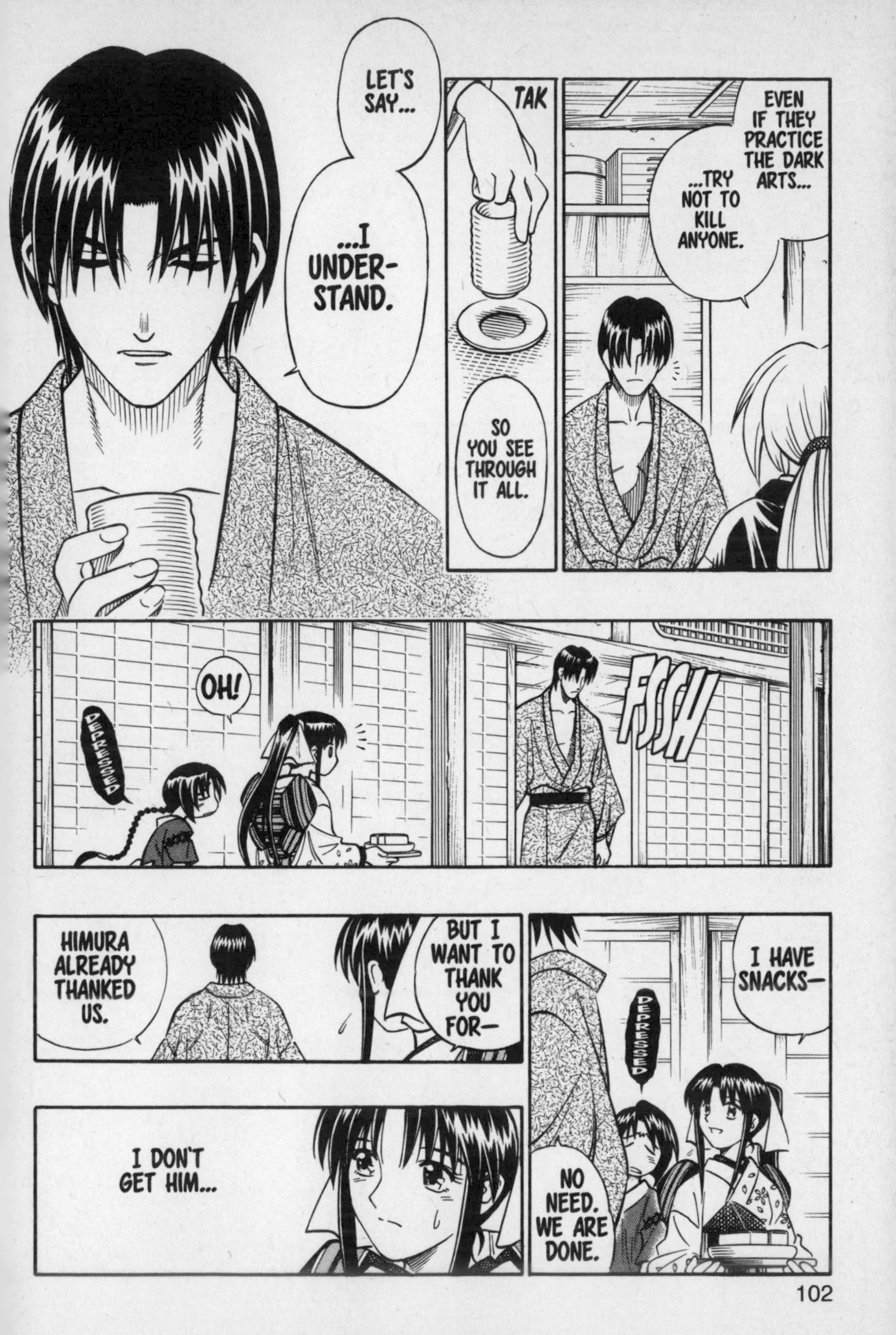
EVEN IF THEY PRACTICE THE DARK ARTS...
...TRY NOT TO KILL ANYONE.
TAK
SO YOU SEE THROUGH IT ALL.
LET'S SAY...
...I UNDERSTAND.
FSSH
OH!
DEPRESSED
I HAVE SNACKS—
DEPRESSED
NO NEED. WE ARE DONE.
BUT I WANT TO THANK YOU FOR—
HIMURA ALREADY THANKED US.
I DON'T GET HIM...

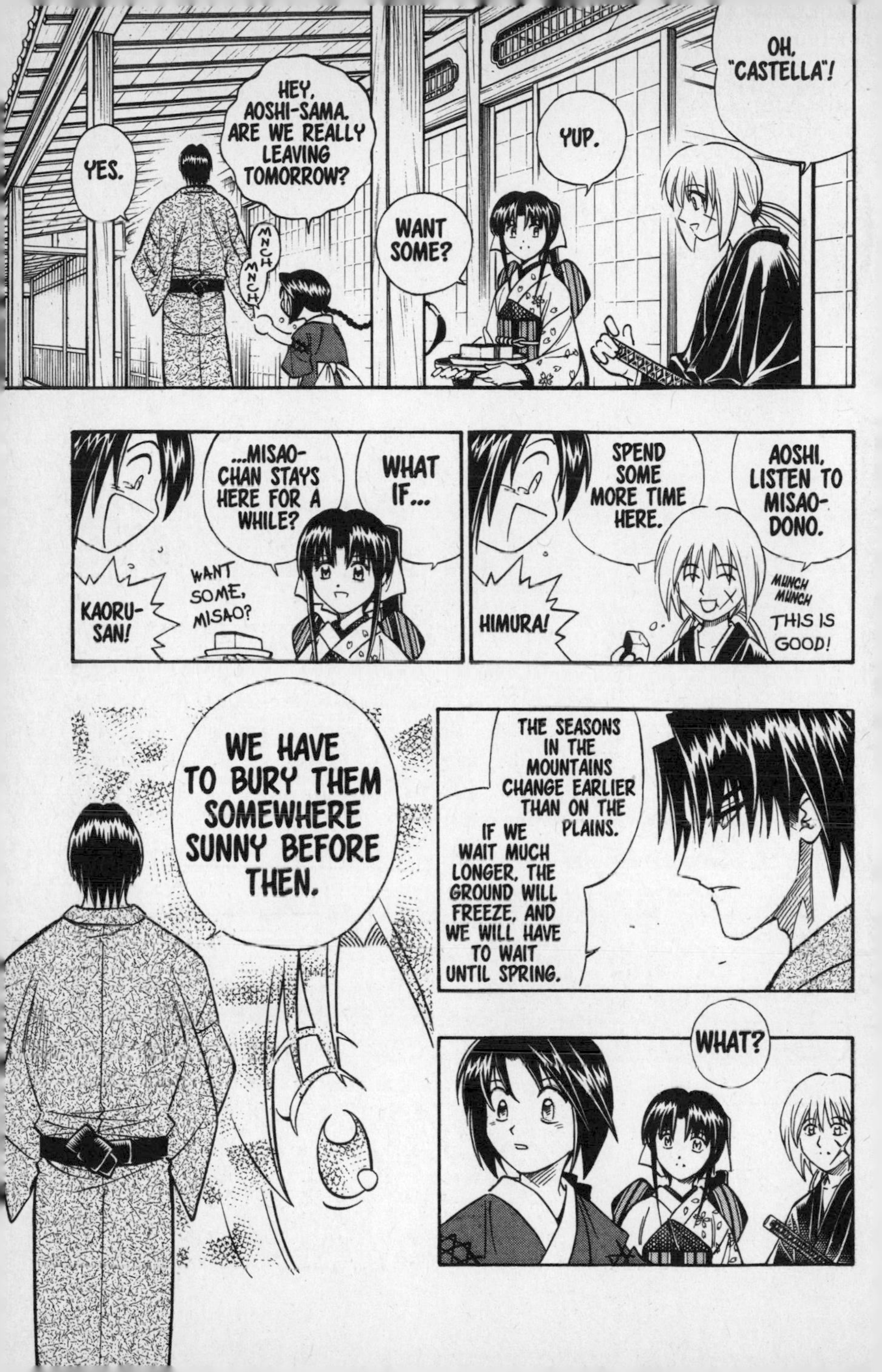
OH, "CASTELLA"!
YUP.
WANT SOME?
HEY, AOSHI-SAMA. ARE WE REALLY LEAVING TOMORROW?
MNCH MNCH
YES.
AOSHI, LISTEN TO MISAO-DONO.
MUNCH MUNCH
THIS IS GOOD!
SPEND SOME MORE TIME HERE.
HIMURA!
WHAT IF...
...MISAO-CHAN STAYS HERE FOR A WHILE?
WANT SOME, MISAO?
KAORU-SAN!
THE SEASONS IN THE MOUNTAINS CHANGE EARLIER THAN ON THE PLAINS.
IF WE WAIT MUCH LONGER, THE GROUND WILL FREEZE, AND WE WILL HAVE TO WAIT UNTIL SPRING.
WHAT?
WE HAVE TO BURY THEM SOMEWHERE SUNNY BEFORE THEN.

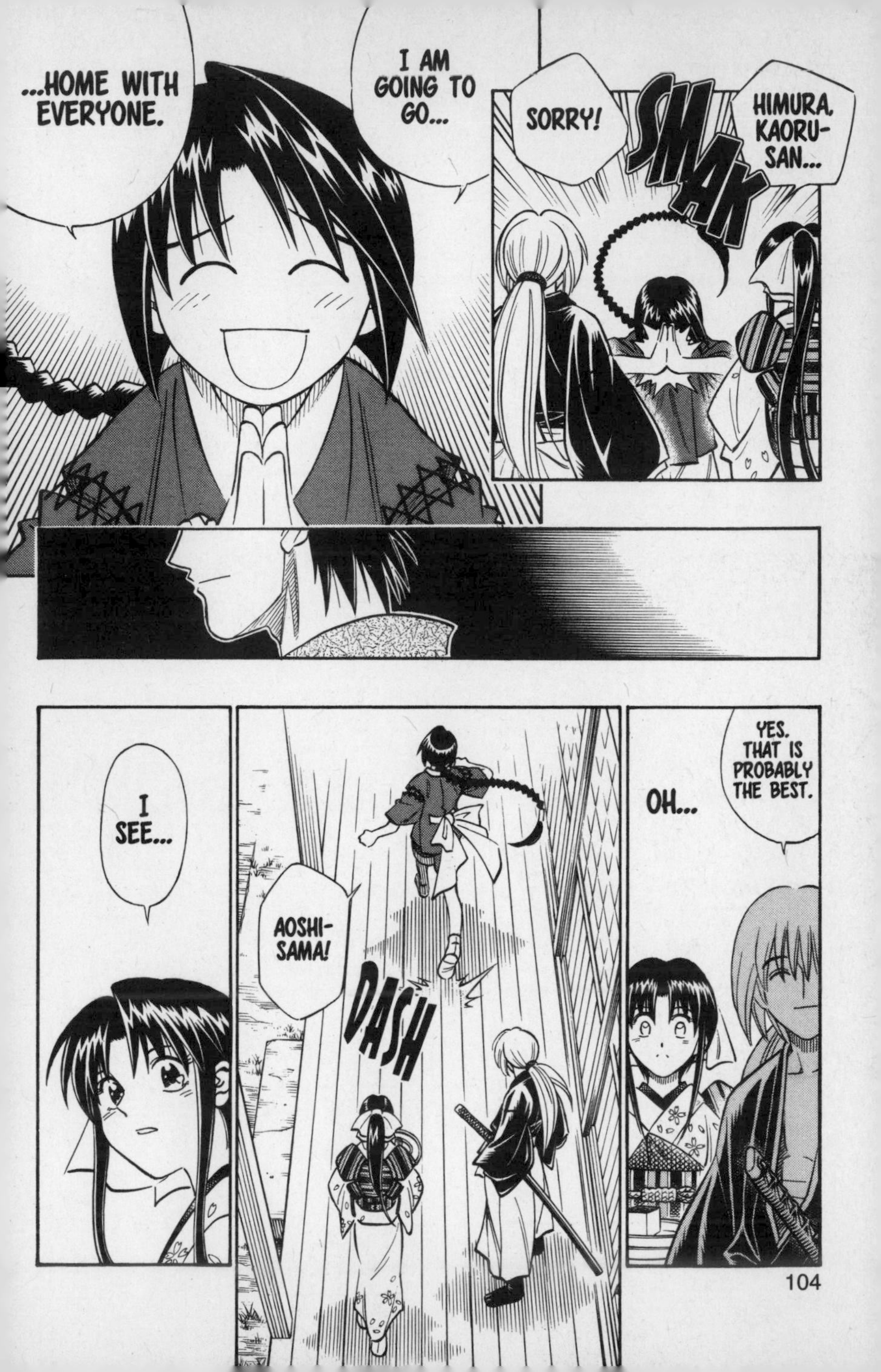
HIMURA, KAORU-SAN...
SHAK
SORRY!
I AM GOING TO GO...
...HOME WITH EVERYONE.
YES. THAT IS PROBABLY THE BEST.
OH...
AOSHI-SAMA!
DASH
I SEE...

READ THIS WAY

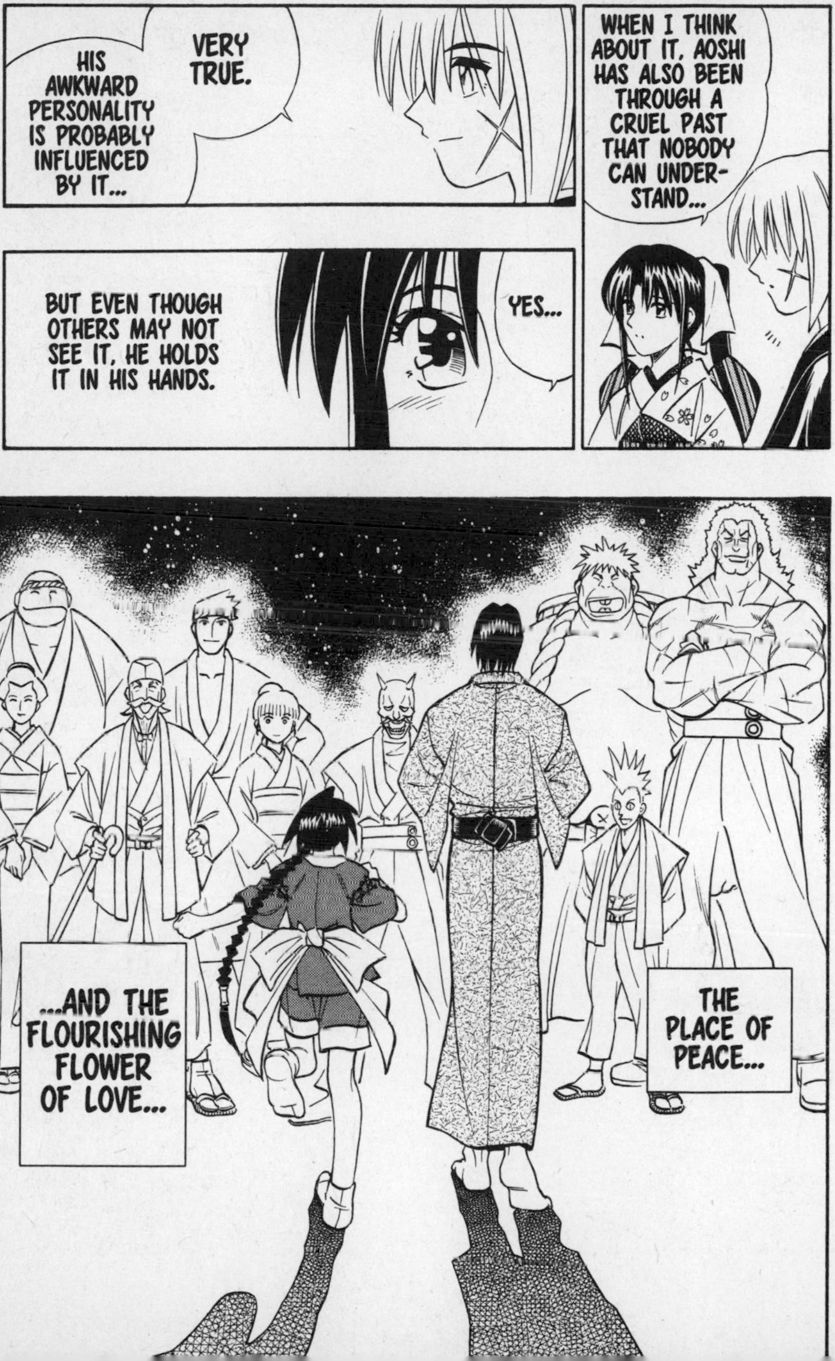

WHEN I THINK ABOUT IT, AOSHI HAS ALSO BEEN THROUGH A CRUEL PAST THAT NOBODY CAN UNDER-STAND...
VERY TRUE.
HIS AWKWARD PERSONALITY IS PROBABLY INFLUENCED BY IT...
YES...
BUT EVEN THOUGH OTHERS MAY NOT SEE IT, HE HOLDS IT IN HIS HANDS.
THE PLACE OF PEACE...
...AND THE FLOURISHING FLOWER OF LOVE...

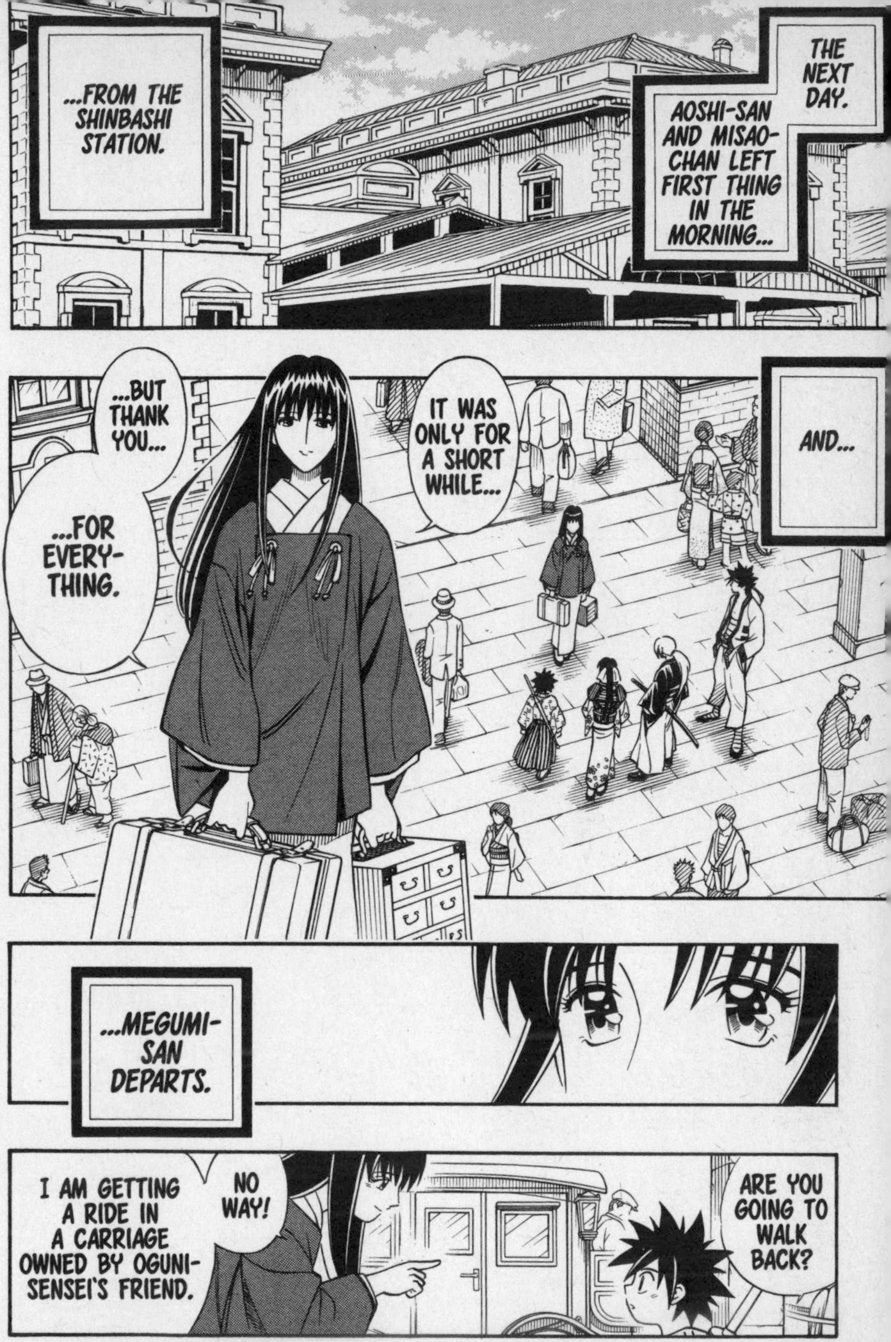
THE NEXT DAY.
AOSHI-SAN AND MISAO-CHAN LEFT FIRST THING IN THE MORNING...
...FROM THE SHINBASHI STATION.
AND...
IT WAS ONLY FOR A SHORT WHILE...
...BUT THANK YOU...
...FOR EVERYTHING.
...MEGUMI-SAN DEPARTS.
ARE YOU GOING TO WALK BACK?
NO WAY!
I AM GETTING A RIDE IN A CARRIAGE OWNED BY OGUNI-SENSEI'S FRIEND.

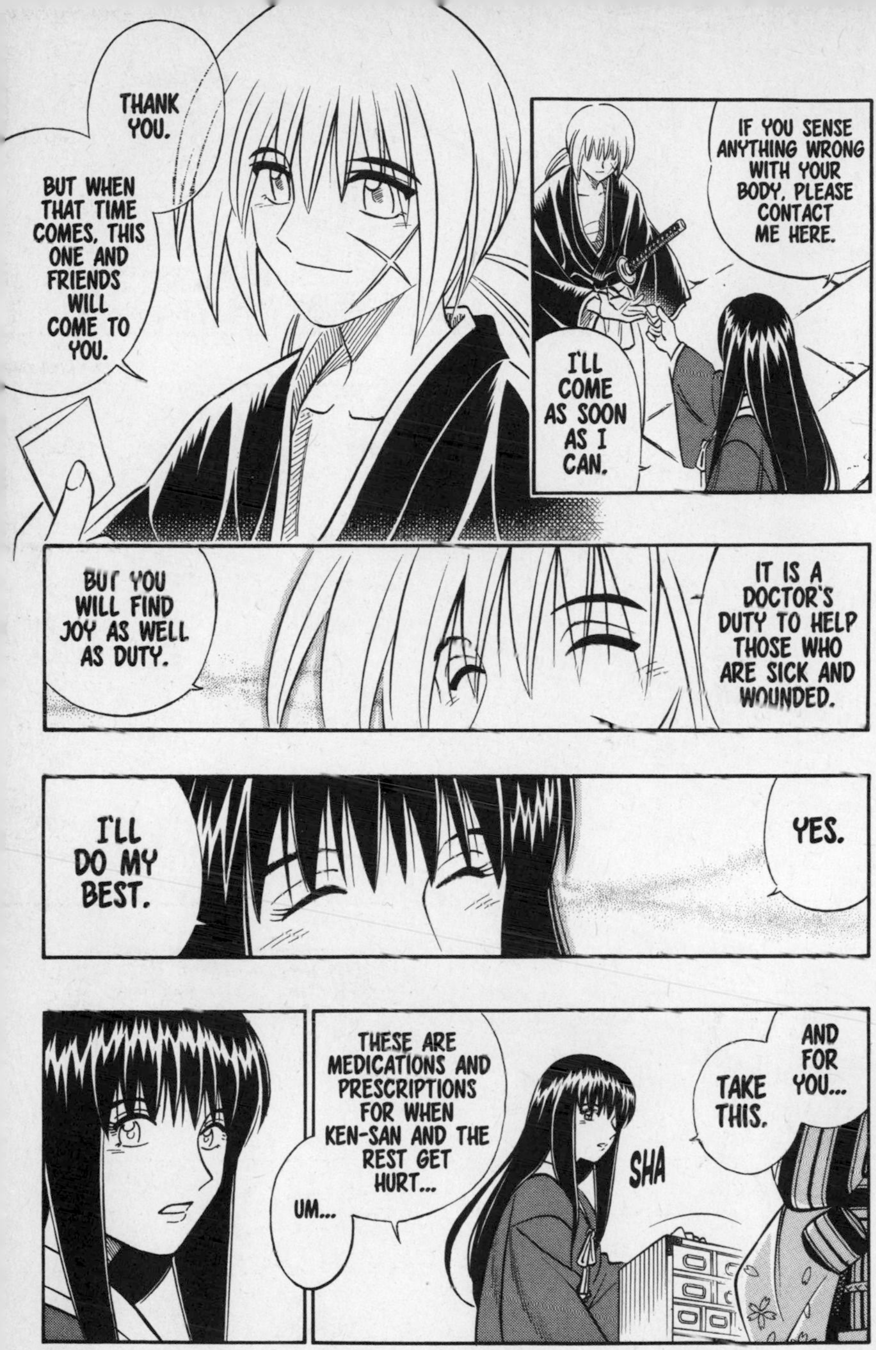
IF YOU SENSE ANYTHING WRONG WITH YOUR BODY, PLEASE CONTACT ME HERE.
I'LL COME AS SOON AS I CAN.
THANK YOU.
BUT WHEN THAT TIME COMES, THIS ONE AND FRIENDS WILL COME TO YOU.
IT IS A DOCTOR'S DUTY TO HELP THOSE WHO ARE SICK AND WOUNDED.
BUT YOU WILL FIND JOY AS WELL AS DUTY.
YES.
I'LL DO MY BEST.
AND FOR YOU...
TAKE THIS.
SHA
THESE ARE MEDICATIONS AND PRESCRIPTIONS FOR WHEN KEN-SAN AND THE REST GET HURT...
UM...

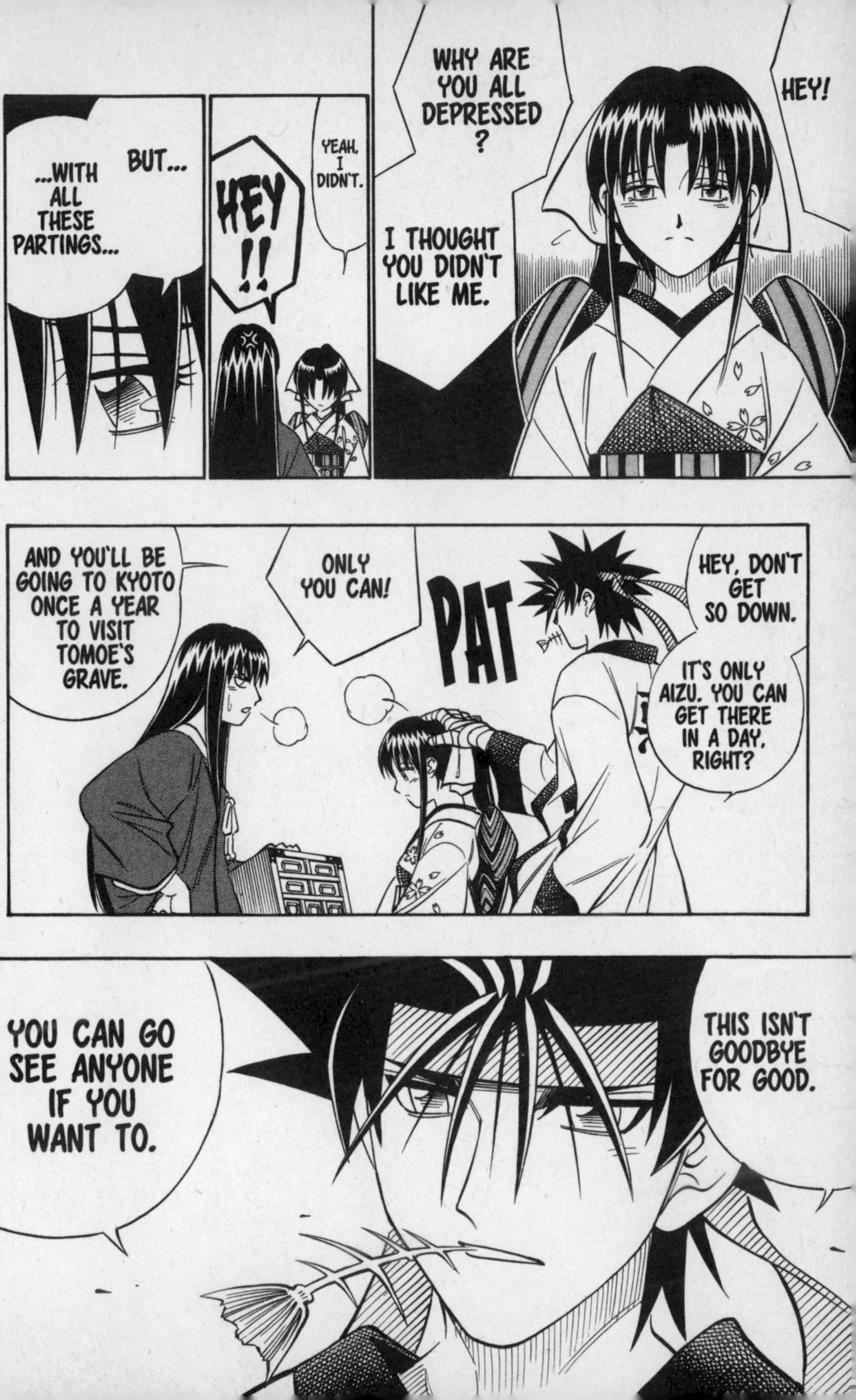
HEY!
WHY ARE YOU ALL DEPRESSED?
I THOUGHT YOU DIDN'T LIKE ME.
YEAH, I DIDN'T.
HEY!!
BUT...
...WITH ALL THESE PARTINGS...
HEY, DON'T GET SO DOWN.
IT'S ONLY AIZU. YOU CAN GET THERE IN A DAY, RIGHT?
PAT
ONLY YOU CAN!
AND YOU'LL BE GOING TO KYOTO ONCE A YEAR TO VISIT TOMOE'S GRAVE.
THIS ISN'T GOODBYE FOR GOOD.
YOU CAN GO SEE ANYONE IF YOU WANT TO.

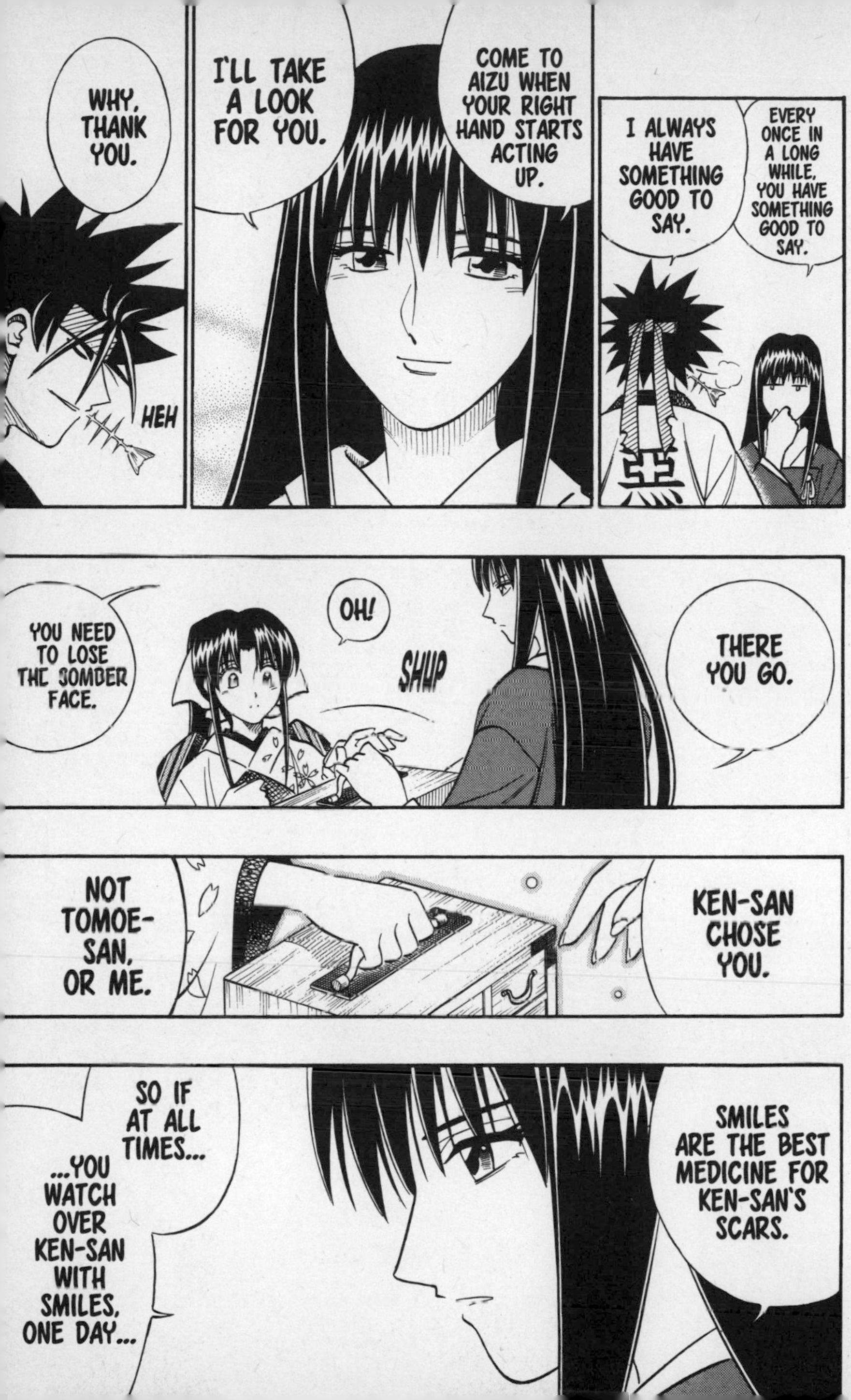
EVERY ONCE IN A LONG WHILE, YOU HAVE SOMETHING GOOD TO SAY.
I ALWAYS HAVE SOMETHING GOOD TO SAY.
COME TO AIZU WHEN YOUR RIGHT HAND STARTS ACTING UP.
I'LL TAKE A LOOK FOR YOU.
WHY, THANK YOU.
HEH
THERE YOU GO.
SHUP
OH!
YOU NEED TO LOSE THE SOMBER FACE.
KEN-SAN CHOSE YOU.
NOT TOMOE-SAN, OR ME.
SMILES ARE THE BEST MEDICINE FOR KEN-SAN'S SCARS.
SO IF AT ALL TIMES...
...YOU WATCH OVER KEN-SAN WITH SMILES, ONE DAY...

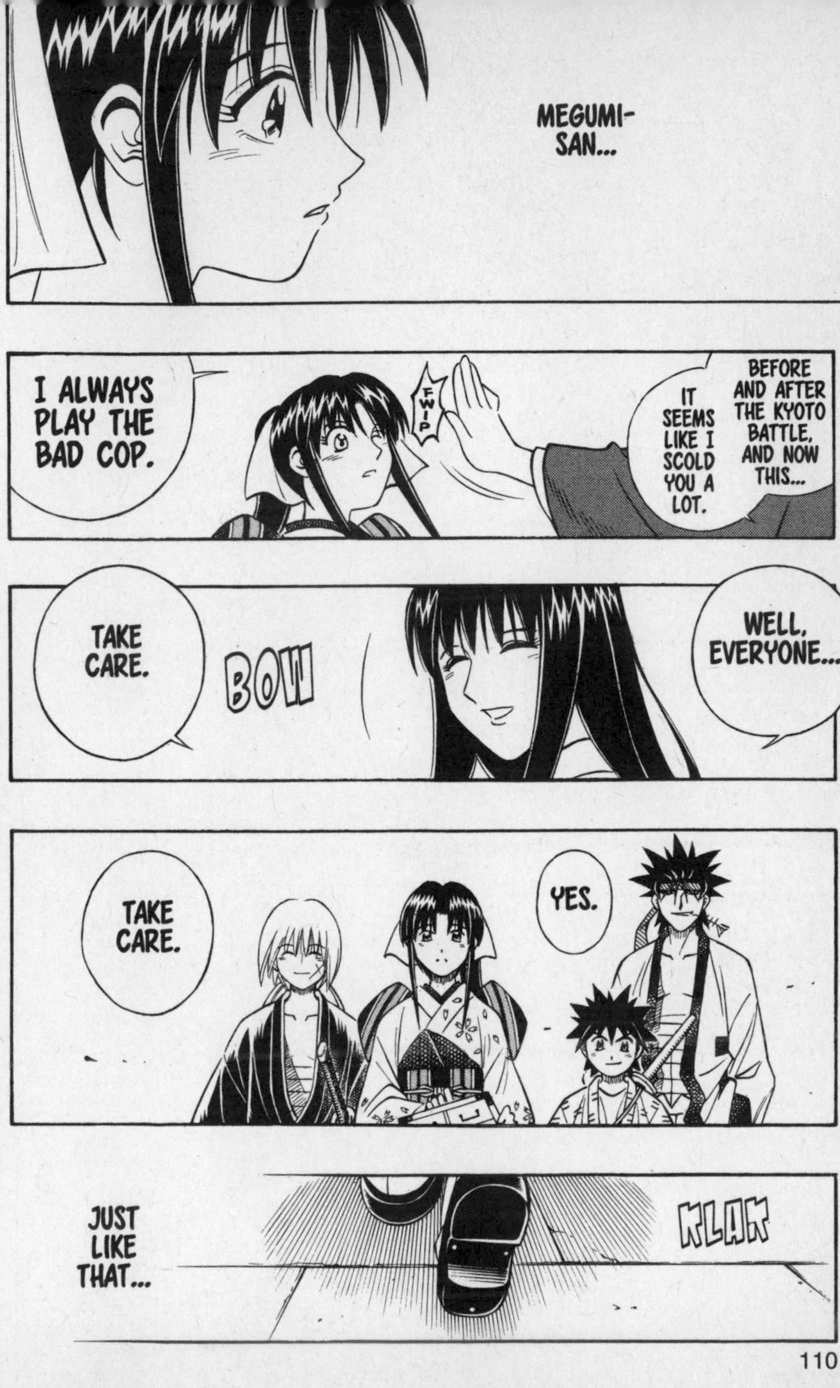
MEGUMI-SAN...
BEFORE AND AFTER THE KYOTO BATTLE, AND NOW THIS...
IT SEEMS LIKE I SCOLD YOU A LOT.
FWIP
I ALWAYS PLAY THE BAD COP.
WELL, EVERYONE...
BOW
TAKE CARE.
YES.
TAKE CARE.
KLAK
JUST LIKE THAT...

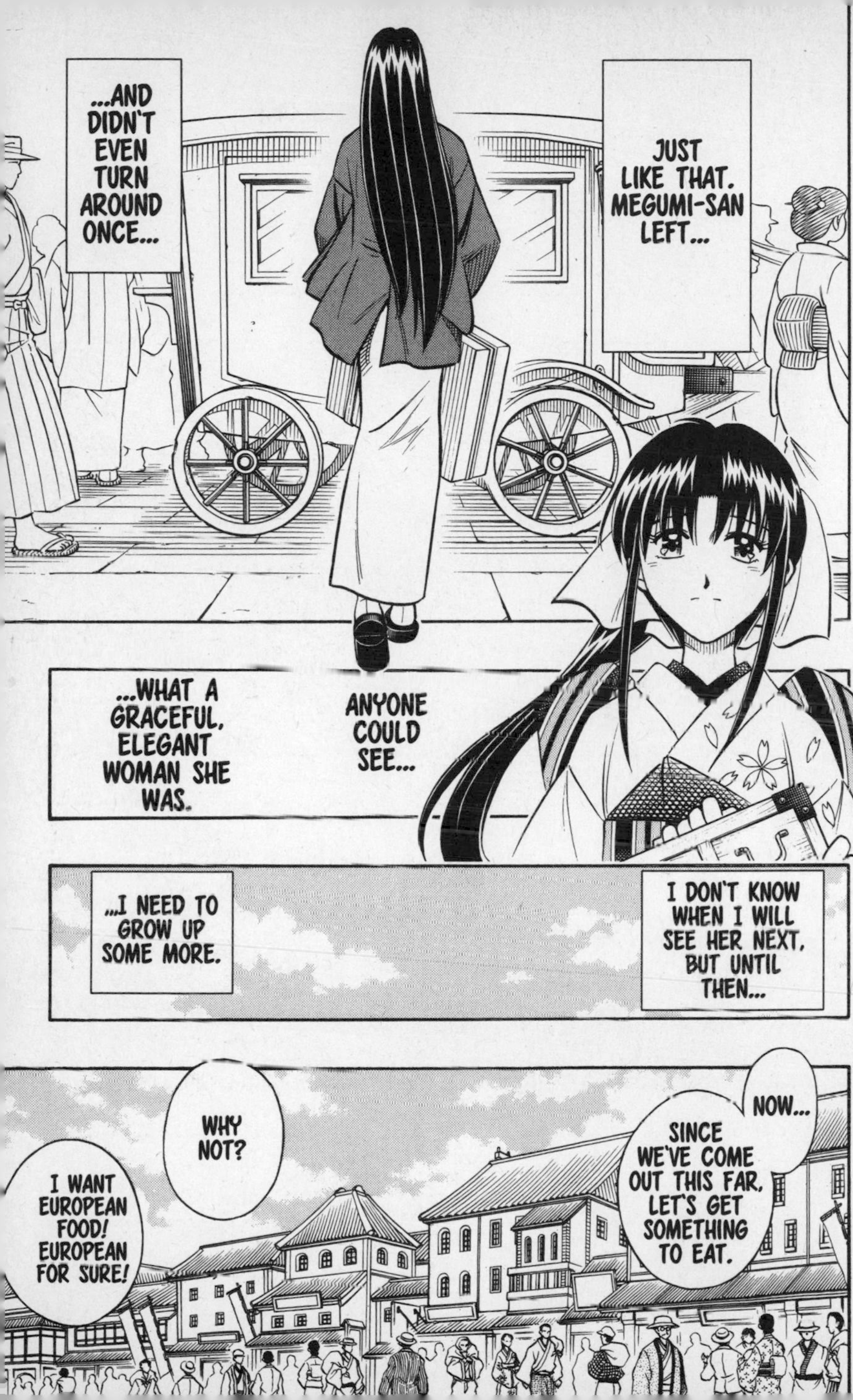
JUST LIKE THAT. MEGUMI-SAN LEFT...
...AND DIDN'T EVEN TURN AROUND ONCE...
ANYONE COULD SEE...
...WHAT A GRACEFUL, ELEGANT WOMAN SHE WAS.
I DON'T KNOW WHEN I WILL SEE HER NEXT, BUT UNTIL THEN...
...I NEED TO GROW UP SOME MORE.
NOW...
SINCE WE'VE COME OUT THIS FAR, LET'S GET SOMETHING TO EAT.
WHY NOT?
I WANT EUROPEAN FOOD! EUROPEAN FOR SURE!

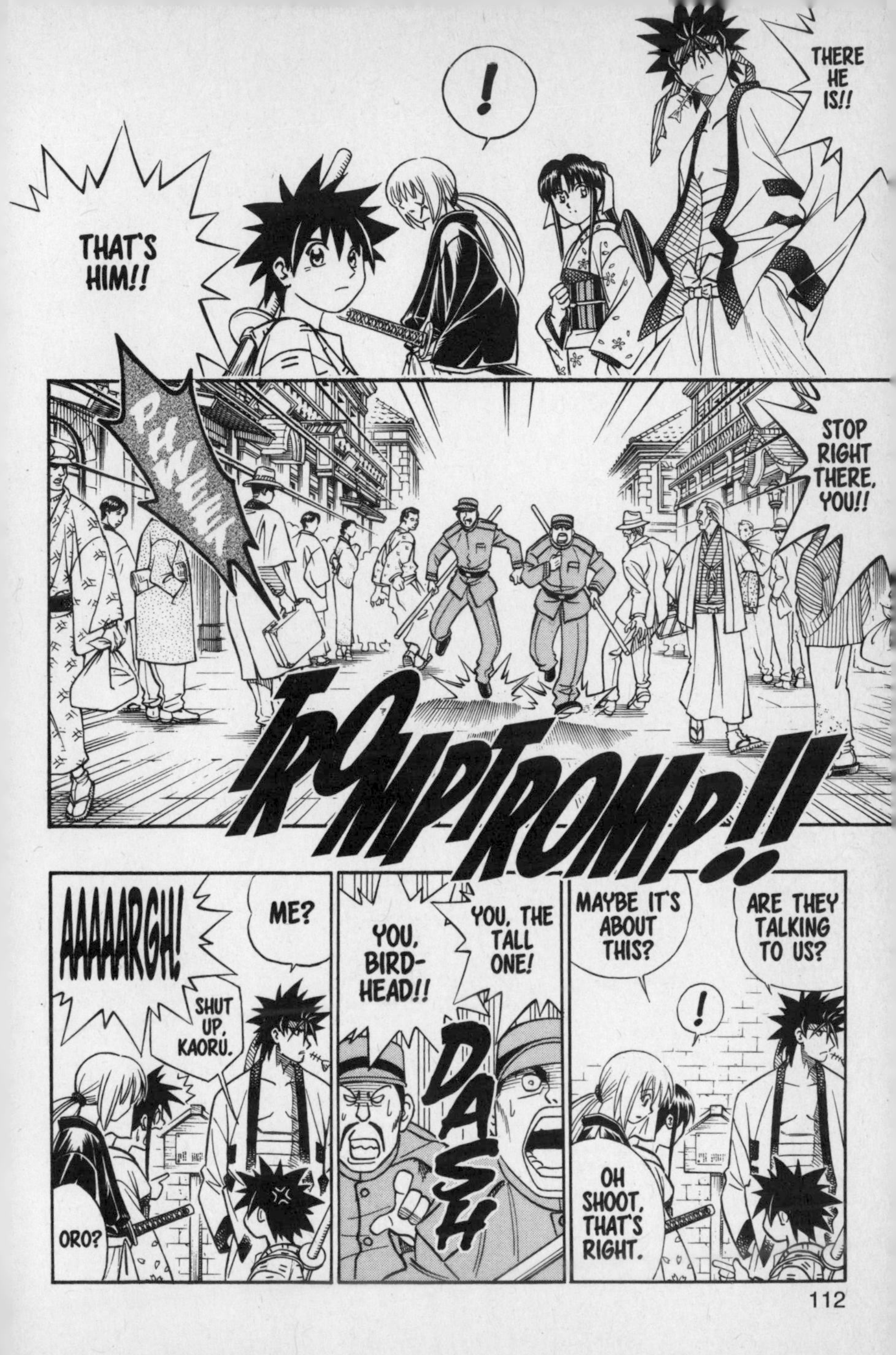
THERE HE IS!!
!
THAT'S HIM!!
PHWEET
STOP RIGHT THERE, YOU!!
TROMPTROMP!!
ARE THEY TALKING TO US?
MAYBE IT'S ABOUT THIS?
!
OH SHOOT, THAT'S RIGHT.
YOU, THE TALL ONE!
YOU, BIRD-HEAD!!
DASH
ME?
AAAAARGH!
SHUT UP, KAORU.
ORO?

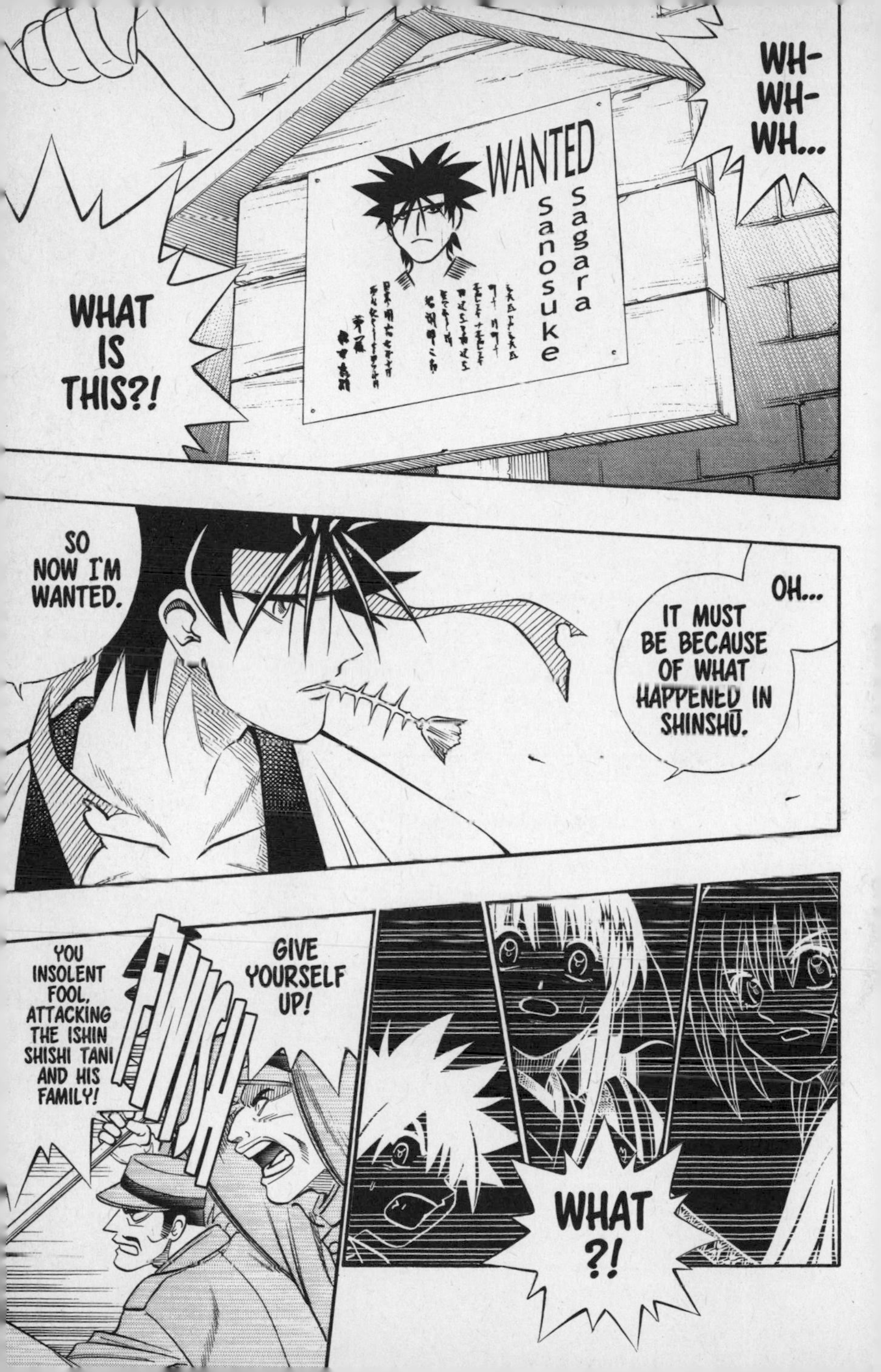
WH- WH- WH...
WHAT IS THIS?!
WANTED
Sagara Sanosuke
OH... IT MUST BE BECAUSE OF WHAT HAPPENED IN SHINSHŪ.
SO NOW I'M WANTED.
WHAT ?!
GIVE YOURSELF UP!
YOU INSOLENT FOOL, ATTACKING THE ISHIN SHISHI TANI AND HIS FAMILY!

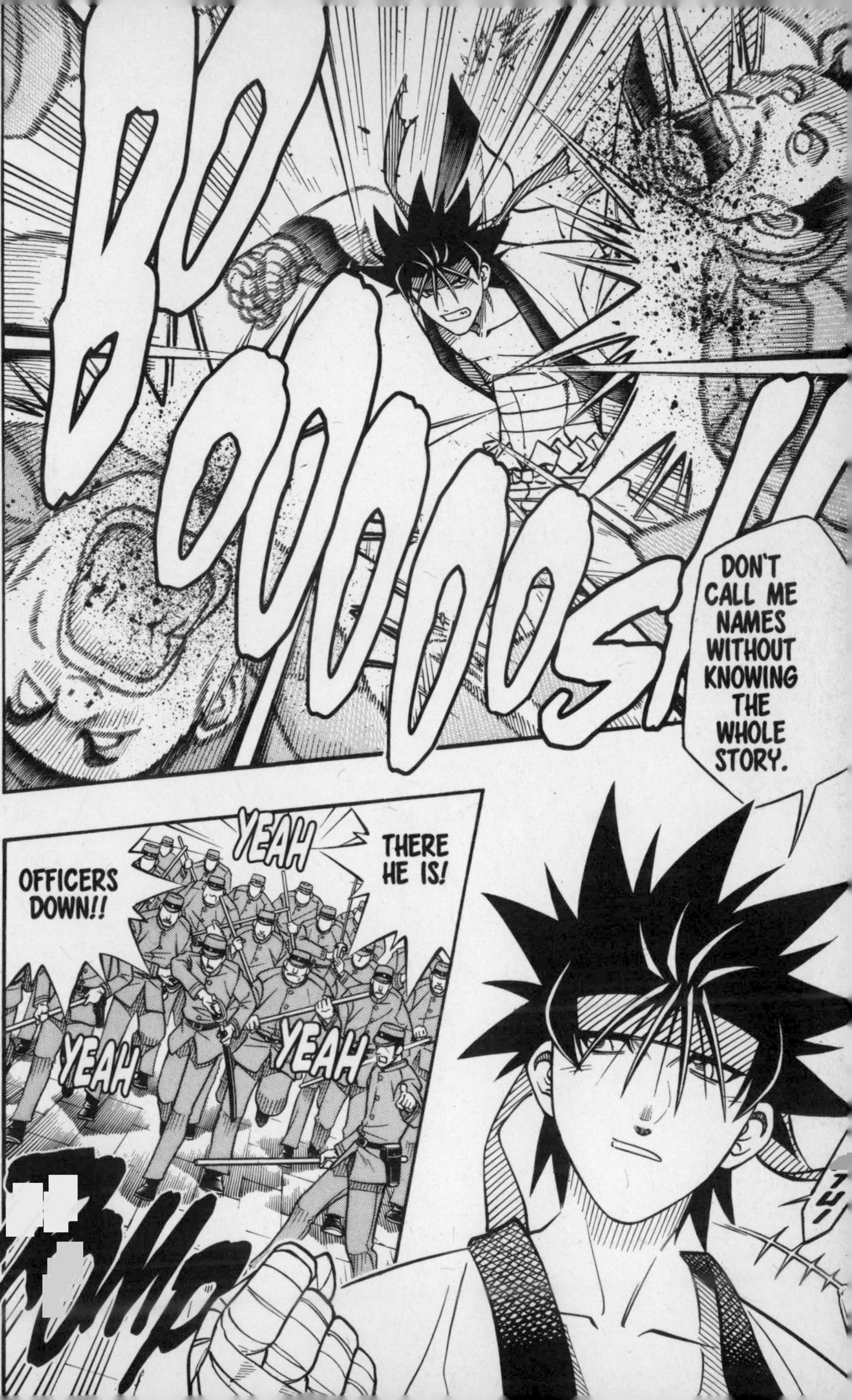
DON'T CALL ME NAMES WITHOUT KNOWING THE WHOLE STORY.
TSU
THERE HE IS!
YEAH
OFFICERS DOWN!!
YEAH
YEAH

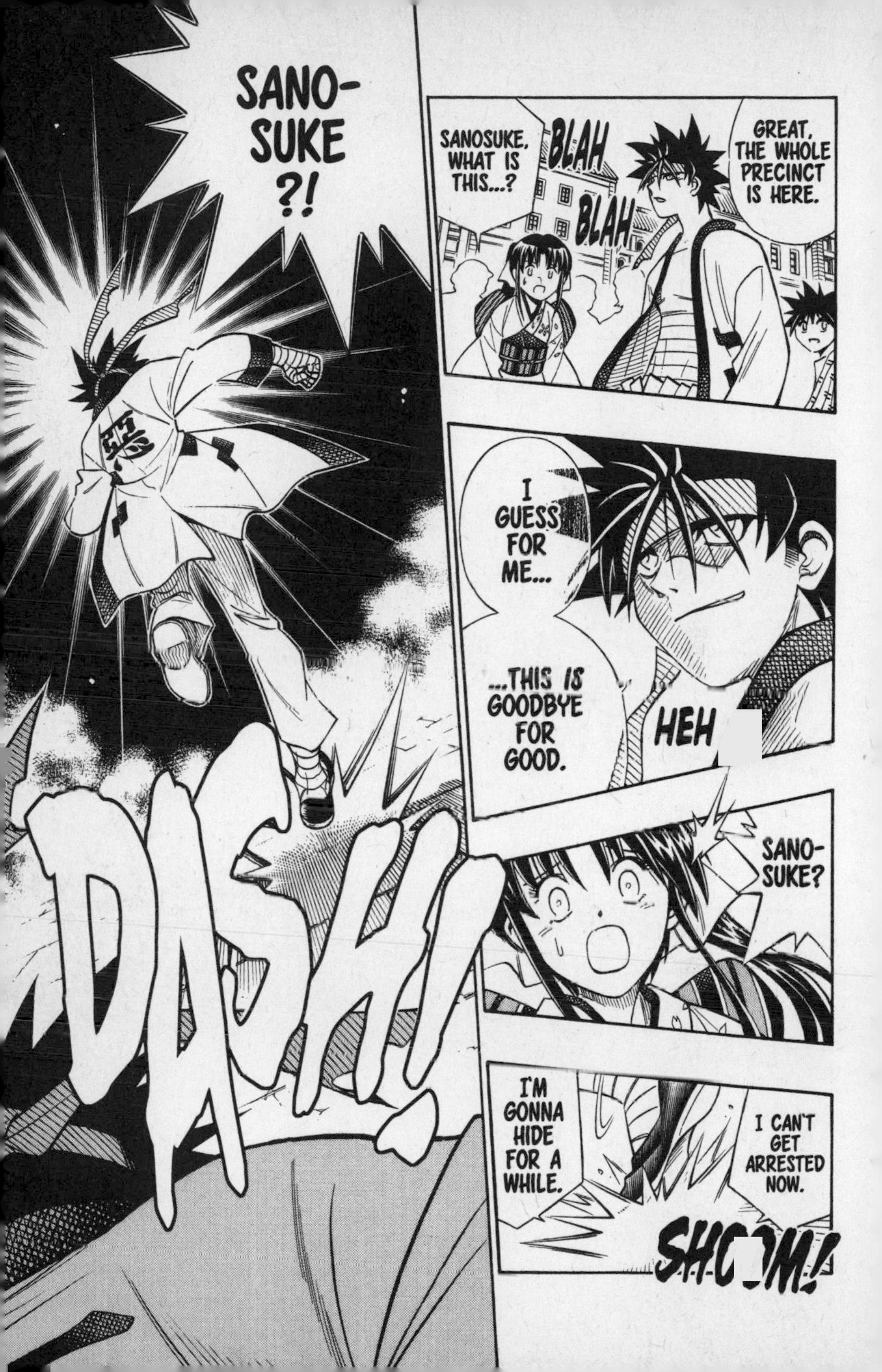
GREAT, THE WHOLE PRECINCT IS HERE.
BLAH
BLAH
SANOSUKE, WHAT IS THIS...?
I GUESS FOR ME...
...THIS IS GOODBYE FOR GOOD.
HEH
SANO-SUKE?
I CAN'T GET ARRESTED NOW.
I'M GONNA HIDE FOR A WHILE.
SHOOM!
SANO-SUKE ?!
DASH!

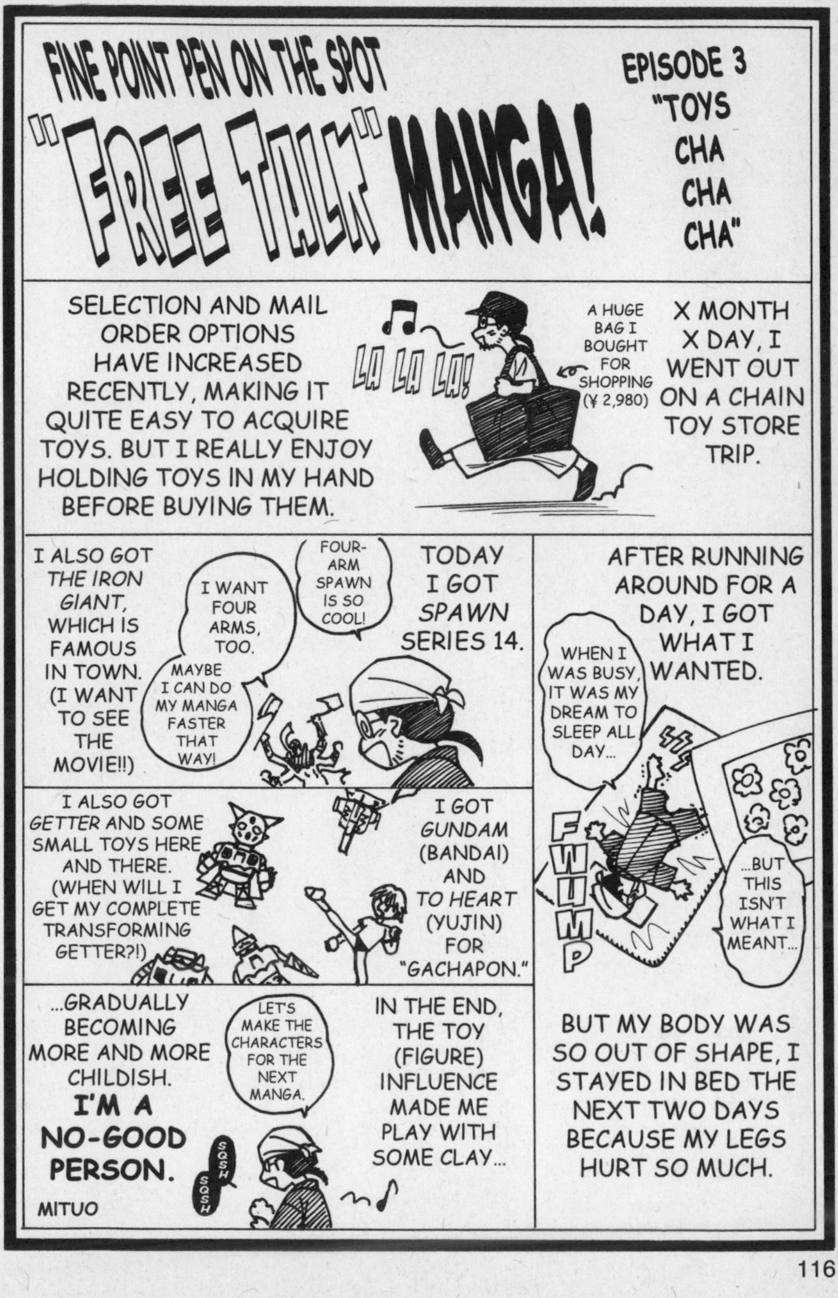
EPISODE 3 "TOYS CHA CHA CHA"
FINE POINT PEN ON THE SPOT
"FREE TALK" MANGA!
X MONTH X DAY, I WENT OUT ON A CHAIN TOY STORE TRIP.
A HUGE BAG I BOUGHT FOR SHOPPING (¥ 2,980)
LA LA LA!
SELECTION AND MAIL ORDER OPTIONS HAVE INCREASED RECENTLY, MAKING IT QUITE EASY TO ACQUIRE TOYS. BUT I REALLY ENJOY HOLDING TOYS IN MY HAND BEFORE BUYING THEM.
AFTER RUNNING AROUND FOR A DAY, I GOT WHAT I WANTED.
WHEN I WAS BUSY, IT WAS MY DREAM TO SLEEP ALL DAY...
...BUT THIS ISN'T WHAT I MEANT...
FWUMP
BUT MY BODY WAS SO OUT OF SHAPE, I STAYED IN BED THE NEXT TWO DAYS BECAUSE MY LEGS HURT SO MUCH.
TODAY I GOT SPAWN SERIES 14.
FOUR-ARM SPAWN IS SO COOL!
I WANT FOUR ARMS, TOO.
MAYBE I CAN DO MY MANGA FASTER THAT WAY!
I ALSO GOT THE IRON GIANT, WHICH IS FAMOUS IN TOWN. (I WANT TO SEE THE MOVIE!!)
I GOT GUNDAM (BANDAI) AND TO HEART (YUJIN) FOR "GACHAPON."
I ALSO GOT GETTER AND SOME SMALL TOYS HERE AND THERE. (WHEN WILL I GET MY COMPLETE TRANSFORMING GETTER?!)
IN THE END, THE TOY (FIGURE) INFLUENCE MADE ME PLAY WITH SOME CLAY...
LET'S MAKE THE CHARACTERS FOR THE NEXT MANGA.
SQSH SQSH
...GRADUALLY BECOMING MORE AND MORE CHILDISH.
I'M A NO-GOOD PERSON.
MITUO

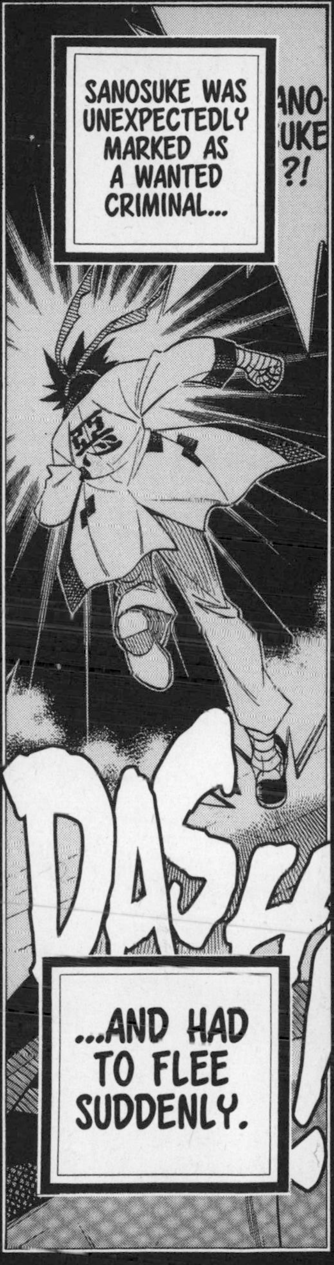
SANOSUKE WAS UNEXPECTEDLY MARKED AS A WANTED CRIMINAL...
ANO- UKE ?!
DAS
...AND HAD TO FLEE SUDDENLY.

Act 254
Years

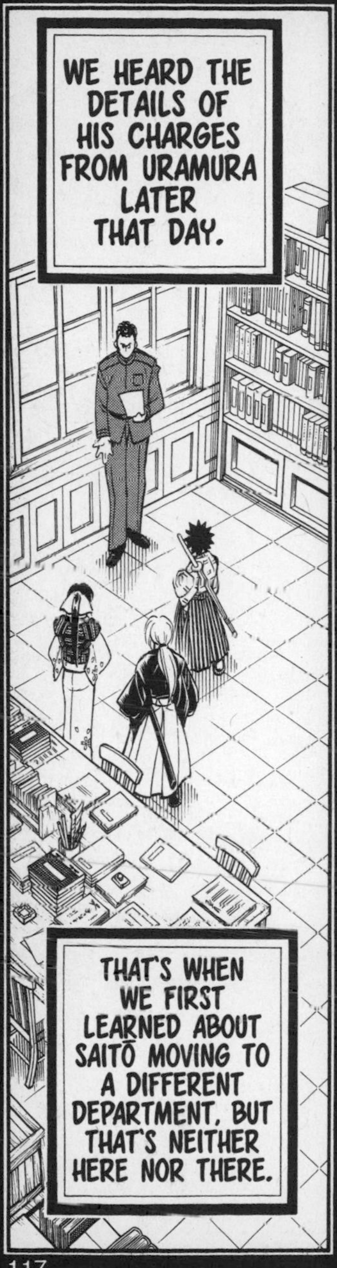
WE HEARD THE DETAILS OF HIS CHARGES FROM URAMURA LATER THAT DAY.
THAT'S WHEN WE FIRST LEARNED ABOUT SAITŌ MOVING TO A DIFFERENT DEPARTMENT, BUT THAT'S NEITHER HERE NOR THERE.

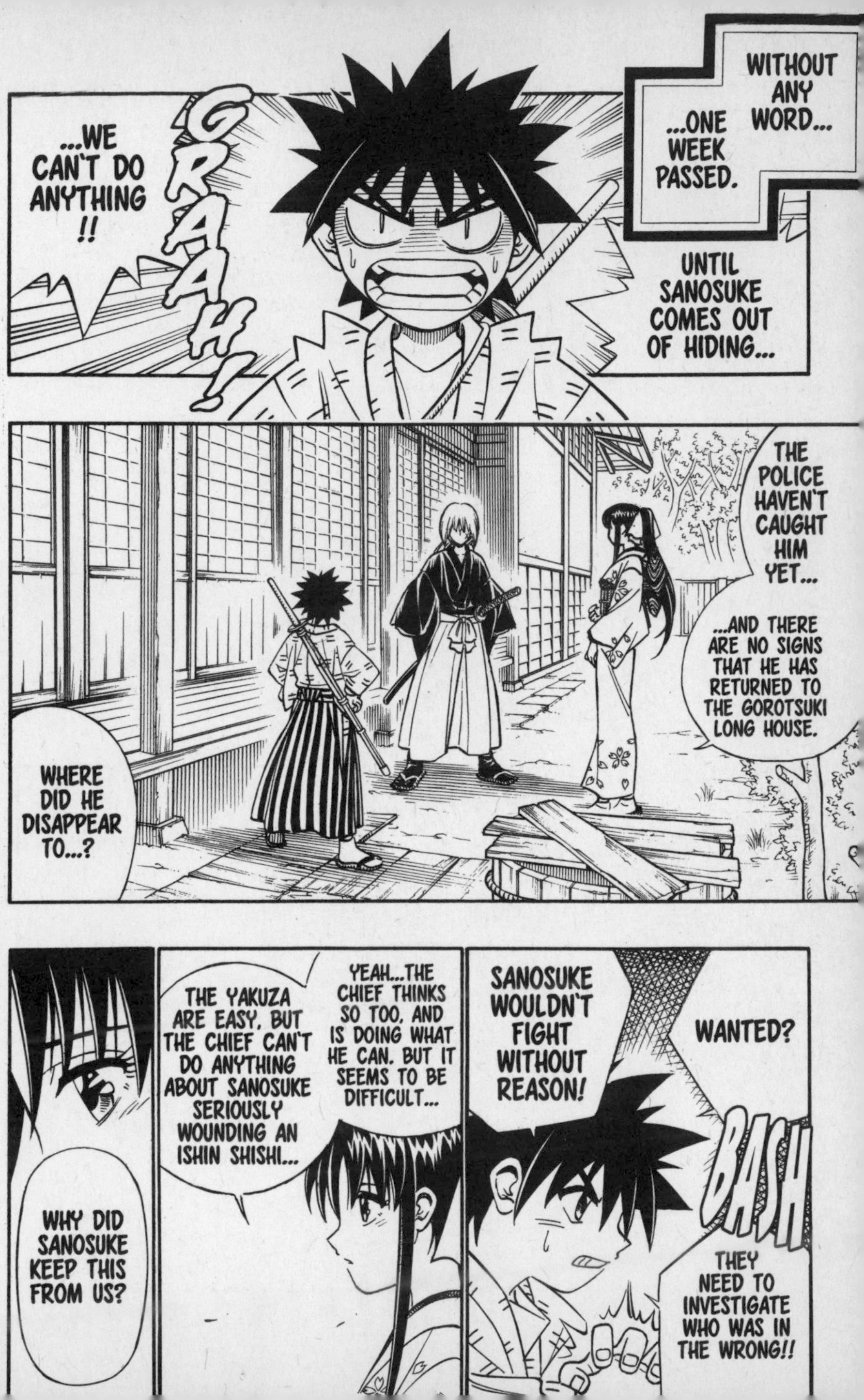
WITHOUT ANY WORD...
...ONE WEEK PASSED.
UNTIL SANOSUKE COMES OUT OF HIDING...
GRAAH!
...WE CAN'T DO ANYTHING!!
THE POLICE HAVEN'T CAUGHT HIM YET...
...AND THERE ARE NO SIGNS THAT HE HAS RETURNED TO THE GOROTSUKI LONG HOUSE.
WHERE DID HE DISAPPEAR TO...?
WANTED?
SANOSUKE WOULDN'T FIGHT WITHOUT REASON!
BASH
THEY NEED TO INVESTIGATE WHO WAS IN THE WRONG!!
YEAH...THE CHIEF THINKS SO TOO, AND IS DOING WHAT HE CAN. BUT IT SEEMS TO BE DIFFICULT...
THE YAKUZA ARE EASY, BUT THE CHIEF CAN'T DO ANYTHING ABOUT SANOSUKE SERIOUSLY WOUNDING AN ISHIN SHISHI...
WHY DID SANOSUKE KEEP THIS FROM US?

READ THIS WAY

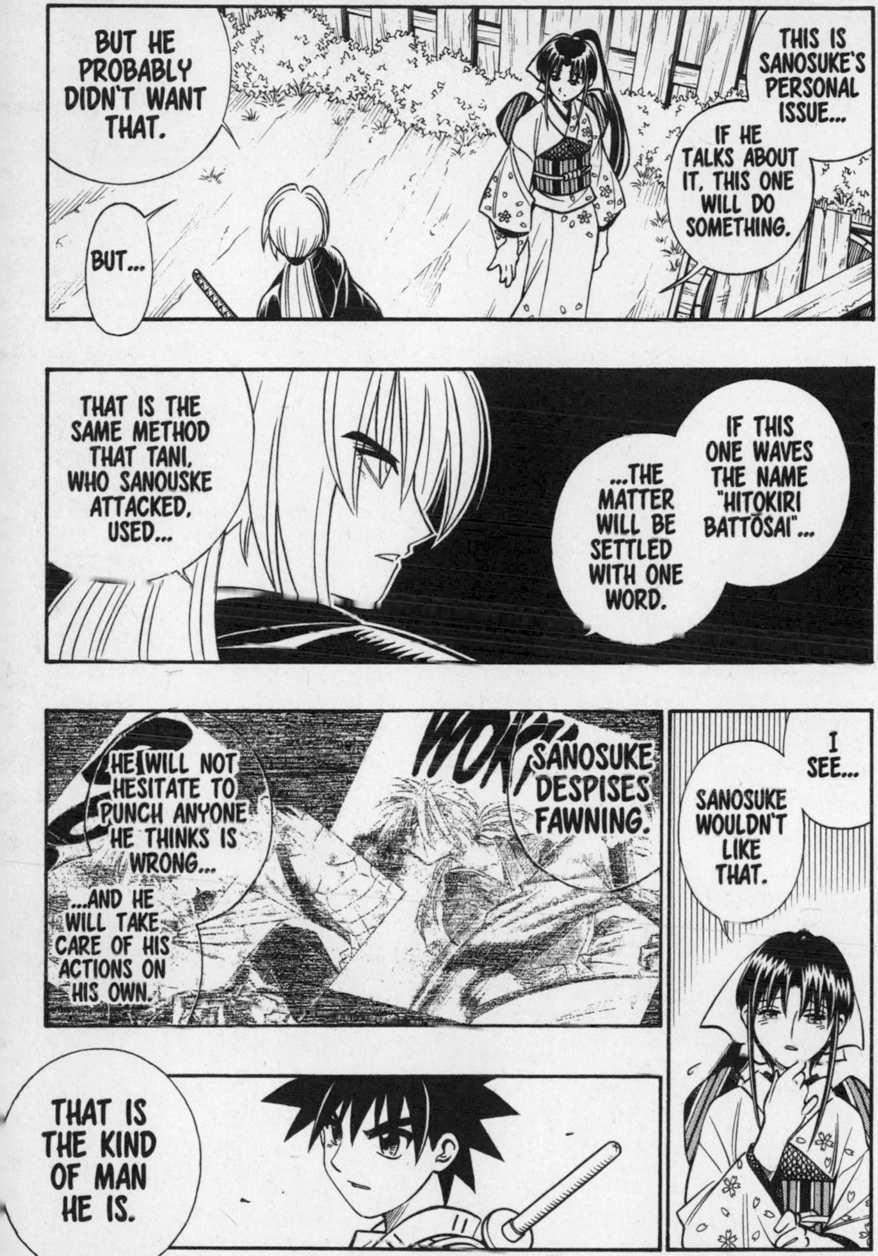
THIS IS SANOSUKE'S PERSONAL ISSUE...
IF HE TALKS ABOUT IT, THIS ONE WILL DO SOMETHING.
BUT HE PROBABLY DIDN'T WANT THAT.
BUT...
IF THIS ONE WAVES THE NAME "HITOKIRI BATTŌSAI"...
...THE MATTER WILL BE SETTLED WITH ONE WORD.
THAT IS THE SAME METHOD THAT TANI, WHO SANOUSKE ATTACKED, USED...
I SEE...
SANOSUKE WOULDN'T LIKE THAT.
SANOSUKE DESPISES FAWNING.
HE WILL NOT HESITATE TO PUNCH ANYONE HE THINKS IS WRONG...
...AND HE WILL TAKE CARE OF HIS ACTIONS ON HIS OWN.
THAT IS THE KIND OF MAN HE IS.

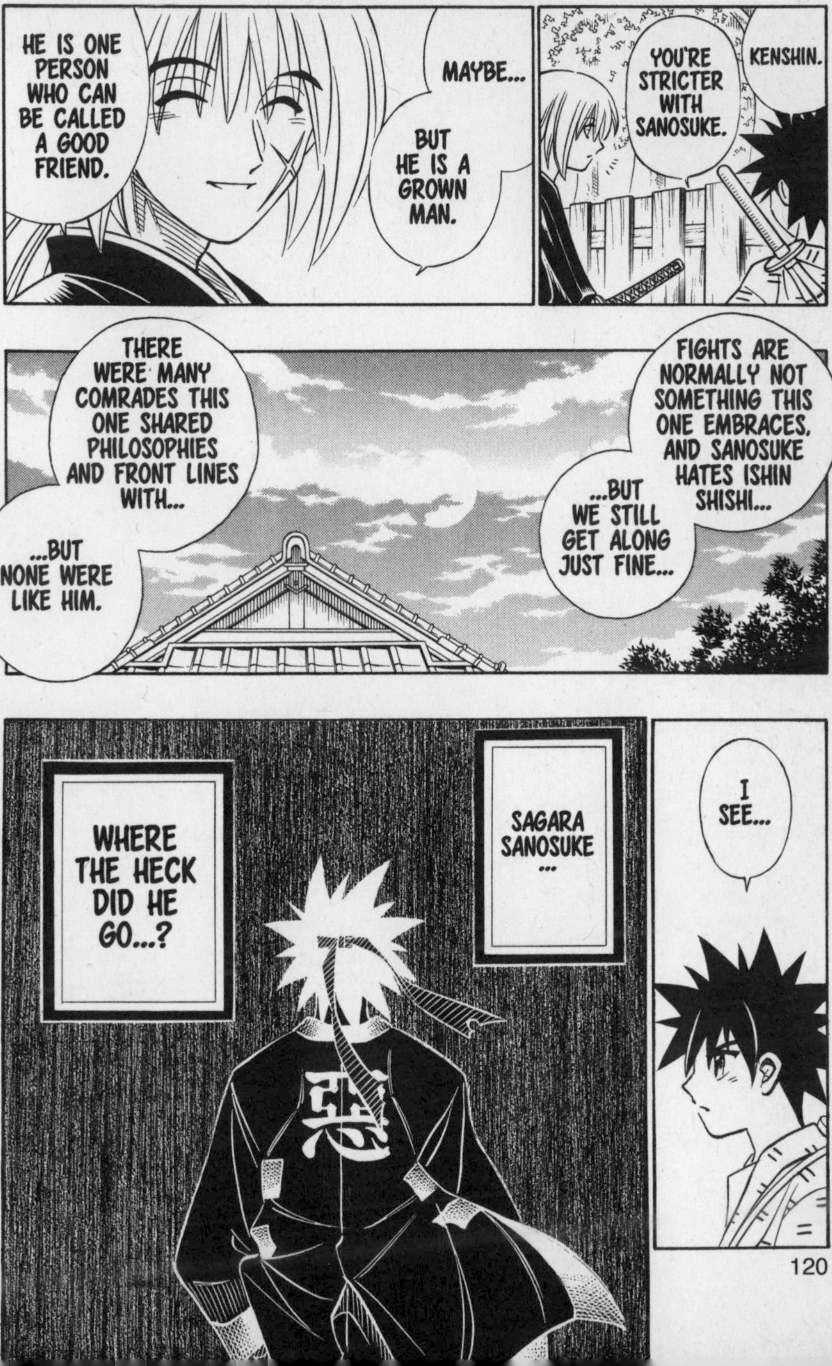
KENSHIN.
YOU'RE STRICTER WITH SANOSUKE.
MAYBE...
BUT HE IS A GROWN MAN.
HE IS ONE PERSON WHO CAN BE CALLED A GOOD FRIEND.
FIGHTS ARE NORMALLY NOT SOMETHING THIS ONE EMBRACES, AND SANOSUKE HATES ISHIN SHISHI...
...BUT WE STILL GET ALONG JUST FINE...
THERE WERE MANY COMRADES THIS ONE SHARED PHILOSOPHIES AND FRONT LINES WITH...
...BUT NONE WERE LIKE HIM.
I SEE...
SAGARA SANOSUKE ...
WHERE THE HECK DID HE GO...?

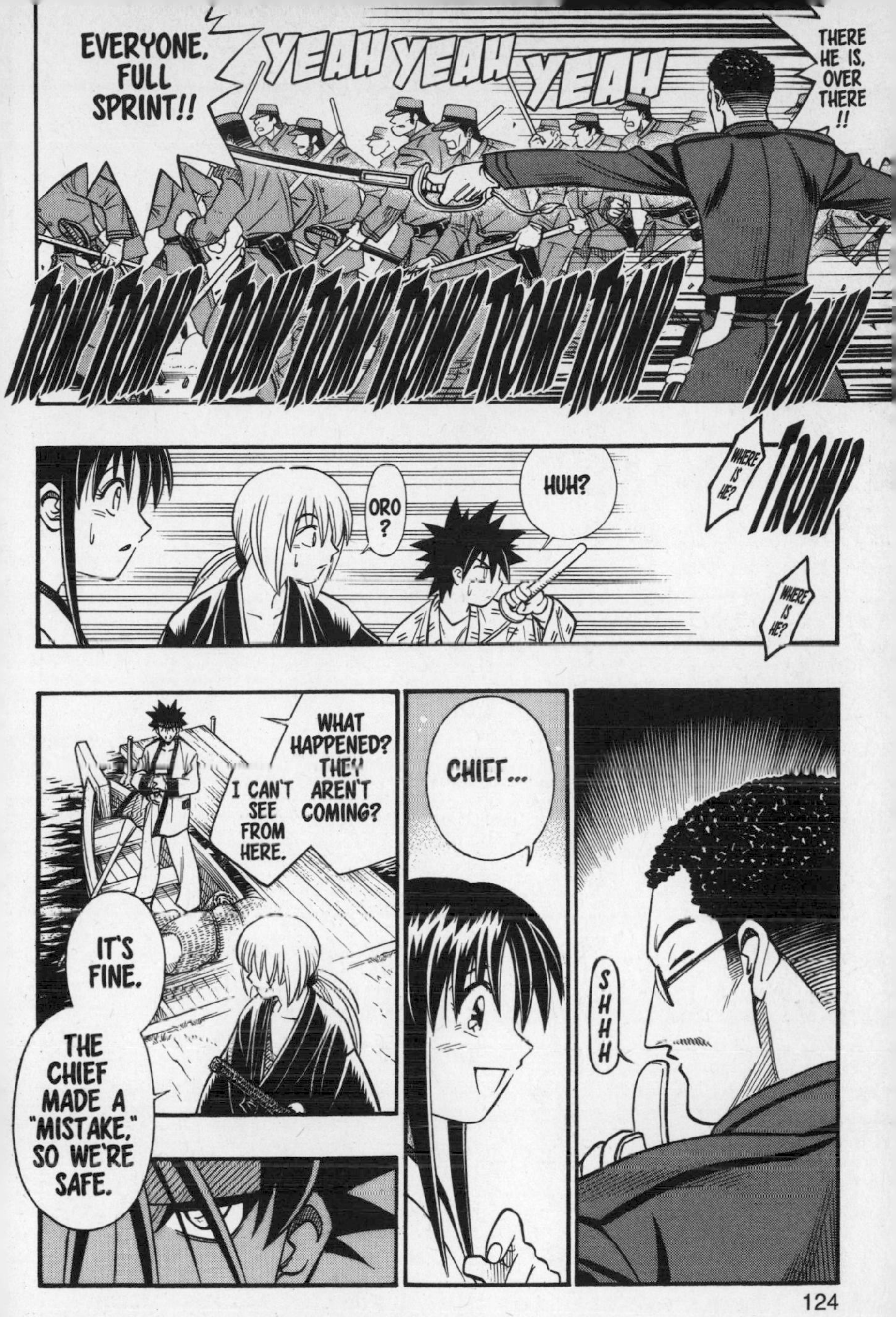
THERE HE IS, OVER THERE!!
YEAH YEAH YEAH
EVERYONE, FULL SPRINT!!
TROMP TROMP TROMP TROMP TROMP TROMP TROMP
TROMP
WHERE IS HE?
WHERE IS HE?
TROMP
HUH?
ORO?
SHHH
CHIEF...
WHAT HAPPENED? THEY AREN'T COMING?
I CAN'T SEE FROM HERE.
IT'S FINE.
THE CHIEF MADE A "MISTAKE," SO WE'RE SAFE.

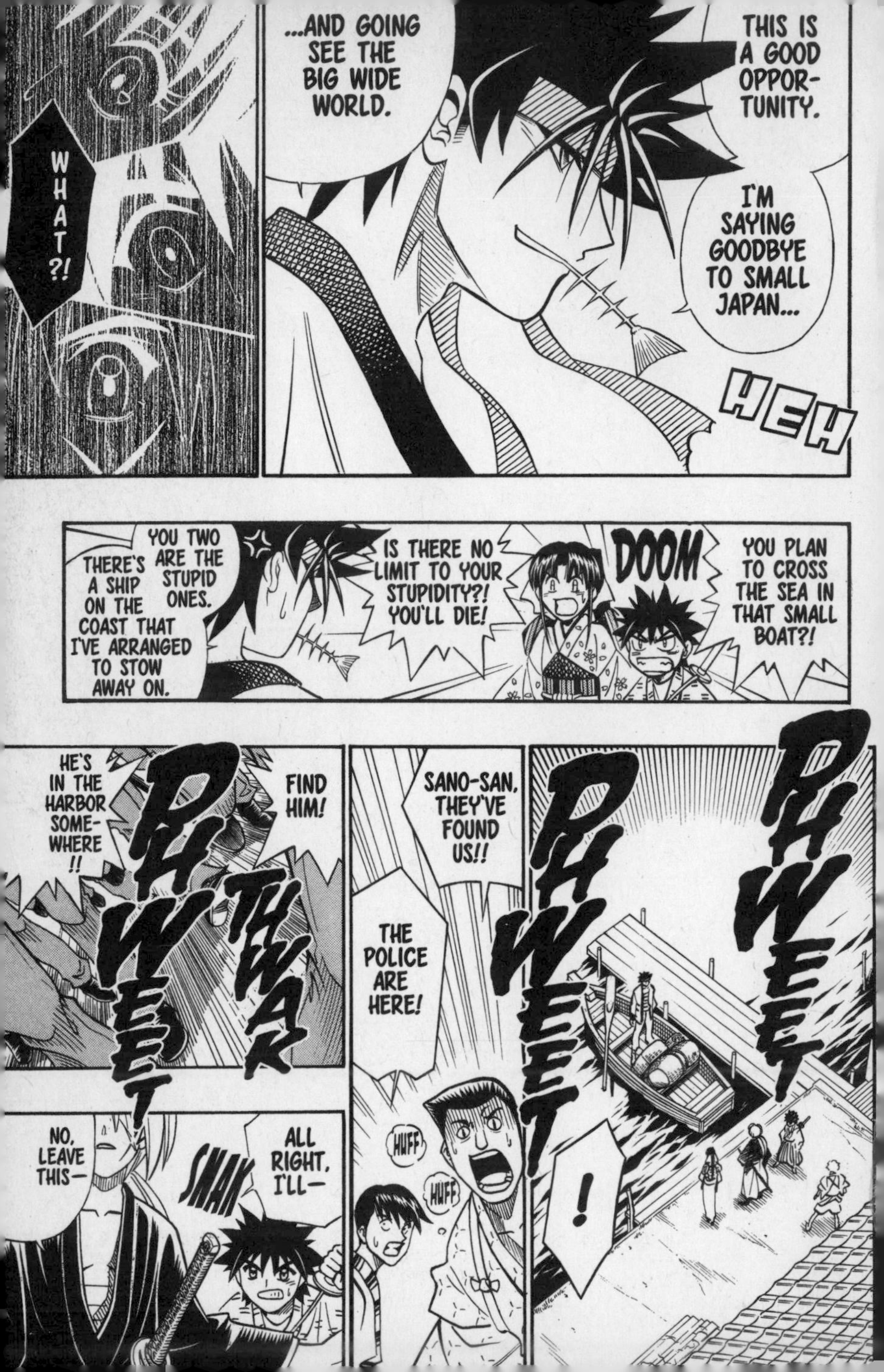
THIS IS A GOOD OPPOR-TUNITY.
I'M SAYING GOODBYE TO SMALL JAPAN...
HEH
...AND GOING SEE THE BIG WIDE WORLD.
WHAT?!
YOU PLAN TO CROSS THE SEA IN THAT SMALL BOAT?!
DOOM
IS THERE NO LIMIT TO YOUR STUPIDITY?! YOU'LL DIE!
YOU TWO ARE THE STUPID ONES.
THERE'S A SHIP ON THE COAST THAT I'VE ARRANGED TO STOW AWAY ON.
PHWEET
PHWEET
!
SANO-SAN, THEY'VE FOUND US!!
THE POLICE ARE HERE!
HUFF
HUFF
FIND HIM!
HE'S IN THE HARBOR SOME-WHERE!!
PHWEET
THWAK
ALL RIGHT, I'LL—
SHAK
NO, LEAVE THIS—

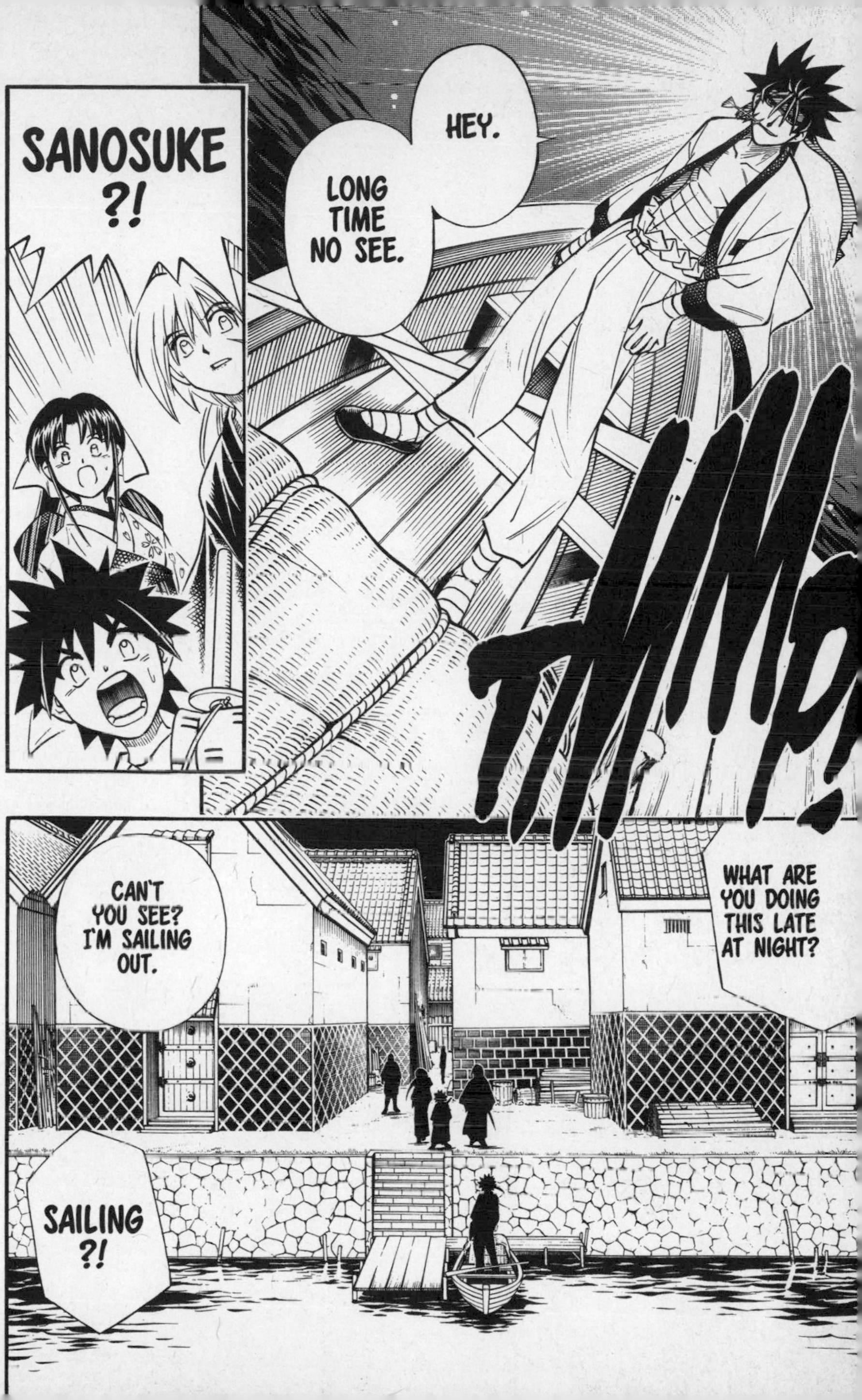
HEY.
LONG TIME NO SEE.
THMP!
SANOSUKE ?!
WHAT ARE YOU DOING THIS LATE AT NIGHT?
CAN'T YOU SEE? I'M SAILING OUT.
SAILING ?!

READ THIS WAY

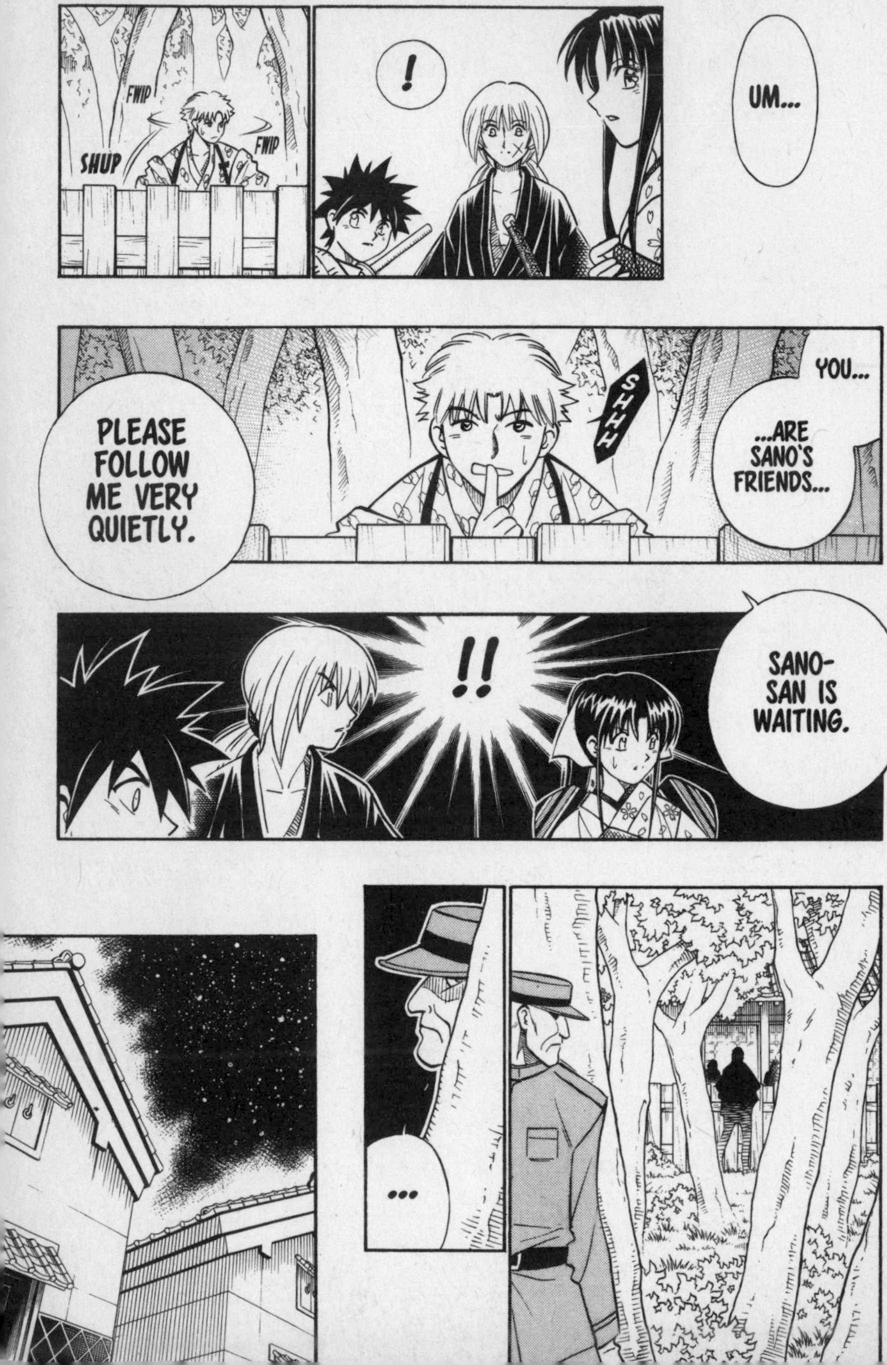
UM...
!
FWIP
FWIP
SHUP
YOU...
...ARE SANO'S FRIENDS...
SHHH
PLEASE FOLLOW ME VERY QUIETLY.
SANO-SAN IS WAITING.
!!
...

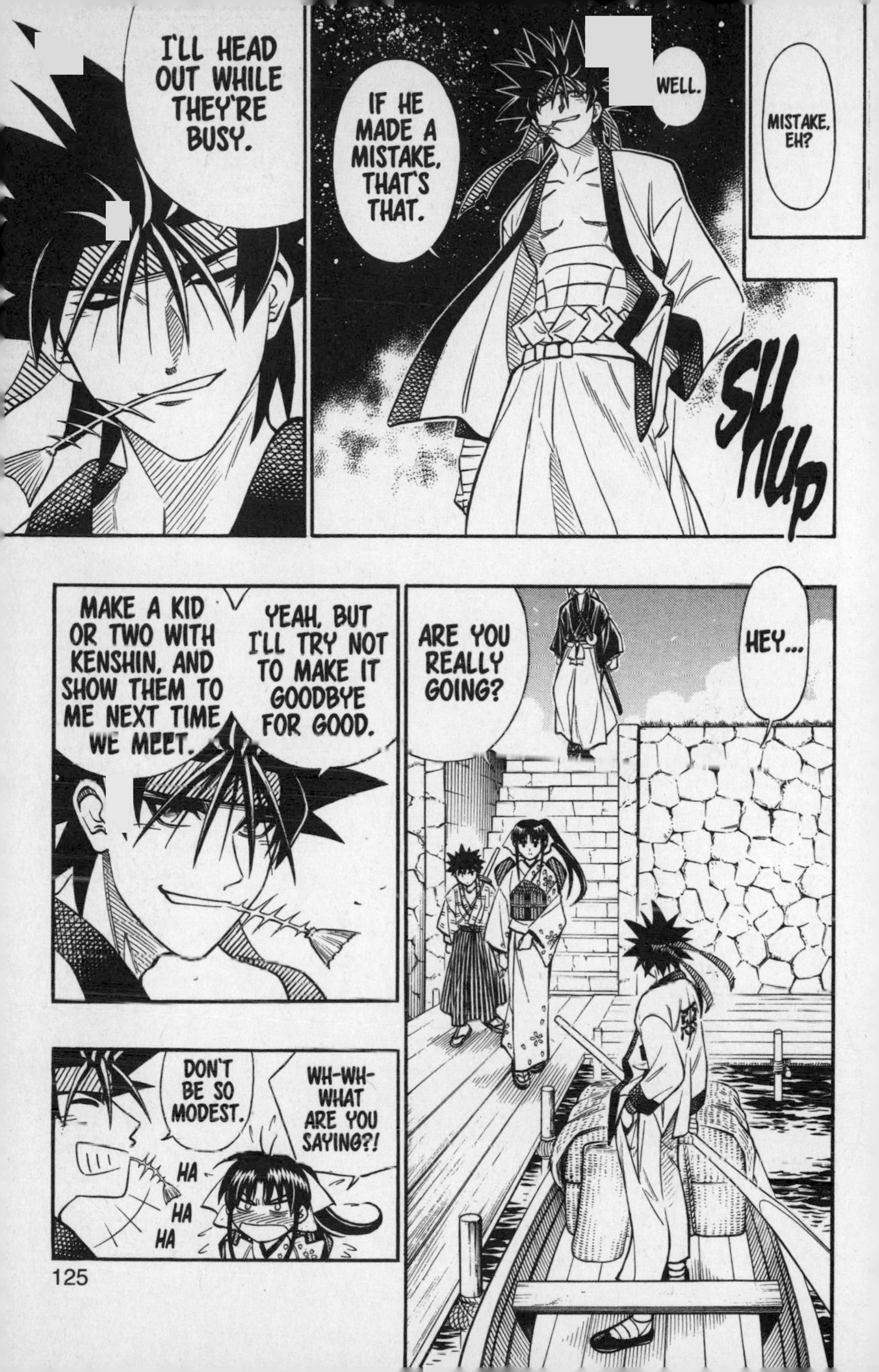
MISTAKE, EH?
WELL.
IF HE MADE A MISTAKE, THAT'S THAT.
SHUP
I'LL HEAD OUT WHILE THEY'RE BUSY.
HEY...
ARE YOU REALLY GOING?
YEAH, BUT I'LL TRY NOT TO MAKE IT GOODBYE FOR GOOD.
MAKE A KID OR TWO WITH KENSHIN, AND SHOW THEM TO ME NEXT TIME WE MEET.
WH-WH-WHAT ARE YOU SAYING?!
DON'T BE SO MODEST.
HA HA HA

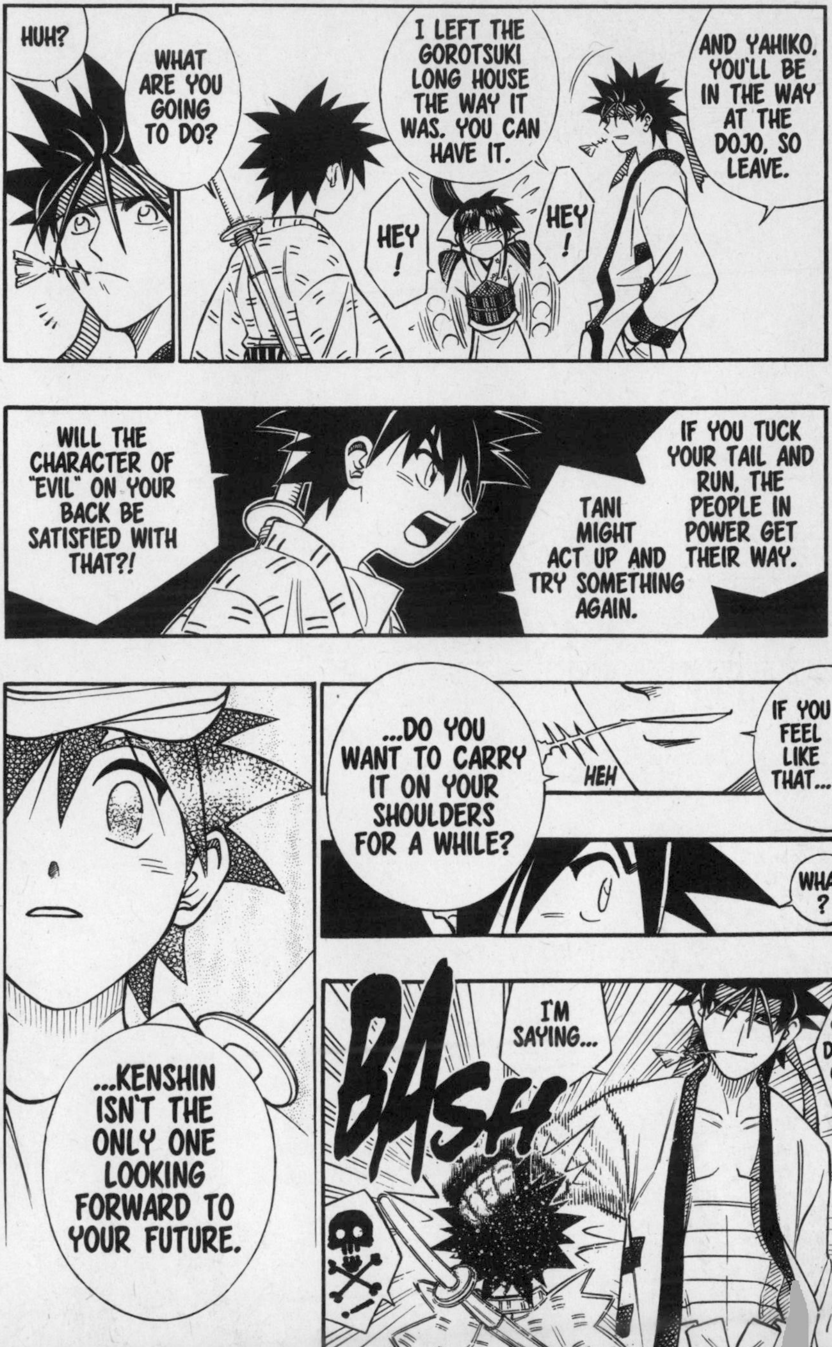
AND YAHIKO, YOU'LL BE IN THE WAY AT THE DOJO, SO LEAVE.
I LEFT THE GOROTSUKI LONG HOUSE THE WAY IT WAS. YOU CAN HAVE IT.
HEY!
HEY!
WHAT ARE YOU GOING TO DO?
HUH?
IF YOU TUCK YOUR TAIL AND RUN, THE PEOPLE IN POWER GET THEIR WAY.
TANI MIGHT ACT UP AND TRY SOMETHING AGAIN.
WILL THE CHARACTER OF "EVIL" ON YOUR BACK BE SATISFIED WITH THAT?!
IF YOU FEEL LIKE THAT...
HEH
...DO YOU WANT TO CARRY IT ON YOUR SHOULDERS FOR A WHILE?
WHAT?
YOU DON'T GET IT?
I'M SAYING...
BASH
...KENSHIN ISN'T THE ONLY ONE LOOKING FORWARD TO YOUR FUTURE.

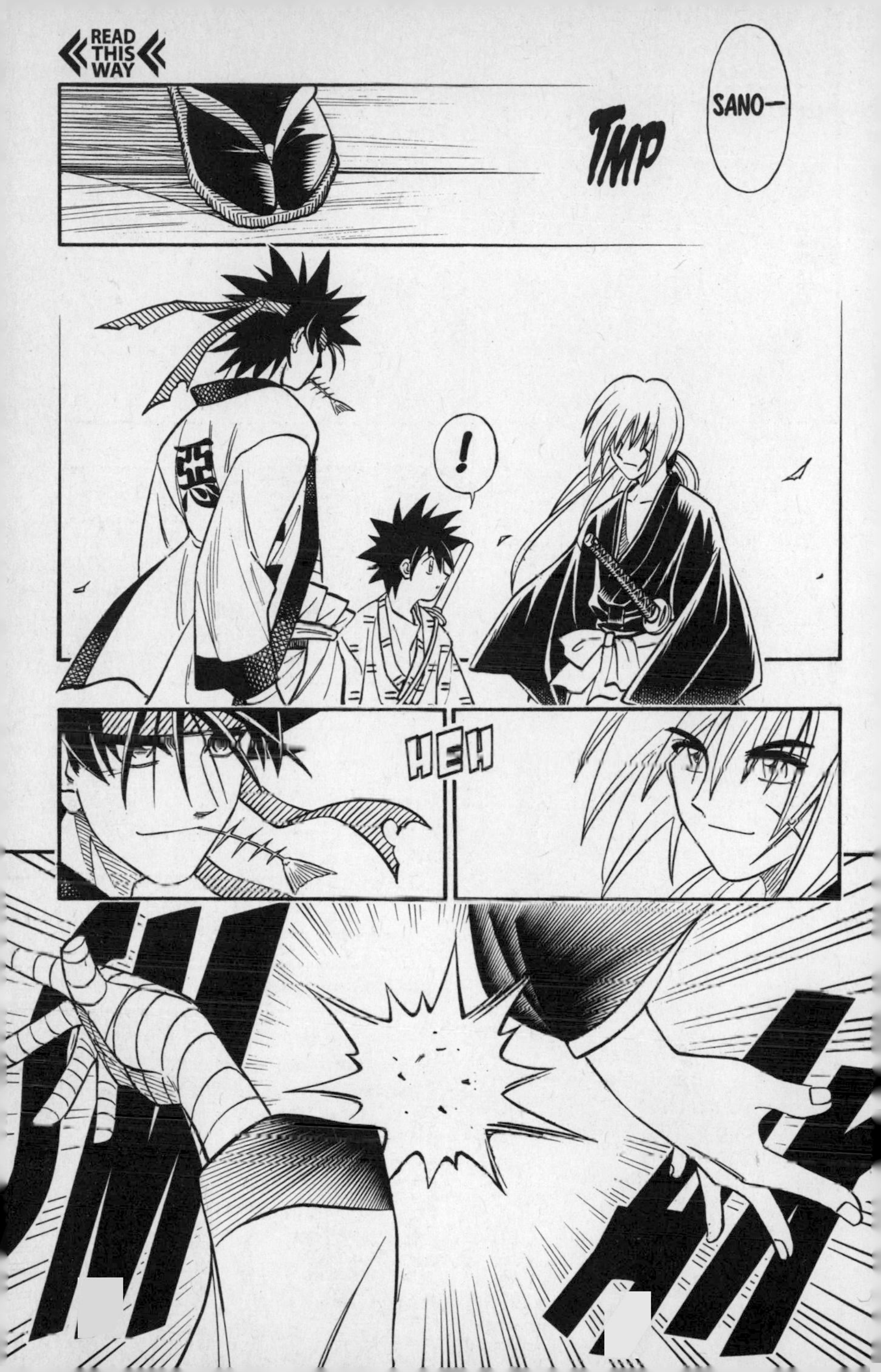
READ THIS WAY
SANO—
TMP
!
HEH

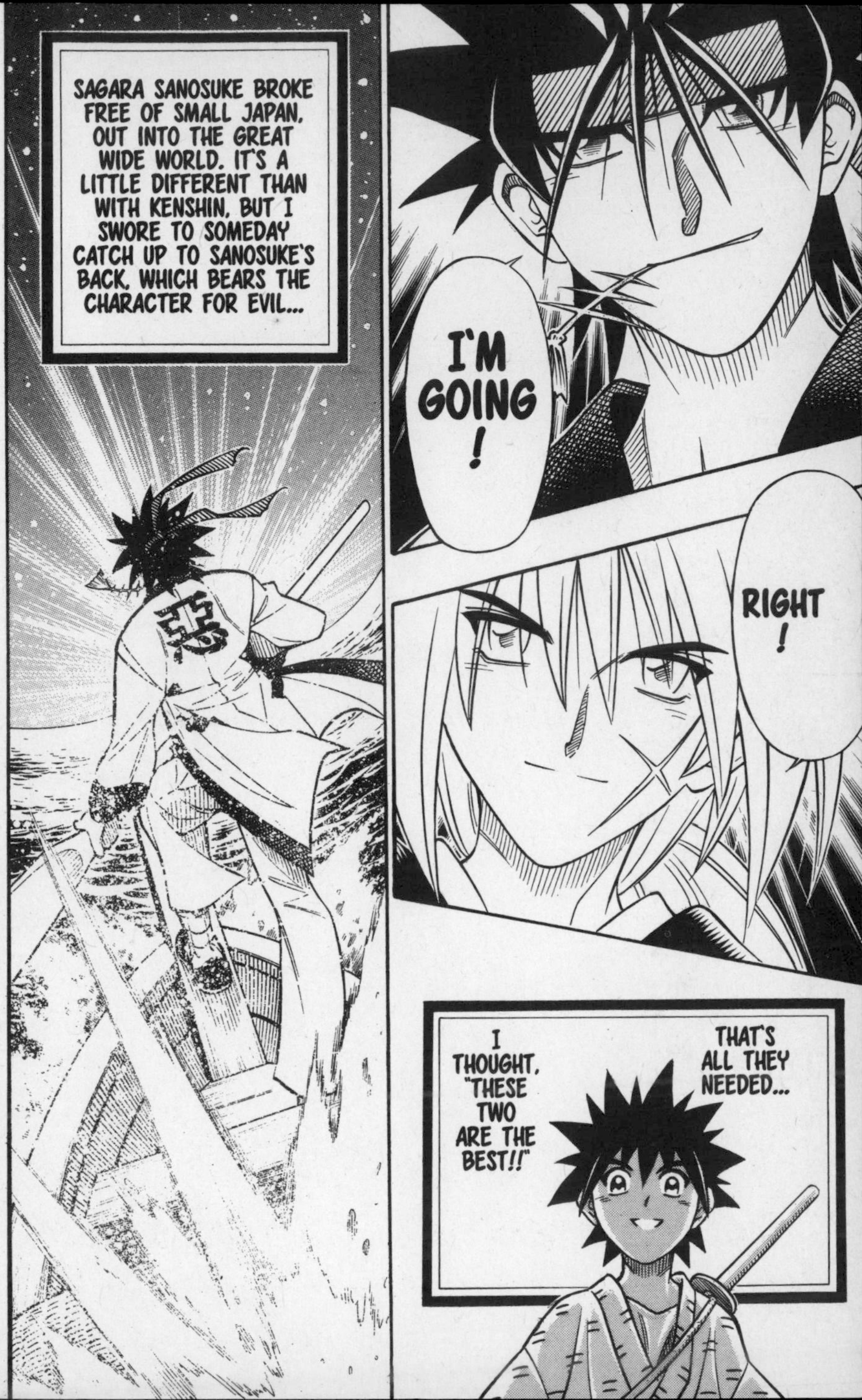
I'M GOING!
RIGHT!
THAT'S ALL THEY NEEDED...
I THOUGHT, "THESE TWO ARE THE BEST!!"
SAGARA SANOSUKE BROKE FREE OF SMALL JAPAN, OUT INTO THE GREAT WIDE WORLD. IT'S A LITTLE DIFFERENT THAN WITH KENSHIN, BUT I SWORE TO SOMEDAY CATCH UP TO SANOSUKE'S BACK, WHICH BEARS THE CHARACTER FOR EVIL...

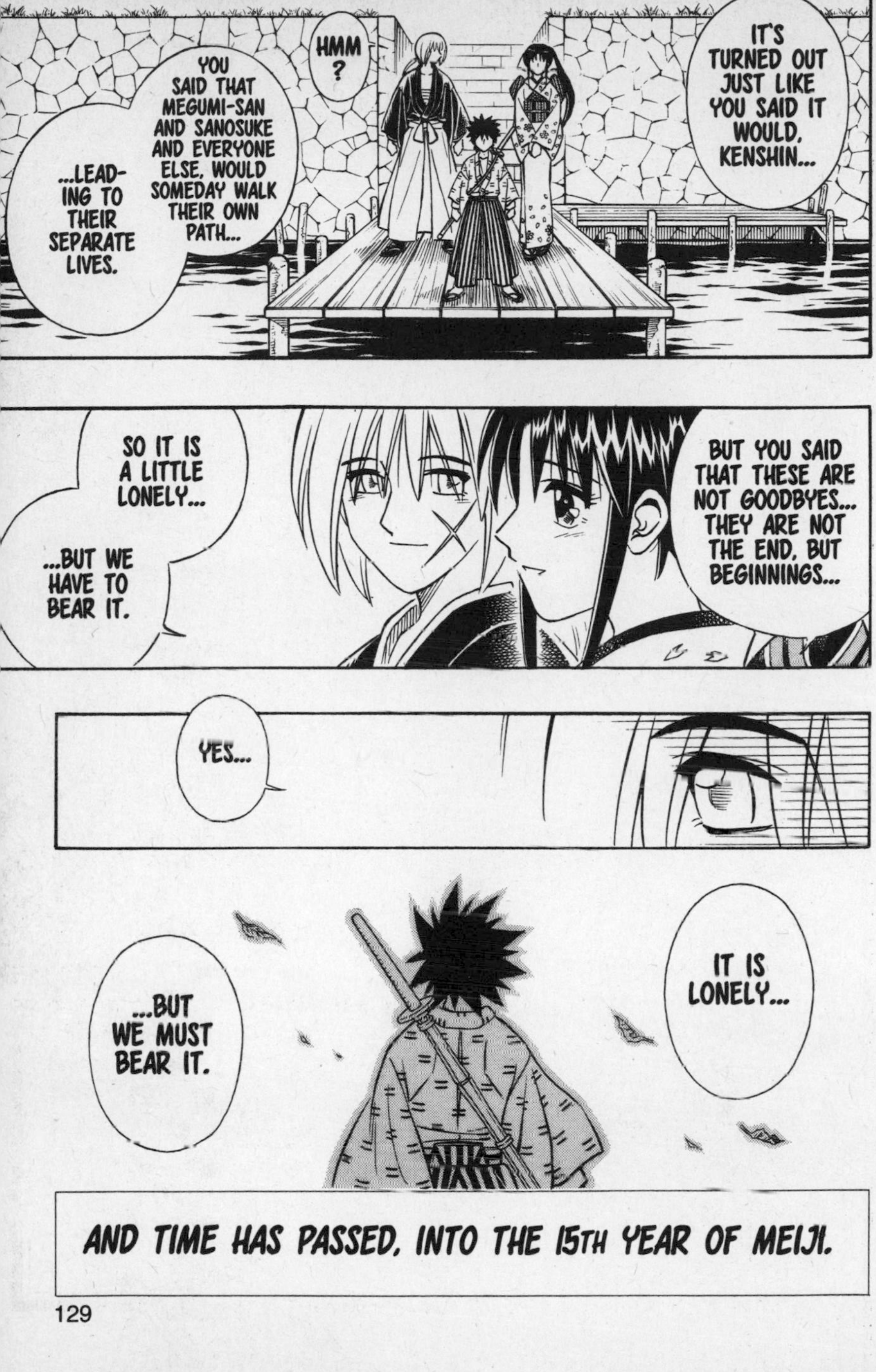
IT'S TURNED OUT JUST LIKE YOU SAID IT WOULD, KENSHIN...
HMM?
YOU SAID THAT MEGUMI-SAN AND SANOSUKE AND EVERYONE ELSE, WOULD SOMEDAY WALK THEIR OWN PATH...
...LEAD-ING TO THEIR SEPARATE LIVES.
BUT YOU SAID THAT THESE ARE NOT GOODBYES... THEY ARE NOT THE END, BUT BEGINNINGS...
SO IT IS A LITTLE LONELY...
...BUT WE HAVE TO BEAR IT.
YES...
IT IS LONELY...
...BUT WE MUST BEAR IT.
AND TIME HAS PASSED, INTO THE 15TH YEAR OF MEIJI.

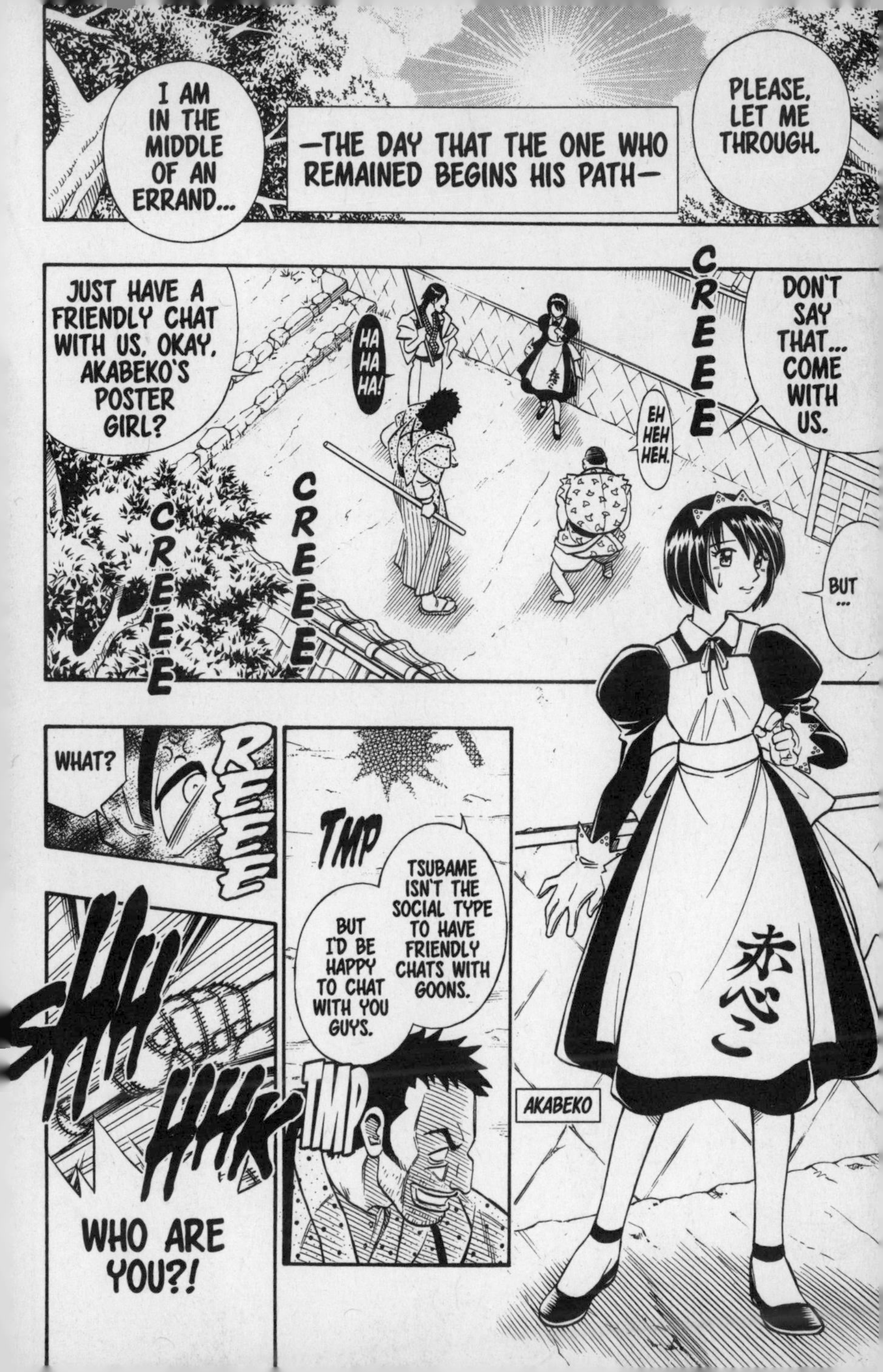
PLEASE, LET ME THROUGH.
—THE DAY THAT THE ONE WHO REMAINED BEGINS HIS PATH—
I AM IN THE MIDDLE OF AN ERRAND...
DON'T SAY THAT... COME WITH US.
CREEE
EH HEH HEH.
HA HA HA!
JUST HAVE A FRIENDLY CHAT WITH US, OKAY, AKABEKO'S POSTER GIRL?
CREEE
CREEE
BUT...
AKABEKO
TMP
TSUBAME ISN'T THE SOCIAL TYPE TO HAVE FRIENDLY CHATS WITH GOONS.
BUT I'D BE HAPPY TO CHAT WITH YOU GUYS.
TMP
REEEE
WHAT?
SHHHHK
WHO ARE YOU?!

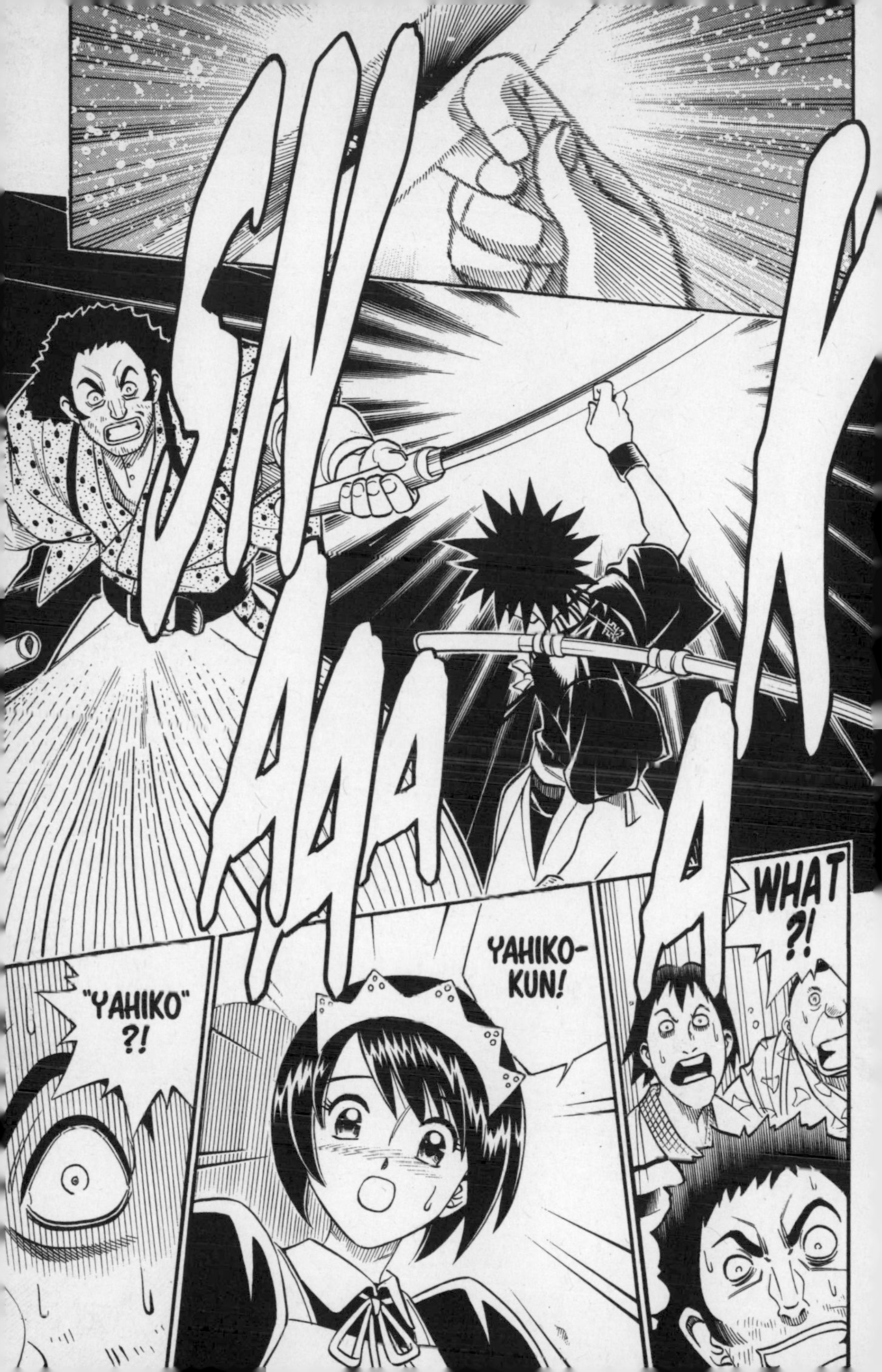
WHAT ?!
YAHIKO-KUN!
"YAHIKO" ?!

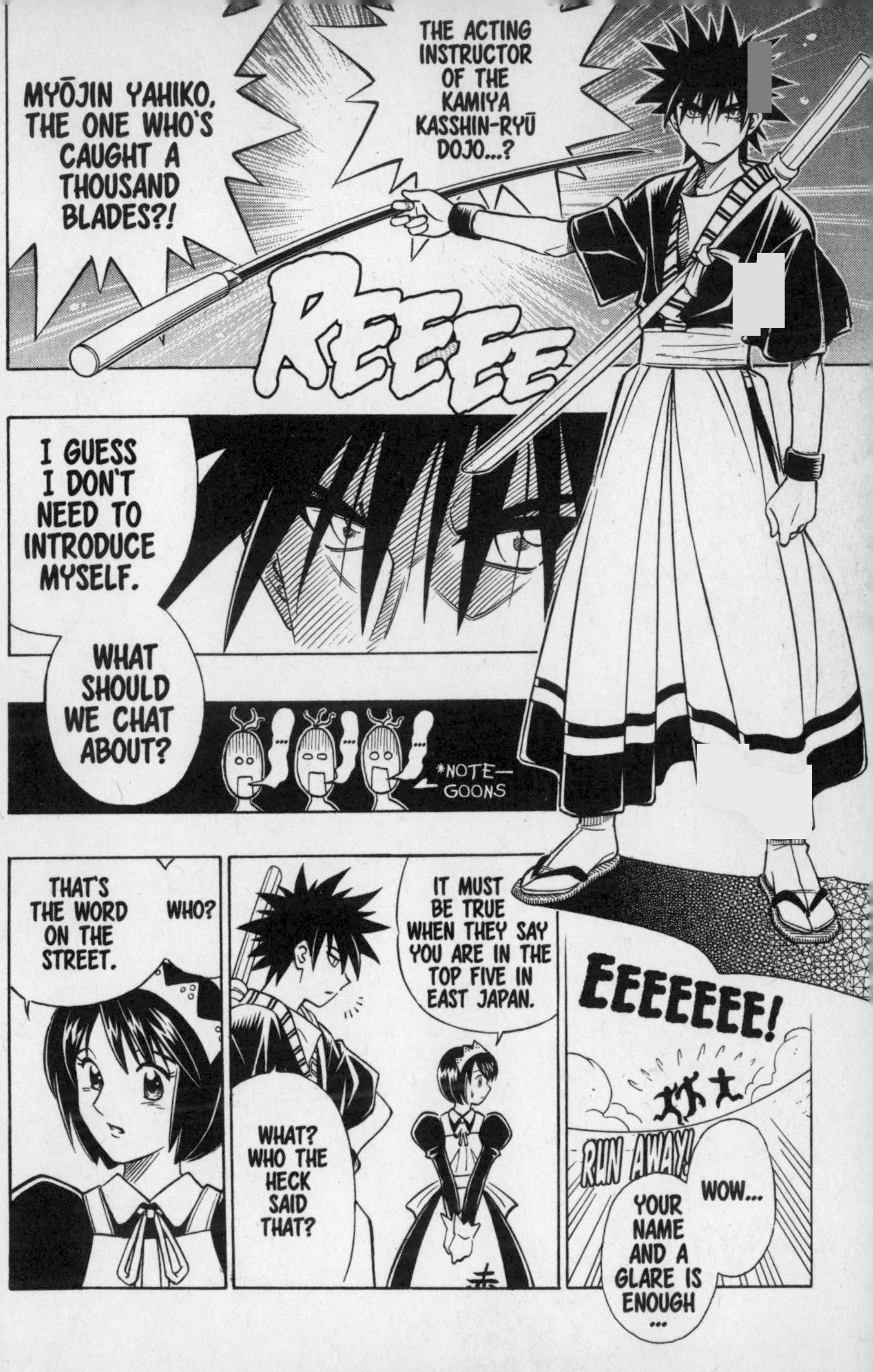
THE ACTING INSTRUCTOR OF THE KAMIYA KASSHIN-RYŪ DOJO...?
MYŌJIN YAHIKO, THE ONE WHO'S CAUGHT A THOUSAND BLADES?!
REEEE
I GUESS I DON'T NEED TO INTRODUCE MYSELF.
WHAT SHOULD WE CHAT ABOUT?
*NOTE—GOONS
EEEEEEE!
RUN AWAY!
WOW...
YOUR NAME AND A GLARE IS ENOUGH...
IT MUST BE TRUE WHEN THEY SAY YOU ARE IN THE TOP FIVE IN EAST JAPAN.
WHAT? WHO THE HECK SAID THAT?
WHO?
THAT'S THE WORD ON THE STREET.

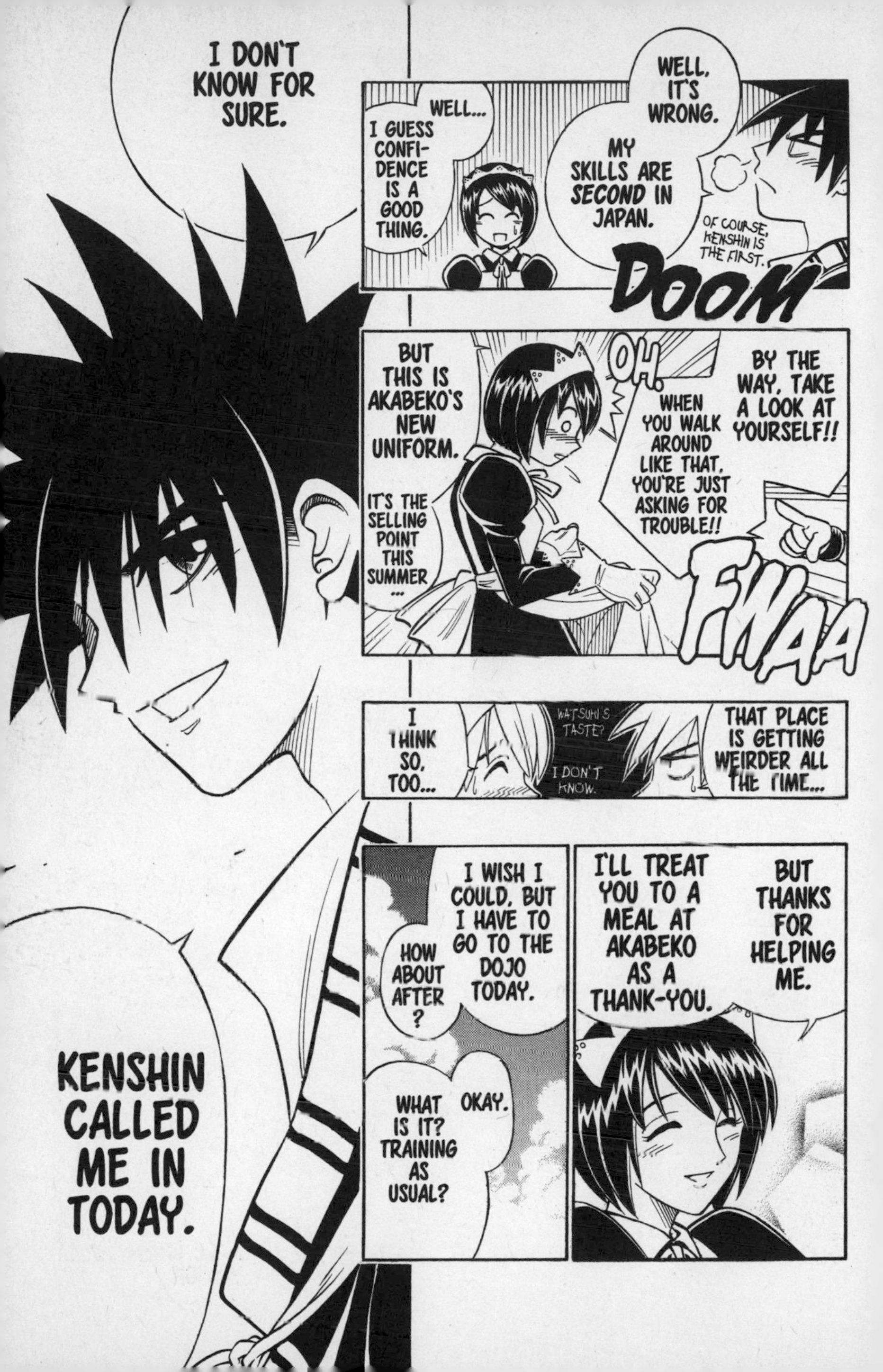

WELL, IT'S WRONG.
MY SKILLS ARE SECOND IN JAPAN.
OF COURSE, KENSHIN IS THE FIRST.
DOOM
WELL...
I GUESS CONFIDENCE IS A GOOD THING.
BY THE WAY, TAKE A LOOK AT YOURSELF!!
WHEN YOU WALK AROUND LIKE THAT, YOU'RE JUST ASKING FOR TROUBLE!!
FNAA
OH.
BUT THIS IS AKABEKO'S NEW UNIFORM.
IT'S THE SELLING POINT THIS SUMMER...
THAT PLACE IS GETTING WEIRDER ALL THE TIME...
WATSUKI'S TASTE?
I DON'T KNOW.
I THINK SO, TOO...
BUT THANKS FOR HELPING ME.
I'LL TREAT YOU TO A MEAL AT AKABEKO AS A THANK-YOU.
I WISH I COULD, BUT I HAVE TO GO TO THE DOJO TODAY.
HOW ABOUT AFTER?
OKAY.
WHAT IS IT? TRAINING AS USUAL?
I DON'T KNOW FOR SURE.
KENSHIN CALLED ME IN TODAY.

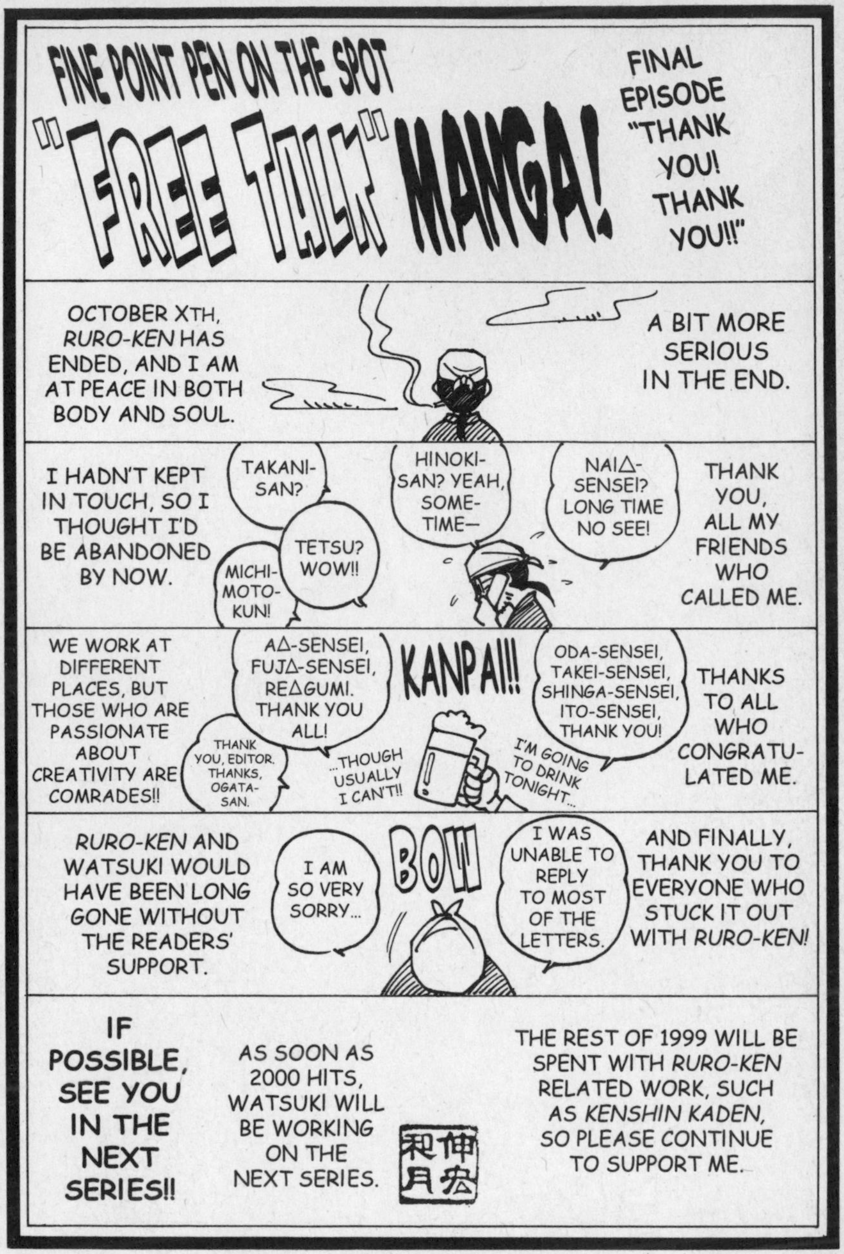
FINAL EPISODE "THANK YOU! THANK YOU!!"
FINE POINT PEN ON THE SPOT
"FREE TALK" MANGA!
A BIT MORE SERIOUS IN THE END.
OCTOBER XTH, RURO-KEN HAS ENDED, AND I AM AT PEACE IN BOTH BODY AND SOUL.
THANK YOU, ALL MY FRIENDS WHO CALLED ME.
NAI△-SENSEI? LONG TIME NO SEE!
HINOKI-SAN? YEAH, SOME-TIME—
TAKANI-SAN?
TETSU? WOW!!
MICHI-MOTO-KUN!
I HADN'T KEPT IN TOUCH, SO I THOUGHT I'D BE ABANDONED BY NOW.
THANKS TO ALL WHO CONGRATU-LATED ME.
ODA-SENSEI, TAKEI-SENSEI, SHINGA-SENSEI, ITO-SENSEI, THANK YOU!
KANPAI!!
A△-SENSEI, FUJ△-SENSEI, RE△GUMI. THANK YOU ALL!
I'M GOING TO DRINK TONIGHT...
...THOUGH USUALLY I CAN'T!!
THANK YOU, EDITOR. THANKS, OGATA-SAN.
WE WORK AT DIFFERENT PLACES, BUT THOSE WHO ARE PASSIONATE ABOUT CREATIVITY ARE COMRADES!!
AND FINALLY, THANK YOU TO EVERYONE WHO STUCK IT OUT WITH RURO-KEN!
I WAS UNABLE TO REPLY TO MOST OF THE LETTERS.
BOW
I AM SO VERY SORRY...
RURO-KEN AND WATSUKI WOULD HAVE BEEN LONG GONE WITHOUT THE READERS' SUPPORT.
THE REST OF 1999 WILL BE SPENT WITH RURO-KEN RELATED WORK, SUCH AS KENSHIN KADEN, SO PLEASE CONTINUE TO SUPPORT ME.
伸宏
和月
AS SOON AS 2000 HITS, WATSUKI WILL BE WORKING ON THE NEXT SERIES.
IF POSSIBLE, SEE YOU IN THE NEXT SERIES!!

BUT... MY HANDWRITING IS SO MESSY... MAYBE I'LL GO TAKE LESSONS...

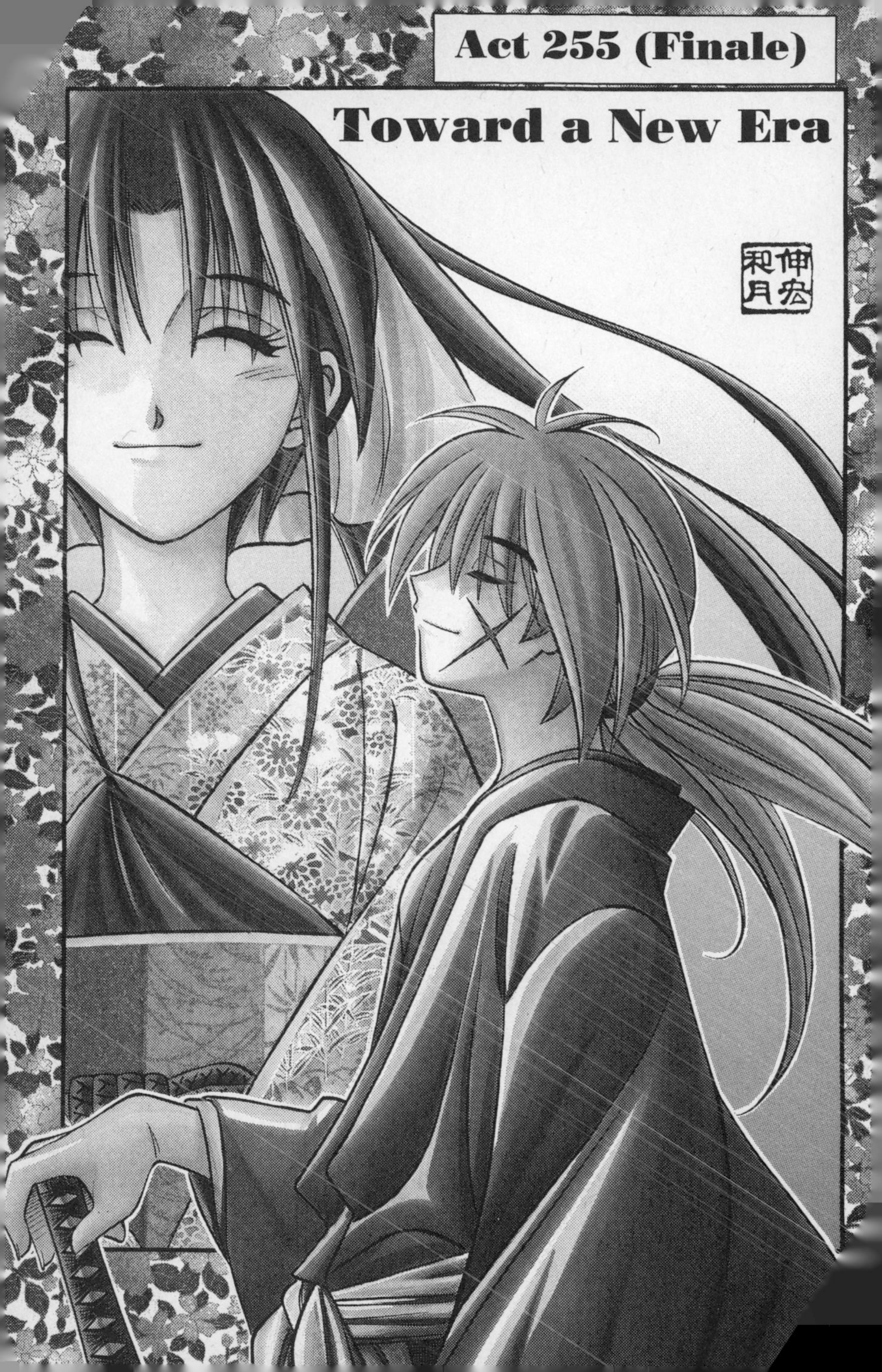
Act 255 (Finale)
Toward a New Era
和月伸宏

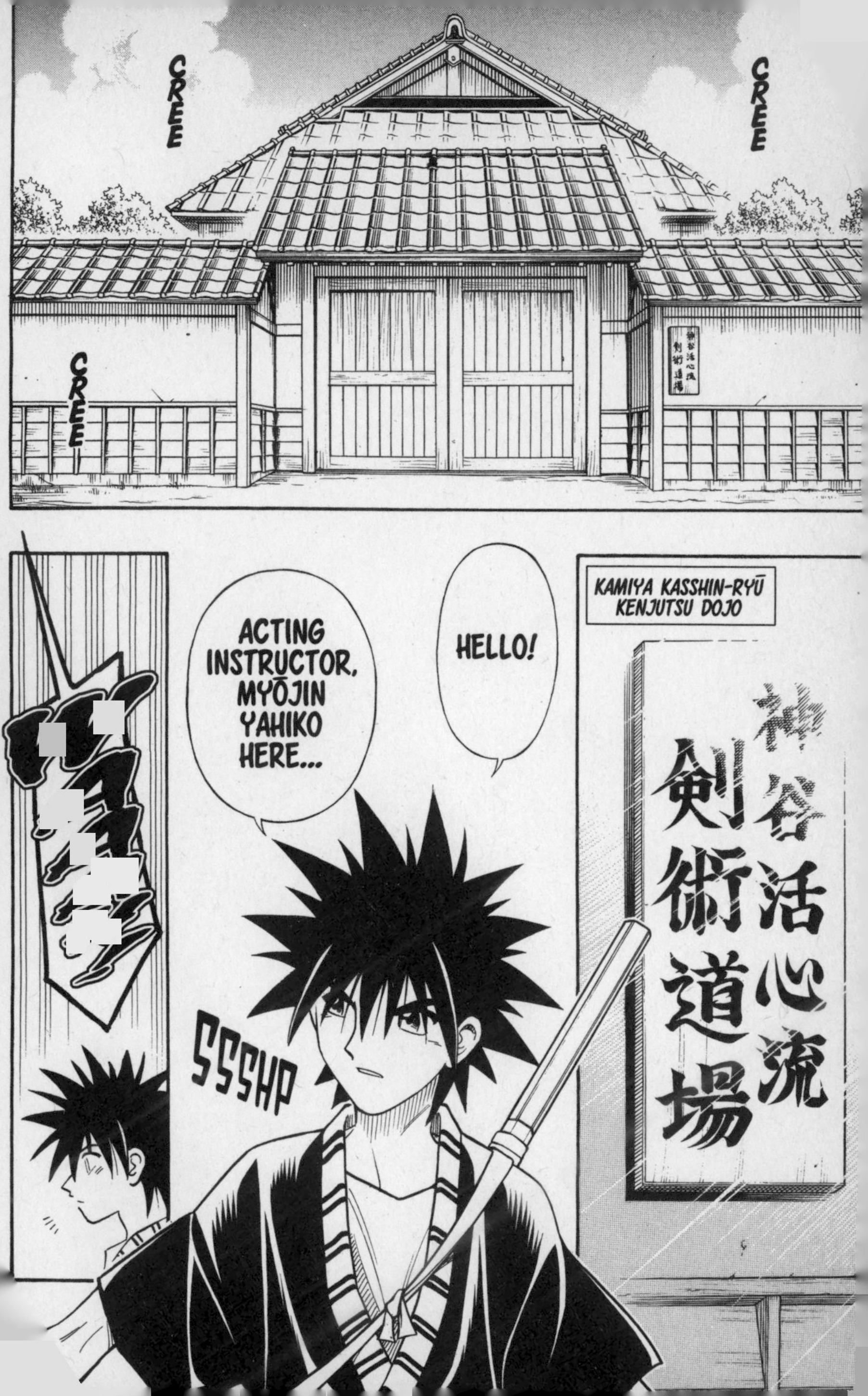
CREE
CREE
CREE
KAMIYA KASSHIN-RYŪ KENJUTSU DOJO
神谷活心流
剣術道場
HELLO!
ACTING INSTRUCTOR, MYŌJIN YAHIKO HERE...
SSSHP

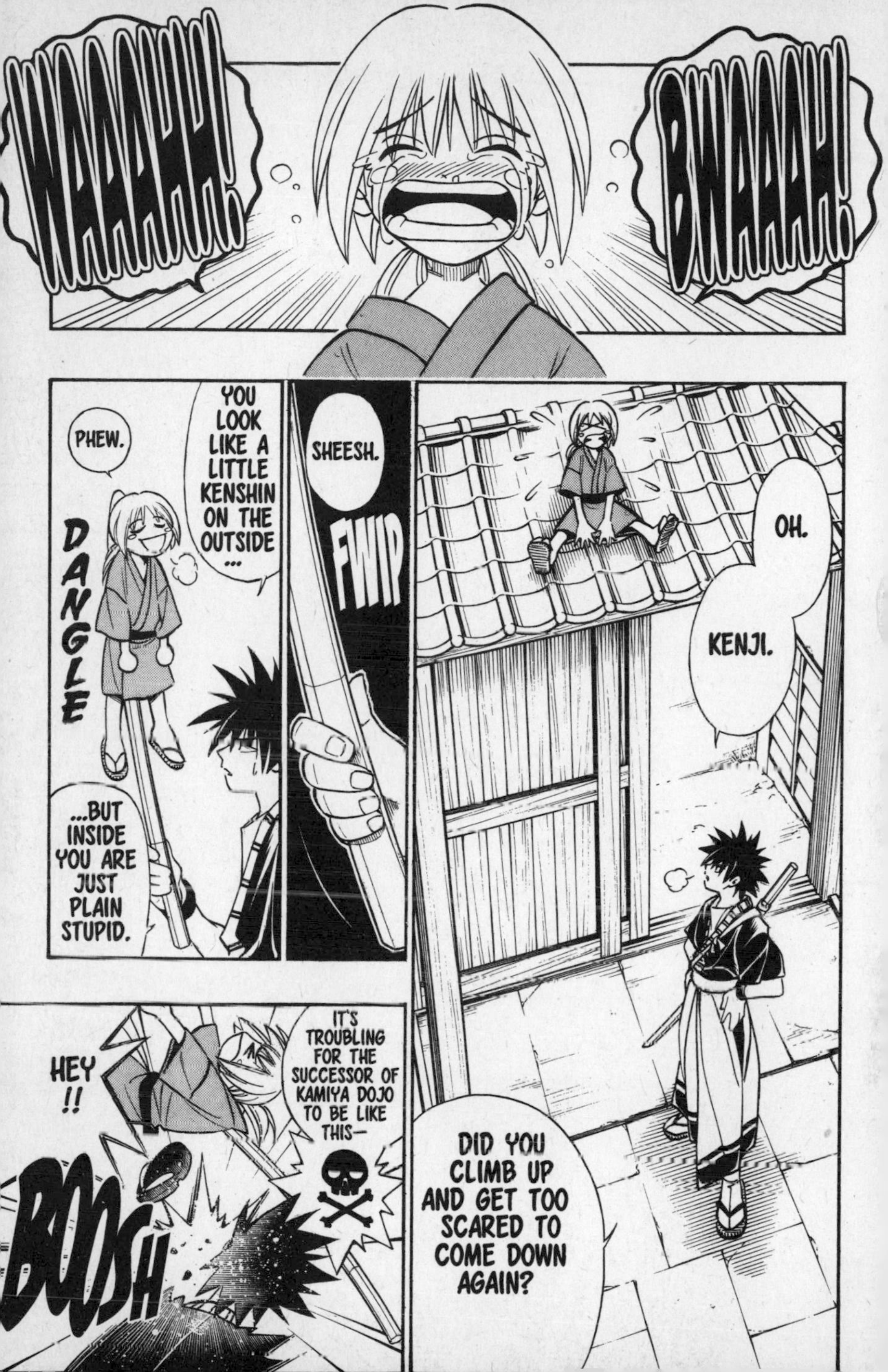
BWAAAH!
WAAAH!
OH.
KENJI.
DID YOU CLIMB UP AND GET TOO SCARED TO COME DOWN AGAIN?
SHEESH.
FWIP
YOU LOOK LIKE A LITTLE KENSHIN ON THE OUTSIDE...
PHEW.
DANGLE
...BUT INSIDE YOU ARE JUST PLAIN STUPID.
IT'S TROUBLING FOR THE SUCCESSOR OF KAMIYA DOJO TO BE LIKE THIS—
HEY!!
BOOSH

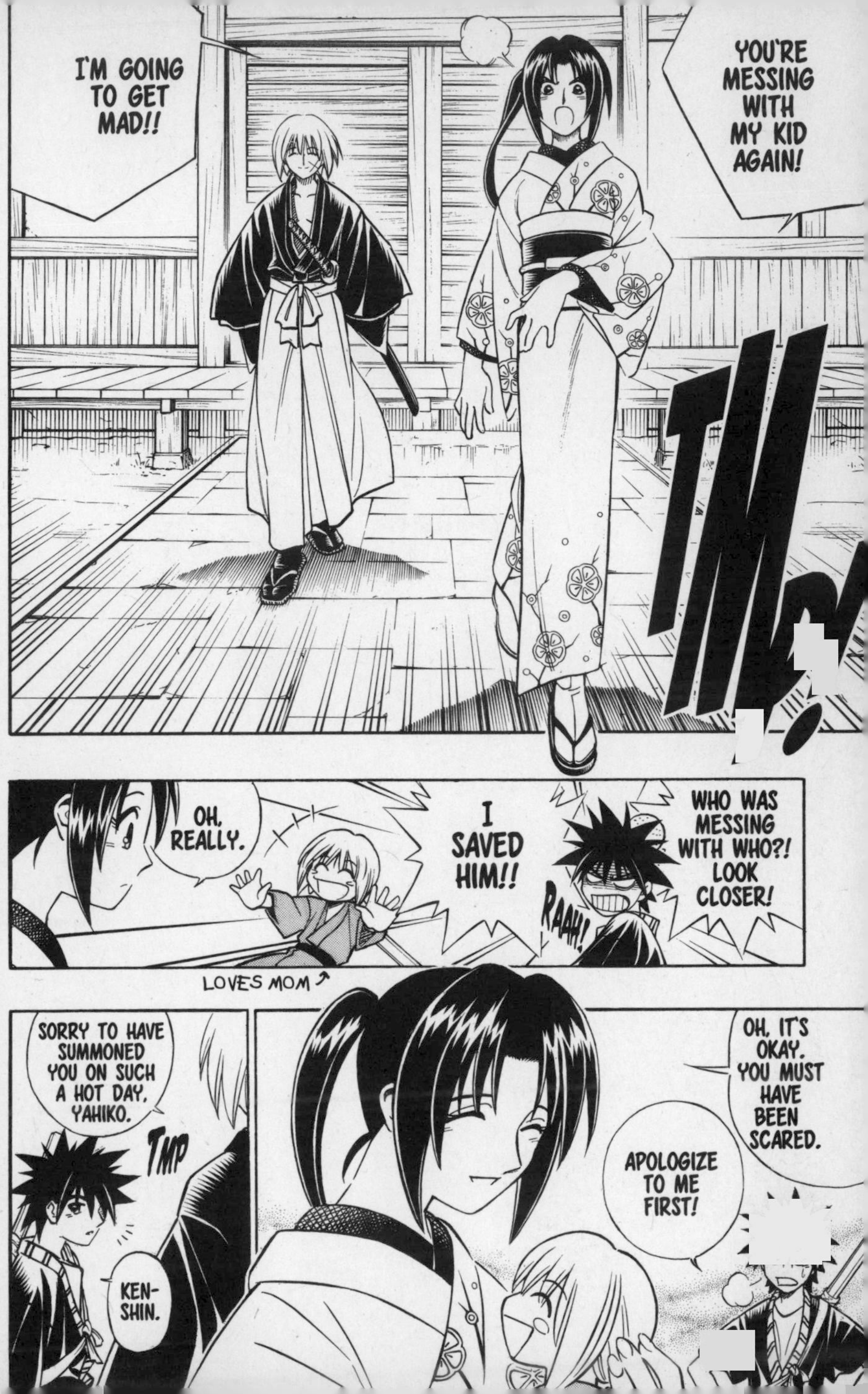

YOU'RE MESSING WITH MY KID AGAIN!
I'M GOING TO GET MAD!!
WHO WAS MESSING WITH WHO?! LOOK CLOSER!
RAAH!
I SAVED HIM!!
OH, REALLY.
LOVES MOM
OH, IT'S OKAY. YOU MUST HAVE BEEN SCARED.
APOLOGIZE TO ME FIRST!
SORRY TO HAVE SUMMONED YOU ON SUCH A HOT DAY, YAHIKO.
TMP
KEN-SHIN.

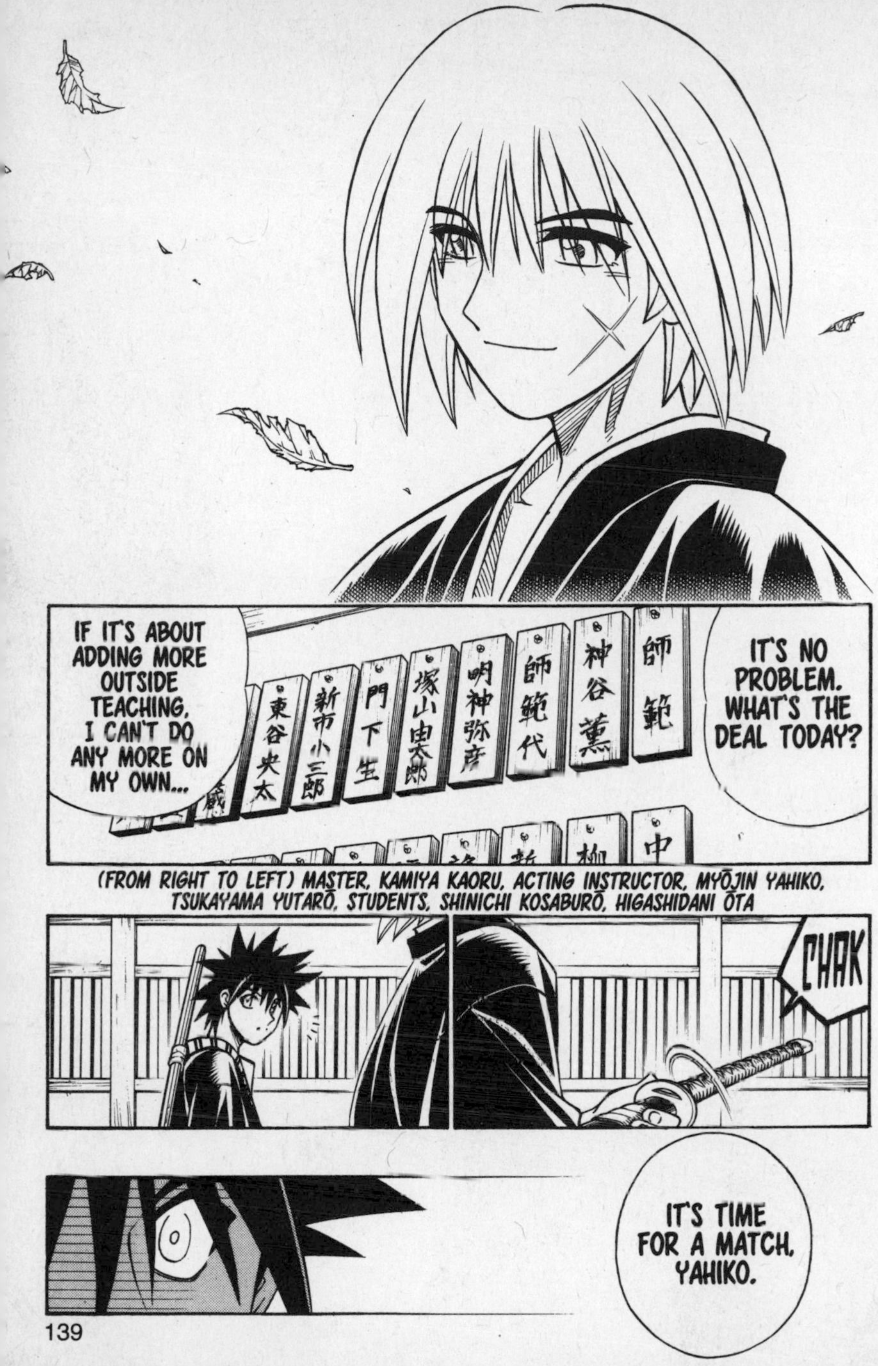
IT'S NO PROBLEM. WHAT'S THE DEAL TODAY?
IF IT'S ABOUT ADDING MORE OUTSIDE TEACHING, I CAN'T DO ANY MORE ON MY OWN...
(FROM RIGHT TO LEFT) MASTER, KAMIYA KAORU, ACTING INSTRUCTOR, MYŌJIN YAHIKO, TSUKAYAMA YUTARŌ, STUDENTS, SHINICHI KOSABURŌ, HIGASHIDANI ŌTA
CHAK
IT'S TIME FOR A MATCH, YAHIKO.

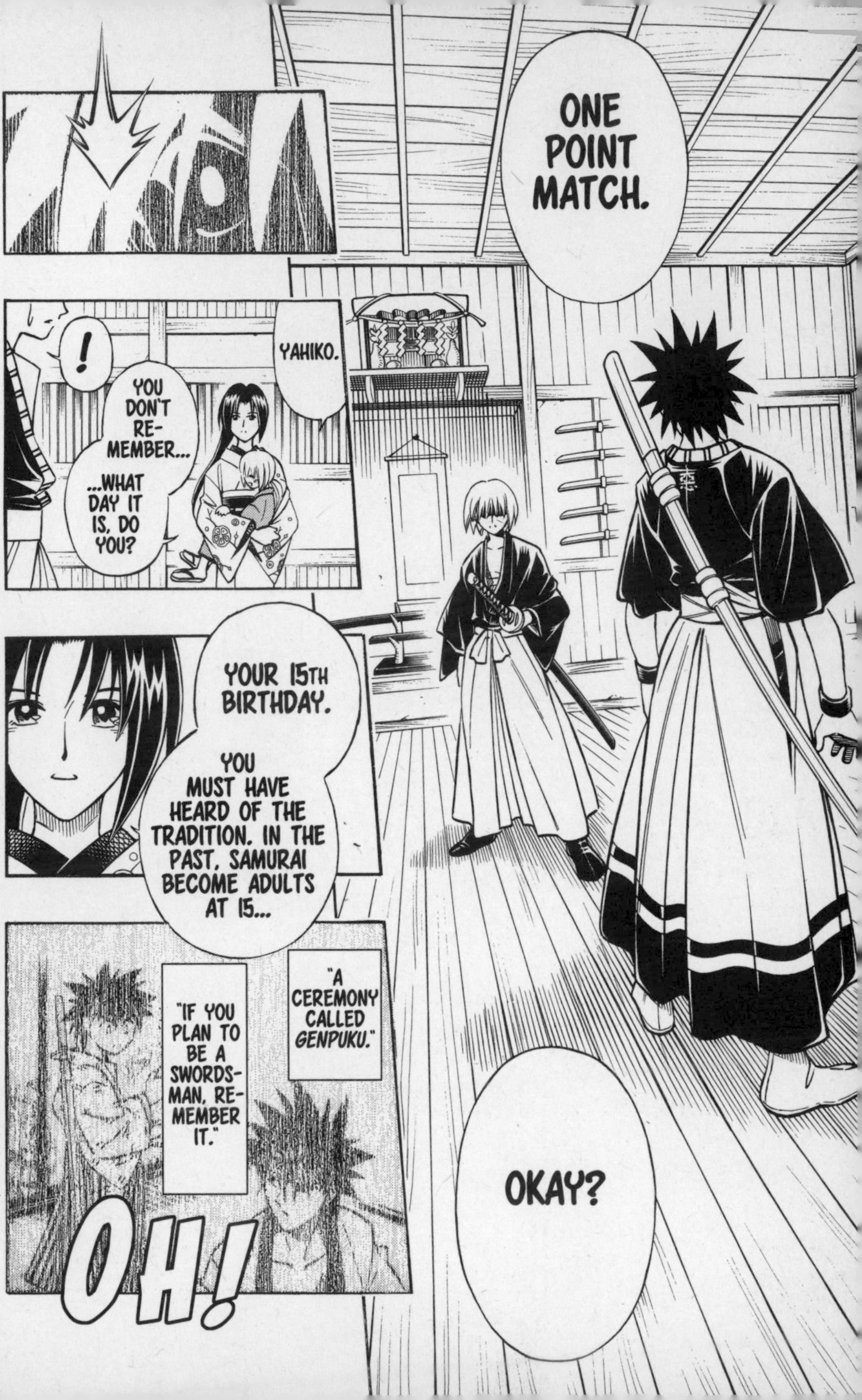
ONE POINT MATCH.
OKAY?
YAHIKO.
!
YOU DON'T RE-MEMBER...
...WHAT DAY IT IS, DO YOU?
YOUR 15TH BIRTHDAY.
YOU MUST HAVE HEARD OF THE TRADITION. IN THE PAST, SAMURAI BECOME ADULTS AT 15...
"A CEREMONY CALLED GENPUKU."
"IF YOU PLAN TO BE A SWORDS-MAN, RE-MEMBER IT."
OH!

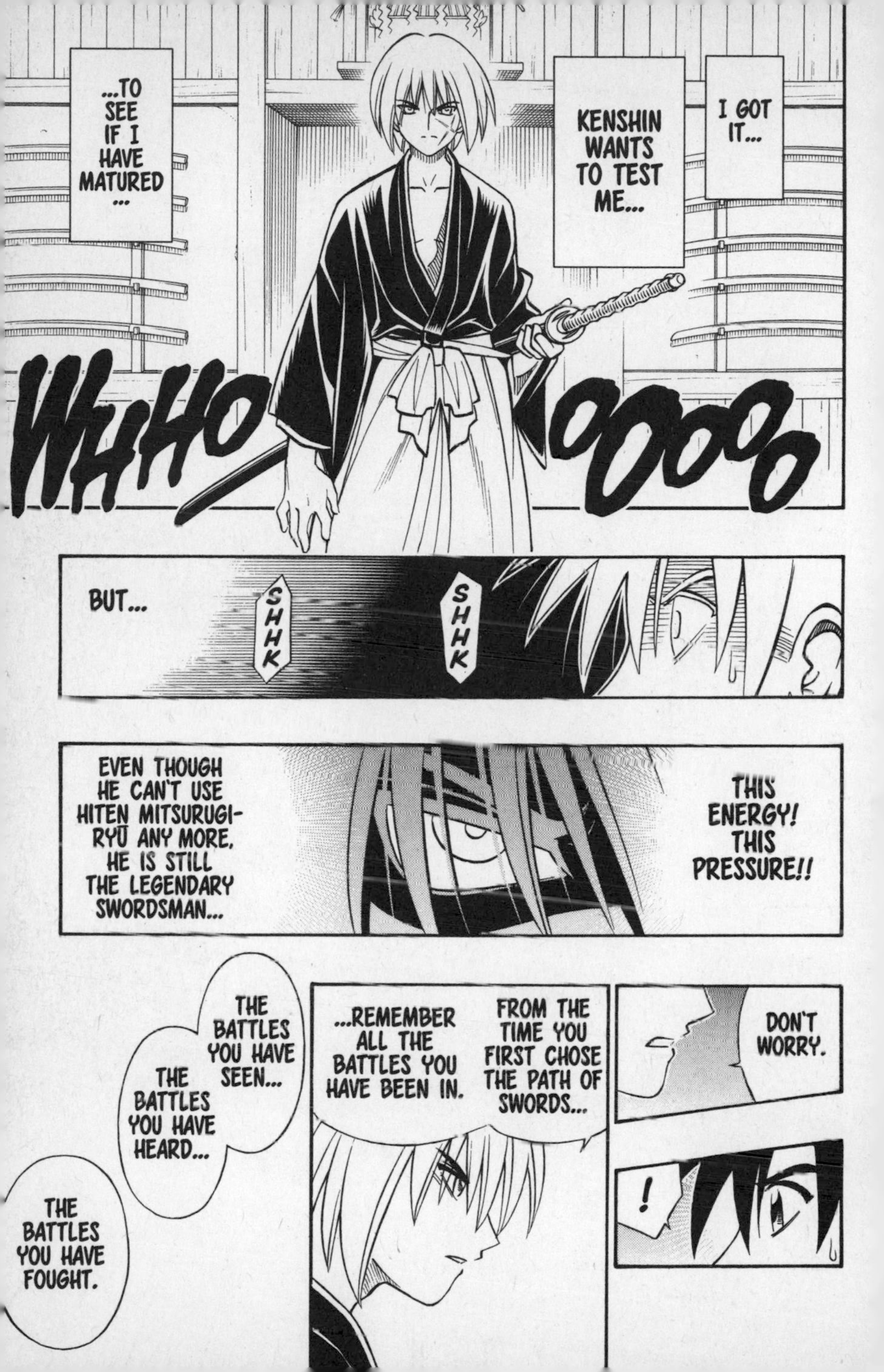

I GOT IT...
KENSHIN WANTS TO TEST ME...
...TO SEE IF I HAVE MATURED...
WHHOOOOOO
SHHK
SHHK
BUT...
THIS ENERGY! THIS PRESSURE!!
EVEN THOUGH HE CAN'T USE HITEN MITSURUGI-RYŪ ANY MORE, HE IS STILL THE LEGENDARY SWORDSMAN...
DON'T WORRY.
!
FROM THE TIME YOU FIRST CHOSE THE PATH OF SWORDS...
...REMEMBER ALL THE BATTLES YOU HAVE BEEN IN.
THE BATTLES YOU HAVE SEEN...
THE BATTLES YOU HAVE HEARD...
THE BATTLES YOU HAVE FOUGHT.

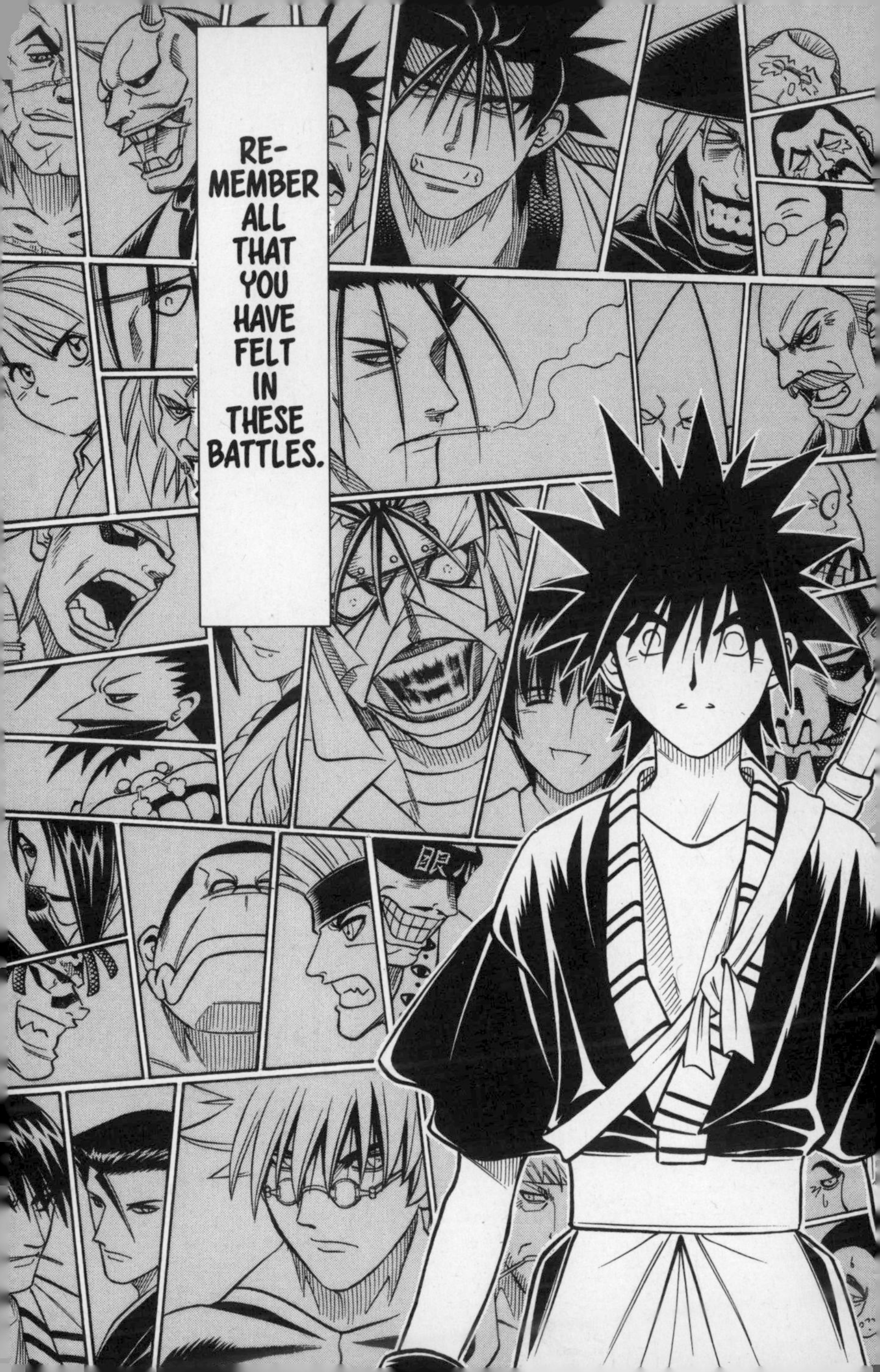
REMEMBER ALL THAT YOU HAVE FELT IN THESE BATTLES.

READ THIS WAY

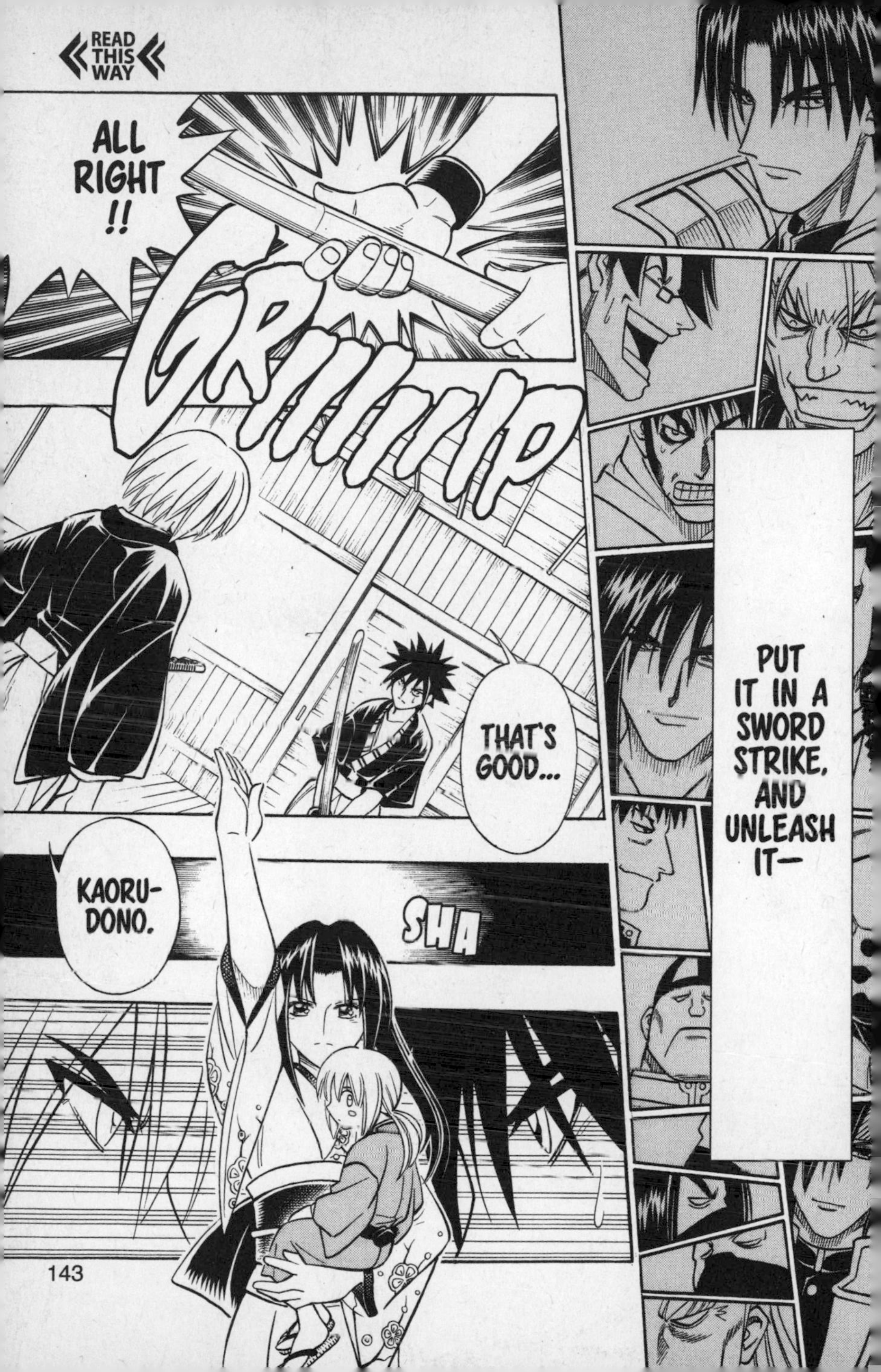

PUT IT IN A SWORD STRIKE, AND UNLEASH IT—
ALL RIGHT !!
GRIIIIP
THAT'S GOOD...
KAORU-DONO.
SHA

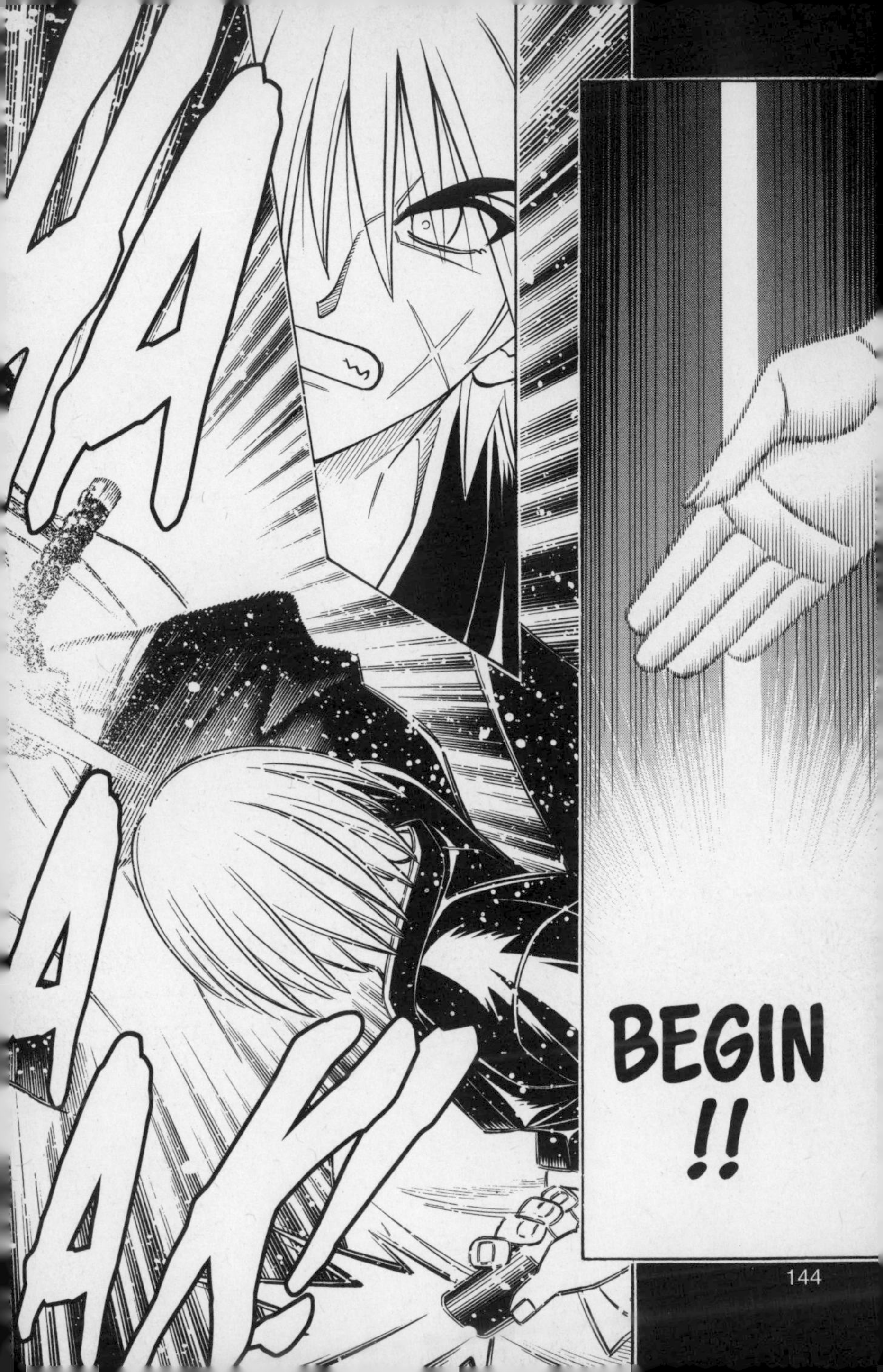
BEGIN
!!

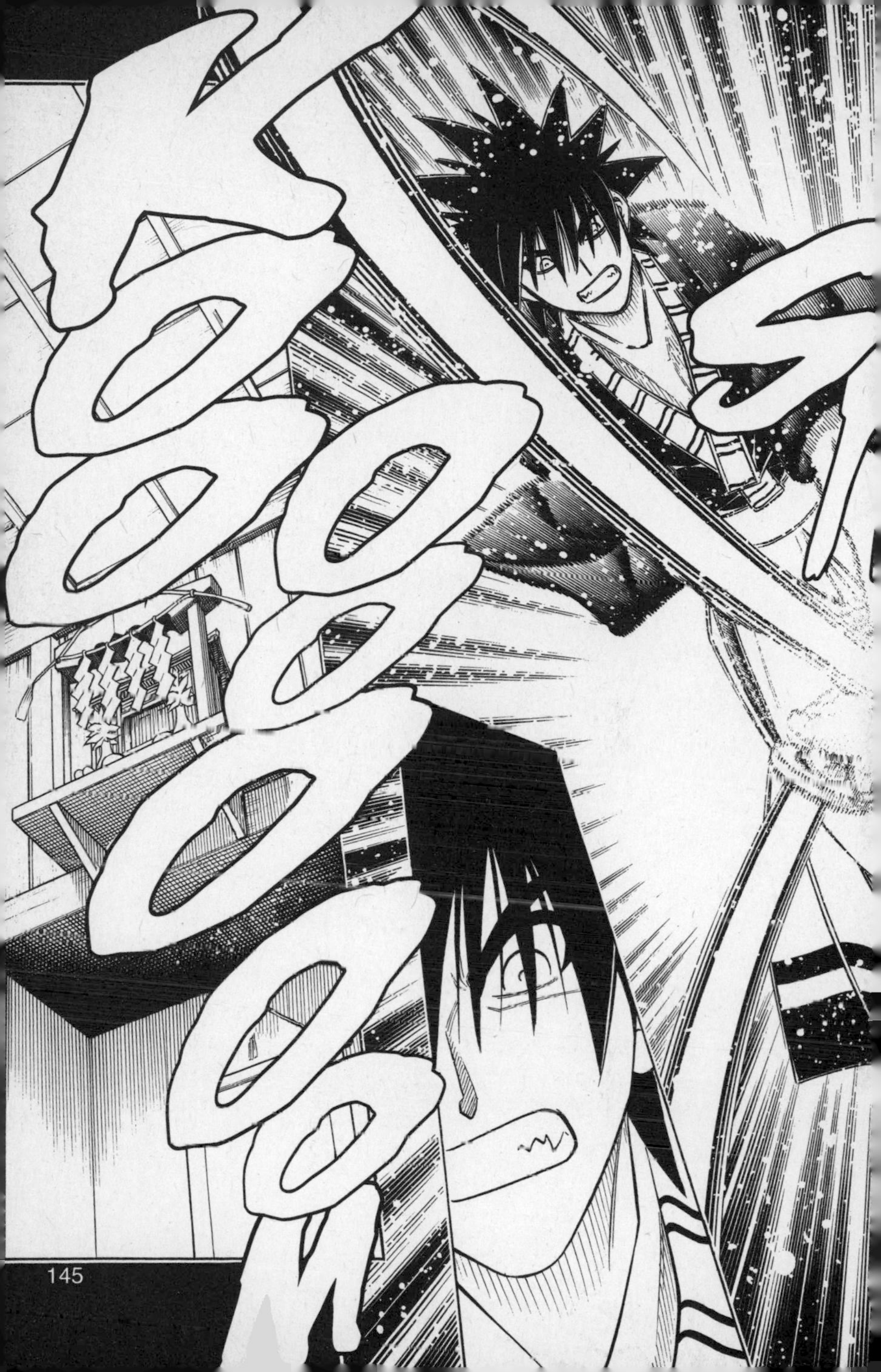

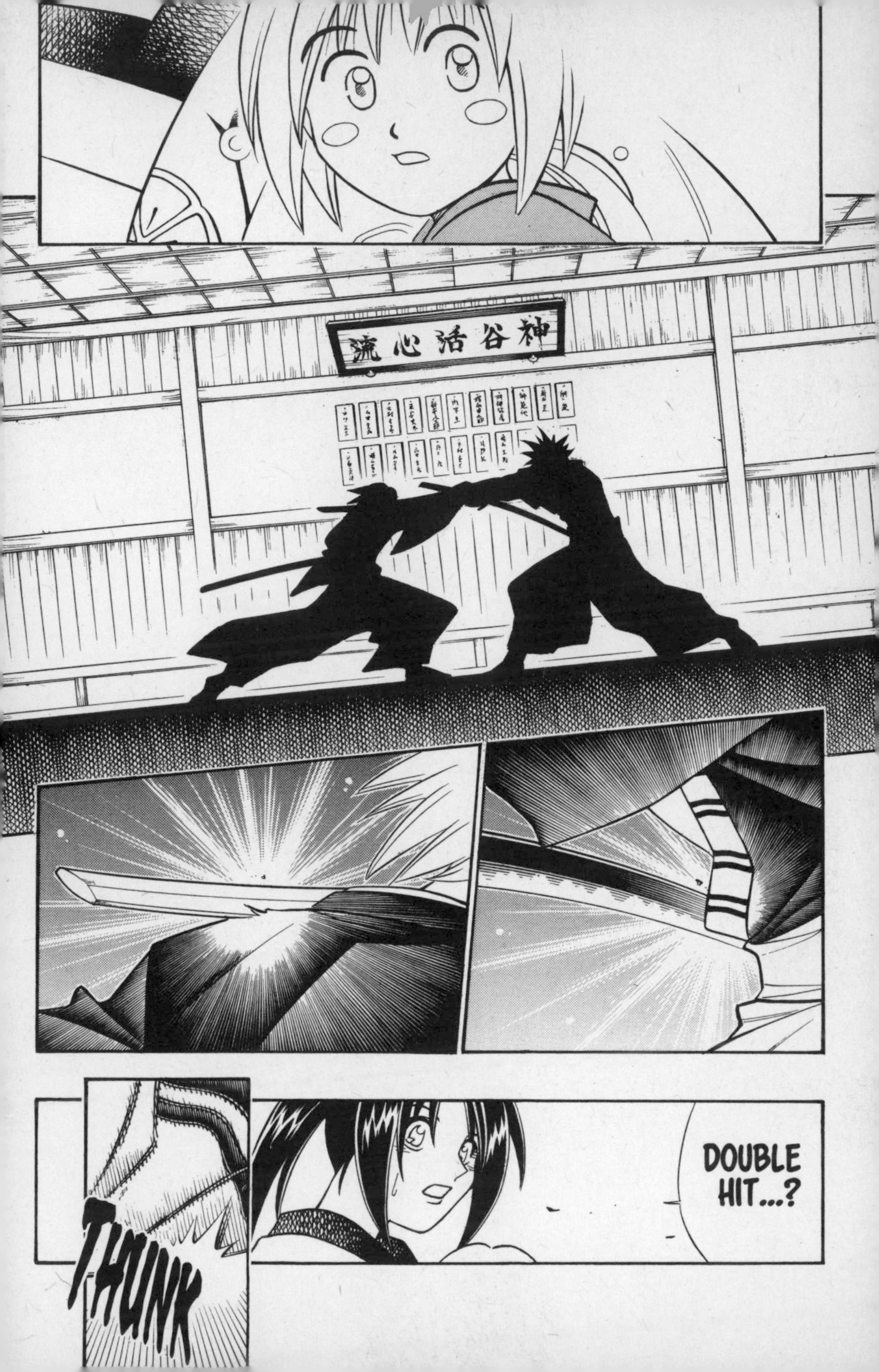
神谷活心流
DOUBLE HIT...?
THUNK

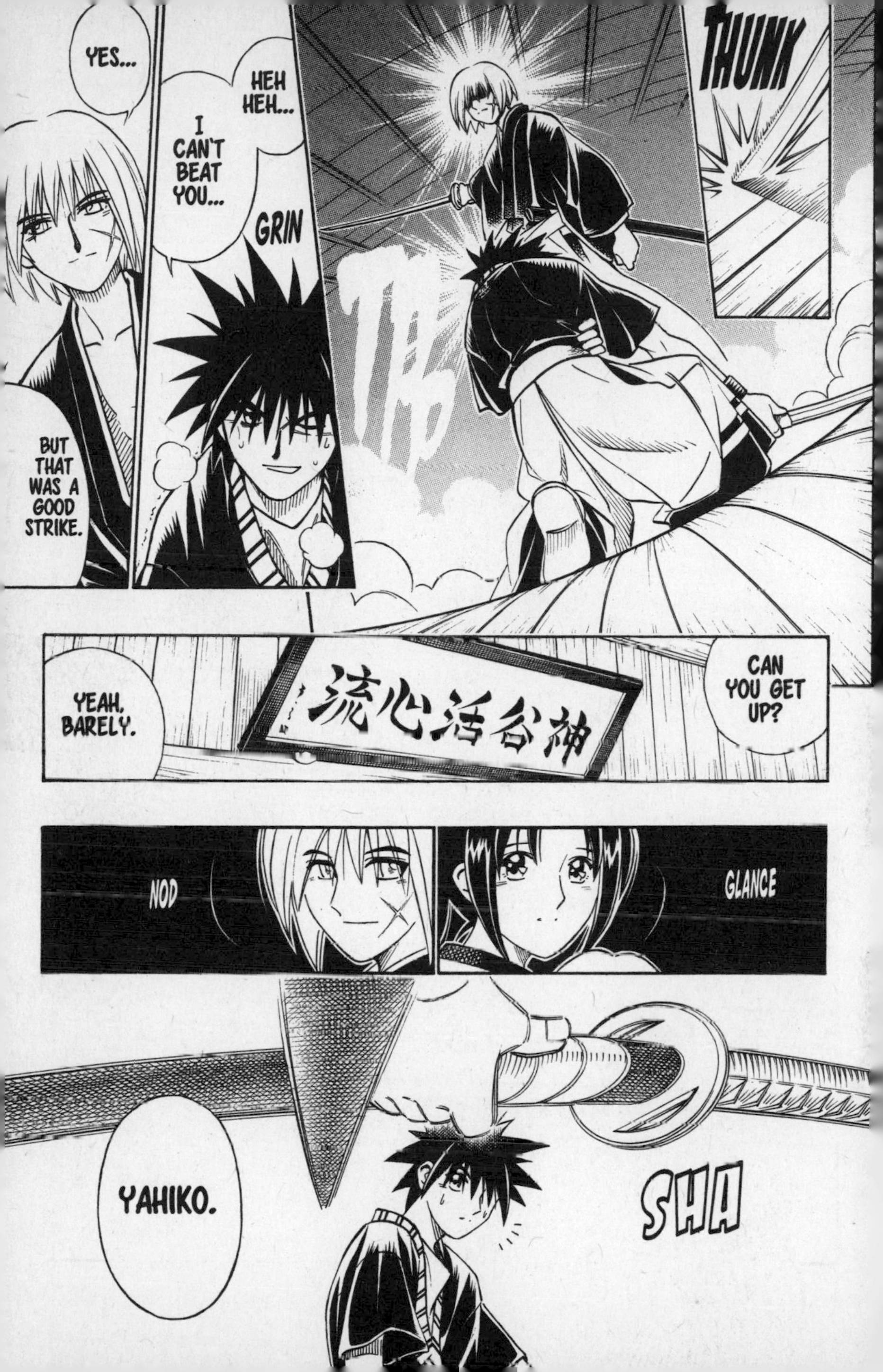
THUNK
HEH HEH...
I CAN'T BEAT YOU...
GRIN
YES...
BUT THAT WAS A GOOD STRIKE.
CAN YOU GET UP?
神谷活心流
YEAH, BARELY.
GLANCE
NOD
SHA
YAHIKO.

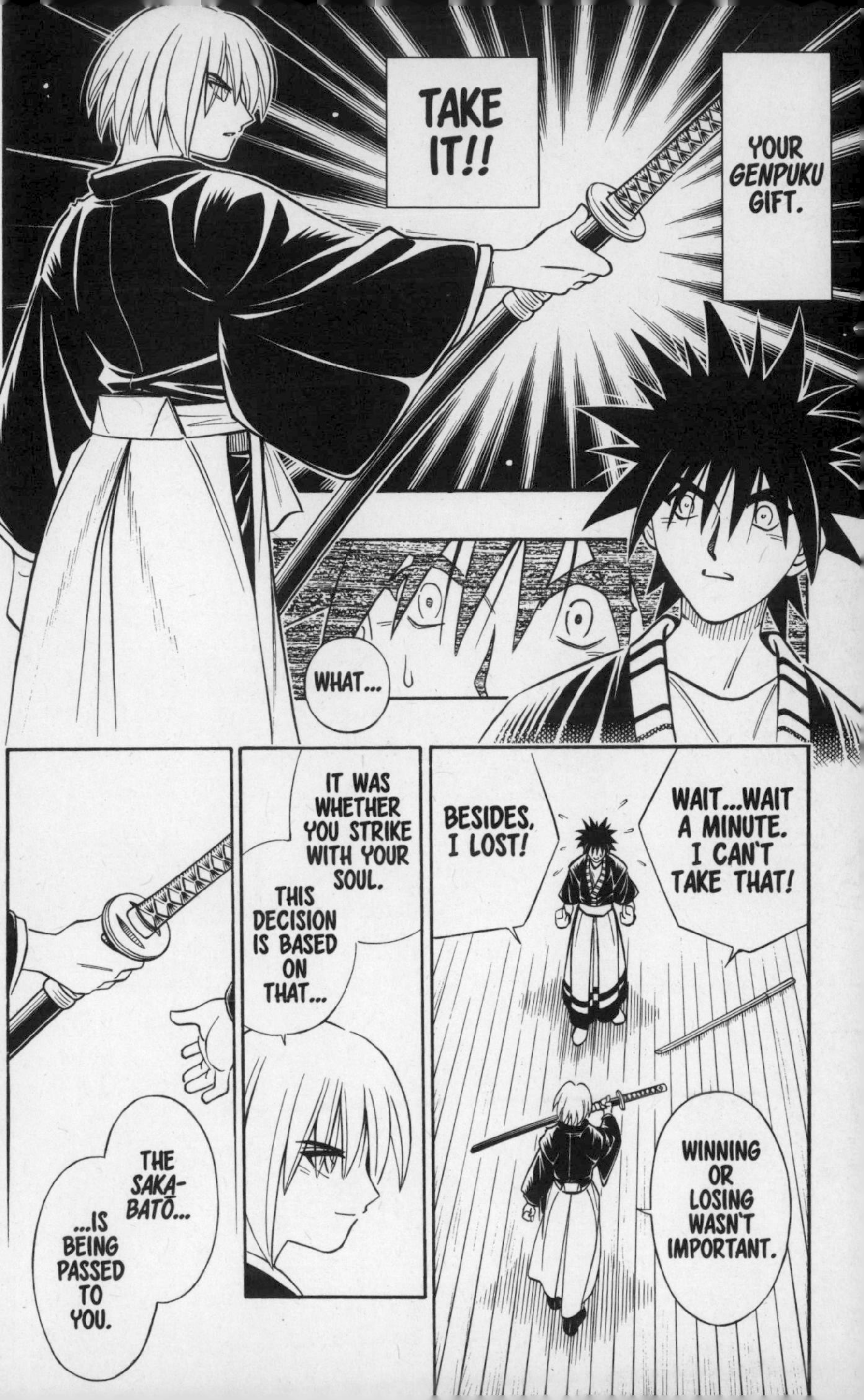
YOUR GENPUKU GIFT.
TAKE IT!!
WHAT...
WAIT...WAIT A MINUTE. I CAN'T TAKE THAT!
BESIDES, I LOST!
WINNING OR LOSING WASN'T IMPORTANT.
IT WAS WHETHER YOU STRIKE WITH YOUR SOUL.
THIS DECISION IS BASED ON THAT...
THE SAKA-BATŌ...
...IS BEING PASSED TO YOU.

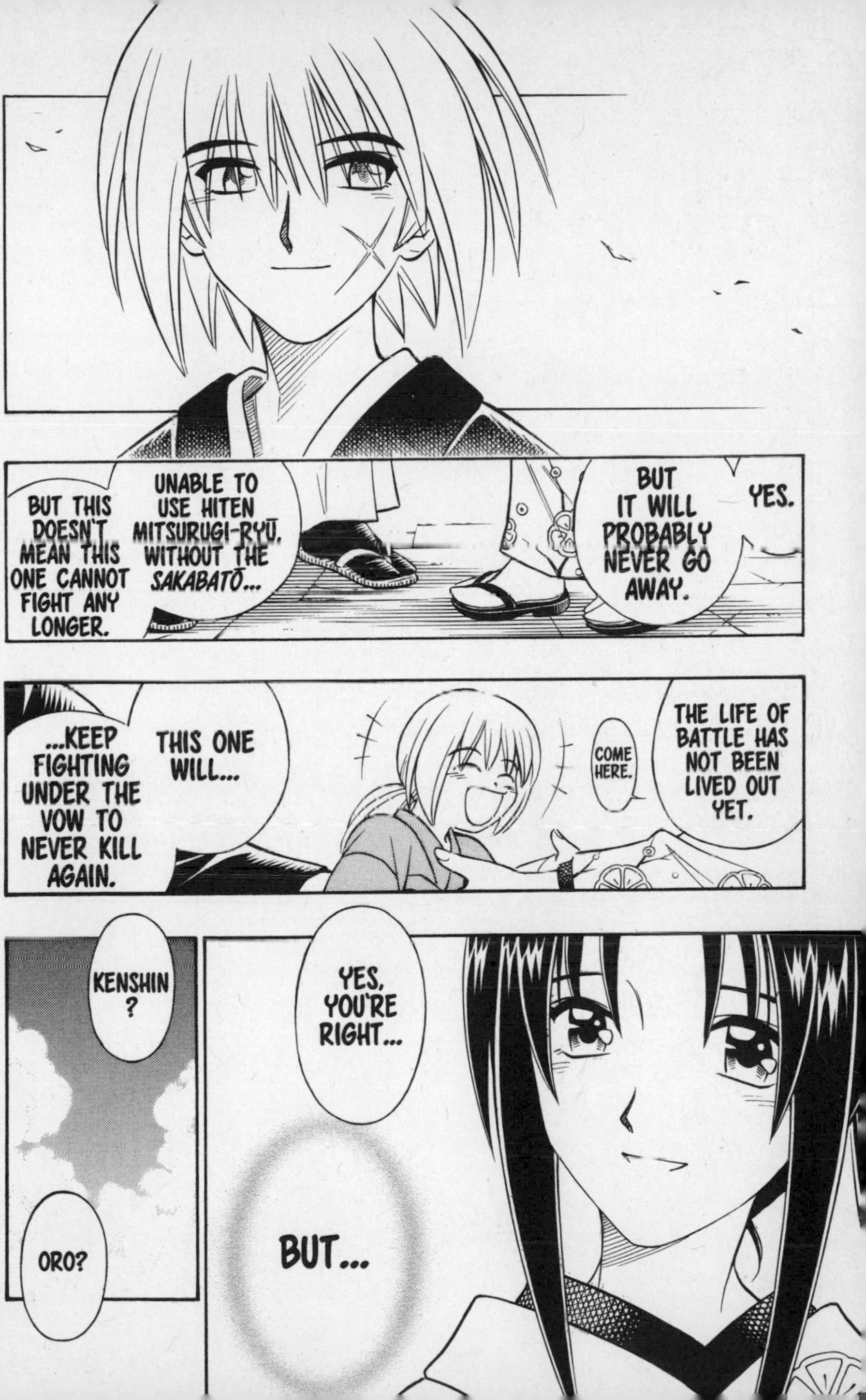
YES.
BUT IT WILL PROBABLY NEVER GO AWAY.
UNABLE TO USE HITEN MITSURUGI-RYŪ WITHOUT THE *SAKABATŌ*...
BUT THIS DOESN'T MEAN THIS ONE CANNOT FIGHT ANY LONGER.
THE LIFE OF BATTLE HAS NOT BEEN LIVED OUT YET.
COME HERE.
THIS ONE WILL...
...KEEP FIGHTING UNDER THE VOW TO NEVER KILL AGAIN.
YES, YOU'RE RIGHT...
BUT...
KENSHIN?
ORO?

READ THIS WAY

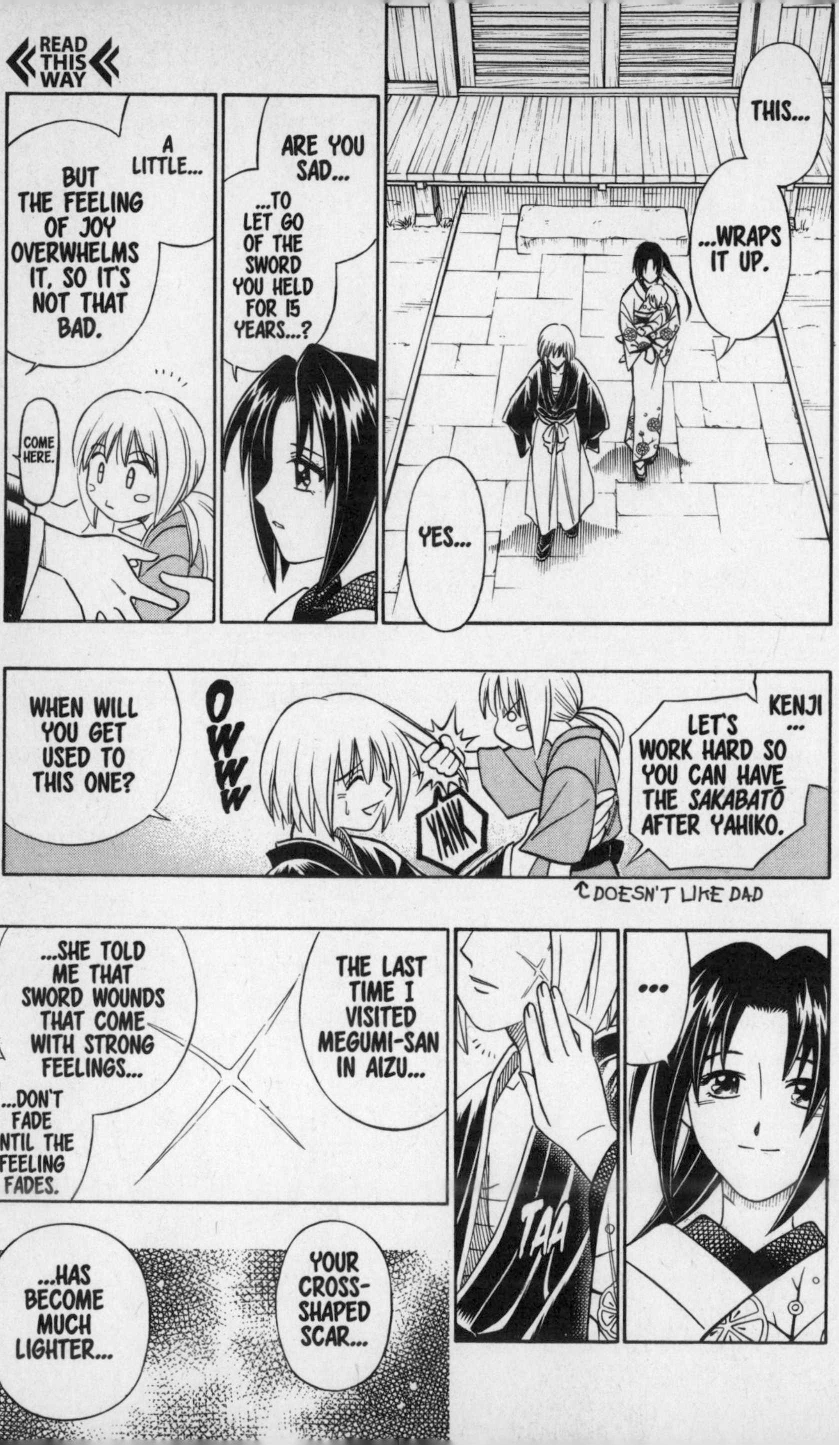
THIS...
...WRAPS IT UP.
YES...
ARE YOU SAD...
...TO LET GO OF THE SWORD YOU HELD FOR 15 YEARS...?
A LITTLE...
BUT THE FEELING OF JOY OVERWHELMS IT, SO IT'S NOT THAT BAD.
COME HERE.
KENJI...
LET'S WORK HARD SO YOU CAN HAVE THE *SAKABATŌ* AFTER YAHIKO.
YANK
OWWW
WHEN WILL YOU GET USED TO THIS ONE?
↑DOESN'T LIKE DAD
...
TAA
THE LAST TIME I VISITED MEGUMI-SAN IN AIZU...
...SHE TOLD ME THAT SWORD WOUNDS THAT COME WITH STRONG FEELINGS...
...DON'T FADE UNTIL THE FEELING FADES.
YOUR CROSS-SHAPED SCAR...
...HAS BECOME MUCH LIGHTER...

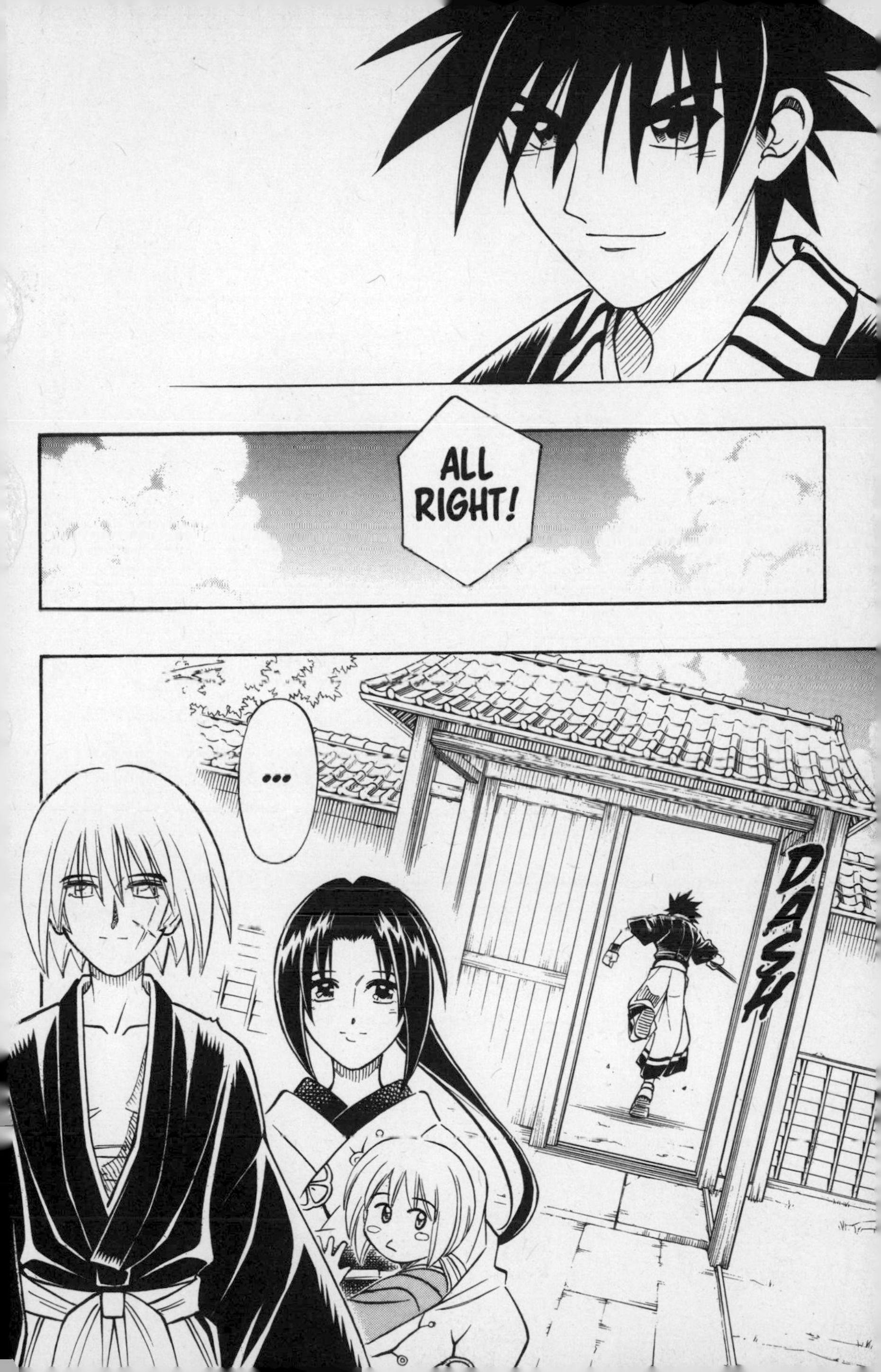
ALL RIGHT!
DASH
...

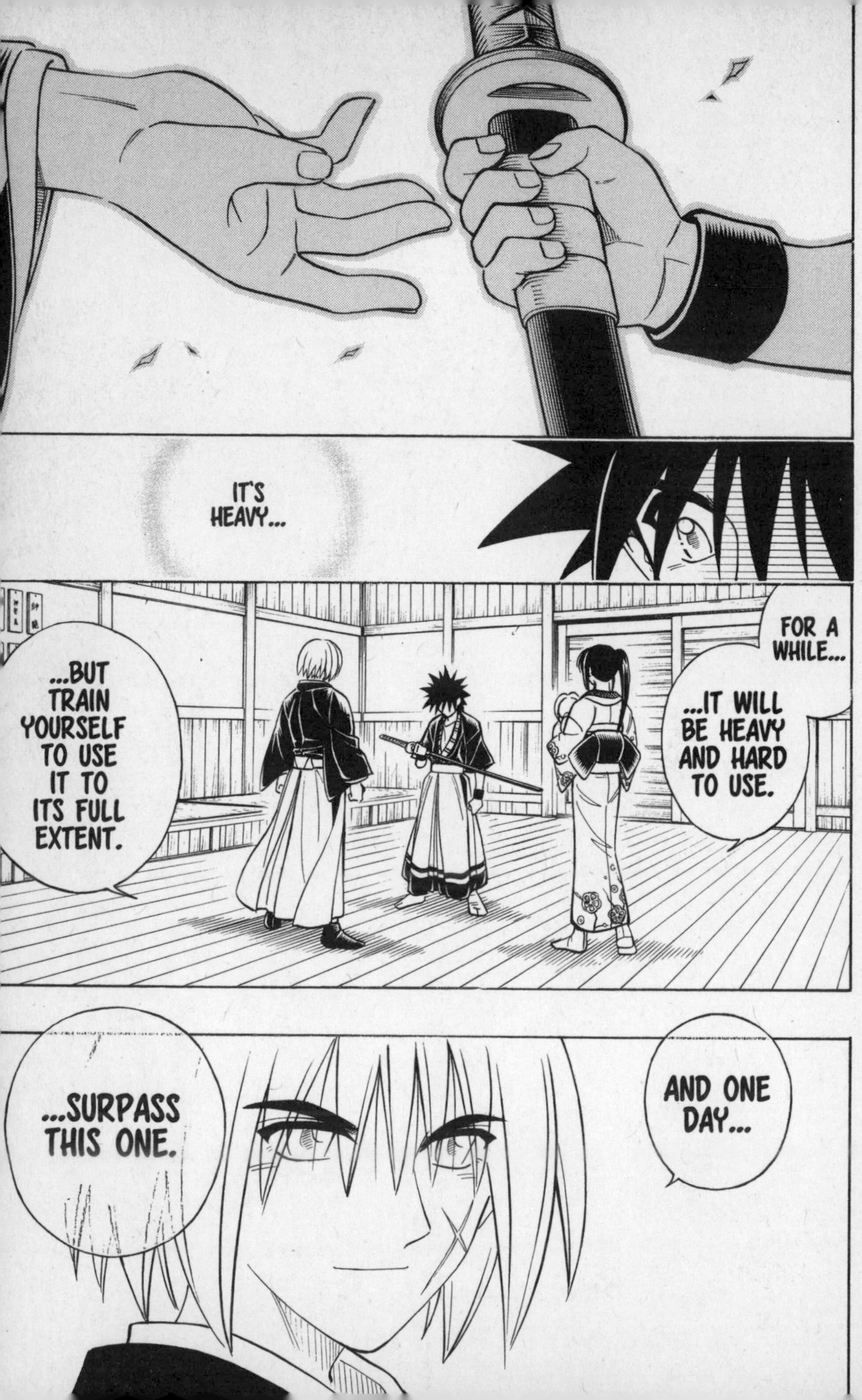
IT'S HEAVY...
FOR A WHILE...
...IT WILL BE HEAVY AND HARD TO USE.
...BUT TRAIN YOURSELF TO USE IT TO ITS FULL EXTENT.
AND ONE DAY...
...SURPASS THIS ONE.

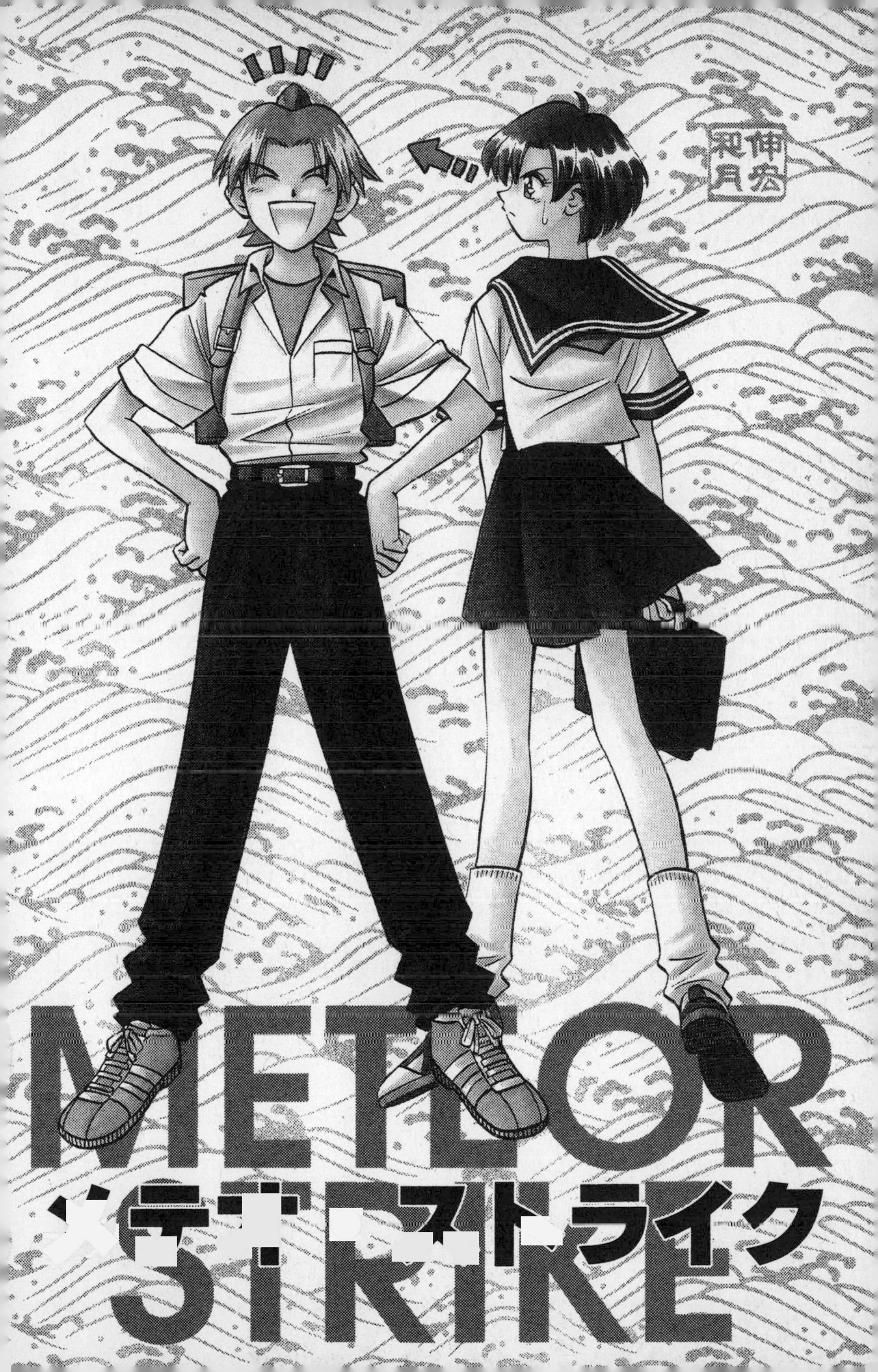
METEOR
STRIKE
ストライク

Meteor Strike

This is a short story I wrote a while back, as one of the projects for *Jump* authors. It was a short story right in the middle of writing for the series, so I tried my hardest to make it the best possible work with the lack of will power, energy, and preparation... But the self-disgust I tumbled into, honestly, made me want to quit drawing manga. I had sworn to never let this work see the light of the day, but due to the page count of this volume, we ended up using it. So, after reading it over, it relaxed me in a nice way. Although it may not deserve a superb score, it seems like it's not that bad, either. (Of course, if I had had one more week and 15 more pages, I would have been happier.)

There are three points to this story. First is the "Meteor." This was an idea I've had for a long time, and this was actually one of the strongest candidates for the new series after *Ruro-Ken*. It's only touched on in the story, but meteors are the most energetic natural phenomena, and the astronomical events closest to us, so I've always thought about using them. Then this short story project came up, and I turned it into a 31 page "Meteor Strike." Since the end of the world predicted by Nostradamus has passed, and Hollywood has put out many movies with this theme, I don't think I'll be able to use it for a while. But I still personally like meteors, and plan to use them sometime. The second point is the "white gloved kid." White gloves are sort of plain and not cool at all, but they give off a sense of strength, making them one of Watsuki's favorites. I've always wanted the main character to have a pair when I write a story set in the present. Shinya is a character I made up on the spot, making him a bit too honest, and his personality overlaps with Kenshin's, which I regret a little. I wanted to put a little more flavor into him. The third point is "Girl with a construction site helmet." The helmet seems masculine by default, so a girl (in a school uniform) wearing it made it somehow good, making me think, "I must get this in!" Watsuki creates heroines that make his taste at the time obvious. Chiho was created with the shojo theme of the moment when a boy's maturity outgrows the girl's, but it did not work out so well. So in the end, a lot wasn't what I wanted it to be. But I really enjoyed drawing Chiho's very helpful nature.

"Meteor Strike" was written in the midst of the struggle of writing *Ruro-Ken*. It has some different flavors than *Ruro-Ken*, making me think it will be a great example, allowing me to look at my new work in a levelheaded manner.

The Secret Life of Characters (54)

—Himura Kenji and the rest in the 15th year of Meiji—

Kenji's personality model can be described with one word—stupid. He's basically equivalent to Iori. Kenji only exists to be Kenshin and Kaoru's son, and is so cliché that I put him in thinking, "Cliché or not, he must be in there!! Right?!" Watsuki is not twisted enough to put negative elements in the ideal family, you there. (Who there?)

Later, Kenji reveals his thoroughbred bloodline. Even without seeing it, he masters Hiten Mitsurugi-ryū moves just from hearing about them. His personality becomes a bit twisted, as common with many geniuses, becoming more cynical than Saitō, and more self-centered than Shishio. Eventually, he becomes rivals with Myōjin Shinya, Yahiko and Tsubame's son, fighting over Hiten Mitsurugi-ryū and the *sakabatō*. This is the story that pops into my head, but I will probably never do a manga about it.

In terms of design, he's just as it is stated in the work, a small Kenshin. Just to touch on some other characters, I cut Kenshin's hair off, which was something I've wanted to try. I was planning to make it a little bit shorter, but I thought people might think it looked like Multi or Aoi from *To Heart*, so I didn't.

Kaoru looked like a different person without the ponytail, but did not look like a mom with the old hairstyle, so after thinking about it for a while, it turned into the simple solution that you see.

Yahiko turned into a cool guy and people will think "I want to see a story with Yahiko as the main character!" Roughly speaking, Yahiko is about Kenshin's height, and about Sanosuke's attitude. I am happy to have many readers notice the small kanji character for *aku* ("evil") on his clothing.

I had the same aim of "I want to read the story where Tsubame is the heroine!" with Tsubame, so I made her as cute as possible. The maid outfit was originally for my next work, but the current trend of having more maids than you can swing a stick at made me think it would be out of style by the time I used it, which is why I put it in now, just for fun (though it is supposed to be a waitress outfit).

The characters I could not show due to page restrictions, such as Sanosuke, Megumi, Misao, Aoshi, and Saitō, will be revealed in *Kenshin Kaden*. Please look forward to it!

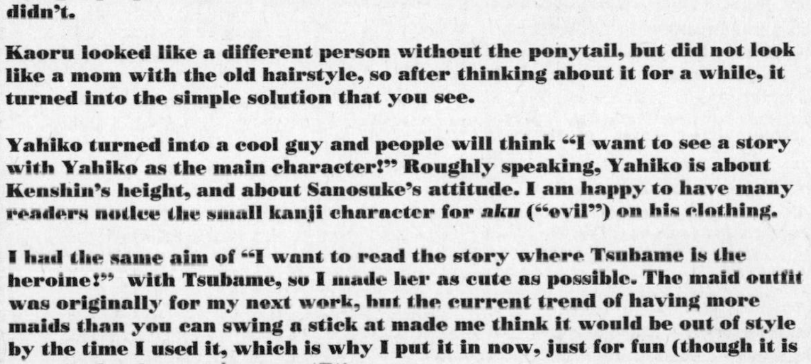
伸宏
和月

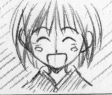

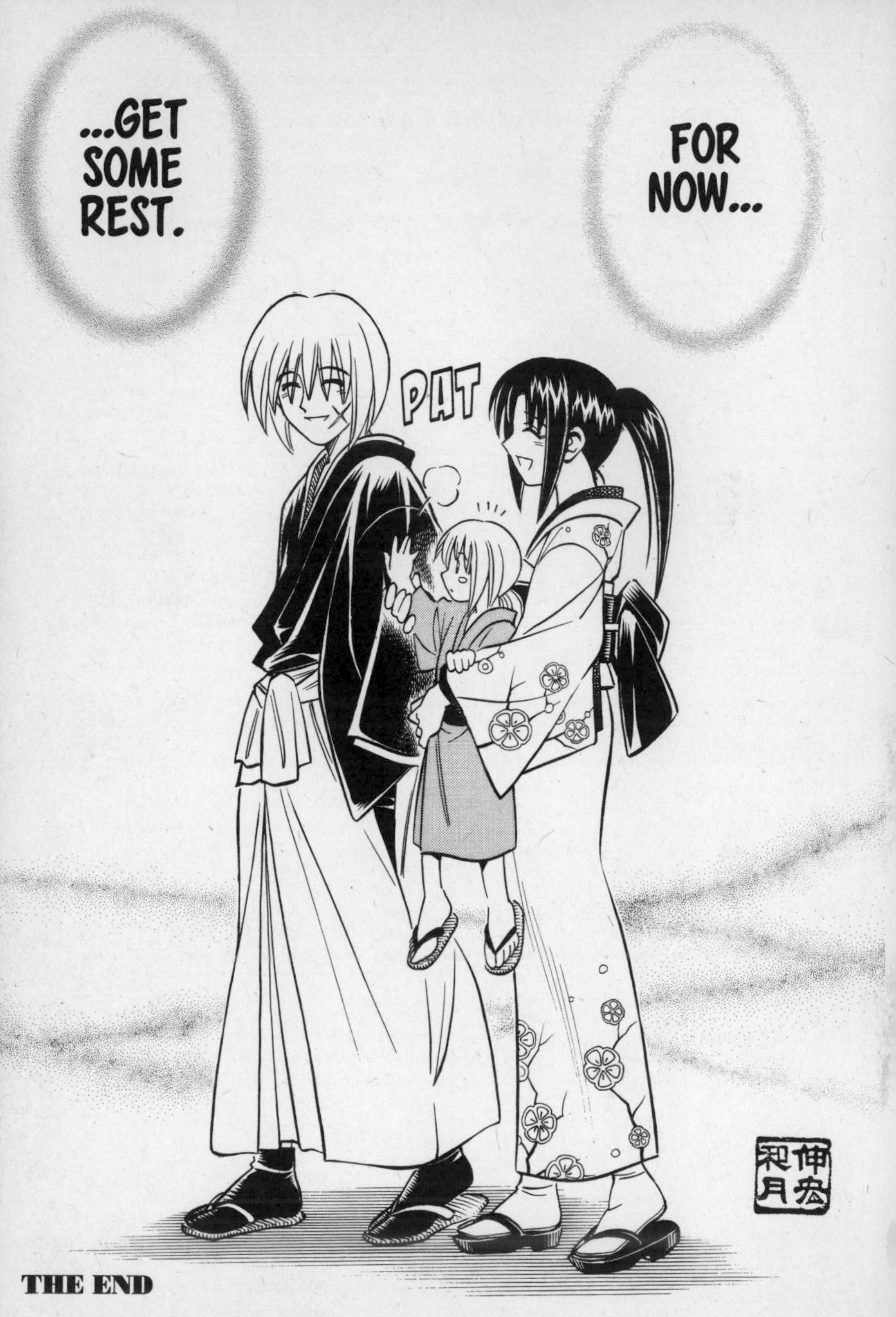
FOR NOW...
...GET SOME REST.
PAT

THE END

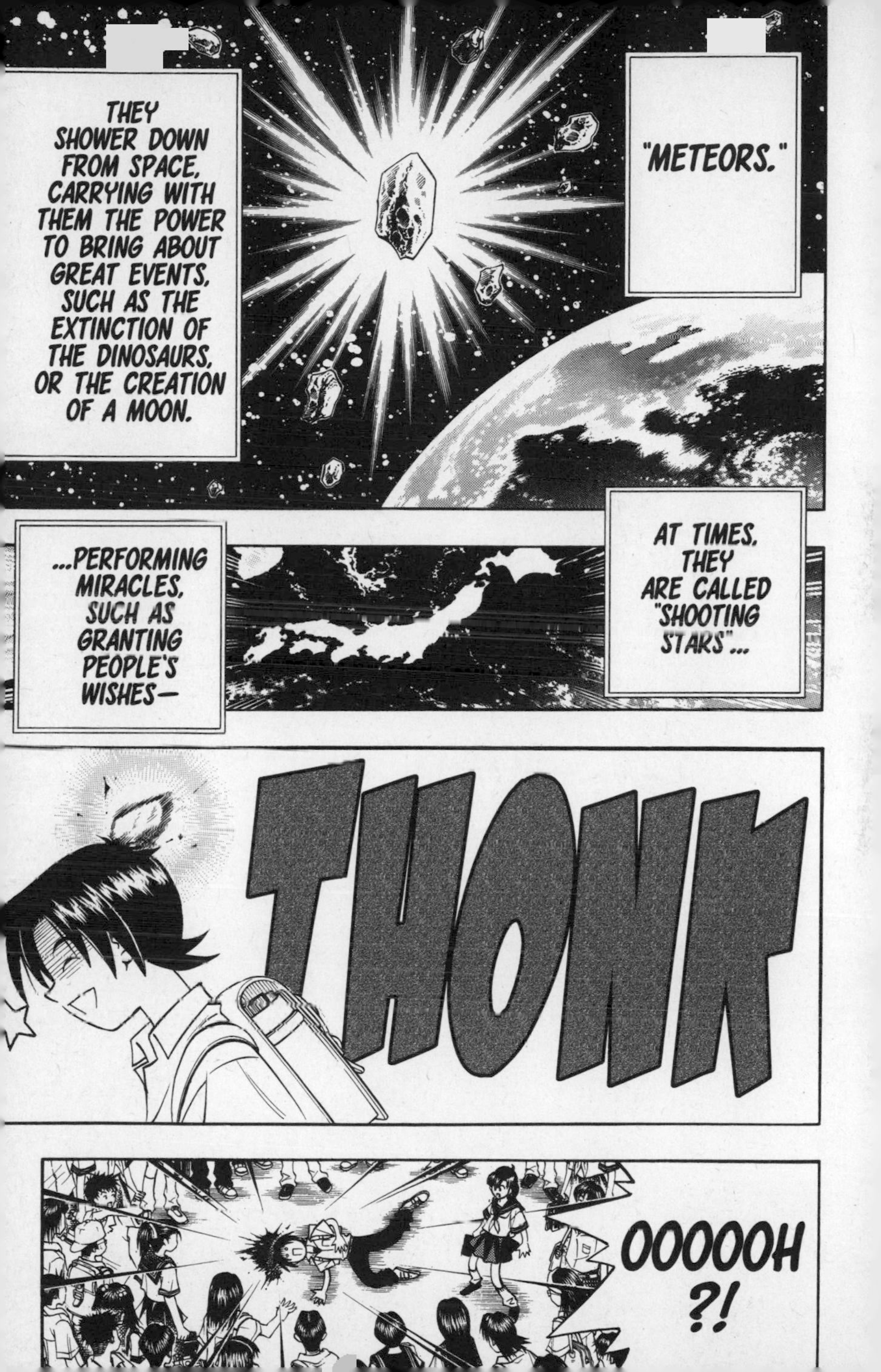
"METEORS."
THEY SHOWER DOWN FROM SPACE, CARRYING WITH THEM THE POWER TO BRING ABOUT GREAT EVENTS, SUCH AS THE EXTINCTION OF THE DINOSAURS, OR THE CREATION OF A MOON.
AT TIMES, THEY ARE CALLED "SHOOTING STARS"...
...PERFORMING MIRACLES, SUCH AS GRANTING PEOPLE'S WISHES—
THONK
OOOOOH ?!

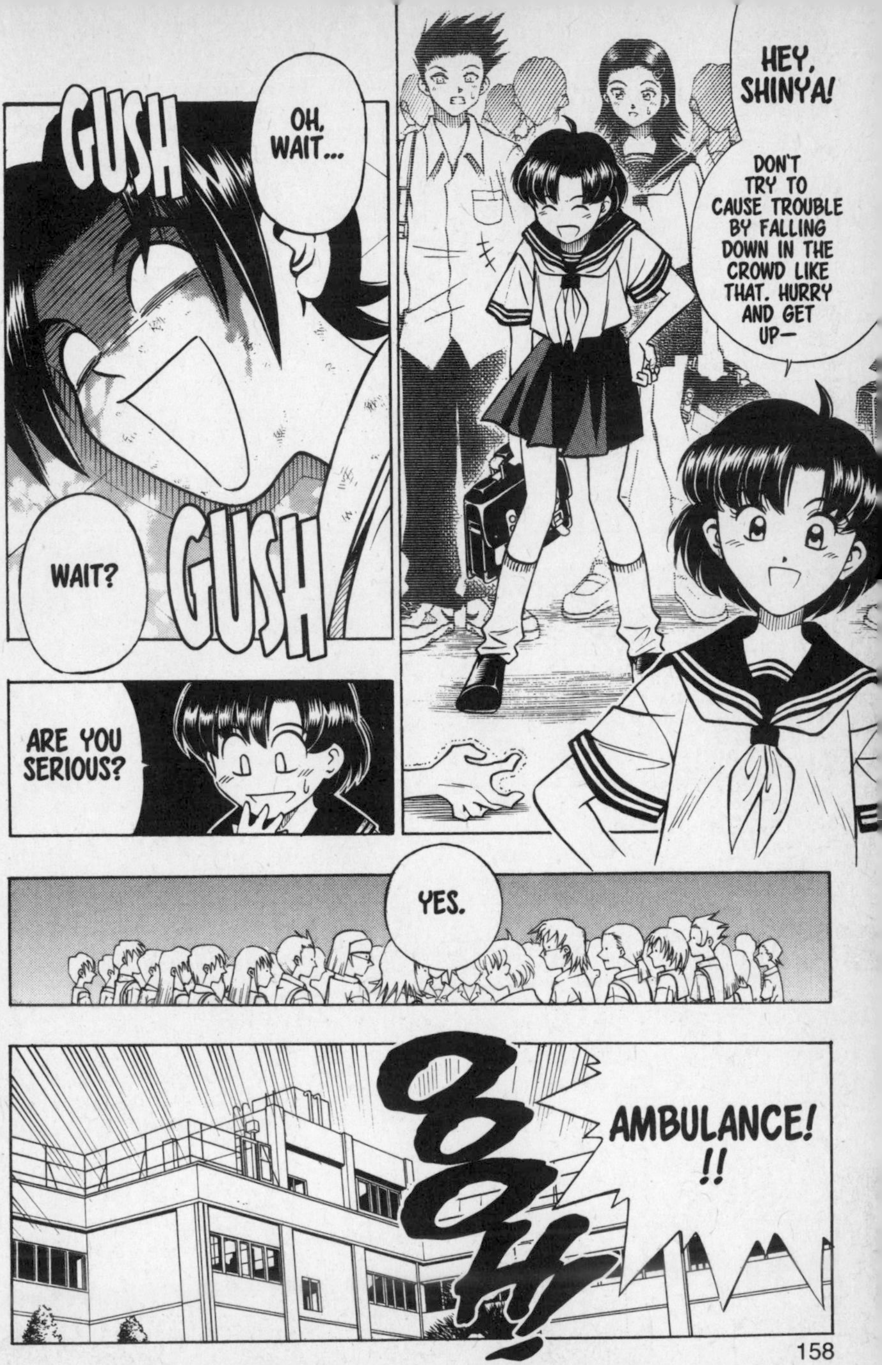
HEY, SHINYA!
DON'T TRY TO CAUSE TROUBLE BY FALLING DOWN IN THE CROWD LIKE THAT. HURRY AND GET UP—
OH, WAIT...
GUSH
GUSH
WAIT?
ARE YOU SERIOUS?
YES.
OOOH!
AMBULANCE! !!

READ THIS WAY

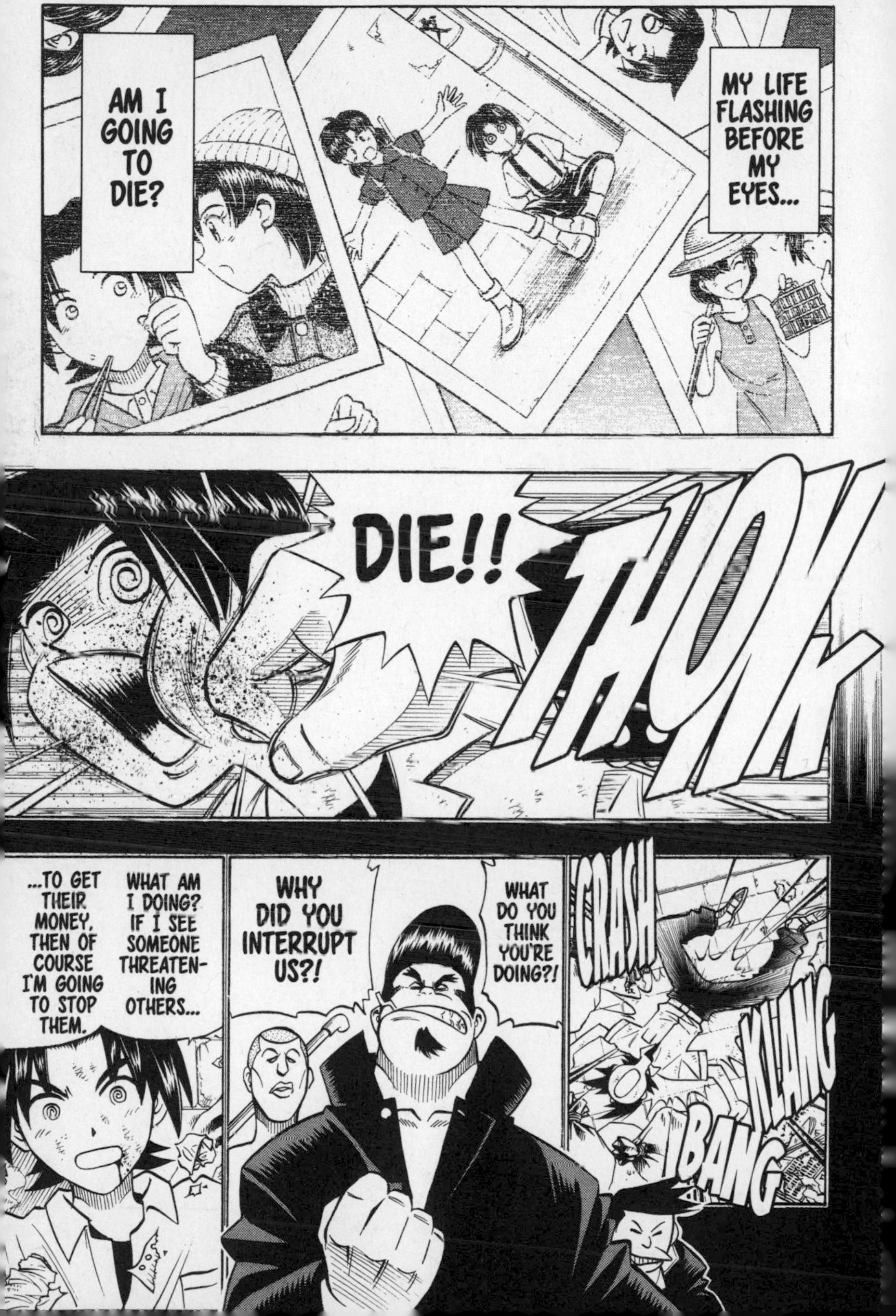
MY LIFE FLASHING BEFORE MY EYES...
AM I GOING TO DIE?
DIE!!
THUNK
CRASH
KLANG
BANG
WHAT DO YOU THINK YOU'RE DOING?!
WHY DID YOU INTERRUPT US?!
WHAT AM I DOING? IF I SEE SOMEONE THREATEN-ING OTHERS...
...TO GET THEIR MONEY, THEN OF COURSE I'M GOING TO STOP THEM.

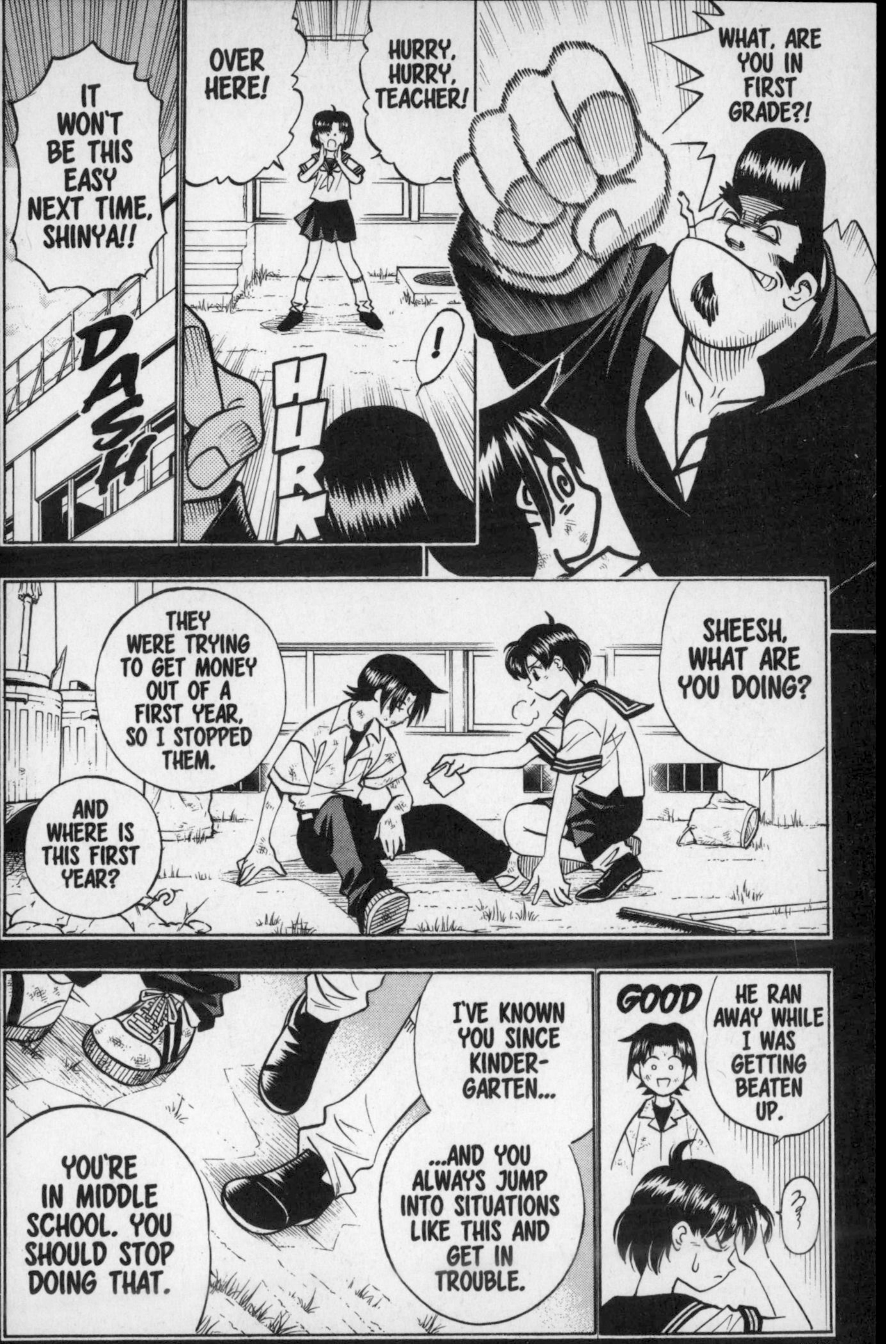
WHAT, ARE YOU IN FIRST GRADE?!
!
HURK
HURRY, HURRY, TEACHER!
OVER HERE!
IT WON'T BE THIS EASY NEXT TIME, SHINYA!!
DASH
SHEESH, WHAT ARE YOU DOING?
THEY WERE TRYING TO GET MONEY OUT OF A FIRST YEAR, SO I STOPPED THEM.
AND WHERE IS THIS FIRST YEAR?
HE RAN AWAY WHILE I WAS GETTING BEATEN UP.
GOOD
I'VE KNOWN YOU SINCE KINDER-GARTEN...
...AND YOU ALWAYS JUMP INTO SITUATIONS LIKE THIS AND GET IN TROUBLE.
YOU'RE IN MIDDLE SCHOOL. YOU SHOULD STOP DOING THAT.

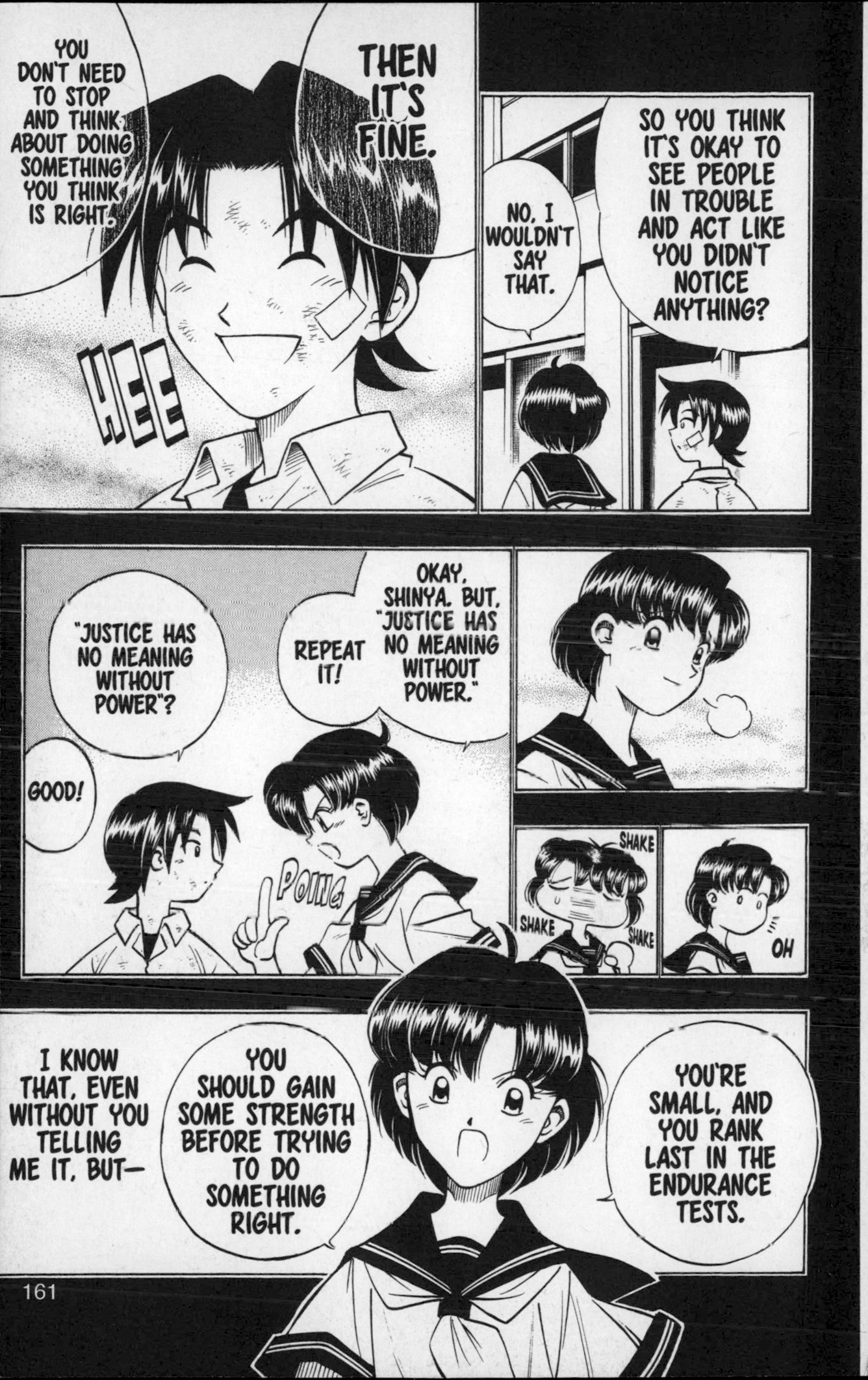
SO YOU THINK IT'S OKAY TO SEE PEOPLE IN TROUBLE AND ACT LIKE YOU DIDN'T NOTICE ANYTHING?
NO, I WOULDN'T SAY THAT.
THEN IT'S FINE.
YOU DON'T NEED TO STOP AND THINK ABOUT DOING SOMETHING YOU THINK IS RIGHT.
HEE
OH
SHAKE
SHAKE
SHAKE
OKAY, SHINYA. BUT, "JUSTICE HAS NO MEANING WITHOUT POWER."
REPEAT IT!
"JUSTICE HAS NO MEANING WITHOUT POWER"?
GOOD!
POING
YOU'RE SMALL, AND YOU RANK LAST IN THE ENDURANCE TESTS.
YOU SHOULD GAIN SOME STRENGTH BEFORE TRYING TO DO SOMETHING RIGHT.
I KNOW THAT, EVEN WITHOUT YOU TELLING ME IT, BUT—

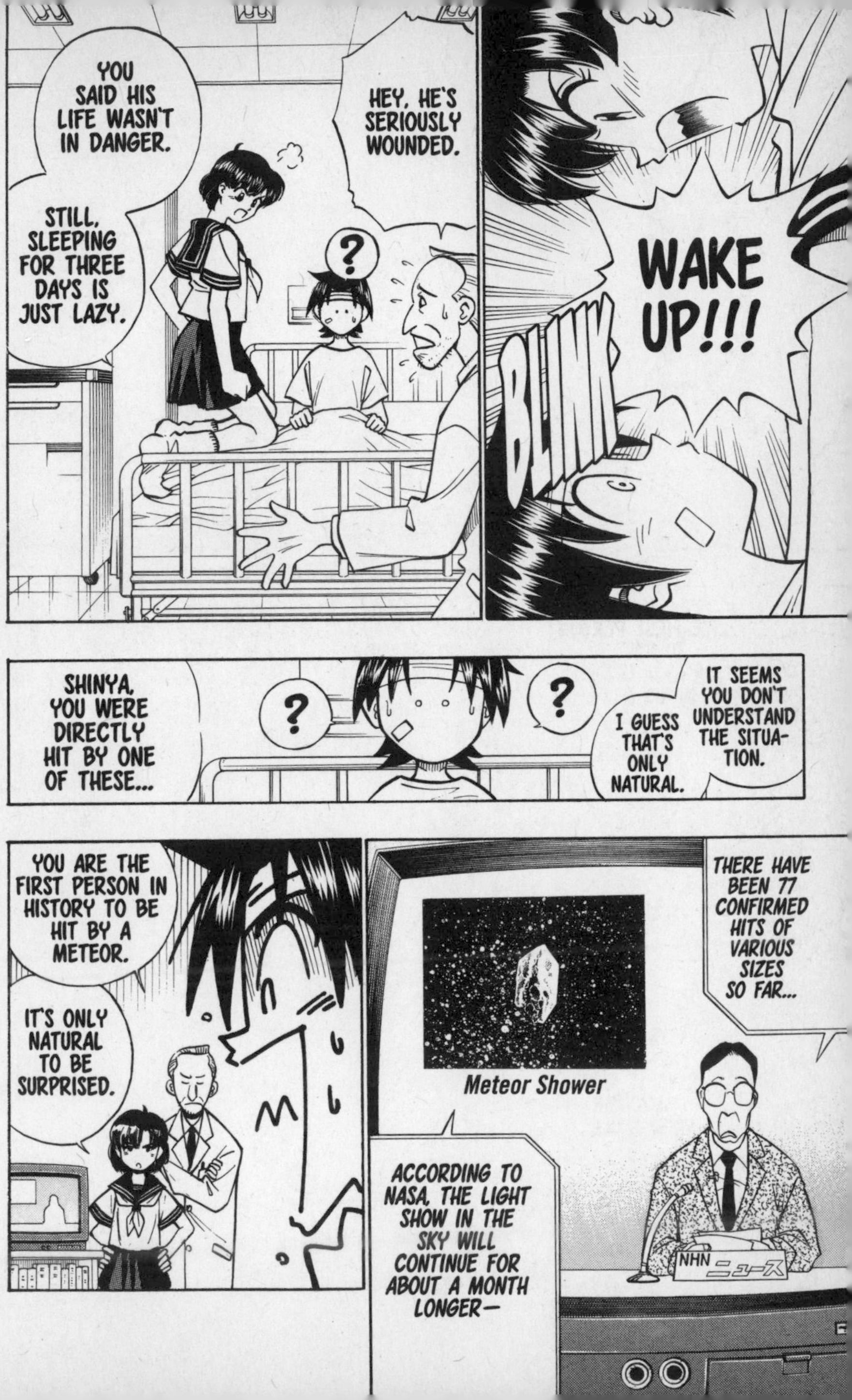
WAKE UP!!!
BLINK
HEY, HE'S SERIOUSLY WOUNDED.
YOU SAID HIS LIFE WASN'T IN DANGER.
STILL, SLEEPING FOR THREE DAYS IS JUST LAZY.
?
IT SEEMS YOU DON'T UNDERSTAND THE SITUA-TION.
I GUESS THAT'S ONLY NATURAL.
?
?
SHINYA, YOU WERE DIRECTLY HIT BY ONE OF THESE...
THERE HAVE BEEN 77 CONFIRMED HITS OF VARIOUS SIZES SO FAR...
Meteor Shower
NHN ニュース
ACCORDING TO NASA, THE LIGHT SHOW IN THE SKY WILL CONTINUE FOR ABOUT A MONTH LONGER—
YOU ARE THE FIRST PERSON IN HISTORY TO BE HIT BY A METEOR.
IT'S ONLY NATURAL TO BE SURPRISED.

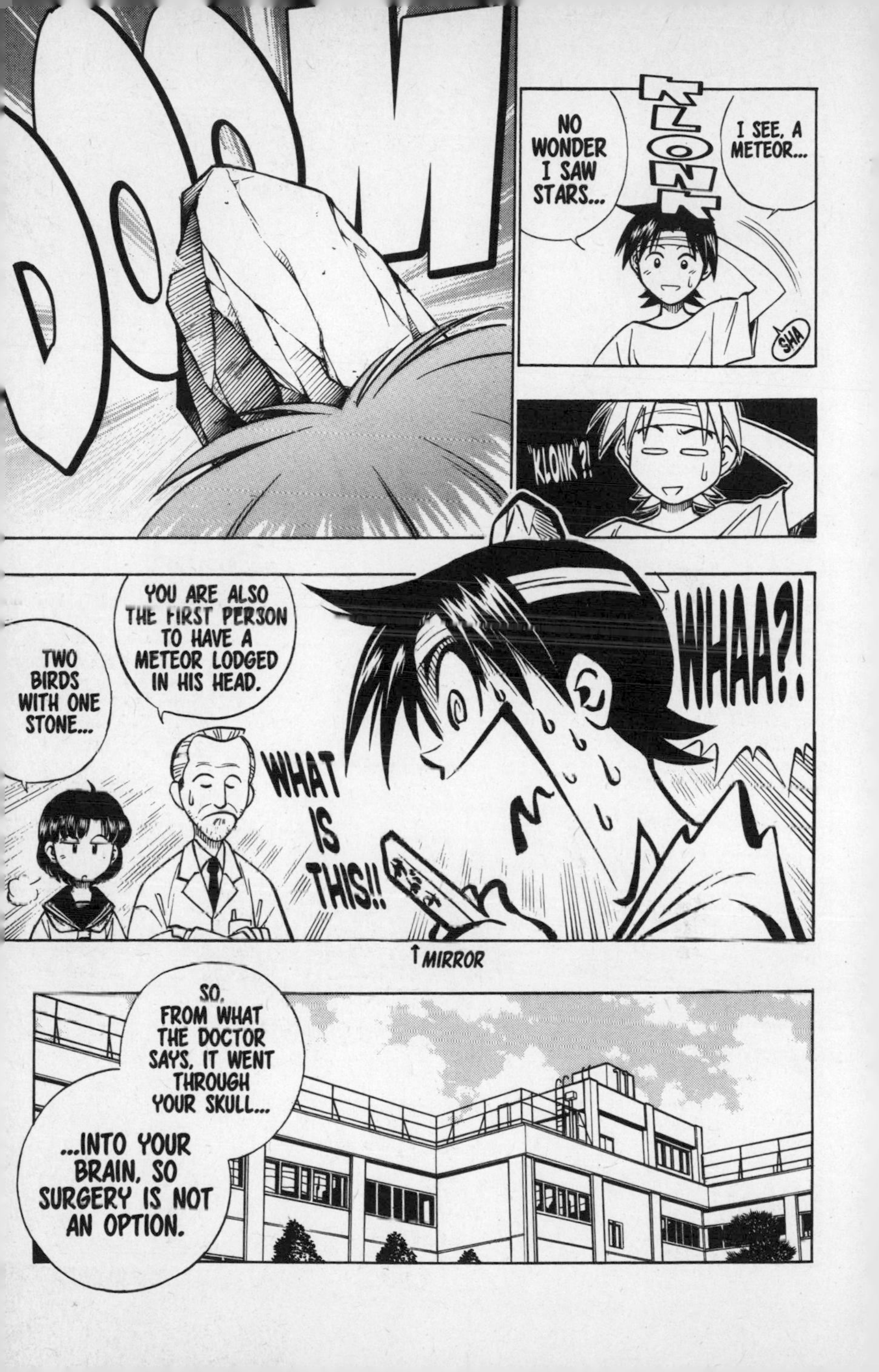
I SEE, A METEOR...
KLONK
NO WONDER I SAW STARS...
SHA
"KLONK"?!
DOOM
WHAA?!
YOU ARE ALSO THE FIRST PERSON TO HAVE A METEOR LODGED IN HIS HEAD.
TWO BIRDS WITH ONE STONE...
WHAT IS THIS!!
↑MIRROR
SO, FROM WHAT THE DOCTOR SAYS, IT WENT THROUGH YOUR SKULL...
...INTO YOUR BRAIN, SO SURGERY IS NOT AN OPTION.

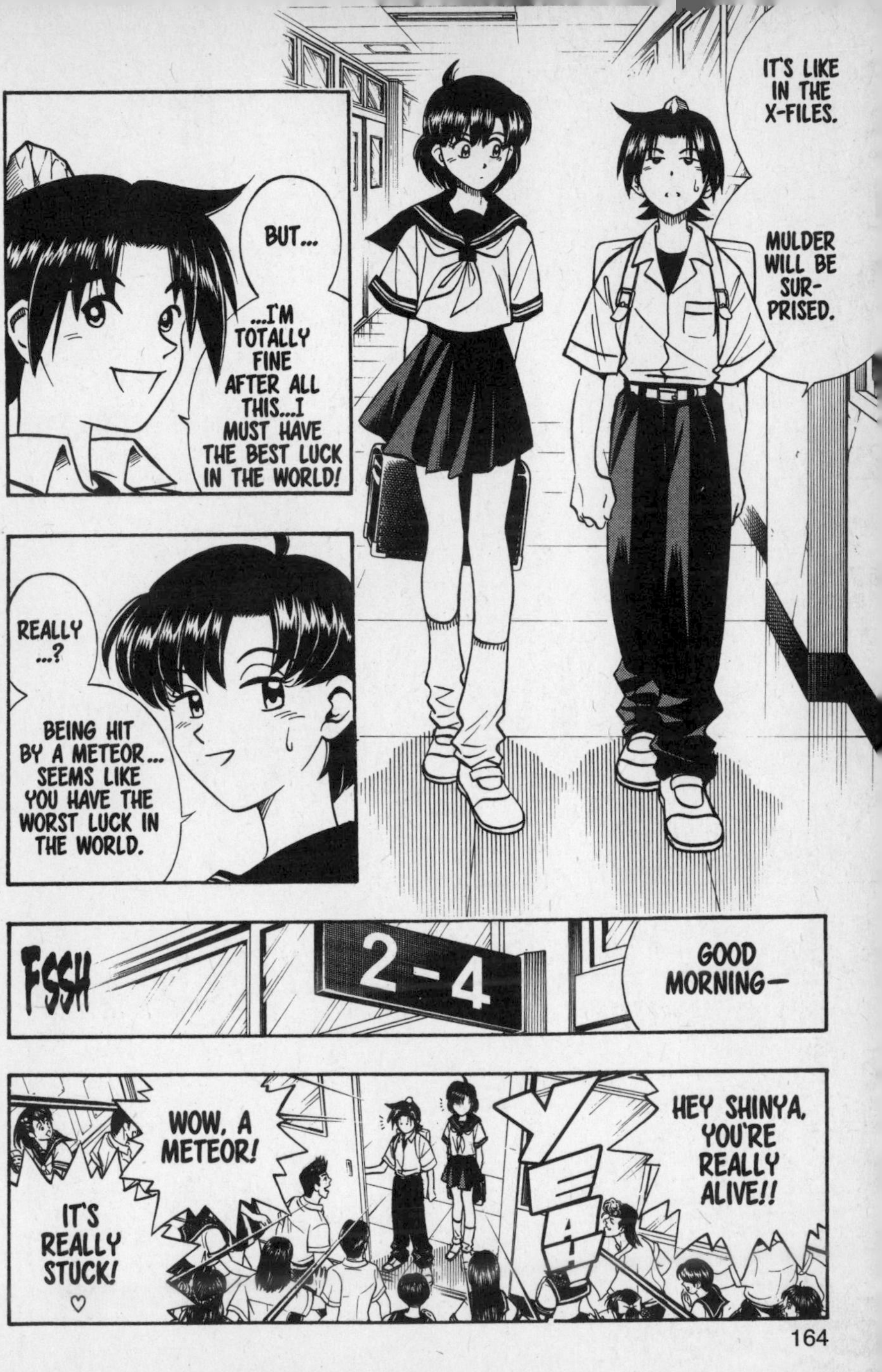
IT'S LIKE IN THE X-FILES.
MULDER WILL BE SUR-PRISED.
BUT...
...I'M TOTALLY FINE AFTER ALL THIS...I MUST HAVE THE BEST LUCK IN THE WORLD!
REALLY ...?
BEING HIT BY A METEOR... SEEMS LIKE YOU HAVE THE WORST LUCK IN THE WORLD.
GOOD MORNING—
2-4
FSSH
HEY SHINYA, YOU'RE REALLY ALIVE!!
YEA!
WOW, A METEOR!
IT'S REALLY STUCK! ♡

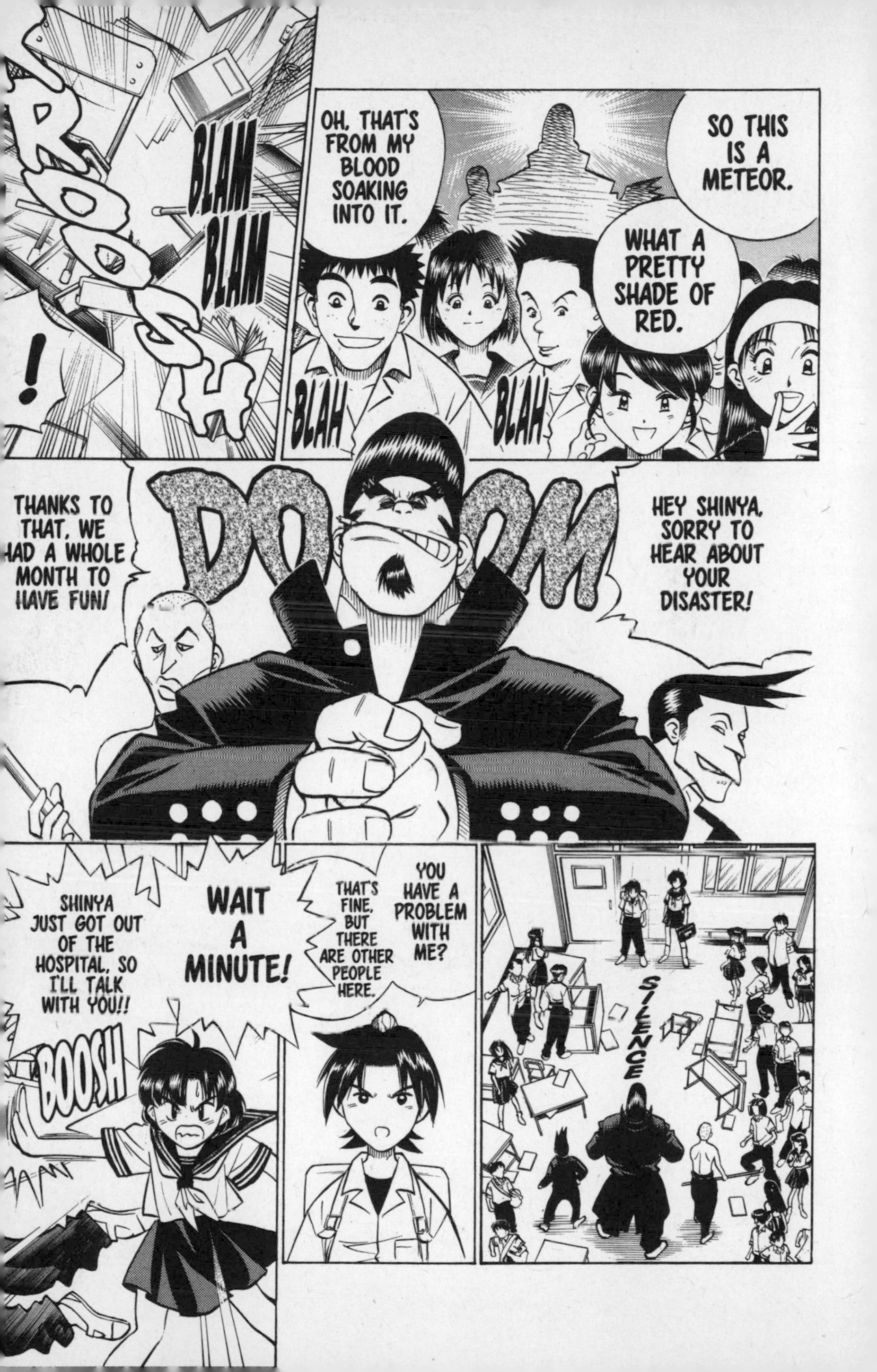
SO THIS IS A METEOR.
WHAT A PRETTY SHADE OF RED.
OH, THAT'S FROM MY BLOOD SOAKING INTO IT.
BLAH
BLAH
BLAM BLAM BLAM
ROOOSH!
HEY SHINYA, SORRY TO HEAR ABOUT YOUR DISASTER!
DOOOM
THANKS TO THAT, WE HAD A WHOLE MONTH TO HAVE FUN!
SILENCE
YOU HAVE A PROBLEM WITH ME?
THAT'S FINE, BUT THERE ARE OTHER PEOPLE HERE.
WAIT A MINUTE!
SHINYA JUST GOT OUT OF THE HOSPITAL, SO I'LL TALK WITH YOU!!
BOOSH

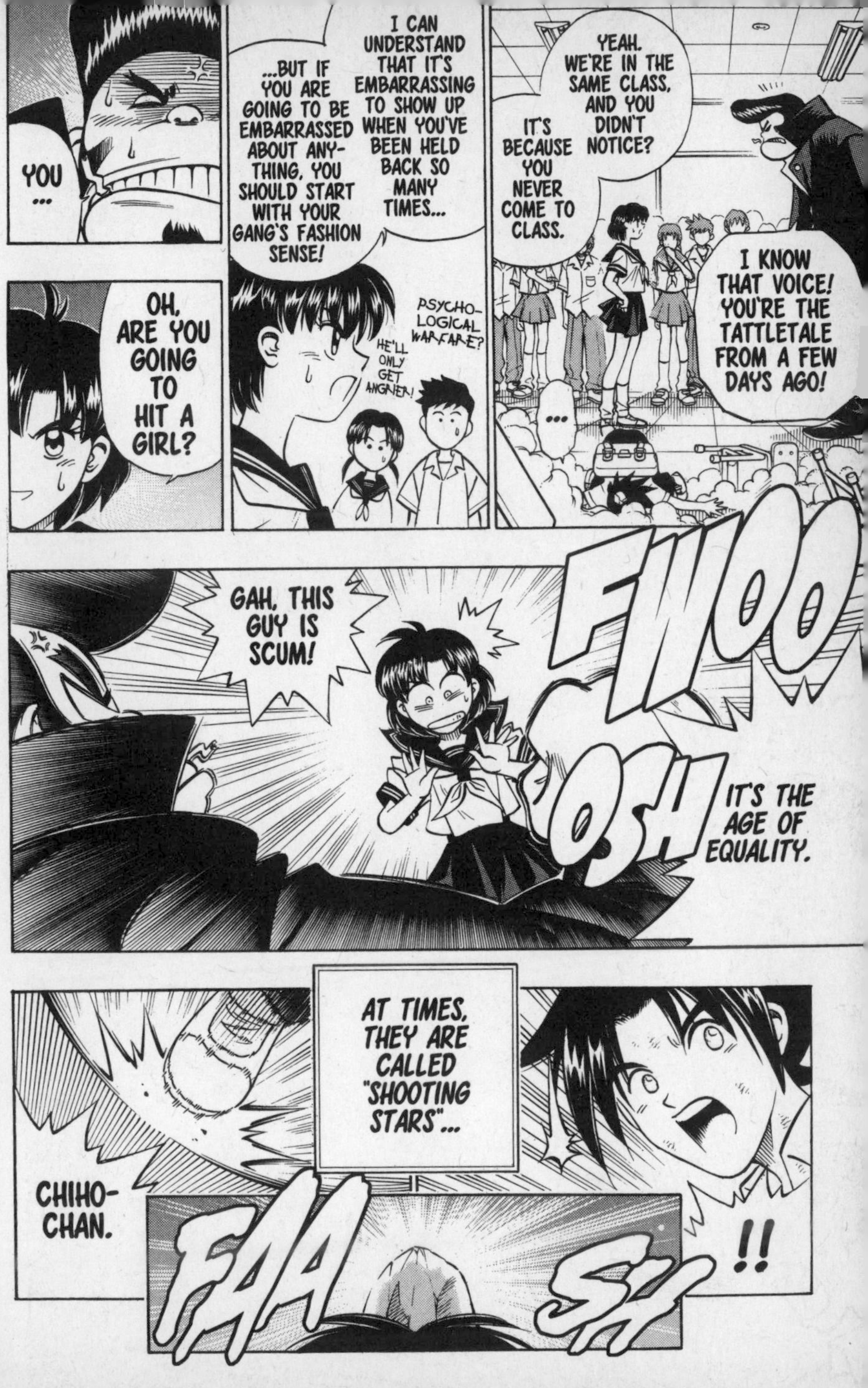
I KNOW THAT VOICE! YOU'RE THE TATTLETALE FROM A FEW DAYS AGO!
YEAH. WE'RE IN THE SAME CLASS, AND YOU DIDN'T NOTICE?
IT'S BECAUSE YOU NEVER COME TO CLASS.
...
I CAN UNDERSTAND THAT IT'S EMBARRASSING TO SHOW UP WHEN YOU'VE BEEN HELD BACK SO MANY TIMES...
...BUT IF YOU ARE GOING TO BE EMBARRASSED ABOUT ANY-THING, YOU SHOULD START WITH YOUR GANG'S FASHION SENSE!
PSYCHO-LOGICAL WARFARE?
HE'LL ONLY GET ANGRIER!
YOU ...
OH, ARE YOU GOING TO HIT A GIRL?
FWOOOSH
IT'S THE AGE OF EQUALITY.
GAH, THIS GUY IS SCUM!
AT TIMES, THEY ARE CALLED "SHOOTING STARS"...
FAASH!!
CHIHO-CHAN.

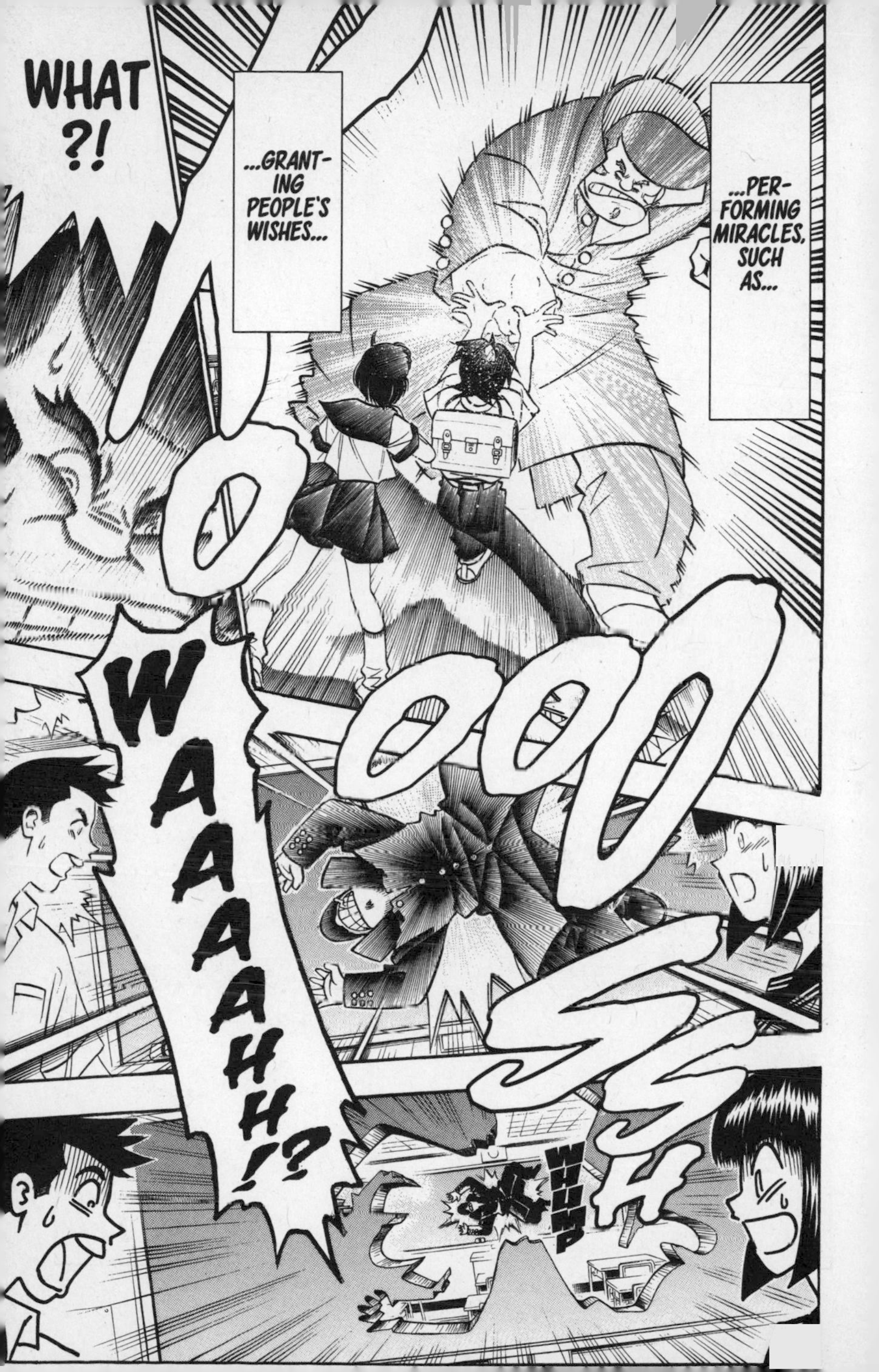
...PER-FORMING MIRACLES, SUCH AS...
...GRANT-ING PEOPLE'S WISHES...
WHAT?!
WOOOOOOSSH
WAAAAAAHH!?
WHUMP

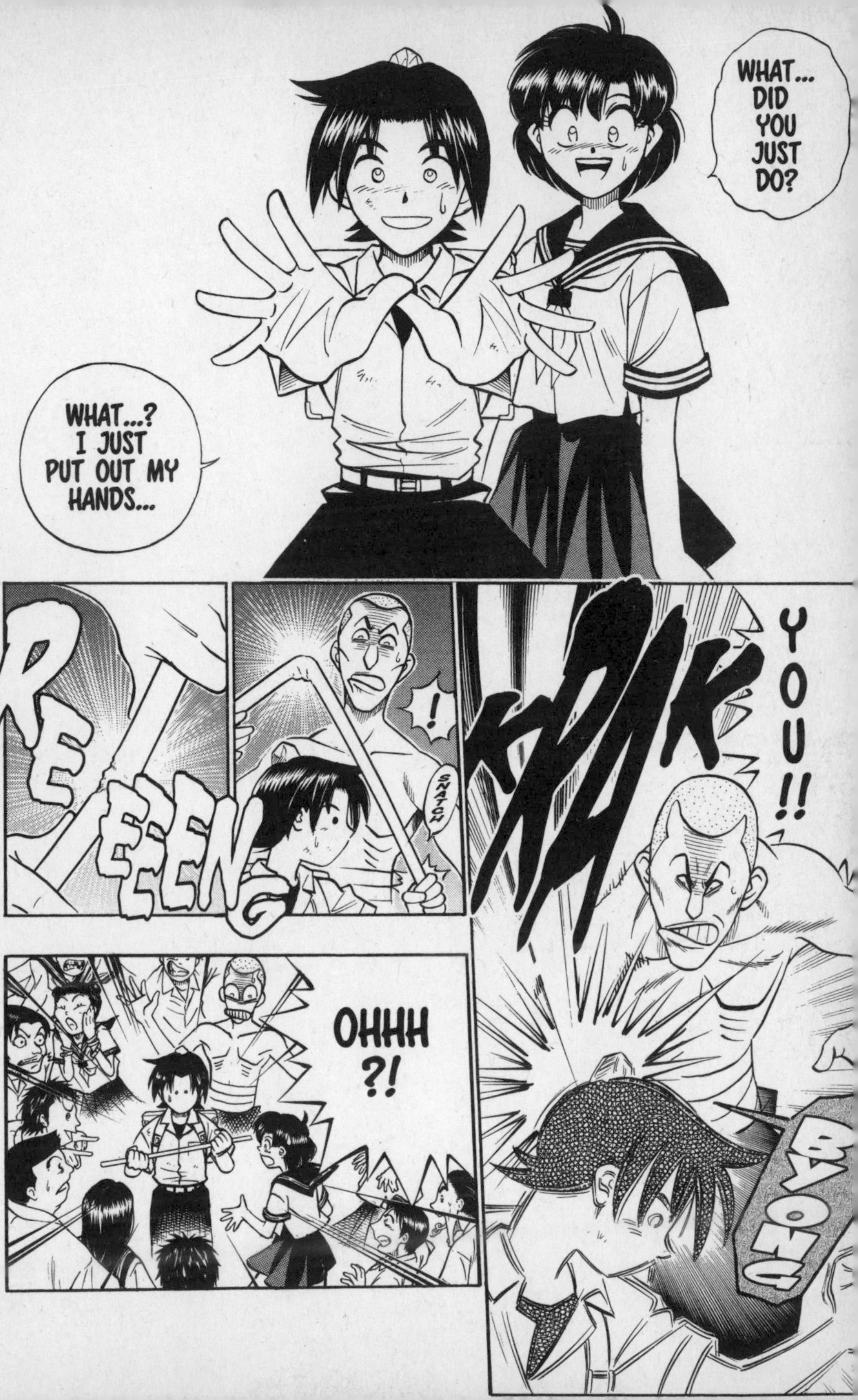
WHAT... DID YOU JUST DO?
WHAT...? I JUST PUT OUT MY HANDS...
YOU!!
BYONG
!
SNATCH
OHHH ?!

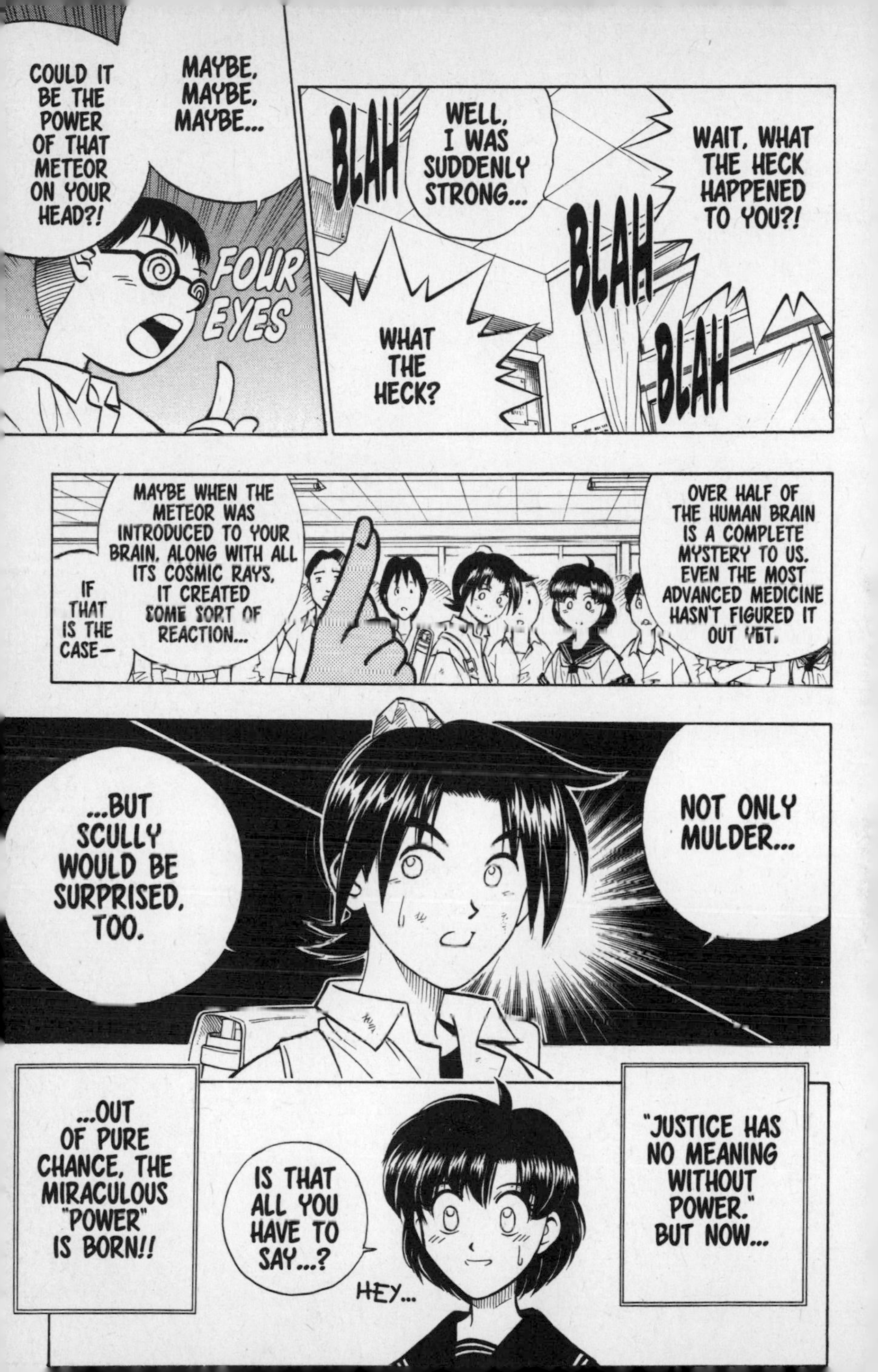
WAIT, WHAT THE HECK HAPPENED TO YOU?!
BLAH
BLAH
WELL, I WAS SUDDENLY STRONG...
BLAH
WHAT THE HECK?
MAYBE, MAYBE, MAYBE...
COULD IT BE THE POWER OF THAT METEOR ON YOUR HEAD?!
FOUR EYES
OVER HALF OF THE HUMAN BRAIN IS A COMPLETE MYSTERY TO US. EVEN THE MOST ADVANCED MEDICINE HASN'T FIGURED IT OUT YET.
MAYBE WHEN THE METEOR WAS INTRODUCED TO YOUR BRAIN, ALONG WITH ALL ITS COSMIC RAYS, IT CREATED SOME SORT OF REACTION...
IF THAT IS THE CASE—
NOT ONLY MULDER...
...BUT SCULLY WOULD BE SURPRISED, TOO.
"JUSTICE HAS NO MEANING WITHOUT POWER." BUT NOW...
HEY...
IS THAT ALL YOU HAVE TO SAY...?
...OUT OF PURE CHANCE, THE MIRACULOUS "POWER" IS BORN!!

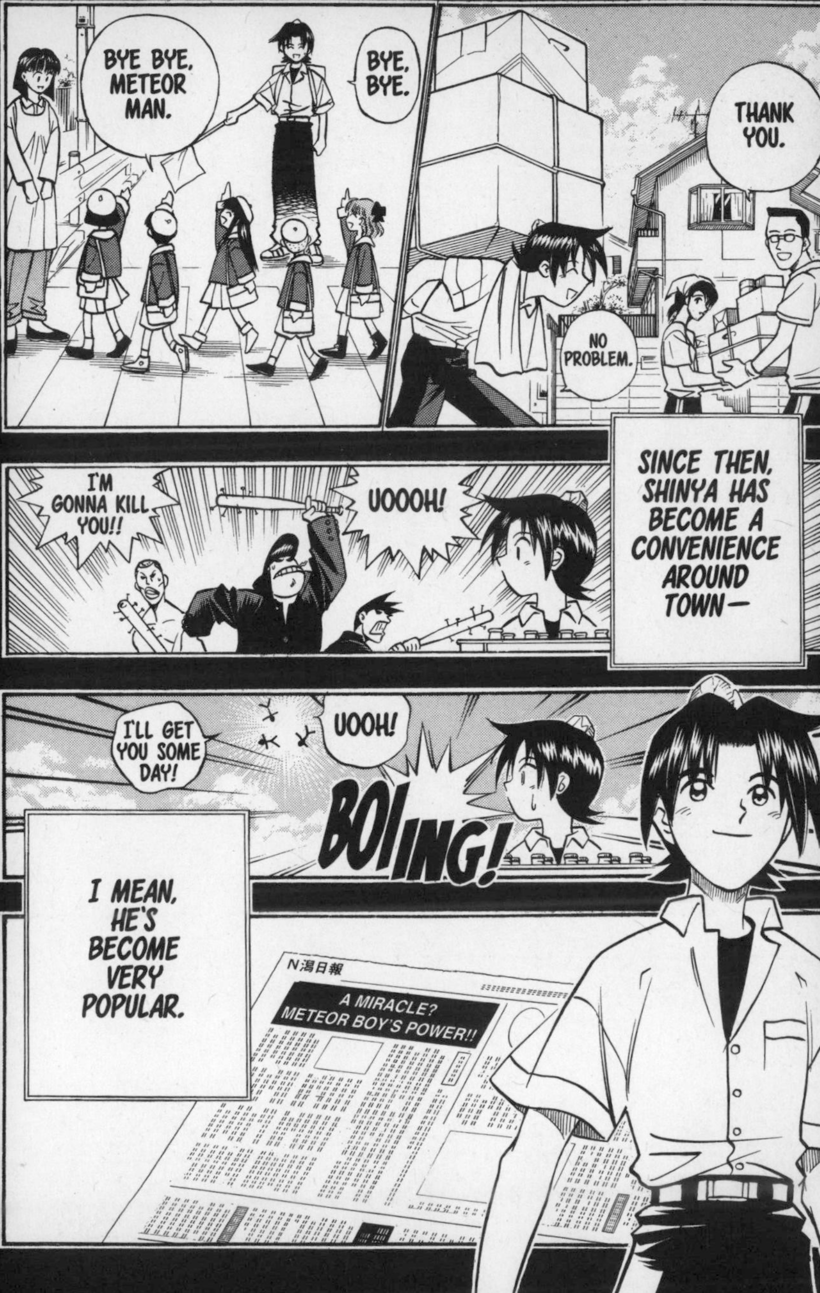
THANK YOU.
NO PROBLEM.
BYE, BYE.
BYE BYE, METEOR MAN.
SINCE THEN, SHINYA HAS BECOME A CONVENIENCE AROUND TOWN—
UOOOH!
I'M GONNA KILL YOU!!
UOOH!
I'LL GET YOU SOME DAY!
BOING!
N潟日報
A MIRACLE? METEOR BOY'S POWER!!
I MEAN, HE'S BECOME VERY POPULAR.

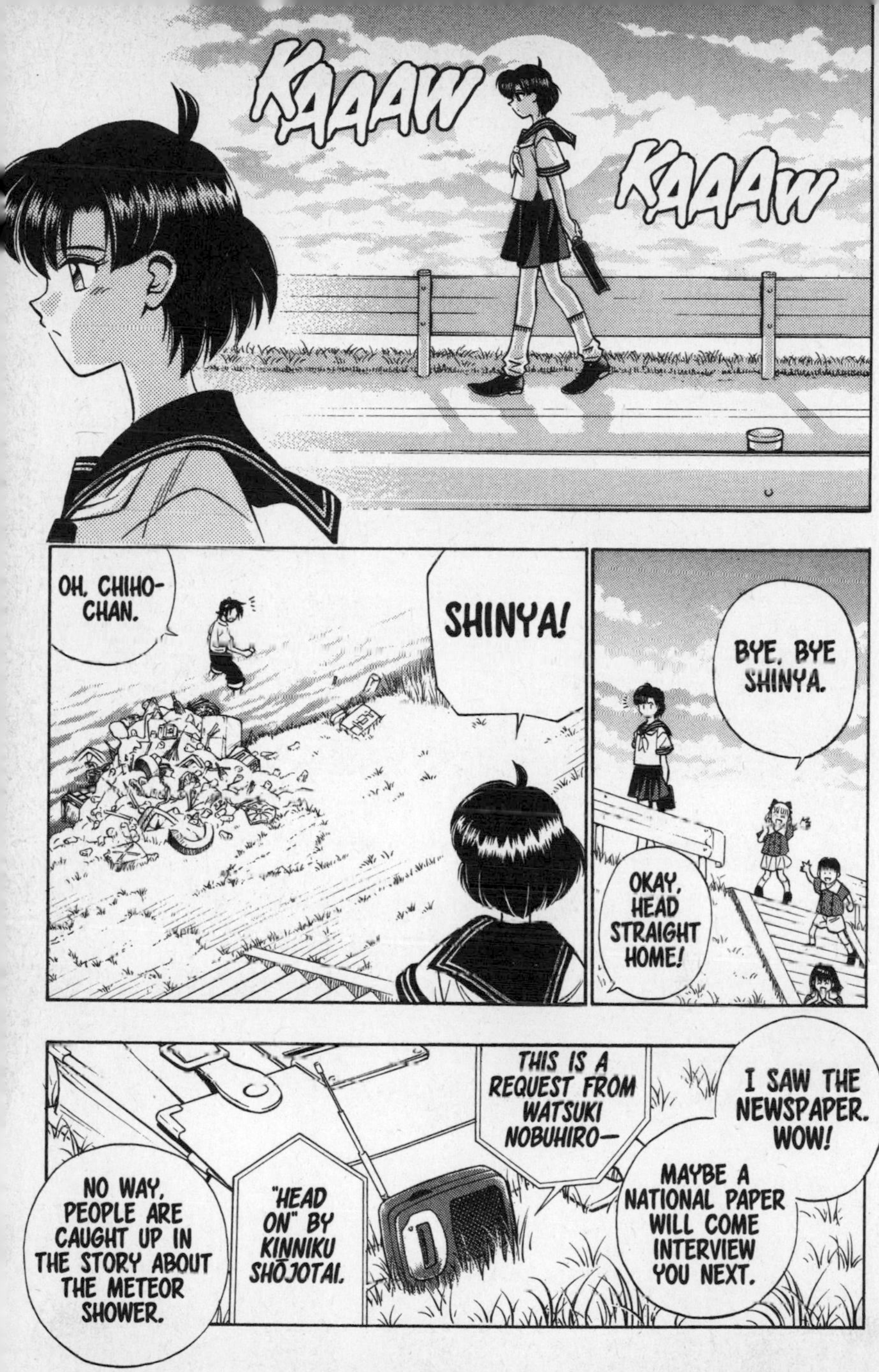
KAAAW
KAAAW
BYE, BYE SHINYA.
OKAY, HEAD STRAIGHT HOME!
SHINYA!
OH, CHIHO-CHAN.
I SAW THE NEWSPAPER. WOW!
THIS IS A REQUEST FROM WATSUKI NOBUHIRO—
MAYBE A NATIONAL PAPER WILL COME INTERVIEW YOU NEXT.
"HEAD ON" BY KINNIKU SHŌJOTAI.
NO WAY, PEOPLE ARE CAUGHT UP IN THE STORY ABOUT THE METEOR SHOWER.

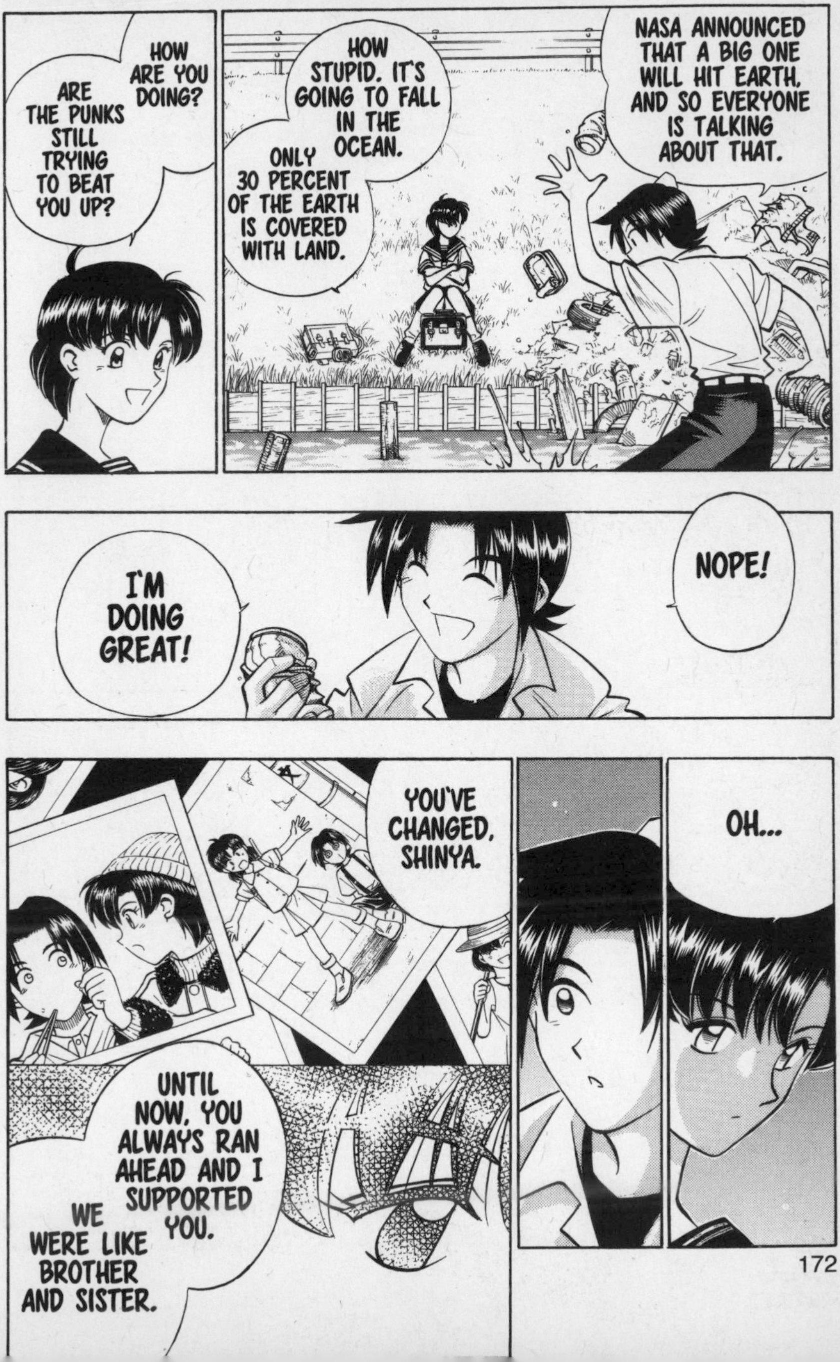
NASA ANNOUNCED THAT A BIG ONE WILL HIT EARTH, AND SO EVERYONE IS TALKING ABOUT THAT.
HOW STUPID. IT'S GOING TO FALL IN THE OCEAN.
ONLY 30 PERCENT OF THE EARTH IS COVERED WITH LAND.
HOW ARE YOU DOING?
ARE THE PUNKS STILL TRYING TO BEAT YOU UP?
NOPE!
I'M DOING GREAT!
OH...
YOU'VE CHANGED, SHINYA.
UNTIL NOW, YOU ALWAYS RAN AHEAD AND I SUPPORTED YOU.
WE WERE LIKE BROTHER AND SISTER.

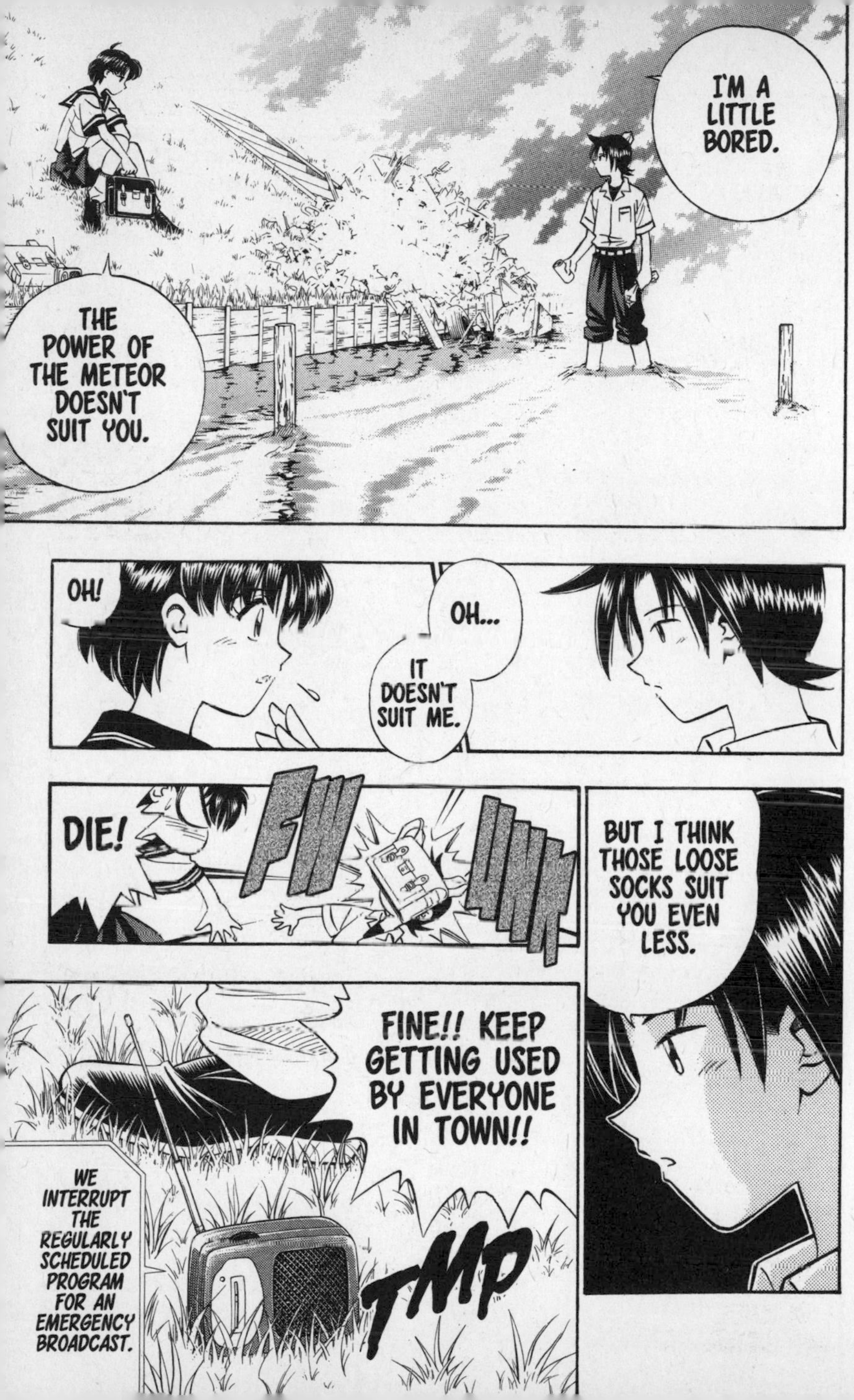
I'M A LITTLE BORED.
THE POWER OF THE METEOR DOESN'T SUIT YOU.
OH...
IT DOESN'T SUIT ME.
OH!
BUT I THINK THOSE LOOSE SOCKS SUIT YOU EVEN LESS.
DIE!
FINE!! KEEP GETTING USED BY EVERYONE IN TOWN!!
TMP
WE INTERRUPT THE REGULARLY SCHEDULED PROGRAM FOR AN EMERGENCY BROADCAST.

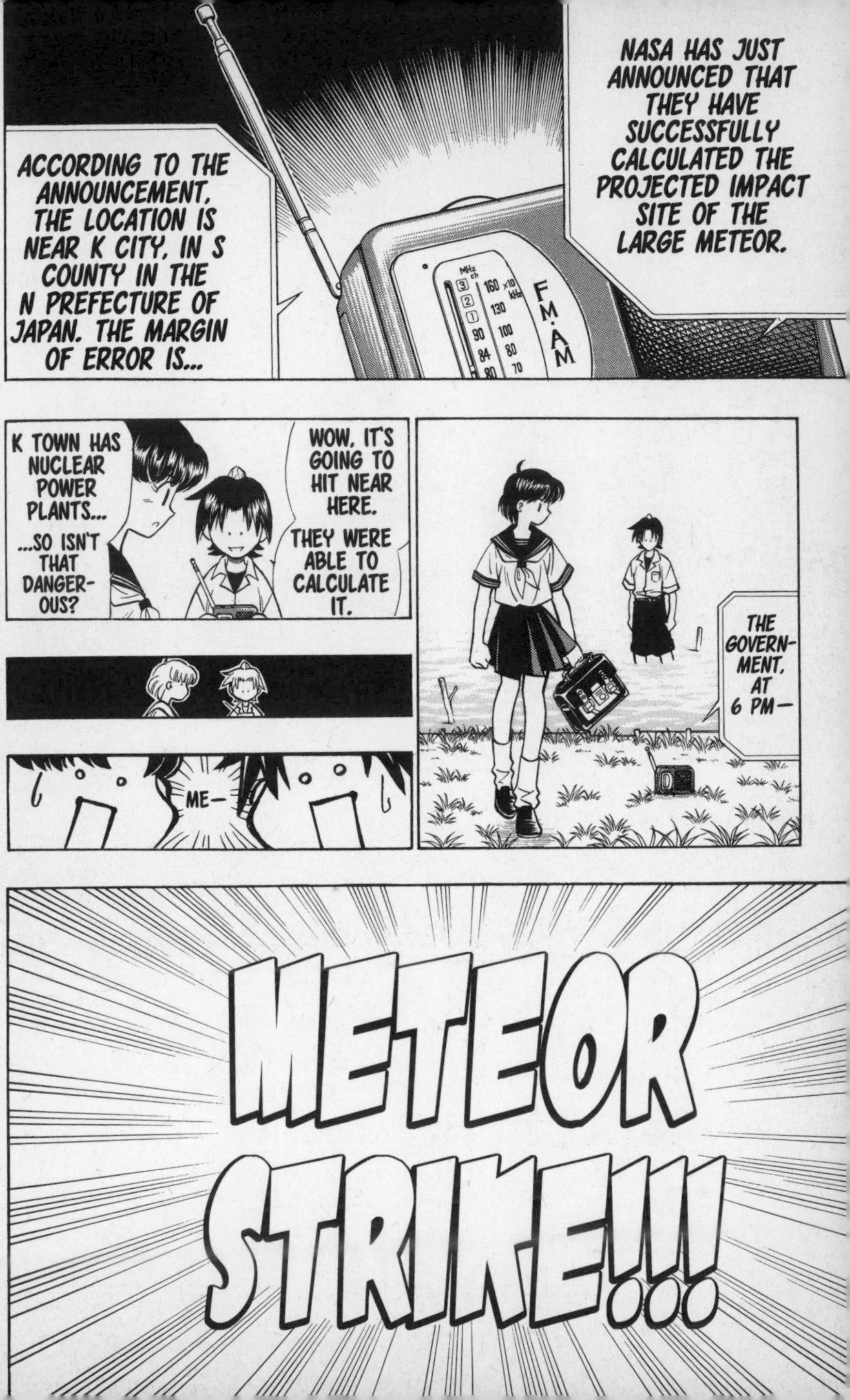
NASA HAS JUST ANNOUNCED THAT THEY HAVE SUCCESSFULLY CALCULATED THE PROJECTED IMPACT SITE OF THE LARGE METEOR.
ACCORDING TO THE ANNOUNCEMENT, THE LOCATION IS NEAR K CITY, IN S COUNTY IN THE N PREFECTURE OF JAPAN. THE MARGIN OF ERROR IS...
F.M.·AM
THE GOVERNMENT, AT 6 PM—
WOW, IT'S GOING TO HIT NEAR HERE.
THEY WERE ABLE TO CALCULATE IT.
K TOWN HAS NUCLEAR POWER PLANTS...
...SO ISN'T THAT DANGEROUS?
ME—
METEOR STRIKE!!!

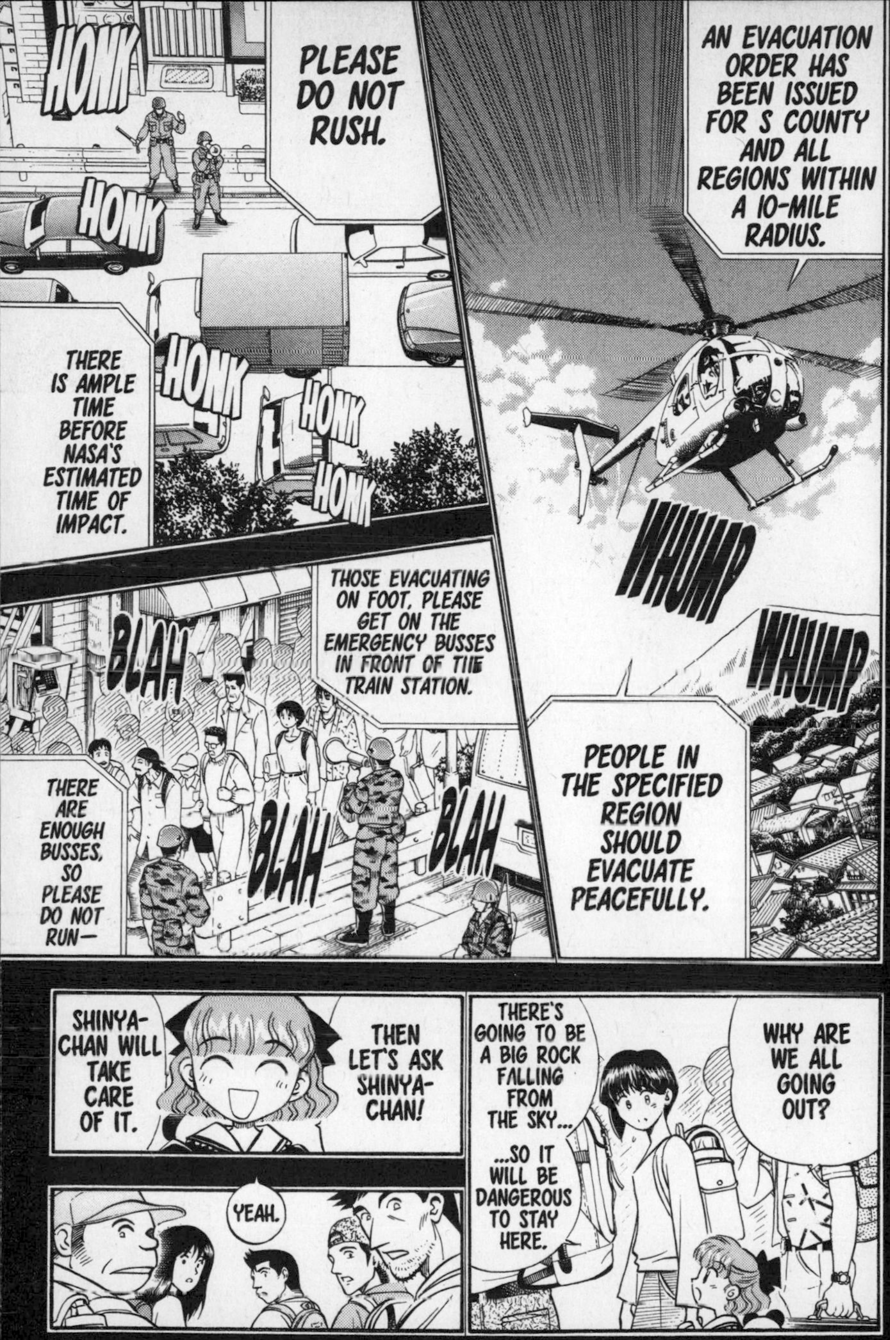
AN EVACUATION ORDER HAS BEEN ISSUED FOR S COUNTY AND ALL REGIONS WITHIN A 10-MILE RADIUS.
WHUMP
WHUMP
PLEASE DO NOT RUSH.
HONK
HONK
HONK
HONK
HONK
THERE IS AMPLE TIME BEFORE NASA'S ESTIMATED TIME OF IMPACT.
PEOPLE IN THE SPECIFIED REGION SHOULD EVACUATE PEACEFULLY.
THOSE EVACUATING ON FOOT, PLEASE GET ON THE EMERGENCY BUSSES IN FRONT OF THE TRAIN STATION.
BLAH
BLAH
BLAH
THERE ARE ENOUGH BUSSES, SO PLEASE DO NOT RUN—
WHY ARE WE ALL GOING OUT?
THERE'S GOING TO BE A BIG ROCK FALLING FROM THE SKY...
...SO IT WILL BE DANGEROUS TO STAY HERE.
THEN LET'S ASK SHINYA-CHAN!
SHINYA-CHAN WILL TAKE CARE OF IT.
YEAH.

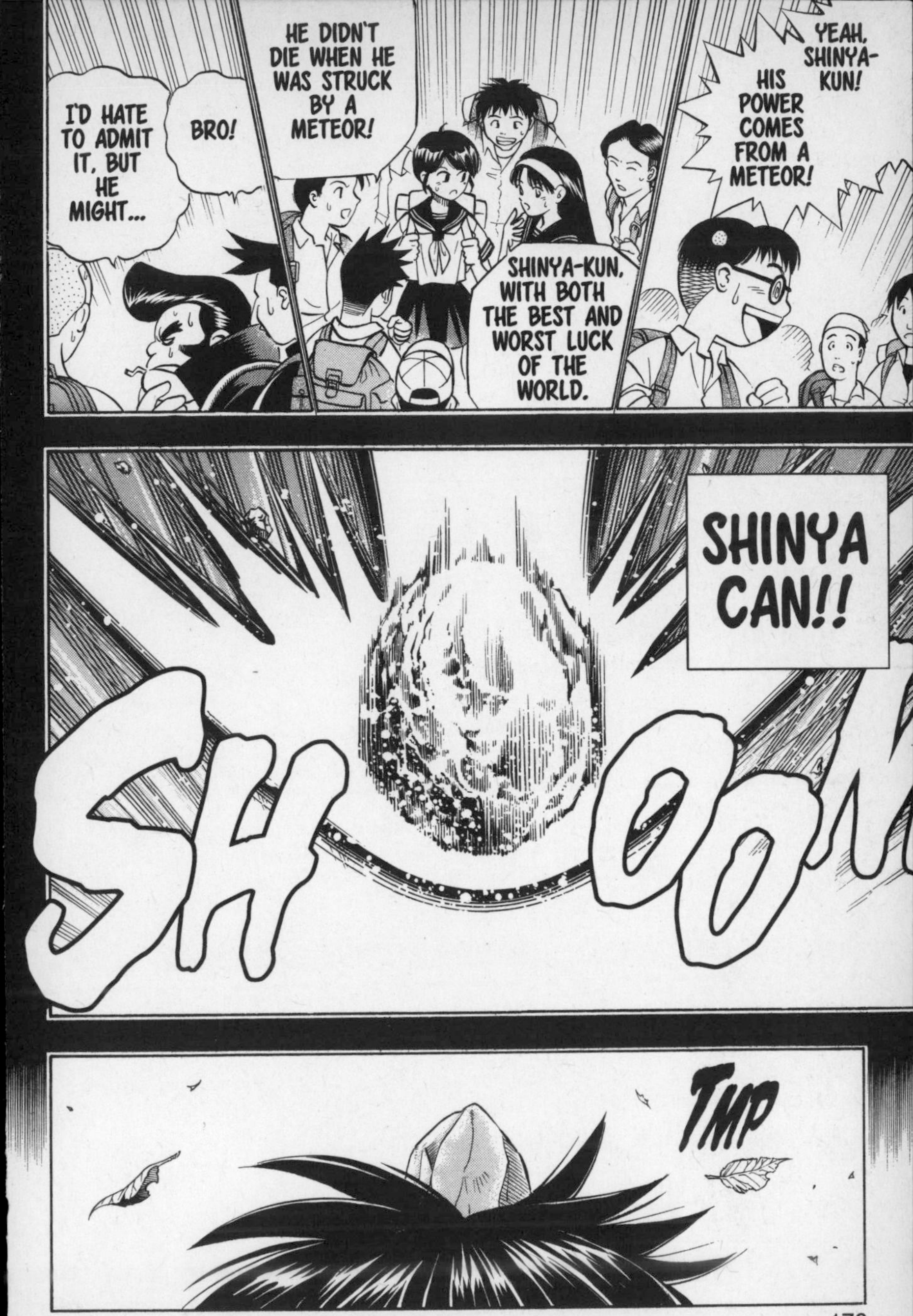
YEAH, SHINYA-KUN!
HIS POWER COMES FROM A METEOR!
HE DIDN'T DIE WHEN HE WAS STRUCK BY A METEOR!
SHINYA-KUN, WITH BOTH THE BEST AND WORST LUCK OF THE WORLD.
BRO!
I'D HATE TO ADMIT IT, BUT HE MIGHT...
SHINYA CAN!!
SHOO
TMP

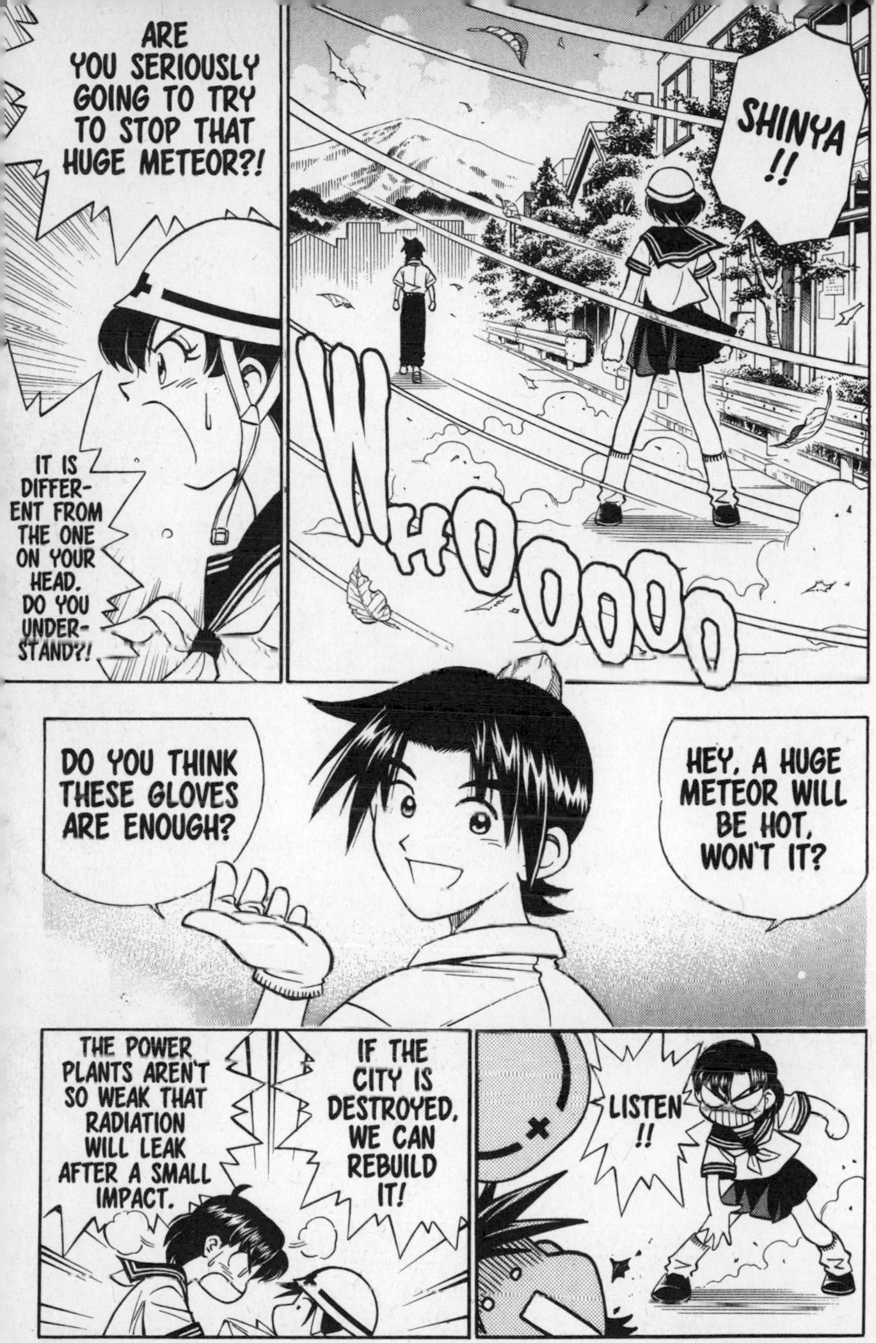
SHINYA !!
WHOOOOO
ARE YOU SERIOUSLY GOING TO TRY TO STOP THAT HUGE METEOR?!
IT IS DIFFERENT FROM THE ONE ON YOUR HEAD. DO YOU UNDERSTAND?!
HEY, A HUGE METEOR WILL BE HOT, WON'T IT?
DO YOU THINK THESE GLOVES ARE ENOUGH?
LISTEN !!
IF THE CITY IS DESTROYED, WE CAN REBUILD IT!
THE POWER PLANTS AREN'T SO WEAK THAT RADIATION WILL LEAK AFTER A SMALL IMPACT.

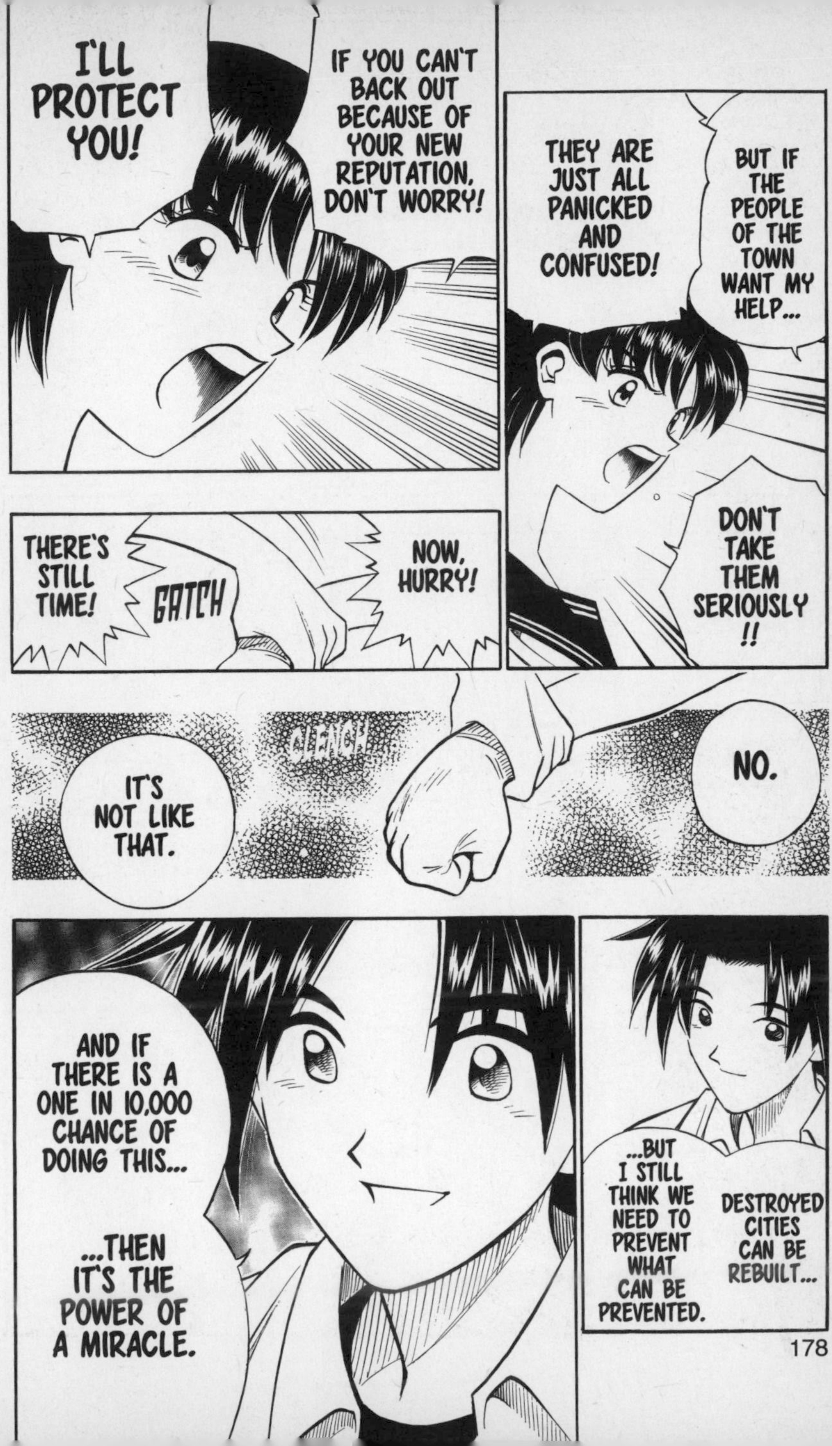

BUT IF THE PEOPLE OF THE TOWN WANT MY HELP...
THEY ARE JUST ALL PANICKED AND CONFUSED!
DON'T TAKE THEM SERIOUSLY !!
IF YOU CAN'T BACK OUT BECAUSE OF YOUR NEW REPUTATION, DON'T WORRY!
I'LL PROTECT YOU!
NOW, HURRY!
GATCH
THERE'S STILL TIME!
NO.
CLENCH
IT'S NOT LIKE THAT.
DESTROYED CITIES CAN BE REBUILT...
...BUT I STILL THINK WE NEED TO PREVENT WHAT CAN BE PREVENTED.
AND IF THERE IS A ONE IN 10,000 CHANCE OF DOING THIS...
...THEN IT'S THE POWER OF A MIRACLE.

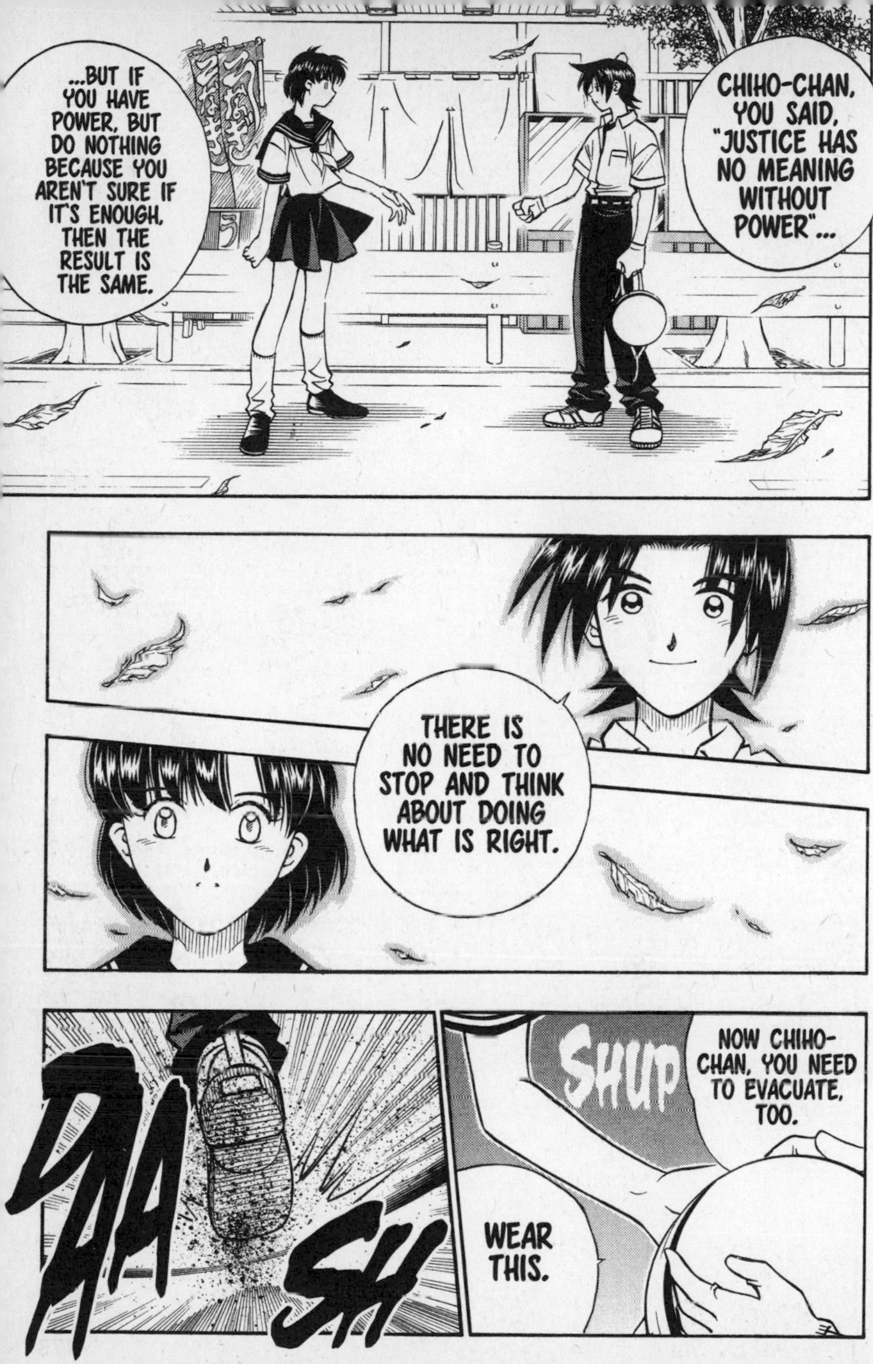
CHIHO-CHAN, YOU SAID, "JUSTICE HAS NO MEANING WITHOUT POWER"...
...BUT IF YOU HAVE POWER, BUT DO NOTHING BECAUSE YOU AREN'T SURE IF IT'S ENOUGH, THEN THE RESULT IS THE SAME.
THERE IS NO NEED TO STOP AND THINK ABOUT DOING WHAT IS RIGHT.
SHUP
NOW CHIHO-CHAN, YOU NEED TO EVACUATE, TOO.
WEAR THIS.
DASH

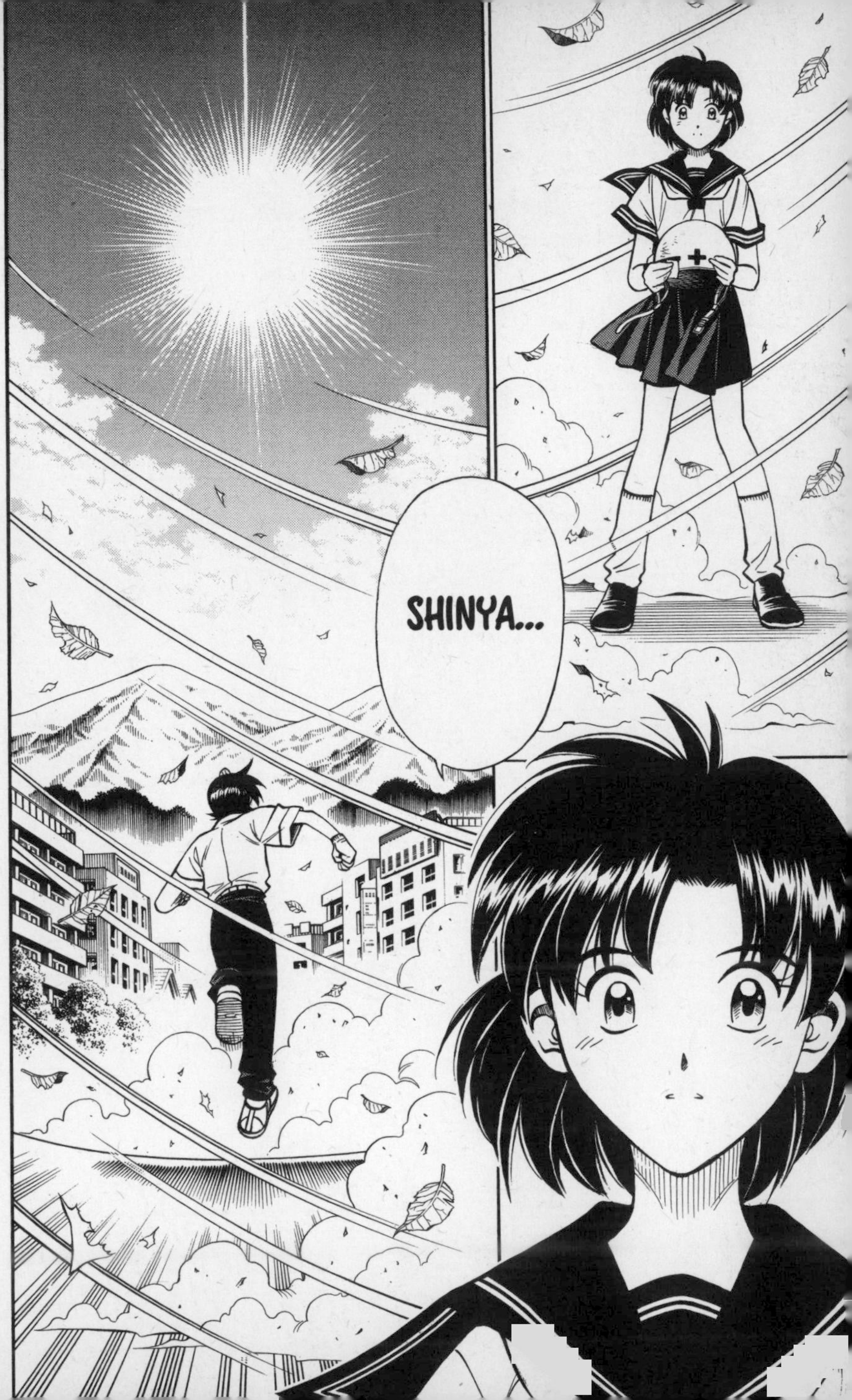
SHINYA...

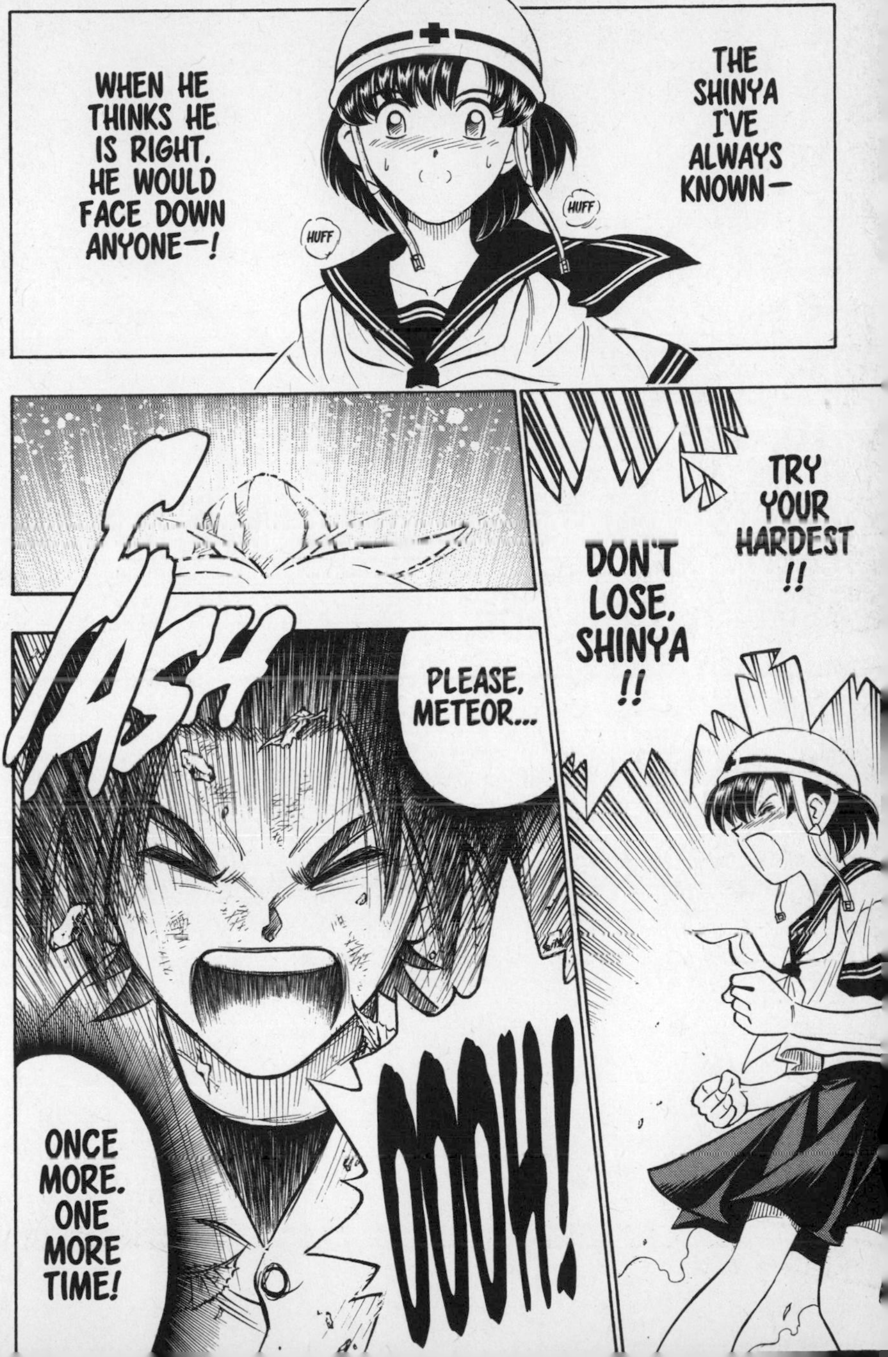
THE SHINYA I'VE ALWAYS KNOWN—
WHEN HE THINKS HE IS RIGHT, HE WOULD FACE DOWN ANYONE—!
HUFF
HUFF
TRY YOUR HARDEST!!
DON'T LOSE, SHINYA!!
ASH
PLEASE, METEOR...
OOOH!
ONCE MORE. ONE MORE TIME!

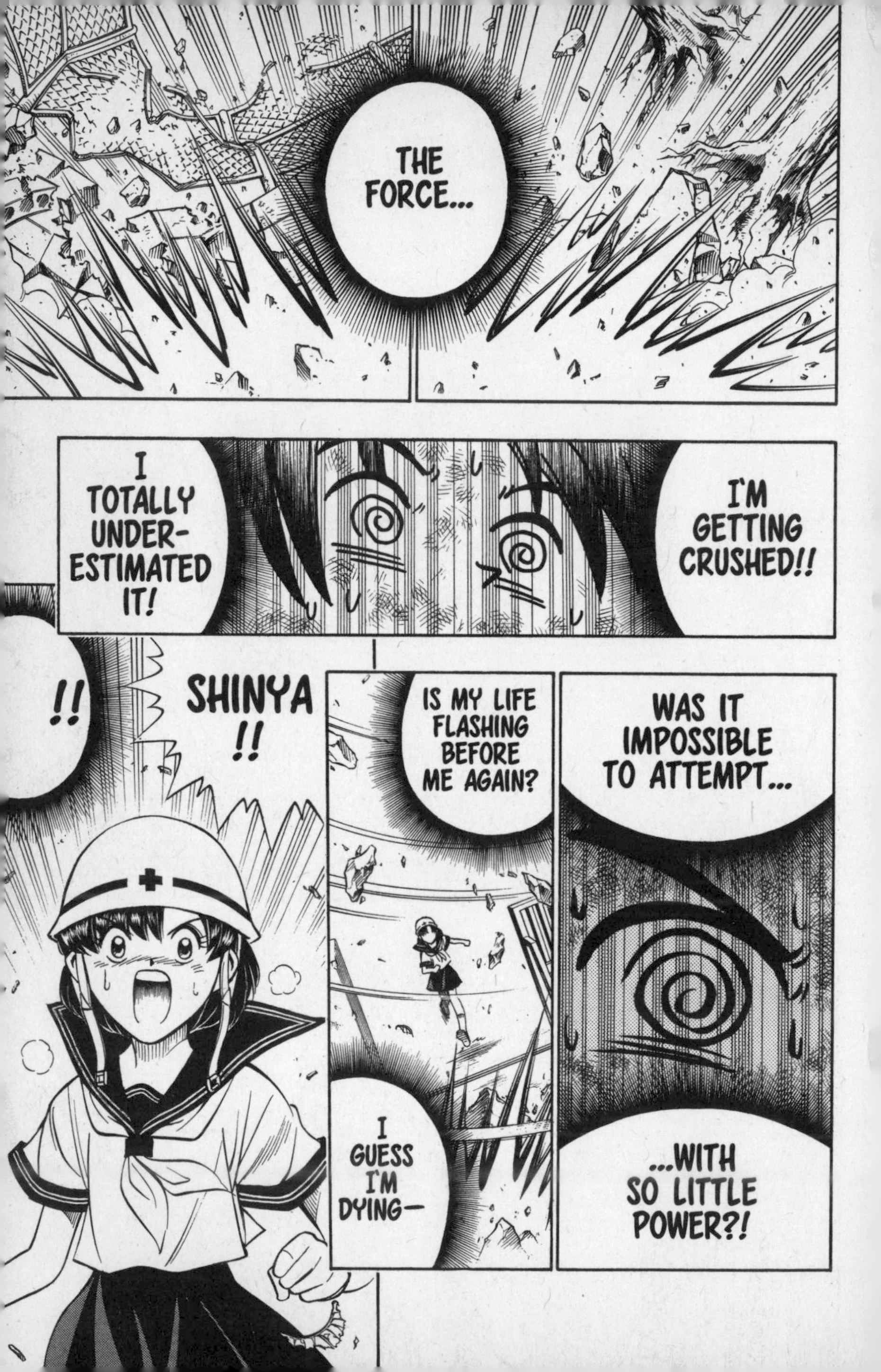
THE FORCE...
I'M GETTING CRUSHED!!
I TOTALLY UNDER-ESTIMATED IT!
WAS IT IMPOSSIBLE TO ATTEMPT...
...WITH SO LITTLE POWER?!
IS MY LIFE FLASHING BEFORE ME AGAIN?
I GUESS I'M DYING—
SHINYA!!
!!

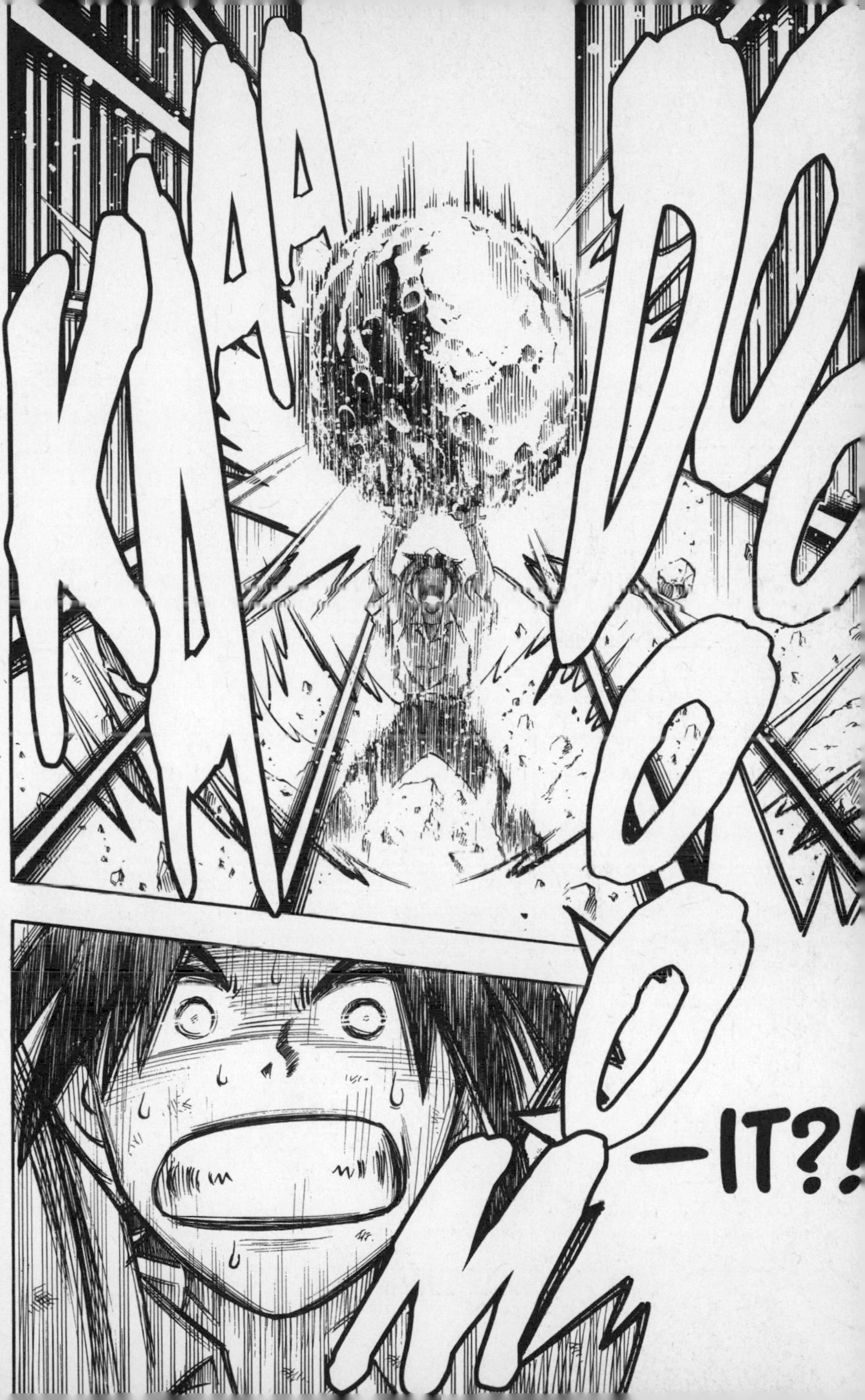
—IT?!

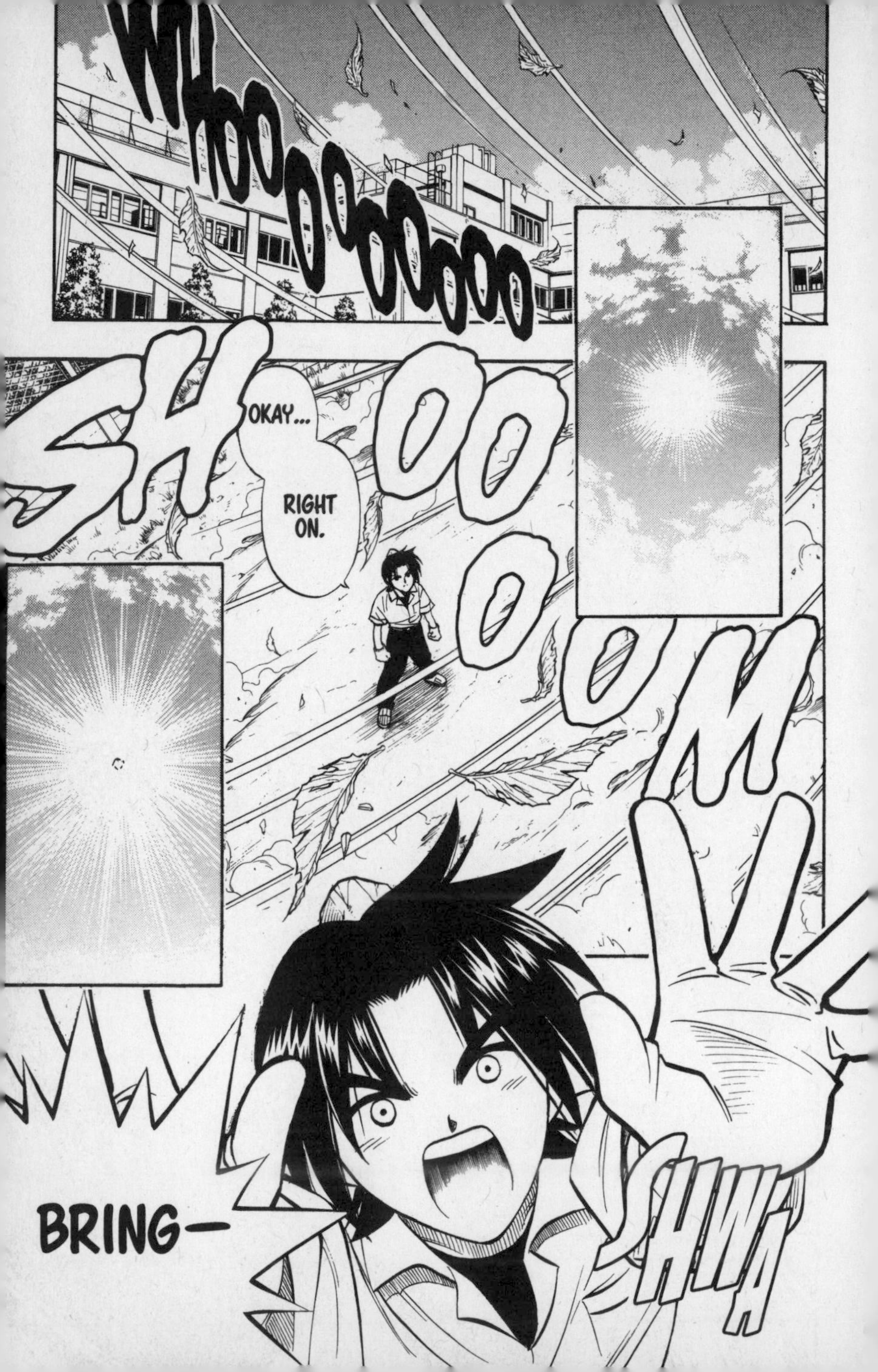
WHOOOOOOOOO
SHOOOOM
OKAY...
RIGHT ON.
BRING—
SHWA

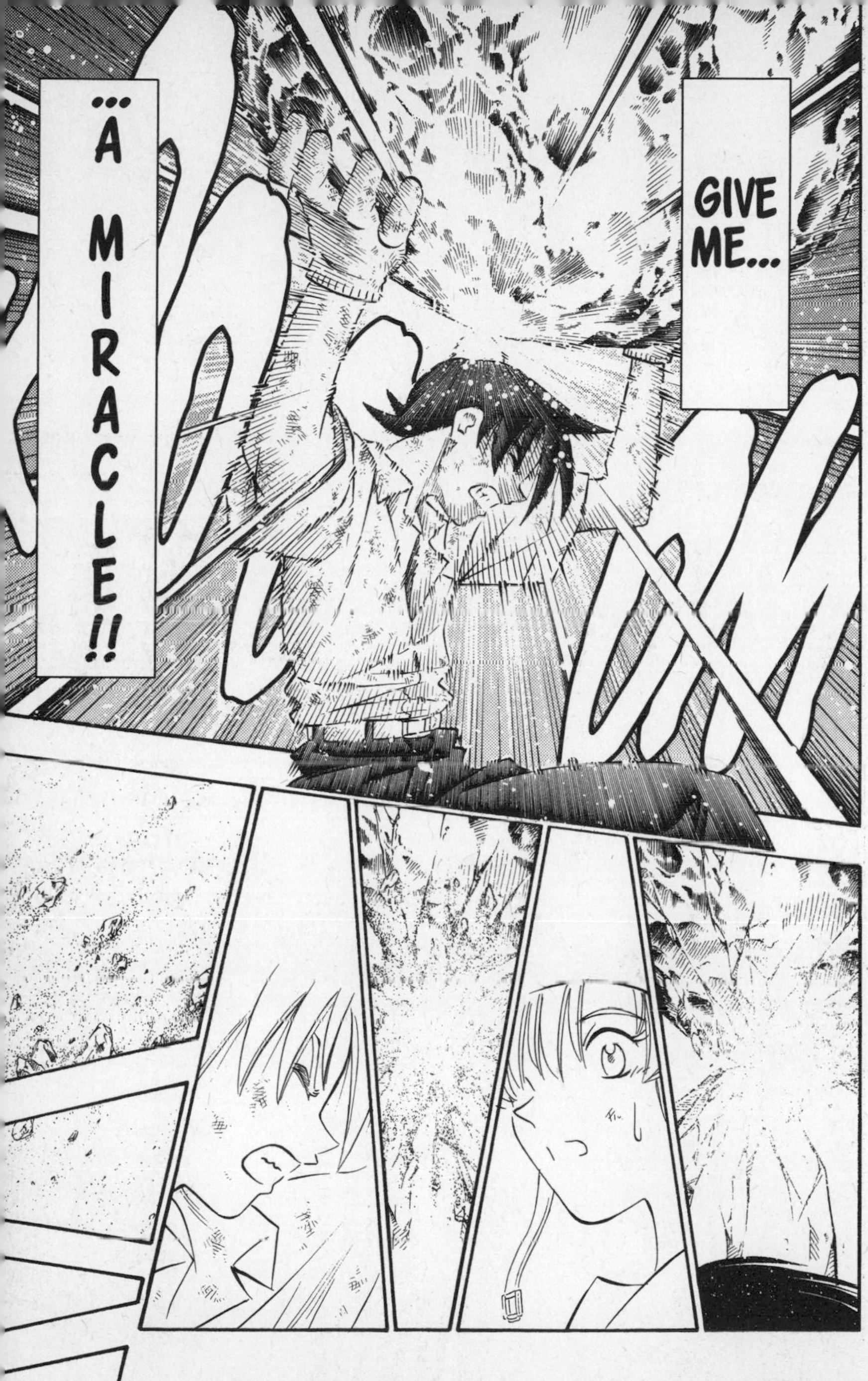
GIVE ME...
...A MIRACLE!!

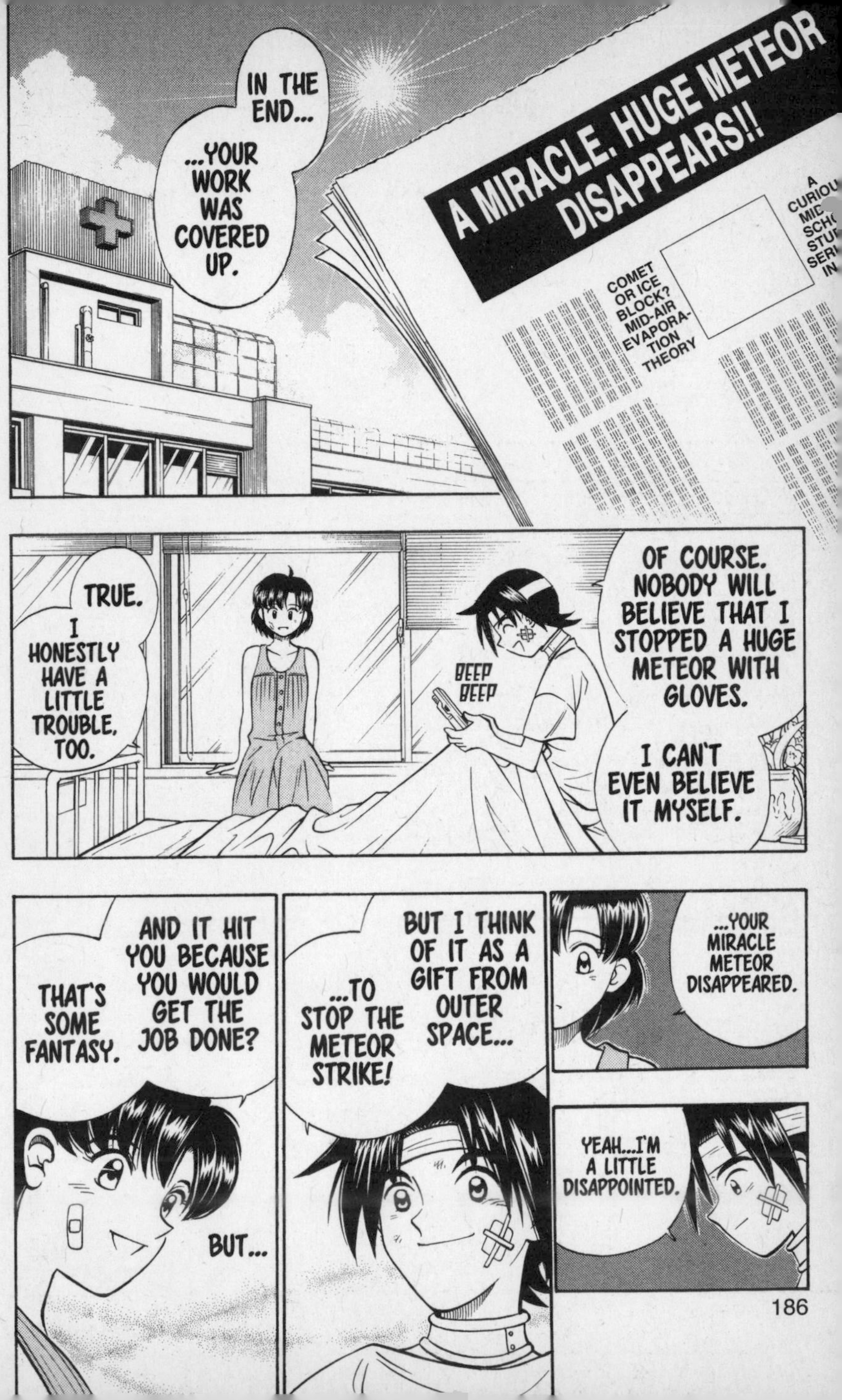
A MIRACLE, HUGE METEOR DISAPPEARS!!
COMET OR ICE BLOCK? MID-AIR EVAPORATION THEORY
IN THE END...
...YOUR WORK WAS COVERED UP.
OF COURSE. NOBODY WILL BELIEVE THAT I STOPPED A HUGE METEOR WITH GLOVES.
I CAN'T EVEN BELIEVE IT MYSELF.
BEEP BEEP
TRUE.
I HONESTLY HAVE A LITTLE TROUBLE, TOO.
...YOUR MIRACLE METEOR DISAPPEARED.
YEAH...I'M A LITTLE DISAPPOINTED.
BUT I THINK OF IT AS A GIFT FROM OUTER SPACE...
...TO STOP THE METEOR STRIKE!
AND IT HIT YOU BECAUSE YOU WOULD GET THE JOB DONE?
THAT'S SOME FANTASY.
BUT...

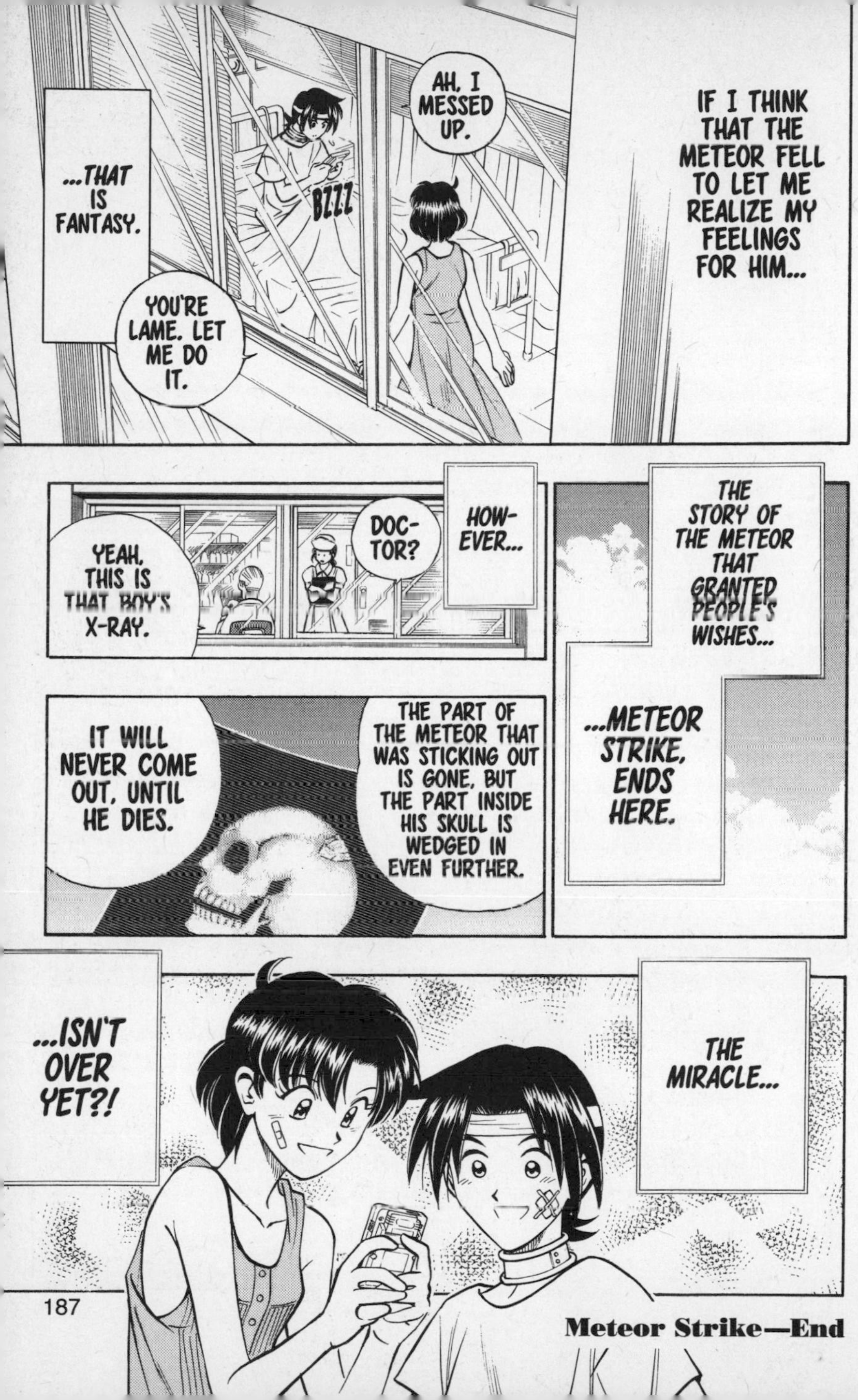
IF I THINK THAT THE METEOR FELL TO LET ME REALIZE MY FEELINGS FOR HIM...
AH, I MESSED UP.
...THAT IS FANTASY.
BZZZ
YOU'RE LAME. LET ME DO IT.
THE STORY OF THE METEOR THAT GRANTED PEOPLE'S WISHES...
...METEOR STRIKE, ENDS HERE.
HOW-EVER...
DOC-TOR?
YEAH, THIS IS THAT BOY'S X-RAY.
THE PART OF THE METEOR THAT WAS STICKING OUT IS GONE, BUT THE PART INSIDE HIS SKULL IS WEDGED IN EVEN FURTHER.
IT WILL NEVER COME OUT, UNTIL HE DIES.
THE MIRACLE...
...ISN'T OVER YET?!
Meteor Strike—End

Afterword

Thank you for reading until the very end. *Rurouni Kenshin—Meiji Swordsman Romantic Story* ends here.

This series started with the objective to "continue for 30 weeks. I will do my best in that time, and learn what I can, using it for my next series." But it ended up lasting five and a half years, or seven years if you start counting from the short story.

Many things have happened during publication. I received an overwhelming amount of mail. Volume one sold out in a blink, and a reprint was issued right away. A CD book was made, and the anime version. I took ten pills at a time to stay awake, and almost passed out. There was a parting of ways with the first chief assistant due to a difference of opinions, and getting depressed after that, and fleeing from work. But deadlines forced me to come back three hours later to finish the work, and cry afterward. I spent endless time thinking about the fine line between plagiarism and inspiration, and the difference between an amateur and a professional. I spoke to many other artists, and got excited, or got depressed. And there was the joy and grief of the survey ranking. And finally, I decided when to end the series. A lot happened, but everything was something I "learned from."

I'll use what I learned on the next project, so I can learn some more! I will try my hardest.

Finally, a professional's work is simultaneously art and merchandise. Because it is merchandise, the buyer is free to enjoy it in whatever way they want. People can read it as a time-killer on the way to work/school, throw it away when they get tired of it, sell it to the used book store... It's all up to the buyer.

However, Watsuki hopes *Rurouni Kenshin—Meiji Swordsman Romantic Story* has a long life in a corner of your bookshelf, though I know this is part of the author's ego.

If it becomes like the manga Watsuki bought during his childhood which still remains on his bookshelf, there could be no greater happiness.

A day in October, 1999, from the studio.
Nobuhiro Watsuki

GLOSSARY of the RESTORATION

A brief guide to select Japanese terms used in **Rurouni Kenshin***. Note that, both here and within the story itself, all names are Japanese style—i.e., last or "family" name first, with personal or "given" name following. This is both because* **Kenshin** *is a "period" story, as well as to decrease confusion—if we were to take the example of Kenshin's* sakabatô *and "reverse" the format of the historically established assassin-name "Hitokiri Battôsai," for example, it would make little sense to then call him "Battôsai Himura."*

Hiten Mitsurugi-ryû
Kenshin's sword technique, used more for defense than offense. An "ancient style that pits one against many," it requires exceptional speed and agility to master.

hitokiri
An assassin. Famous swordsmen of the period were sometimes thus known to adopt "professional" names—**Kawakami Gensai**, for example, was also known as "Hitokiri Gensai."

Ishin Shishi
Loyalist or pro-Imperialist **patriots** who fought to restore the Emperor to his ancient seat of power

jinchû
Hitokiri were fond of the word *tenchû*, or "judgment from the heavens," which expressed their belief that judgment lay in their hands. Enishi calls his form of revenge **jinchû**, meaning that if the heavens won't cast judgment on Kenshin, he will with his own brand of justice.

Kamiya Kasshin-ryû
Sword-arts or *kenjutsu* school established by Kaoru's father, who rejected the ethics of **Satsujin-ken** for **Katsujin-ken**

Katsujin-ken
"Swords that give life"; the sword-arts style developed over ten years by Kaoru's father and founding principle of **Kamiya Kasshin-ryû**

Kawakami Gensai
Real-life, historical inspiration for the character of **Himura Kenshin**

aku
Kanji character for "evil," worn by Sanosuke as a remembrance of his beloved, betrayed Captain Sagara and the *Sekihô* Army

Bakumatsu
Final, chaotic days of the Tokugawa regime

castella
Sponge cake said to be of Portuguese origin

-chan
Honorific. Can be used either as a diminutive (e.g., with a small child— "Little Hanako or Kentarô"), or with those who are grown, to indicate affection ("My dear...").

-dono
Honorific. Even more respectful than **-san**; the effect in modern-day Japanese conversation would be along the lines of "Milord So-and-So." As used by Kenshin, it indicates both respect and humility.

Edo
Capital city of the **Tokugawa Bakufu**; renamed **Tokyo** ("Eastern Capital") after the Meiji Restoration

Himura Kenshin
Kenshin's "real" name, revealed to Kaoru only at her urging

Satsujin-ken
"Swords that give death"; a style of swordsmanship rejected by Kaoru's father

Shinsengumi
Elite, notorious, government-sanctioned and exceptionally skilled swordsman-supporters of the military government (**Bakufu**) which had ruled Japan for nearly 250 years, the **Shinsengumi** ("newly selected corps") were established in 1863 to suppress the **loyalists** and to restore law and order to the blood-soaked streets of **Kyoto**

shôgun
Feudal military ruler of Japan

shôgunate
See **Tokugawa Bakufu**

"Swift Death to Evil"
Although there is some debate on who originated the term (some say it was the personal slogan of Saitô Hajime; others hold it to be a more general motto of the Shinsengumi itself), a more liberal translation of *"Aku • Soku • Zan"* might be "Evil Unto Evil"...where, in this case, the "evil" would be beheading, or death.

Tokugawa Bakufu
Military feudal government which dominated Japan from 1603 to 1867

Tokyo
The renaming of *"Edo"* to *"Tokyo"* is a marker of the start of the **Meiji Restoration**

watô
Enishi's trademark weapon; along with its accompanying martial-art *Watôjutsu*, Enishi's *watô* combines the speed and sharpness of a Japanese blade with the power and grace of the continent

-kun
Honorific. Used in the modern day among male students, or those who grew up together, but another usage—the one you're more likely to find in *Rurouni Kenshin*—is the "superior-to-inferior" form, intended as a way to emphasize a difference in status or rank, as well as to indicate familiarity or affection.

Kyoto
Home of the Emperor and imperial court from A.D. 794 until shortly after the **Meiji Restoration** in 1868

loyalists
Those who supported the return of the Emperor to power; **Ishin Shishi**

Meiji Restoration
1853-1868; culminated in the collapse of the **Tokugawa Bakufu** and the restoration of imperial rule. So called after Emperor Meiji, whose chosen name was written with the characters for "culture and enlightenment."

patriots
Another term for **Ishin Shishi**... and, when used by Sano, not a flattering one

rurouni
Wanderer, vagabond

sakabatô
Reversed-edge sword (the dull edge on the side the sharp should be, and vice versa); carried by Kenshin as a symbol of his resolution never to kill again

-sama
Honorific. The respectful equivalent of *-san*, *-sama* is used primarily in addressing persons of much higher rank than one's self...or, in a romantic sense, in addressing those upon whom one is crushing, wicked hard.

-san
Honorific. Carries the meaning of "Mr.," "Ms.," "Miss," etc., but used more extensively in Japanese than its English equivalent (note that even an enemy may be addressed as *"-san"*).

SPECIAL MANGA PREVIEW!

The latest series from Nobuhiro Watsuki, the creator of Rurouni Kenshin!

Buso Renkin
ブソウレンキン

1
SHONEN JUMP ADVANCED
Story & Art by
NOBUHIRO WATSUKI

- Only $7.99

- On Sale August 2006

- What Kazuki thought was a dream turns out to be a living, breathing nightmare!

THE WORLD'S MOST CUTTING-EDGE MANGA

SHONEN JUMP ADVANCED

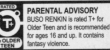

PARENTAL ADVISORY
BUSO RENKIN is rated T+ for Older Teen and is recommended for ages 16 and up. It contains fantasy violence.
RATED T+ FOR OLDER TEEN

High school student Kazuki Muto dies while trying to save a mysterious girl from a horrible demon, only to wake up the next morning and realize it was all a nightmare. But when he can't shake the strange feeling in his chest, Kazuki has to wonder...was it really just a dream? It isn't long before Kazuki learns the terrifying truth and finds himself entangled in a world of eerie monsters that can only be destroyed with the help of the *Buso Renkin*!

VIZ media

BUSOU RENKIN © 2003 by Nobuhiro Watsuki. All rights reserved.
First published in Japan in 2003 by SHUEISHA Inc., Tokyo.

CHAPTER 1: NEW LIFE

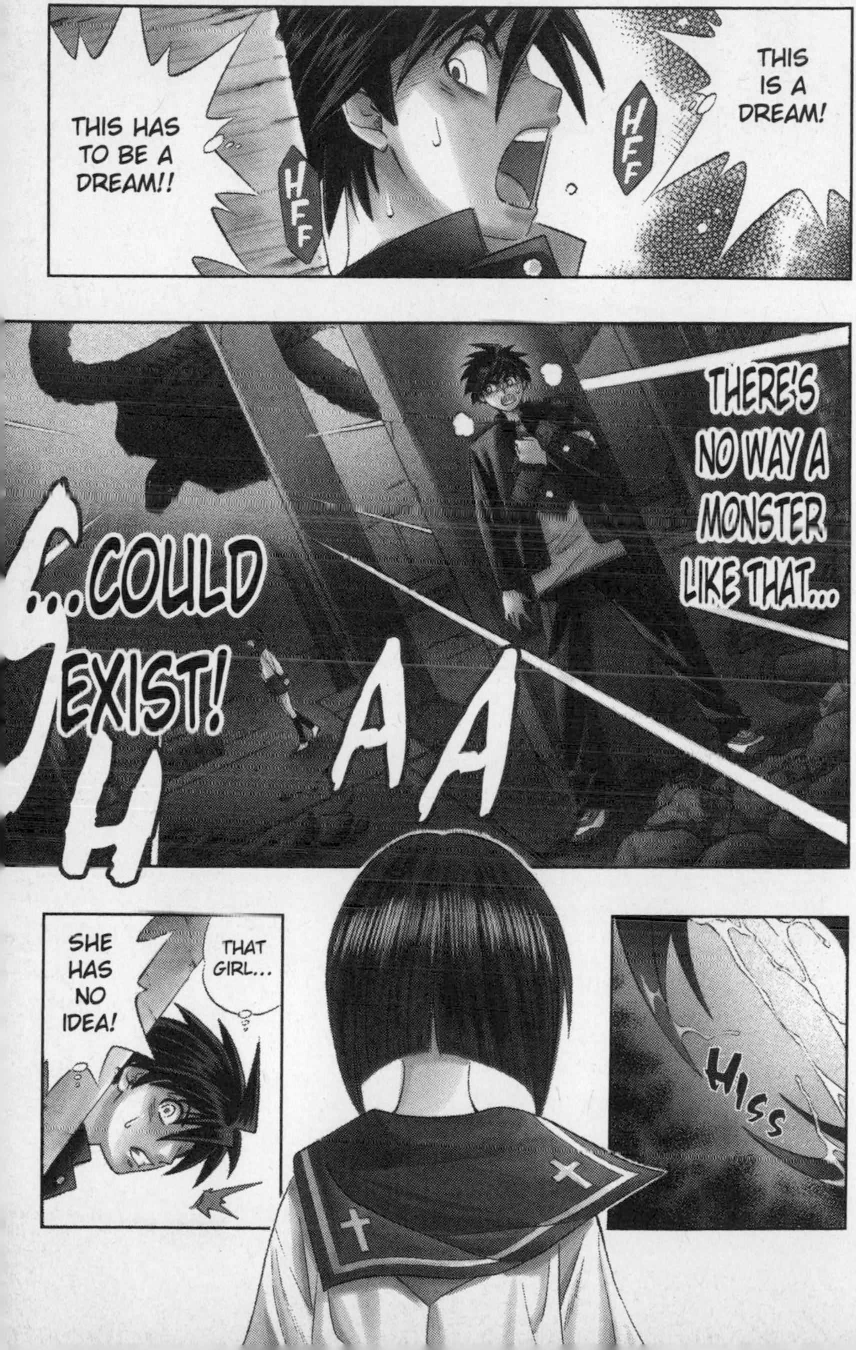
THIS IS A DREAM!
HFF
HFF
THIS HAS TO BE A DREAM!!
THERE'S NO WAY A MONSTER LIKE THAT...
...COULD EXIST!
HAAA
HISS
THAT GIRL...
SHE HAS NO IDEA!

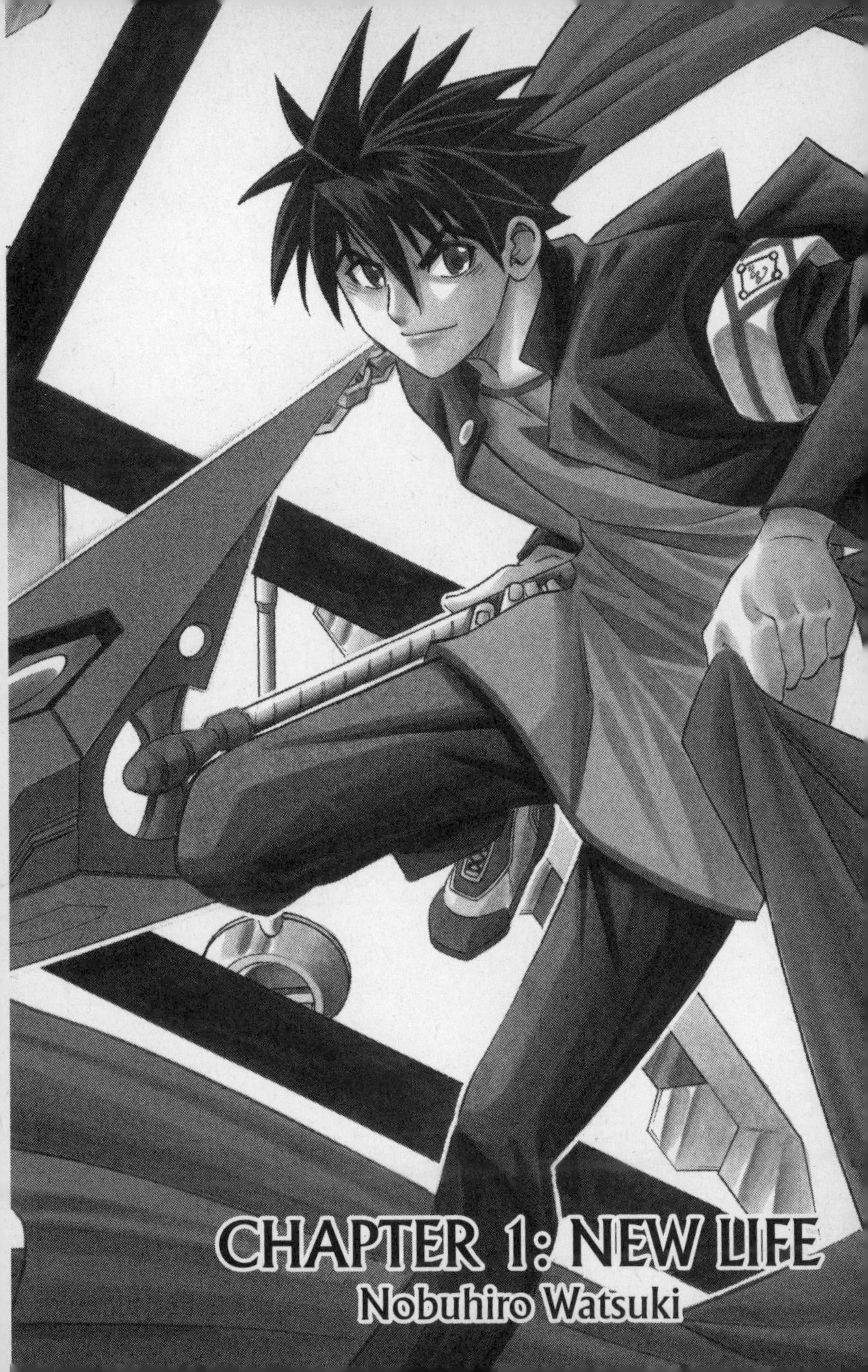
CHAPTER 1: NEW LIFE
Nobuhiro Watsuki

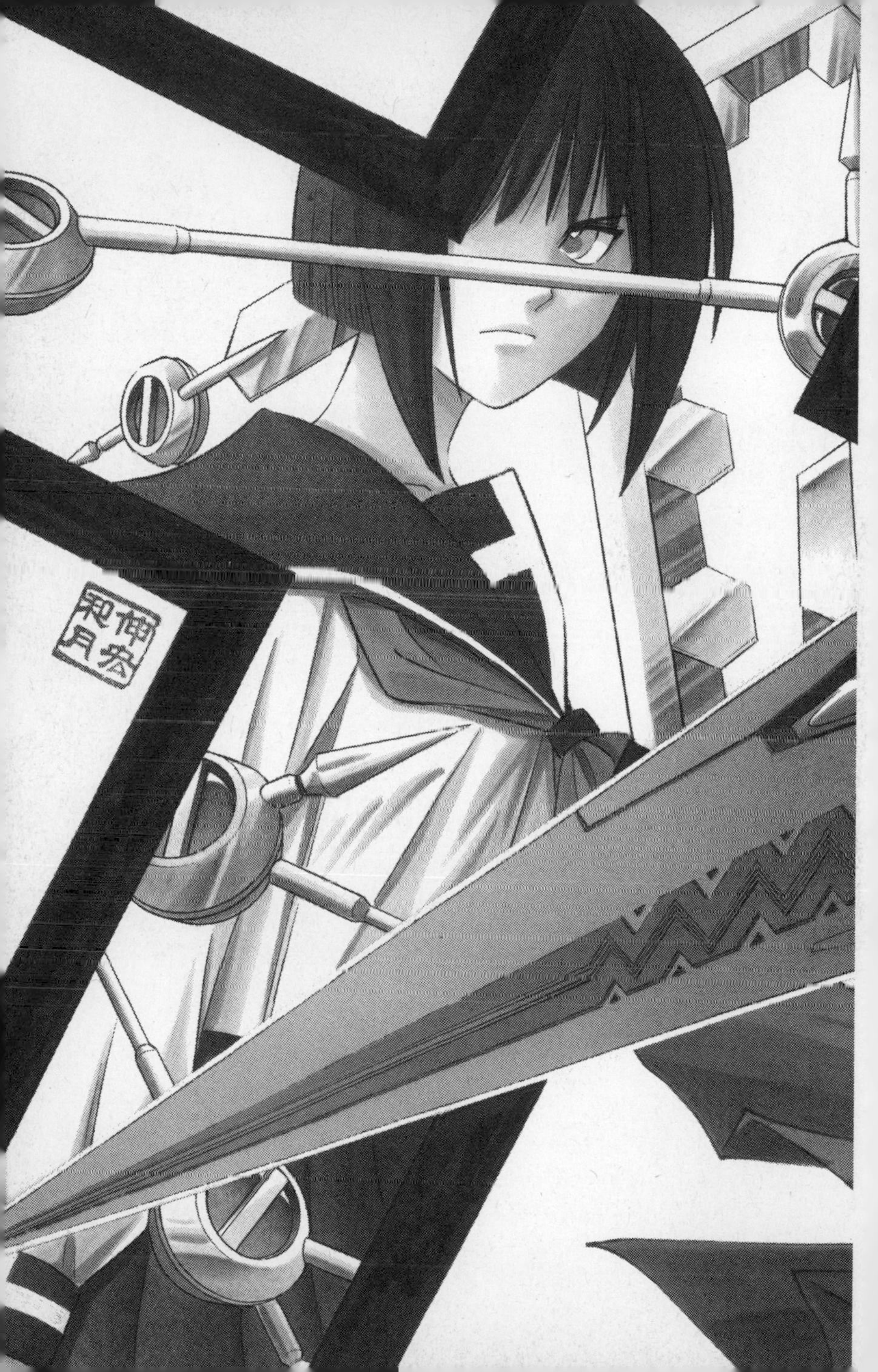
神谷和月

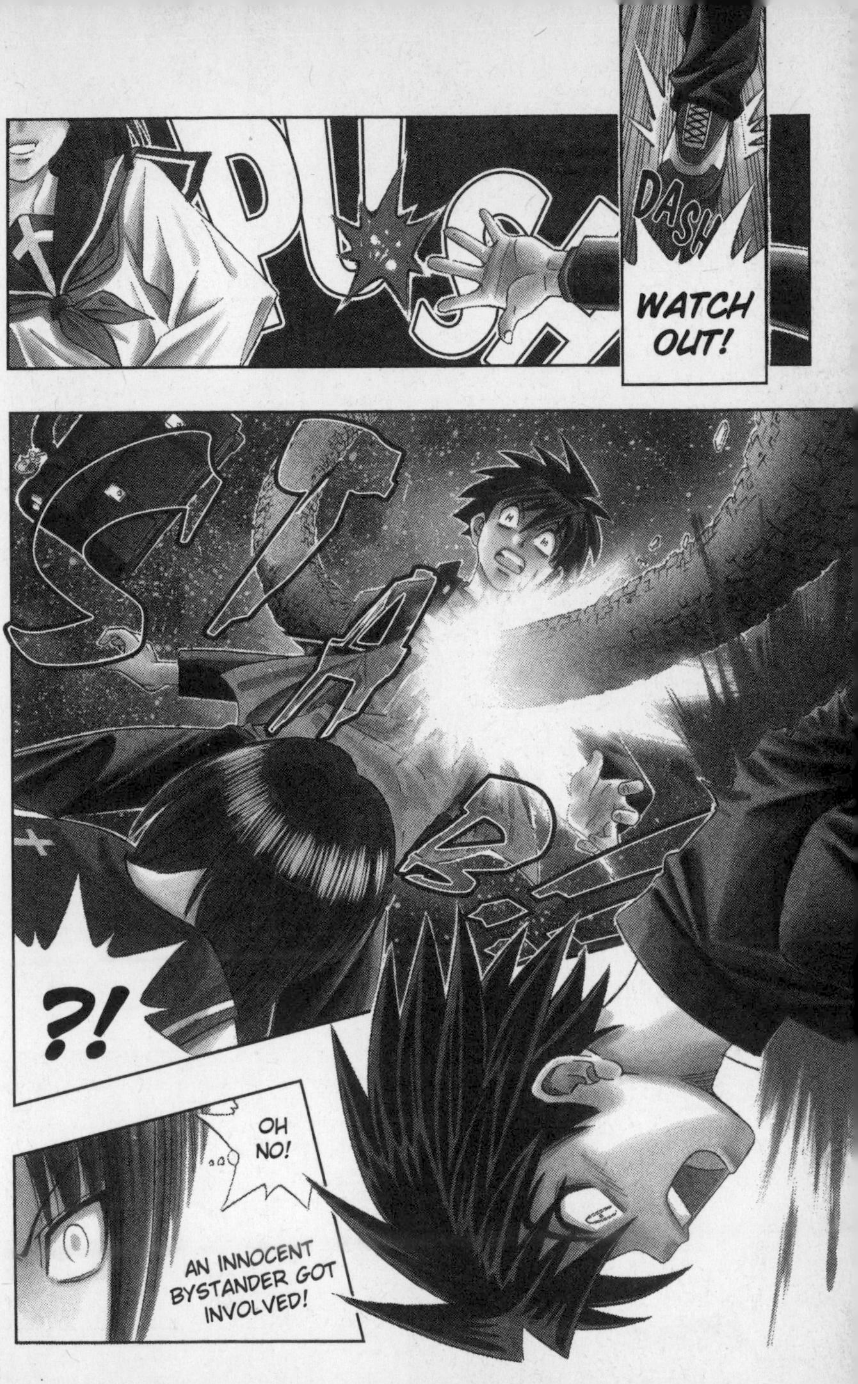
DASH
WATCH OUT!
?!
OH NO!
AN INNOCENT BYSTANDER GOT INVOLVED!

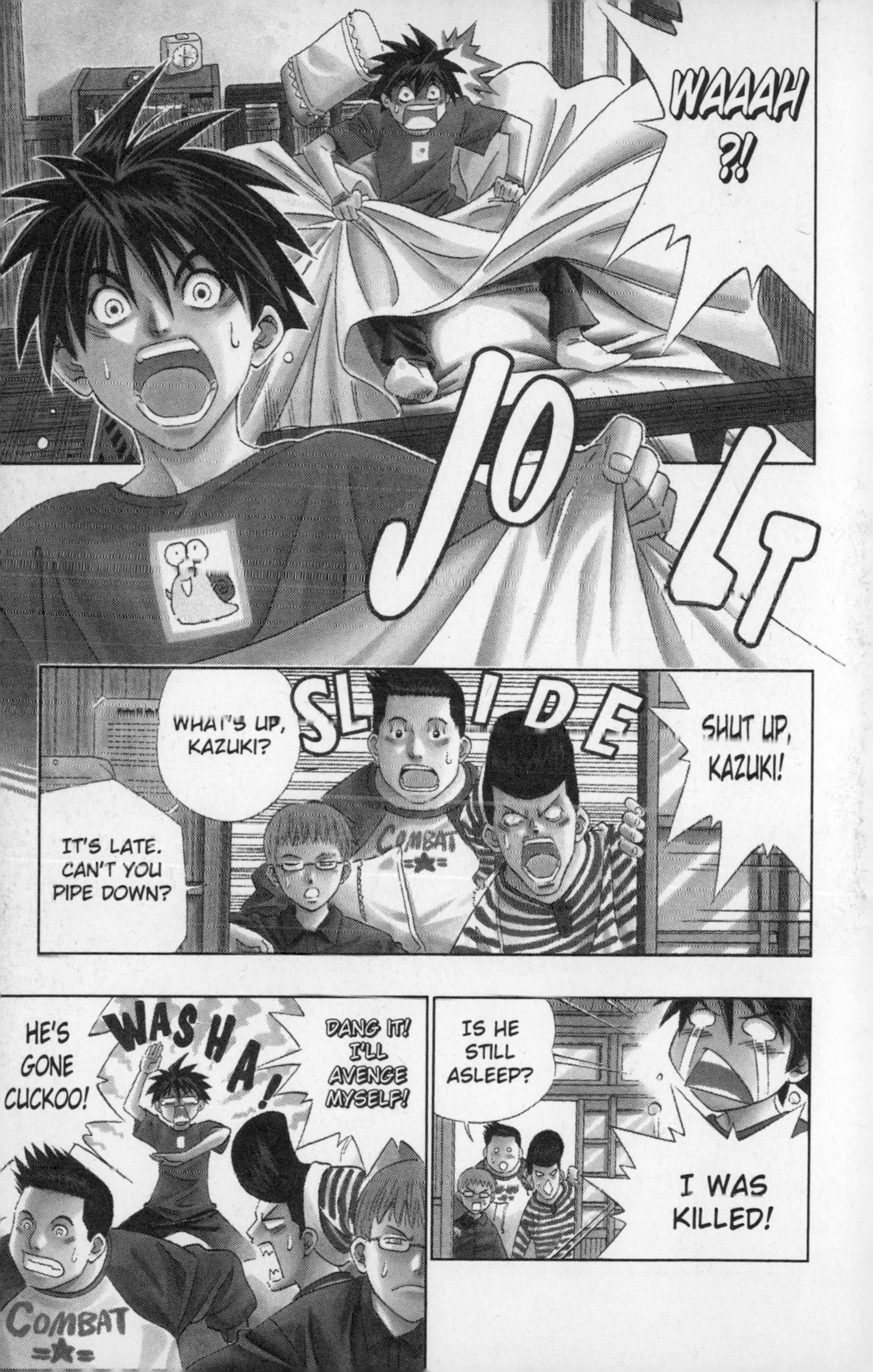
WAAAH ?!
JOLT
SHUT UP, KAZUKI!
SLIDE
WHAT'S UP, KAZUKI?
IT'S LATE. CAN'T YOU PIPE DOWN?
IS HE STILL ASLEEP?
I WAS KILLED!
DANG IT! I'LL AVENGE MYSELF!
WASHA!
HE'S GONE CUCKOO!
COMBAT

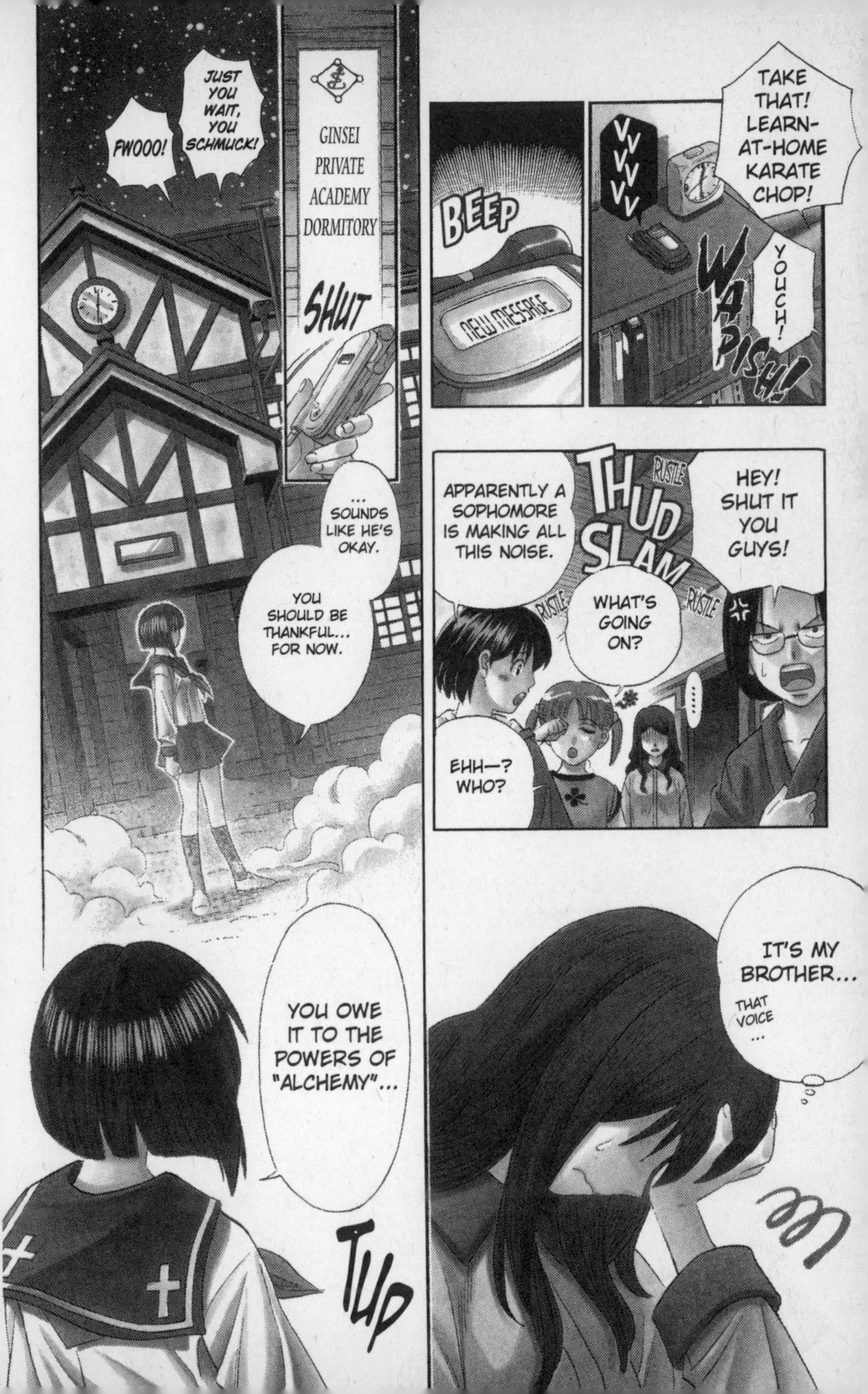
TAKE THAT! LEARN-AT-HOME KARATE CHOP!
VVVVVV
YOUCH!
WAPISH!
BEEP
NEW MESSAGE
HEY! SHUT IT YOU GUYS!
RUSTLE
THUD
SLAM
RUSTLE
APPARENTLY A SOPHOMORE IS MAKING ALL THIS NOISE.
WHAT'S GOING ON?
.....
EHH—? WHO?
JUST YOU WAIT, YOU SCHMUCK!
FWOOO!
GINSEI PRIVATE ACADEMY DORMITORY
SHUT
... SOUNDS LIKE HE'S OKAY.
YOU SHOULD BE THANKFUL... FOR NOW.
IT'S MY BROTHER...
THAT VOICE ...
YOU OWE IT TO THE POWERS OF "ALCHEMY"...
TUP

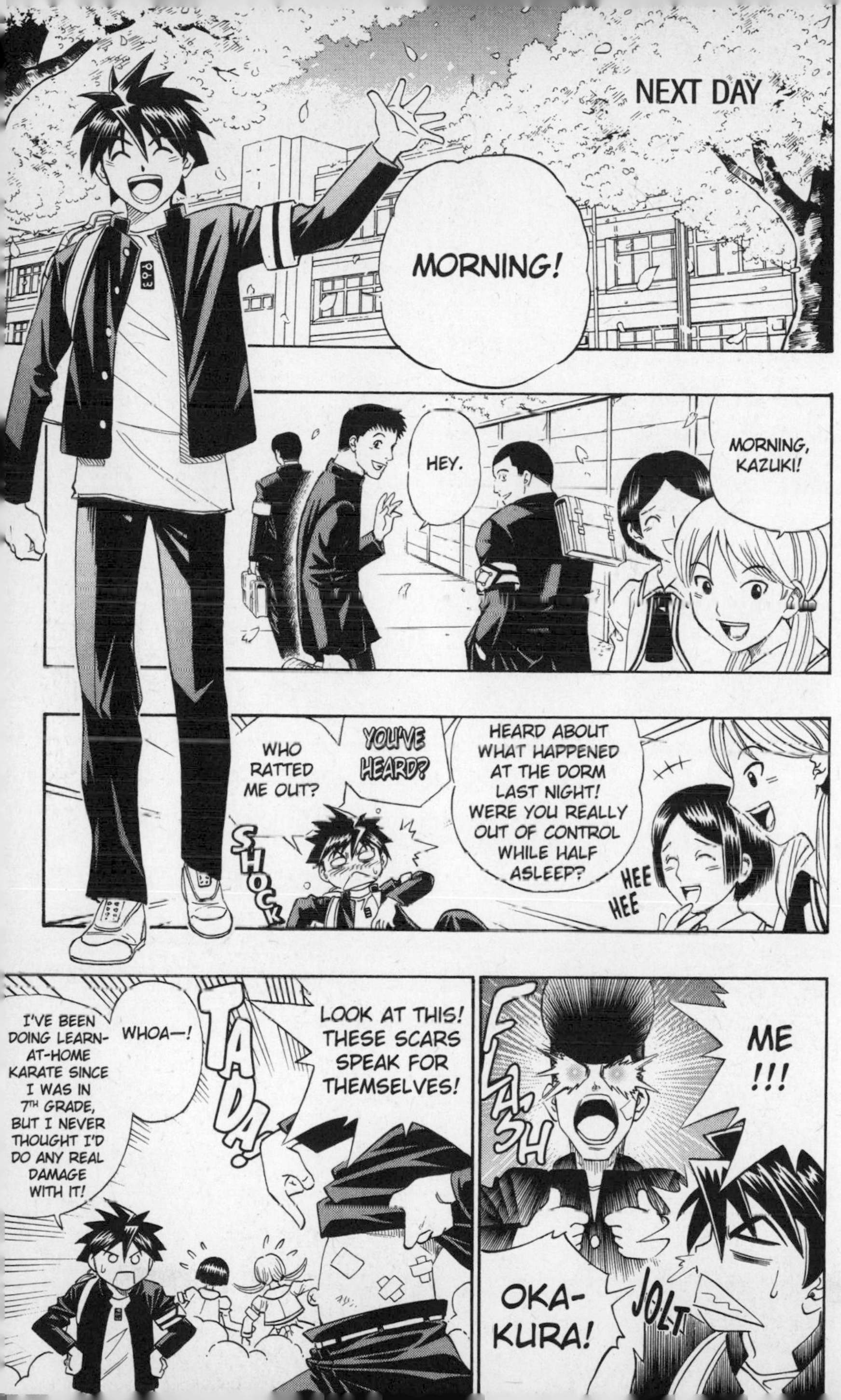
NEXT DAY
MORNING!
MORNING, KAZUKI!
HEY.
HEARD ABOUT WHAT HAPPENED AT THE DORM LAST NIGHT! WERE YOU REALLY OUT OF CONTROL WHILE HALF ASLEEP?
HEE HEE
YOU'VE HEARD?
WHO RATTED ME OUT?
SHOCK
ME !!!
FLASH
OKA-KURA!
JOLT
LOOK AT THIS! THESE SCARS SPEAK FOR THEMSELVES!
TA DA!
WHOA—!
I'VE BEEN DOING LEARN-AT-HOME KARATE SINCE I WAS IN 7TH GRADE, BUT I NEVER THOUGHT I'D DO ANY REAL DAMAGE WITH IT!

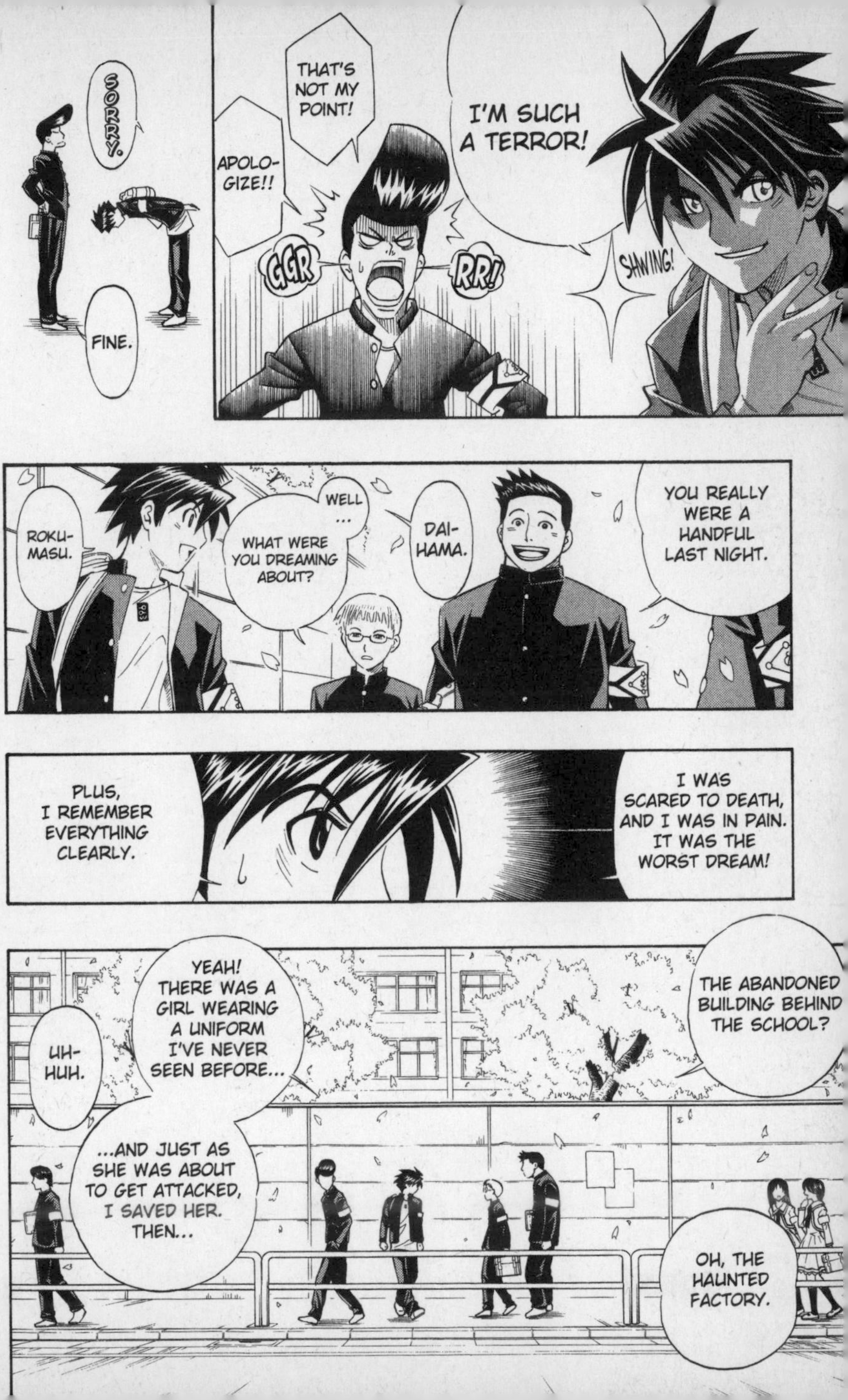
I'M SUCH A TERROR!
SHWING!
THAT'S NOT MY POINT!
APOLOGIZE!!
GGR
RR!
SORRY.
FINE.
YOU REALLY WERE A HANDFUL LAST NIGHT.
DAI-HAMA.
WELL ...
WHAT WERE YOU DREAMING ABOUT?
ROKU-MASU.
I WAS SCARED TO DEATH, AND I WAS IN PAIN. IT WAS THE WORST DREAM!
PLUS, I REMEMBER EVERYTHING CLEARLY.
THE ABANDONED BUILDING BEHIND THE SCHOOL?
OH, THE HAUNTED FACTORY.
YEAH! THERE WAS A GIRL WEARING A UNIFORM I'VE NEVER SEEN BEFORE...
UH-HUH.
...AND JUST AS SHE WAS ABOUT TO GET ATTACKED, I SAVED HER. THEN...

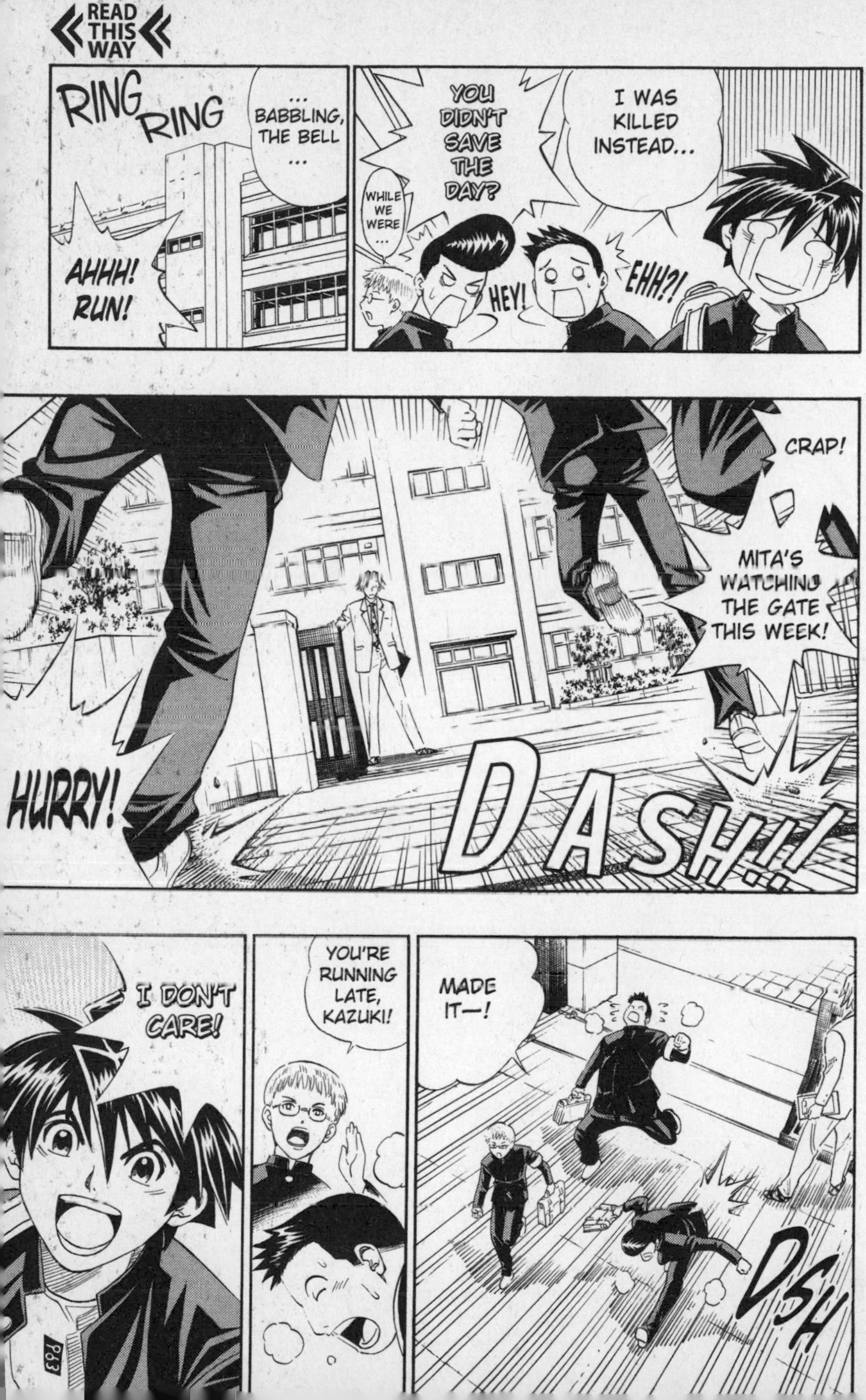
READ THIS WAY
I WAS KILLED INSTEAD...
EHH?!
YOU DIDN'T SAVE THE DAY?
HEY!
WHILE WE WERE ...
... BABBLING, THE BELL ...
RING RING
AHHH! RUN!
CRAP!
MITA'S WATCHING THE GATE THIS WEEK!
DASH!!
HURRY!
MADE IT—!
DSH
YOU'RE RUNNING LATE, KAZUKI!
I DON'T CARE!

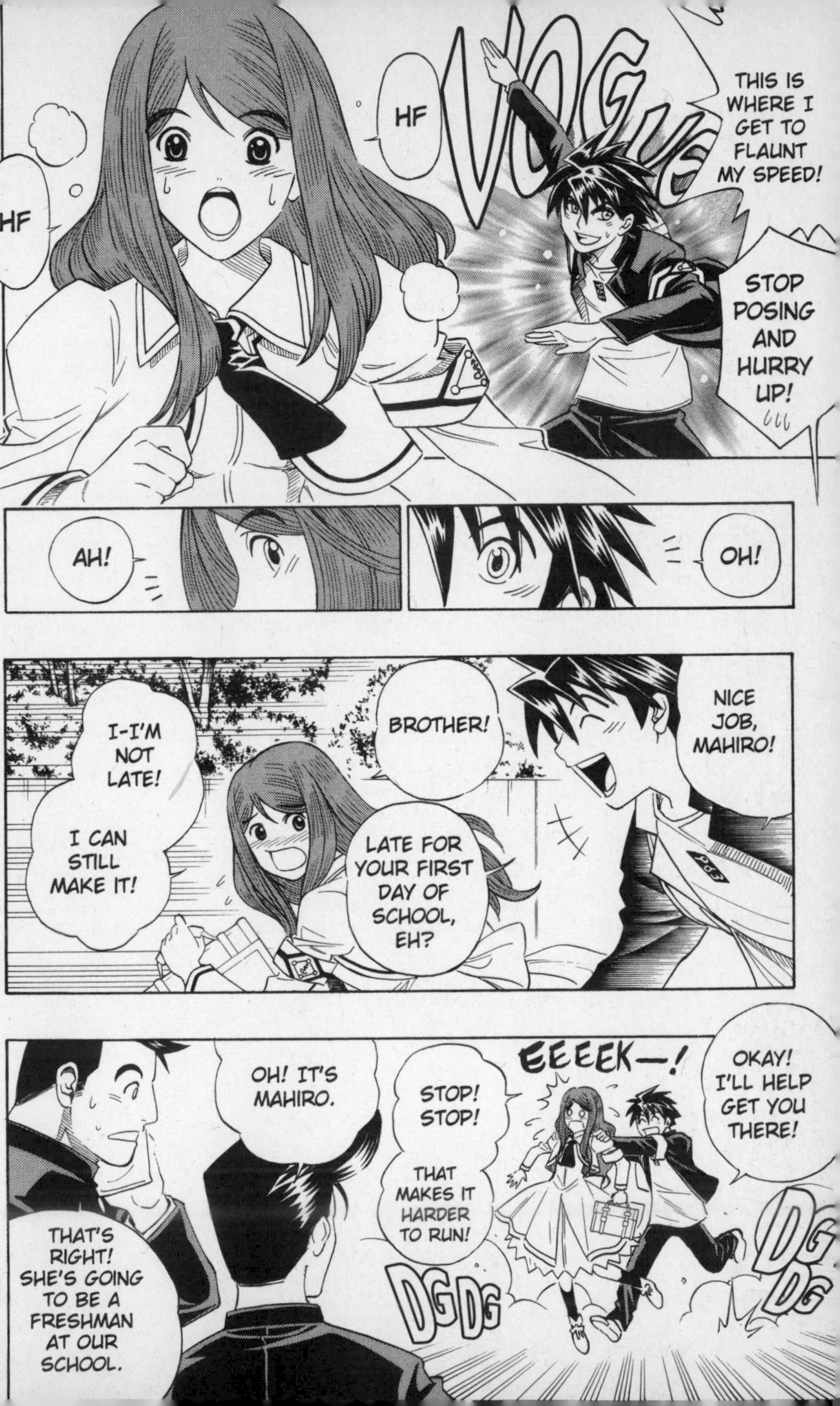
THIS IS WHERE I GET TO FLAUNT MY SPEED!
VOG
STOP POSING AND HURRY UP!
HF
HF
OH!
AH!
NICE JOB, MAHIRO!
BROTHER!
LATE FOR YOUR FIRST DAY OF SCHOOL, EH?
I-I'M NOT LATE!
I CAN STILL MAKE IT!
OKAY! I'LL HELP GET YOU THERE!
EEEEK—!
STOP! STOP!
THAT MAKES IT HARDER TO RUN!
DG DG
DGDG
OH! IT'S MAHIRO.
THAT'S RIGHT! SHE'S GOING TO BE A FRESHMAN AT OUR SCHOOL.

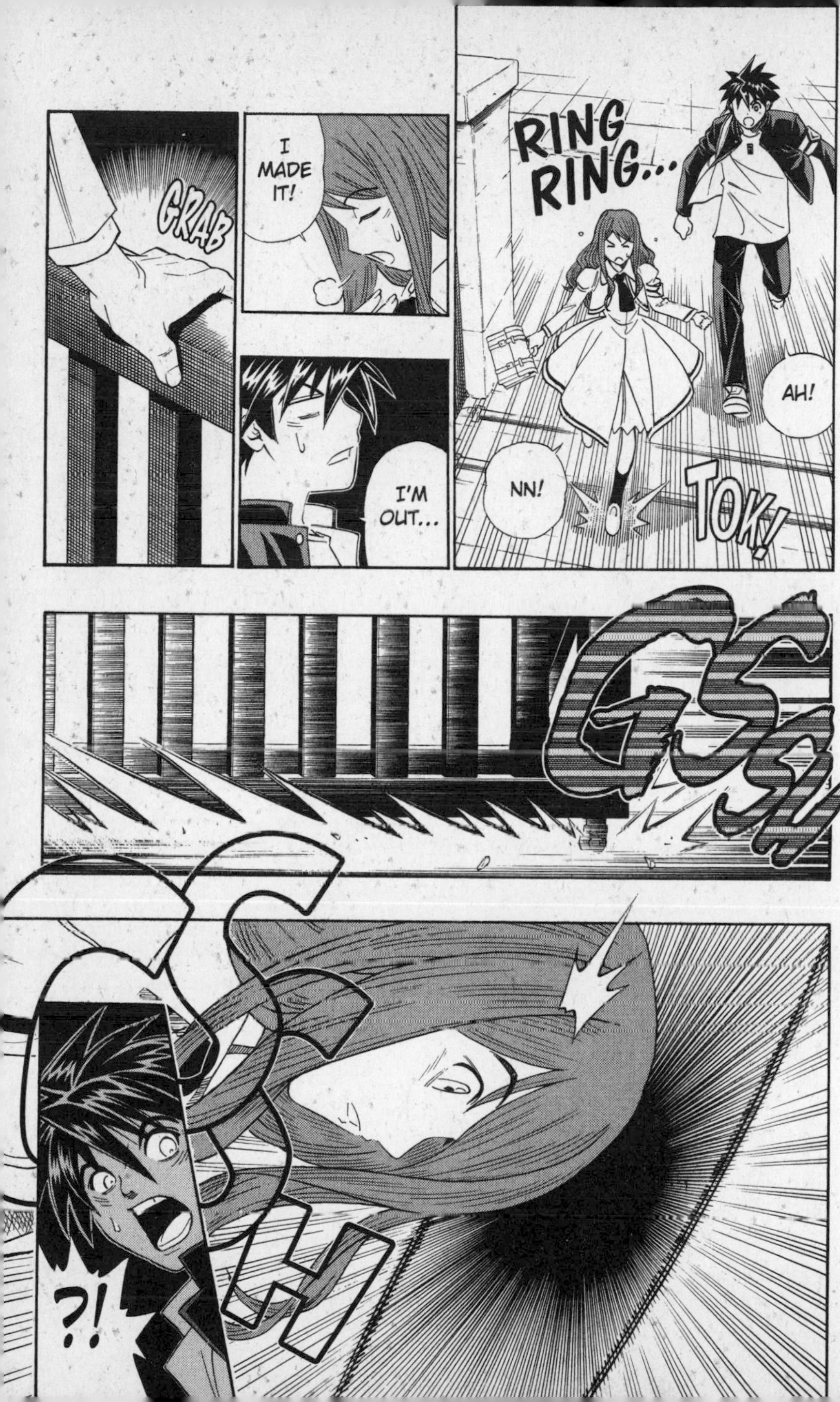
RING RING...
AH!
NN!
TOK!
I MADE IT!
I'M OUT...
GRAB
GASH
?!

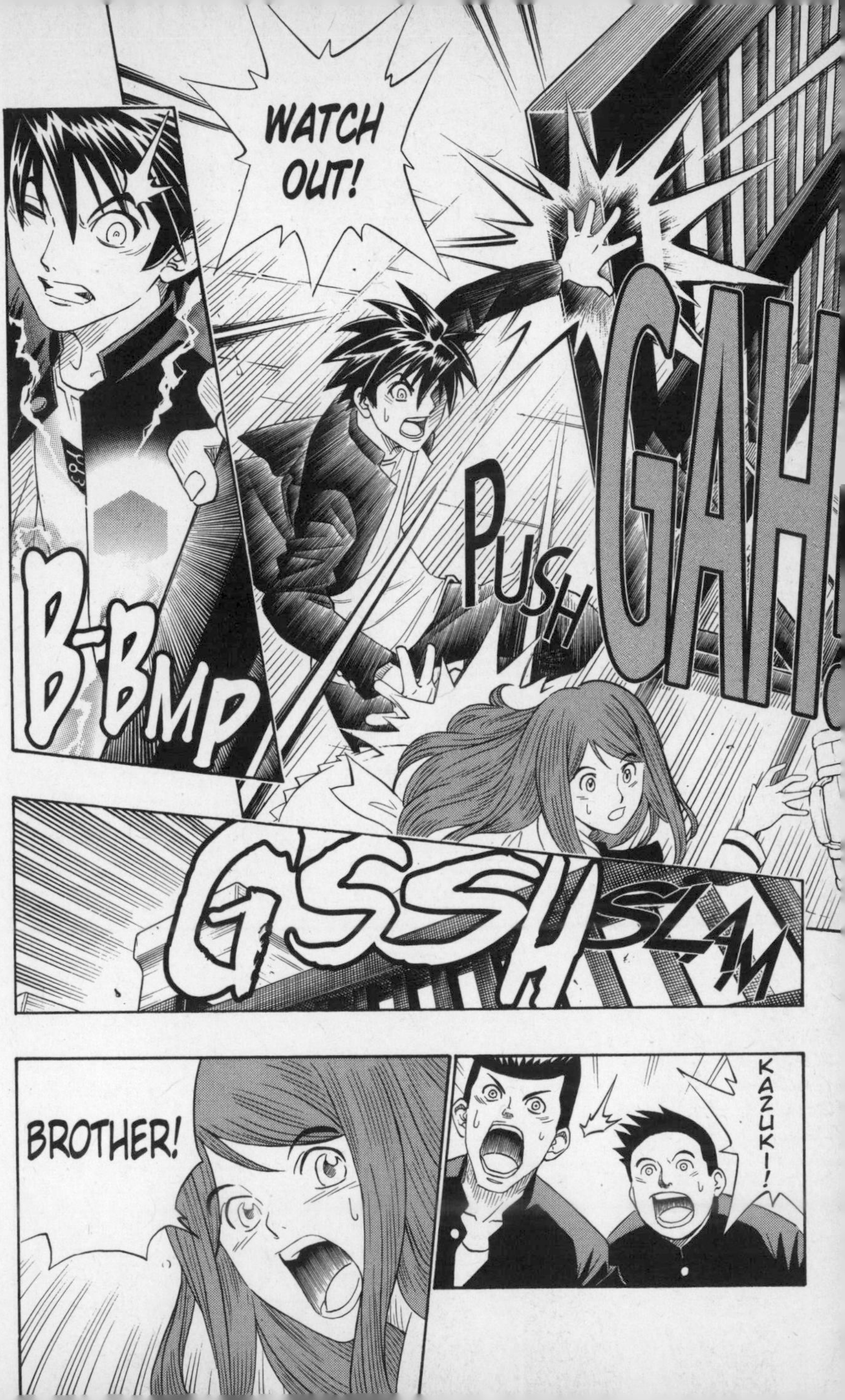
WATCH OUT!
GAH!
PUSH
B-BMP
GSSH
SLAM
KAZUKI!
BROTHER!

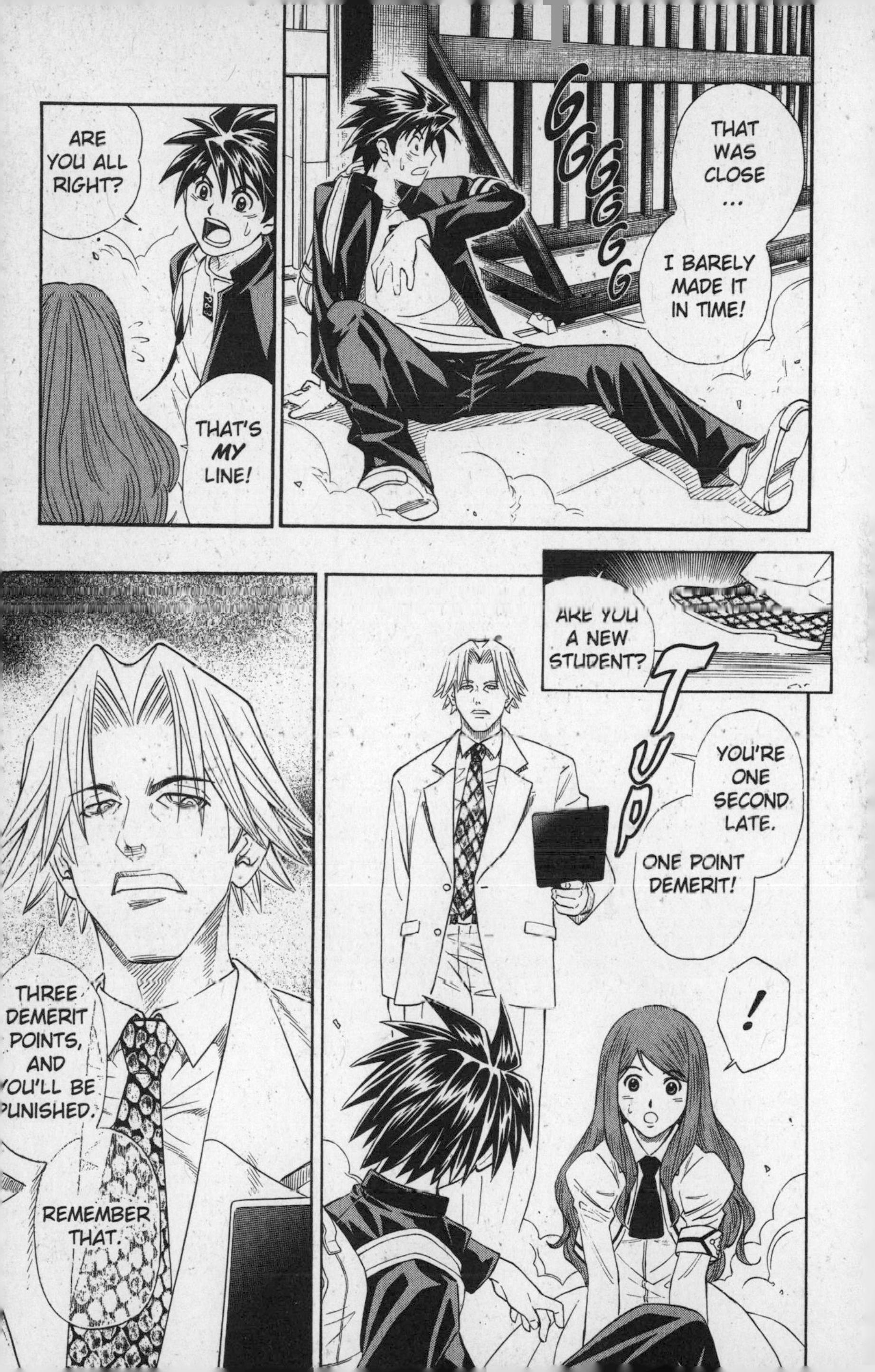
THAT WAS CLOSE ...
I BARELY MADE IT IN TIME!
GGGGGG
ARE YOU ALL RIGHT?
THAT'S MY LINE!
ARE YOU A NEW STUDENT?
TUP
YOU'RE ONE SECOND LATE.
ONE POINT DEMERIT!
!
THREE DEMERIT POINTS, AND YOU'LL BE PUNISHED.
REMEMBER THAT.

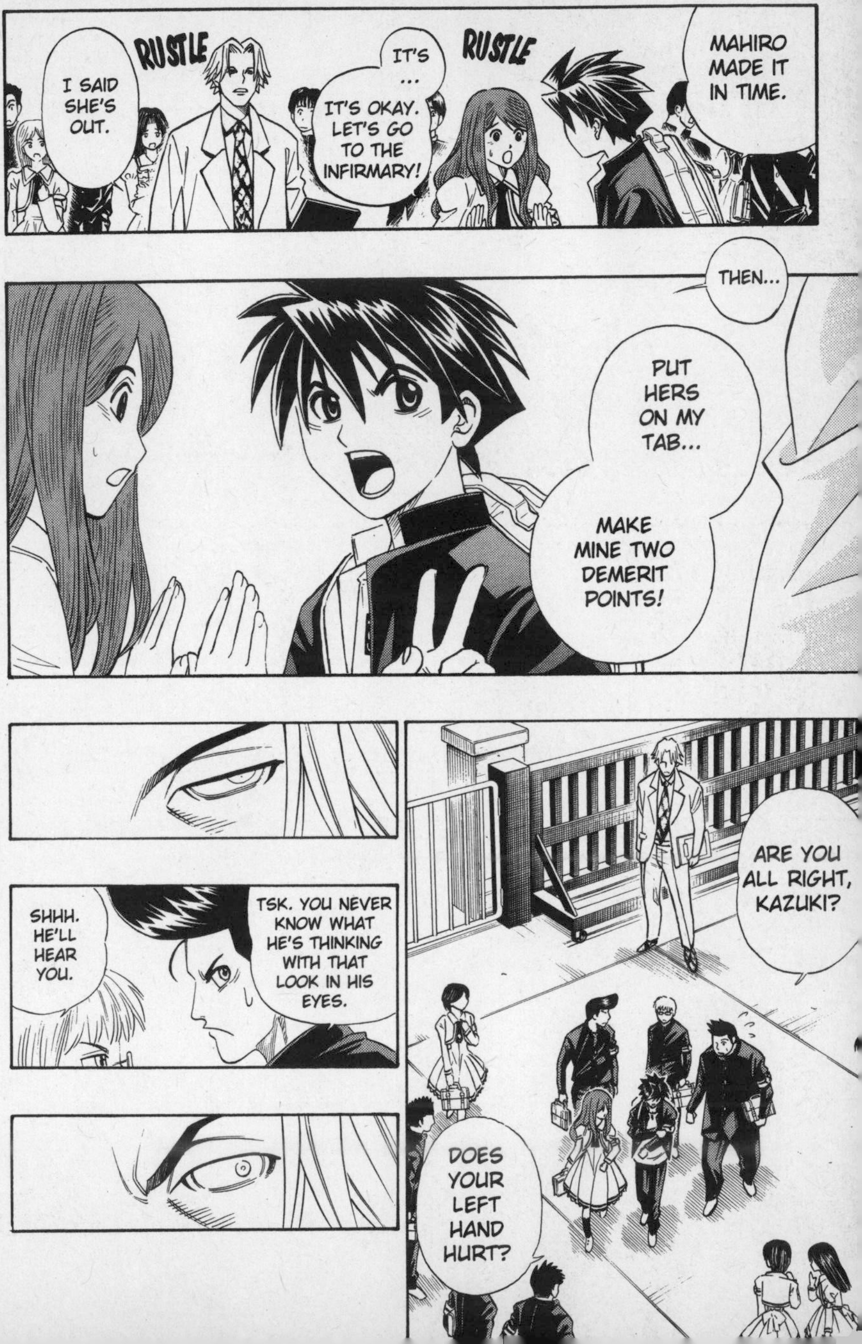
MAHIRO MADE IT IN TIME.
RUSTLE
IT'S ...
IT'S OKAY. LET'S GO TO THE INFIRMARY!
RUSTLE
I SAID SHE'S OUT.
THEN...
PUT HERS ON MY TAB...
MAKE MINE TWO DEMERIT POINTS!
ARE YOU ALL RIGHT, KAZUKI?
DOES YOUR LEFT HAND HURT?
TSK. YOU NEVER KNOW WHAT HE'S THINKING WITH THAT LOOK IN HIS EYES.
SHHH. HE'LL HEAR YOU.

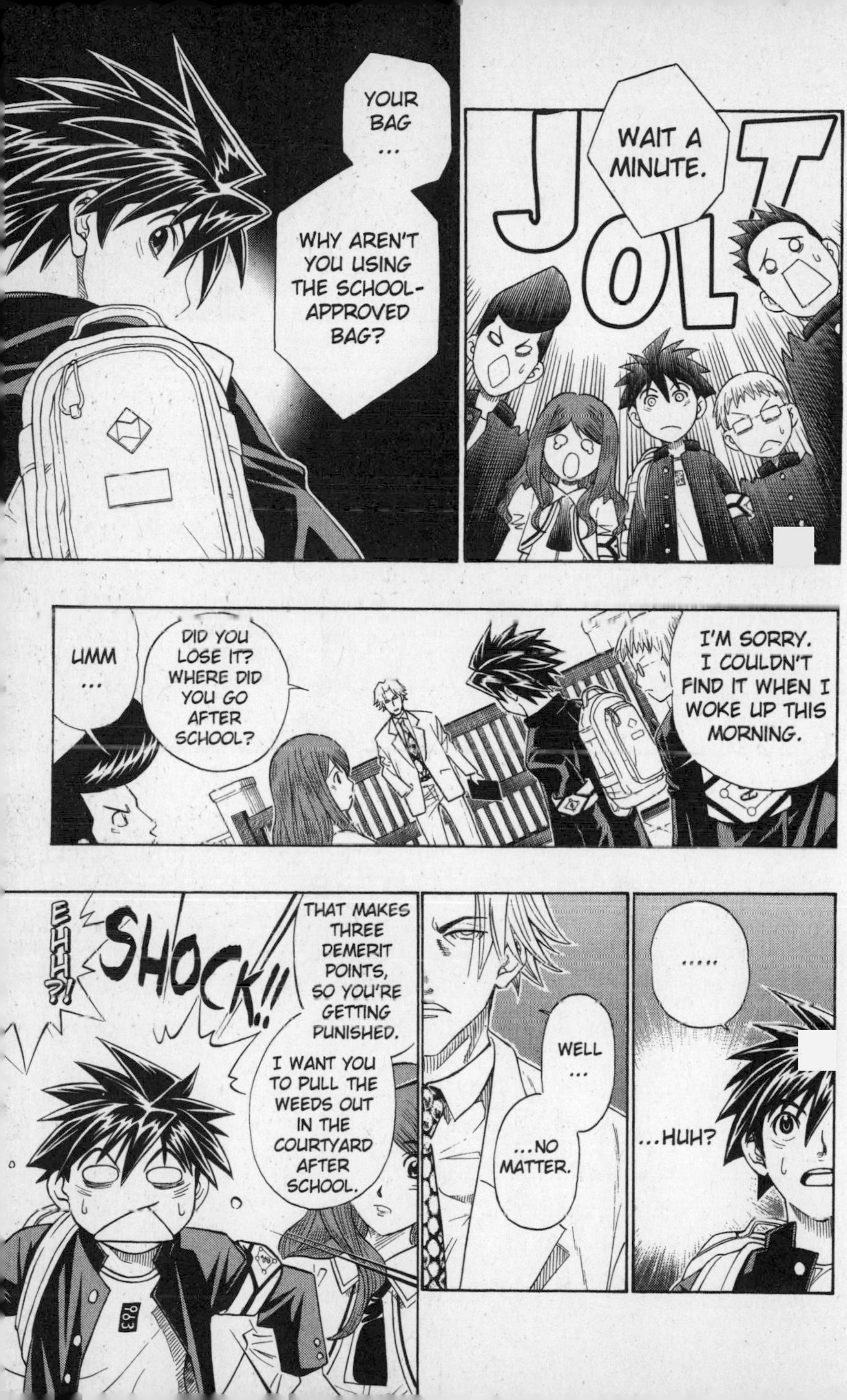
JOLT
WAIT A MINUTE.
YOUR BAG ...
WHY AREN'T YOU USING THE SCHOOL-APPROVED BAG?
I'M SORRY. I COULDN'T FIND IT WHEN I WOKE UP THIS MORNING.
DID YOU LOSE IT? WHERE DID YOU GO AFTER SCHOOL?
UMM ...
.....
...HUH?
WELL ...
...NO MATTER.
THAT MAKES THREE DEMERIT POINTS, SO YOU'RE GETTING PUNISHED.
I WANT YOU TO PULL THE WEEDS OUT IN THE COURTYARD AFTER SCHOOL.
SHOCK!!
EHHH?!

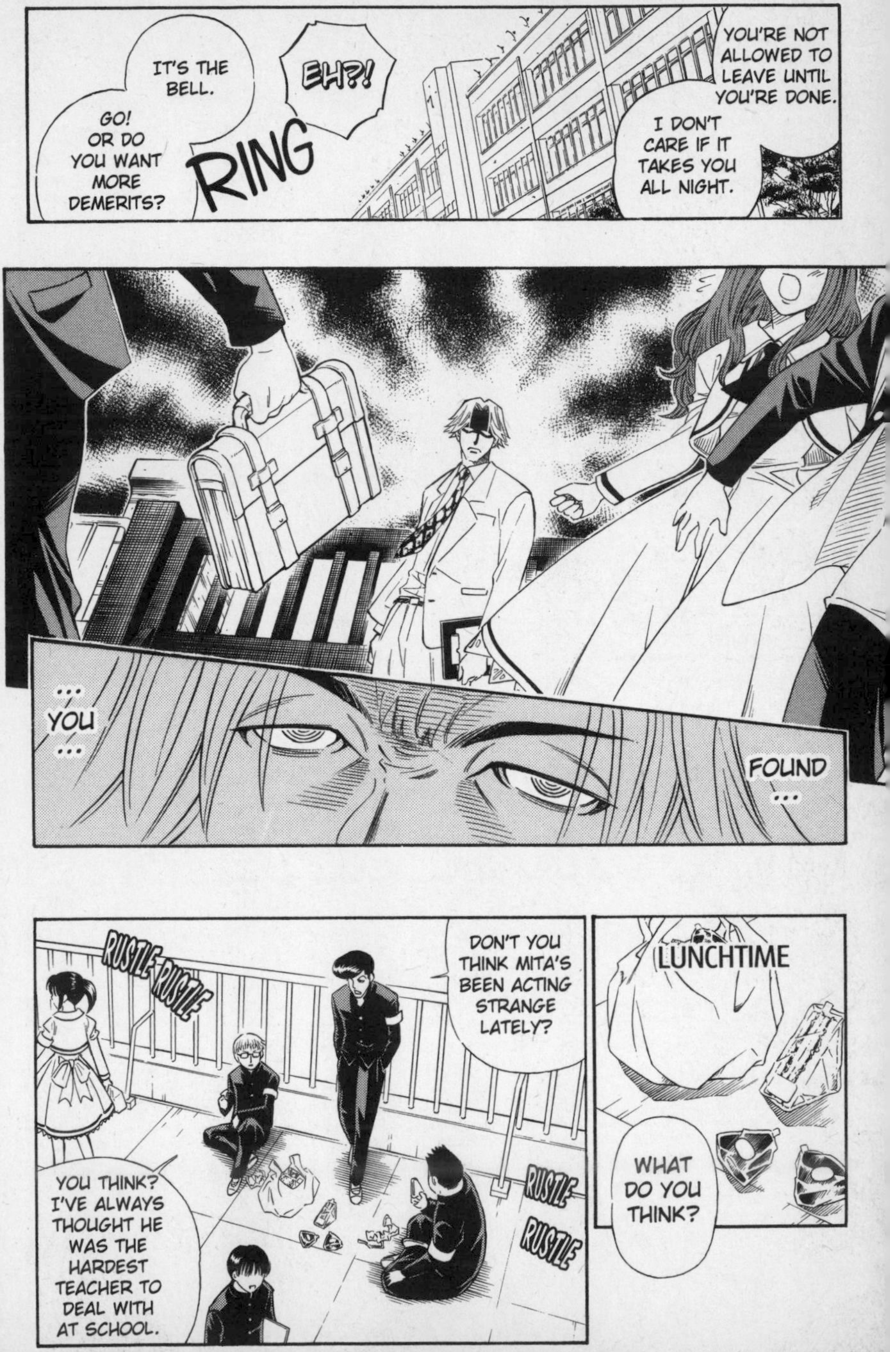
YOU'RE NOT ALLOWED TO LEAVE UNTIL YOU'RE DONE.
I DON'T CARE IF IT TAKES YOU ALL NIGHT.
EH?!
IT'S THE BELL.
RING
GO! OR DO YOU WANT MORE DEMERITS?
FOUND ...
... YOU ...
LUNCHTIME
WHAT DO YOU THINK?
DON'T YOU THINK MITA'S BEEN ACTING STRANGE LATELY?
RUSTLE RUSTLE
YOU THINK? I'VE ALWAYS THOUGHT HE WAS THE HARDEST TEACHER TO DEAL WITH AT SCHOOL.
RUSTLE
RUSTLE

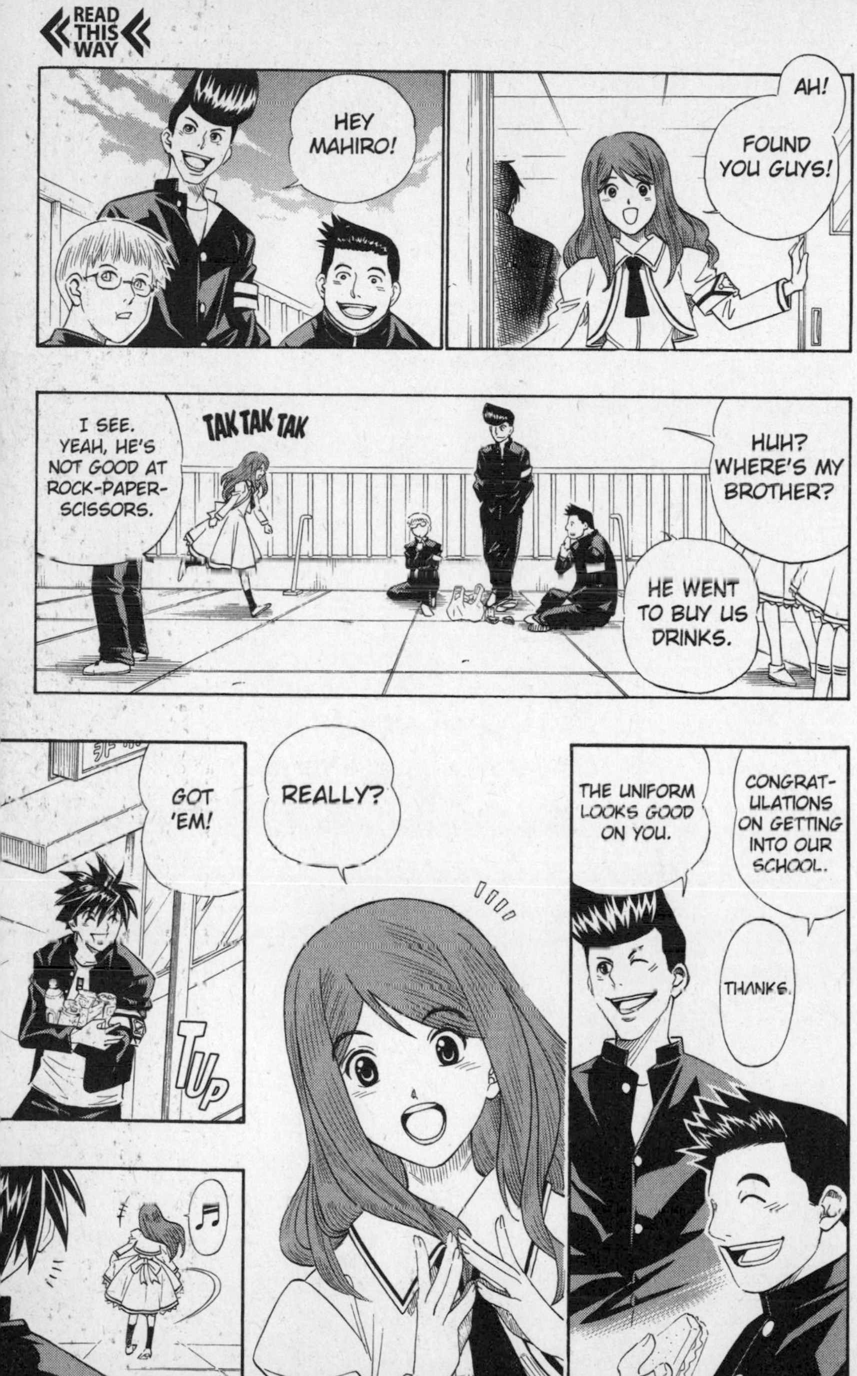
READ THIS WAY
AH!
FOUND YOU GUYS!
HEY MAHIRO!
HUH? WHERE'S MY BROTHER?
HE WENT TO BUY US DRINKS.
TAK TAK TAK
I SEE. YEAH, HE'S NOT GOOD AT ROCK-PAPER-SCISSORS.
CONGRAT-ULATIONS ON GETTING INTO OUR SCHOOL.
THE UNIFORM LOOKS GOOD ON YOU.
THANKS.
REALLY?
GOT 'EM!
TUP
♪

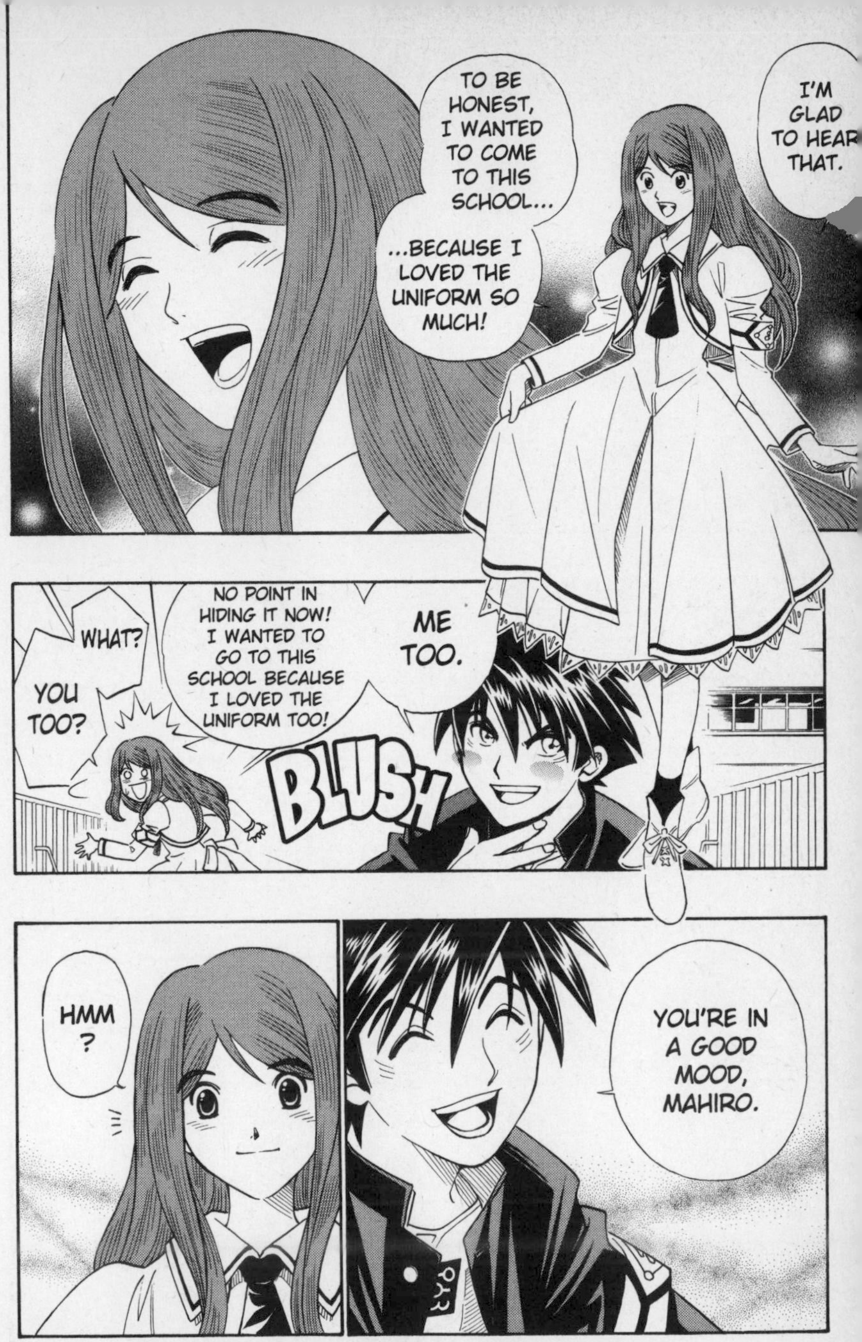
I'M GLAD TO HEAR THAT.
TO BE HONEST, I WANTED TO COME TO THIS SCHOOL...
...BECAUSE I LOVED THE UNIFORM SO MUCH!
ME TOO.
WHAT?
YOU TOO?
NO POINT IN HIDING IT NOW! I WANTED TO GO TO THIS SCHOOL BECAUSE I LOVED THE UNIFORM TOO!
BLUSH
YOU'RE IN A GOOD MOOD, MAHIRO.
HMM?

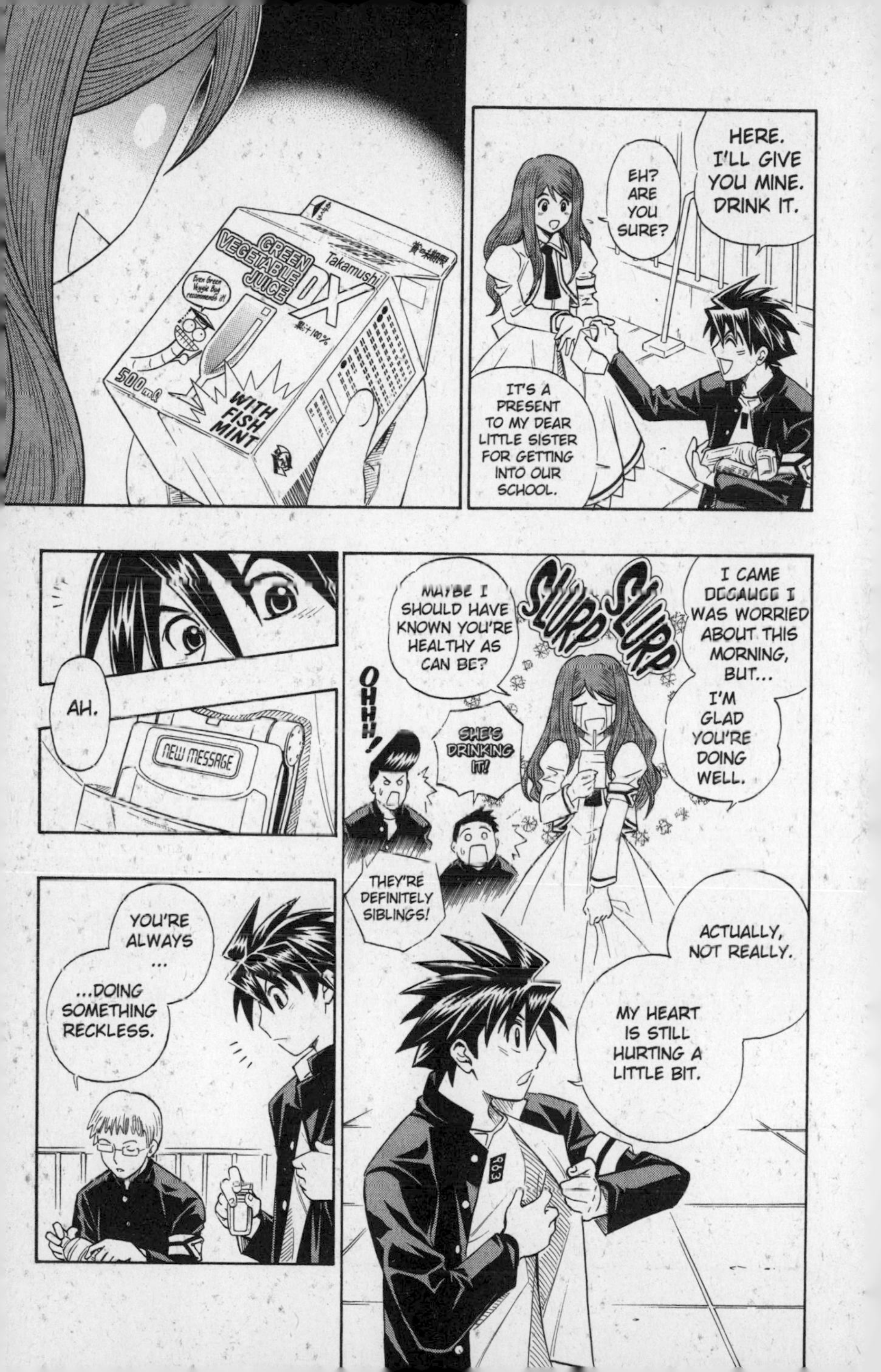
HERE. I'LL GIVE YOU MINE. DRINK IT.
EH? ARE YOU SURE?
IT'S A PRESENT TO MY DEAR LITTLE SISTER FOR GETTING INTO OUR SCHOOL.
GREEN VEGETABLE JUICE
Takamushi
DX
Even Green Veggie Bug recommends it!
500ml
WITH FISH MINT
I CAME BECAUSE I WAS WORRIED ABOUT THIS MORNING, BUT...
I'M GLAD YOU'RE DOING WELL.
SLURP SLURP
MAYBE I SHOULD HAVE KNOWN YOU'RE HEALTHY AS CAN BE?
OHHH!
SHE'S DRINKING IT!
THEY'RE DEFINITELY SIBLINGS!
ACTUALLY, NOT REALLY.
MY HEART IS STILL HURTING A LITTLE BIT.
AH.
NEW MESSAGE
YOU'RE ALWAYS ...
...DOING SOMETHING RECKLESS.

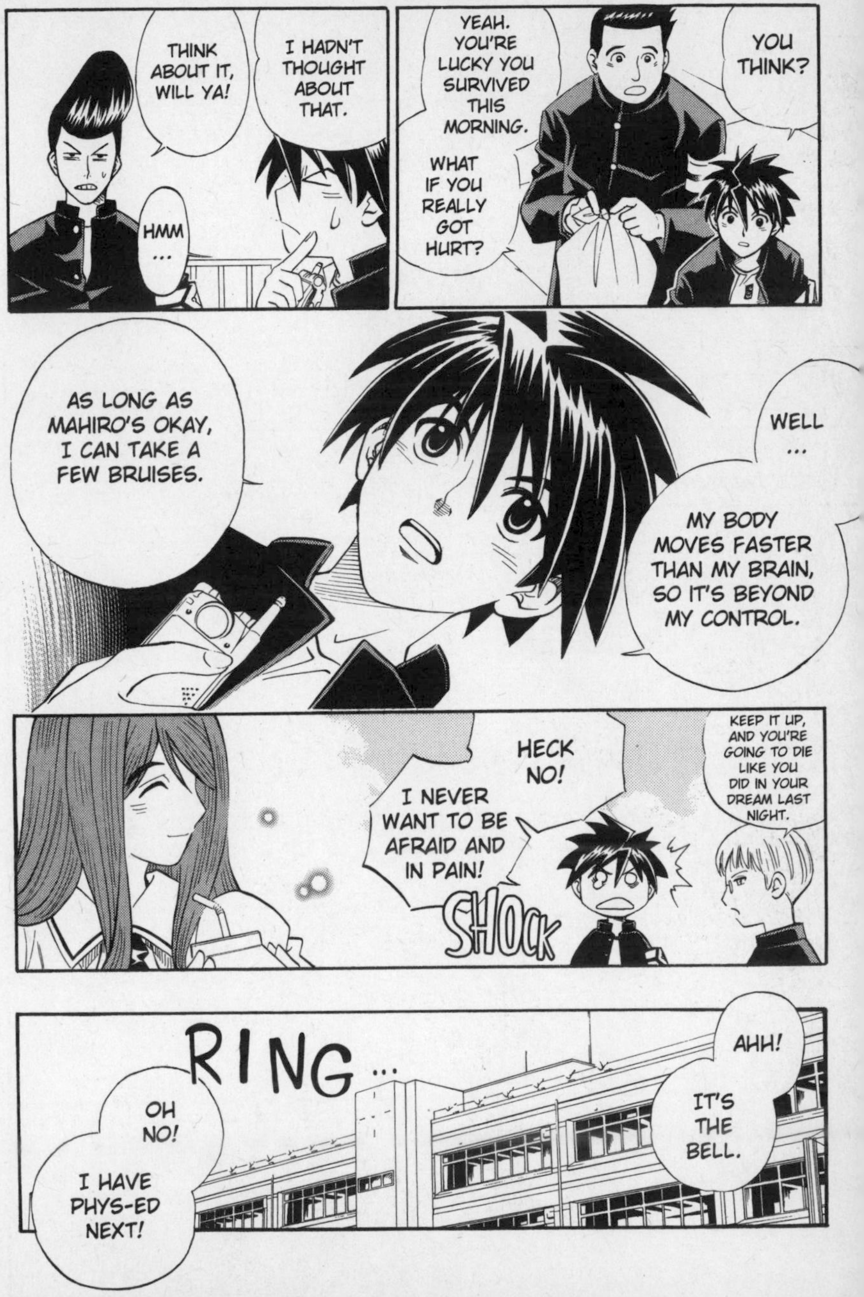
YOU THINK?
YEAH. YOU'RE LUCKY YOU SURVIVED THIS MORNING.
WHAT IF YOU REALLY GOT HURT?
I HADN'T THOUGHT ABOUT THAT.
THINK ABOUT IT, WILL YA!
HMM ...
WELL ...
MY BODY MOVES FASTER THAN MY BRAIN, SO IT'S BEYOND MY CONTROL.
AS LONG AS MAHIRO'S OKAY, I CAN TAKE A FEW BRUISES.
KEEP IT UP, AND YOU'RE GOING TO DIE LIKE YOU DID IN YOUR DREAM LAST NIGHT.
HECK NO!
I NEVER WANT TO BE AFRAID AND IN PAIN!
SHOCK
AHH!
IT'S THE BELL.
RING ...
OH NO!
I HAVE PHYS-ED NEXT!

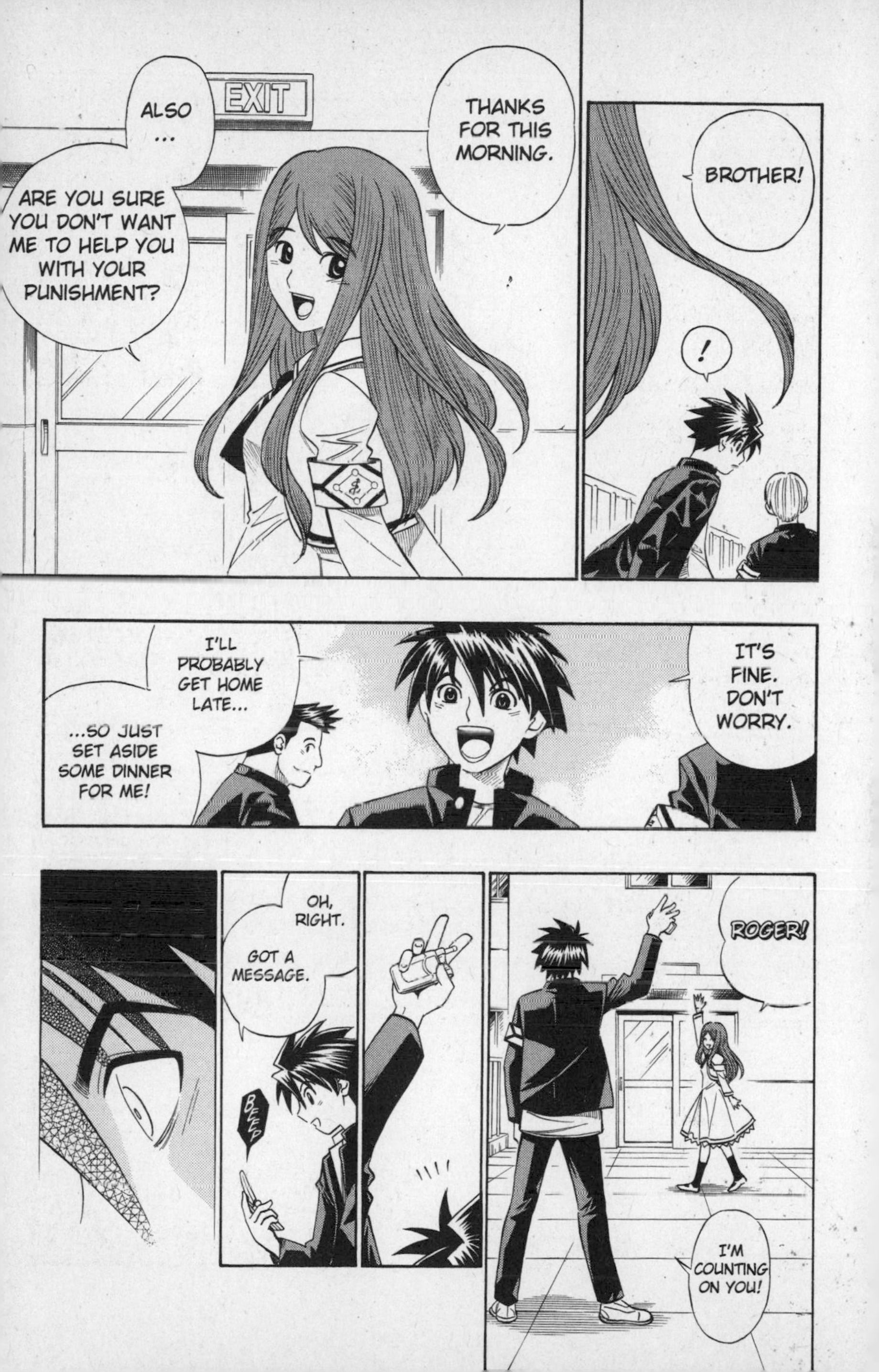
BROTHER!
!
THANKS FOR THIS MORNING.
EXIT
ALSO ...
ARE YOU SURE YOU DON'T WANT ME TO HELP YOU WITH YOUR PUNISHMENT?
IT'S FINE. DON'T WORRY.
I'LL PROBABLY GET HOME LATE...
...SO JUST SET ASIDE SOME DINNER FOR ME!
ROGER!
I'M COUNTING ON YOU!
OH, RIGHT.
GOT A MESSAGE.
BEEP

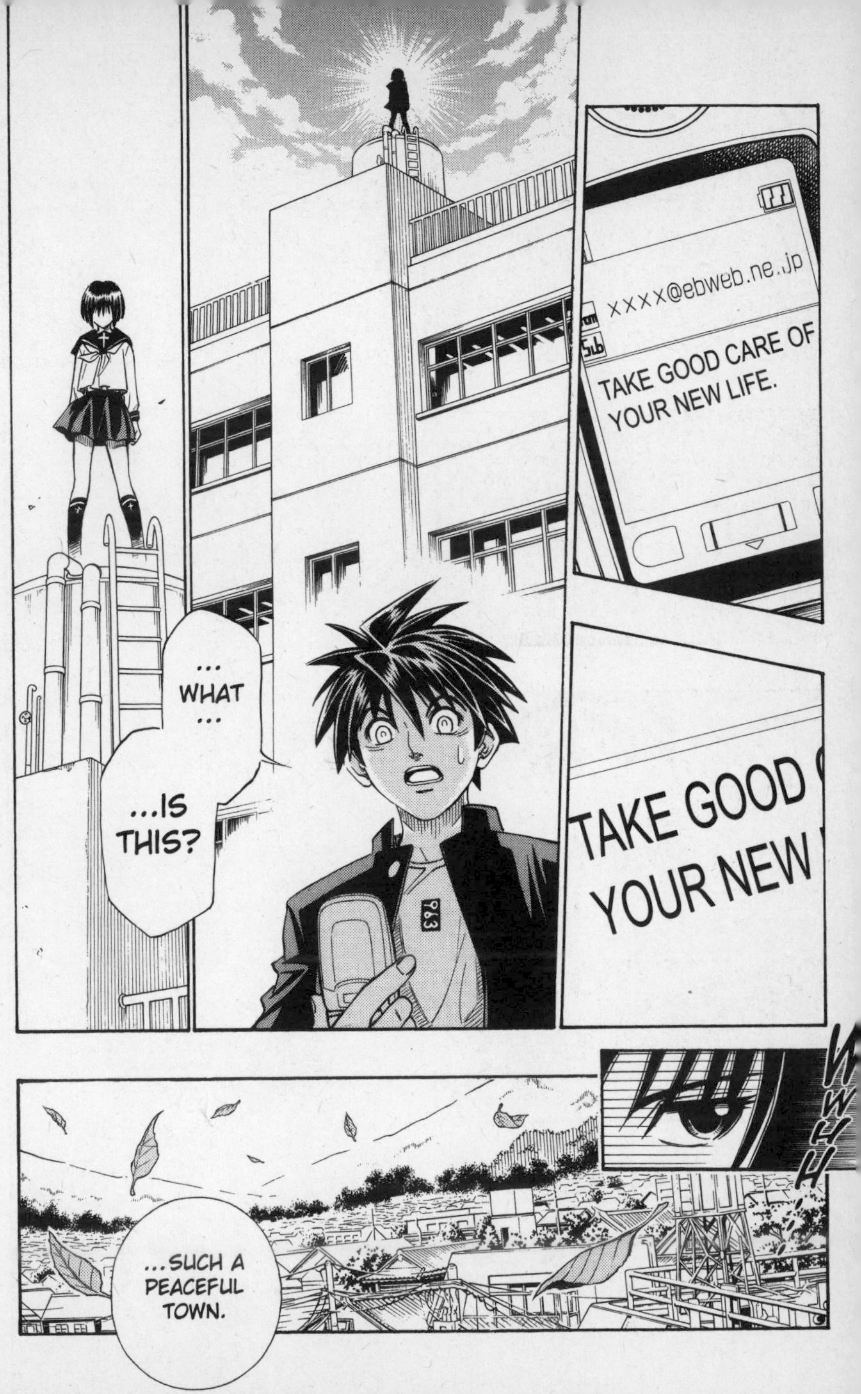
XXXX@ebweb.ne.jp
TAKE GOOD CARE OF YOUR NEW LIFE.
TAKE GOOD
YOUR NEW
... WHAT ...
...IS THIS?
...SUCH A PEACEFUL TOWN.

READ THIS WAY

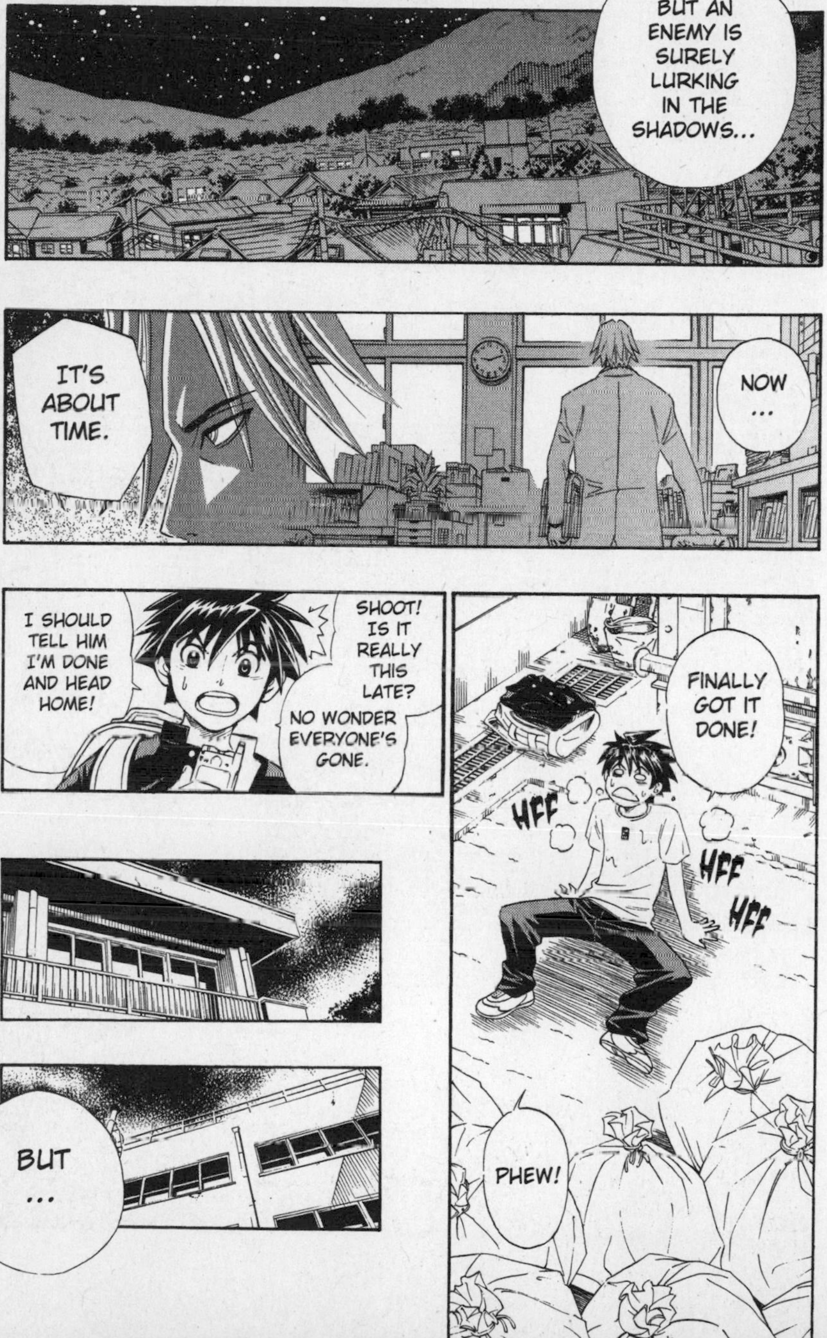
BUT AN ENEMY IS SURELY LURKING IN THE SHADOWS...
NOW ...
IT'S ABOUT TIME.
FINALLY GOT IT DONE!
HFF
HFF
HFF
PHEW!
SHOOT! IS IT REALLY THIS LATE?
NO WONDER EVERYONE'S GONE.
I SHOULD TELL HIM I'M DONE AND HEAD HOME!
BUT ...

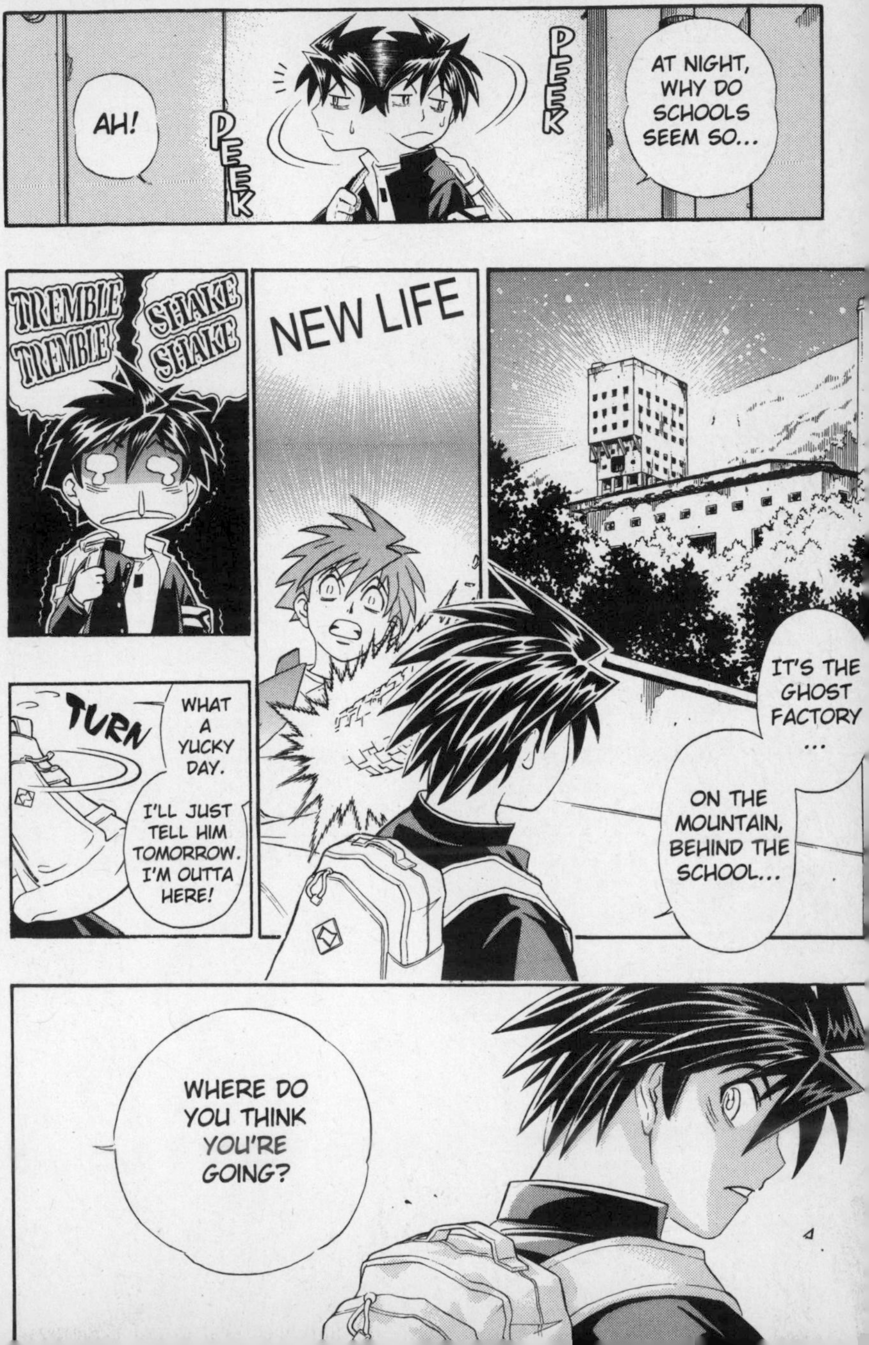
AT NIGHT, WHY DO SCHOOLS SEEM SO...
PEEK
PEEK
AH!
IT'S THE GHOST FACTORY ...
ON THE MOUNTAIN, BEHIND THE SCHOOL...
NEW LIFE
SHAKE SHAKE
TREMBLE TREMBLE
WHAT A YUCKY DAY.
I'LL JUST TELL HIM TOMORROW. I'M OUTTA HERE!
TURN
WHERE DO YOU THINK YOU'RE GOING?

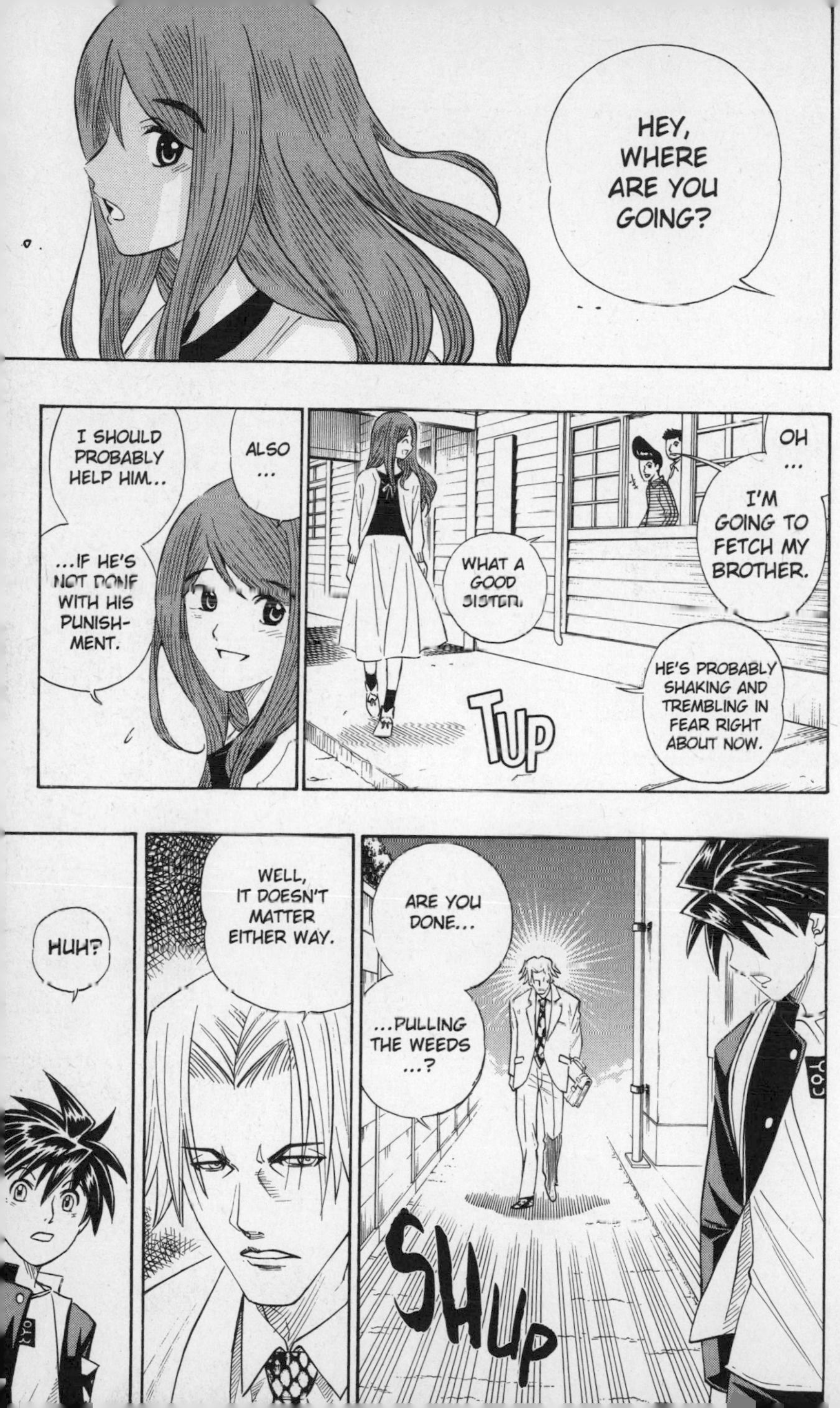
HEY, WHERE ARE YOU GOING?
OH ... I'M GOING TO FETCH MY BROTHER.
WHAT A GOOD SISTER.
HE'S PROBABLY SHAKING AND TREMBLING IN FEAR RIGHT ABOUT NOW.
TUP
ALSO ...
I SHOULD PROBABLY HELP HIM...
...IF HE'S NOT DONE WITH HIS PUNISHMENT.
ARE YOU DONE...
...PULLING THE WEEDS ...?
SHUP
WELL, IT DOESN'T MATTER EITHER WAY.
HUH?

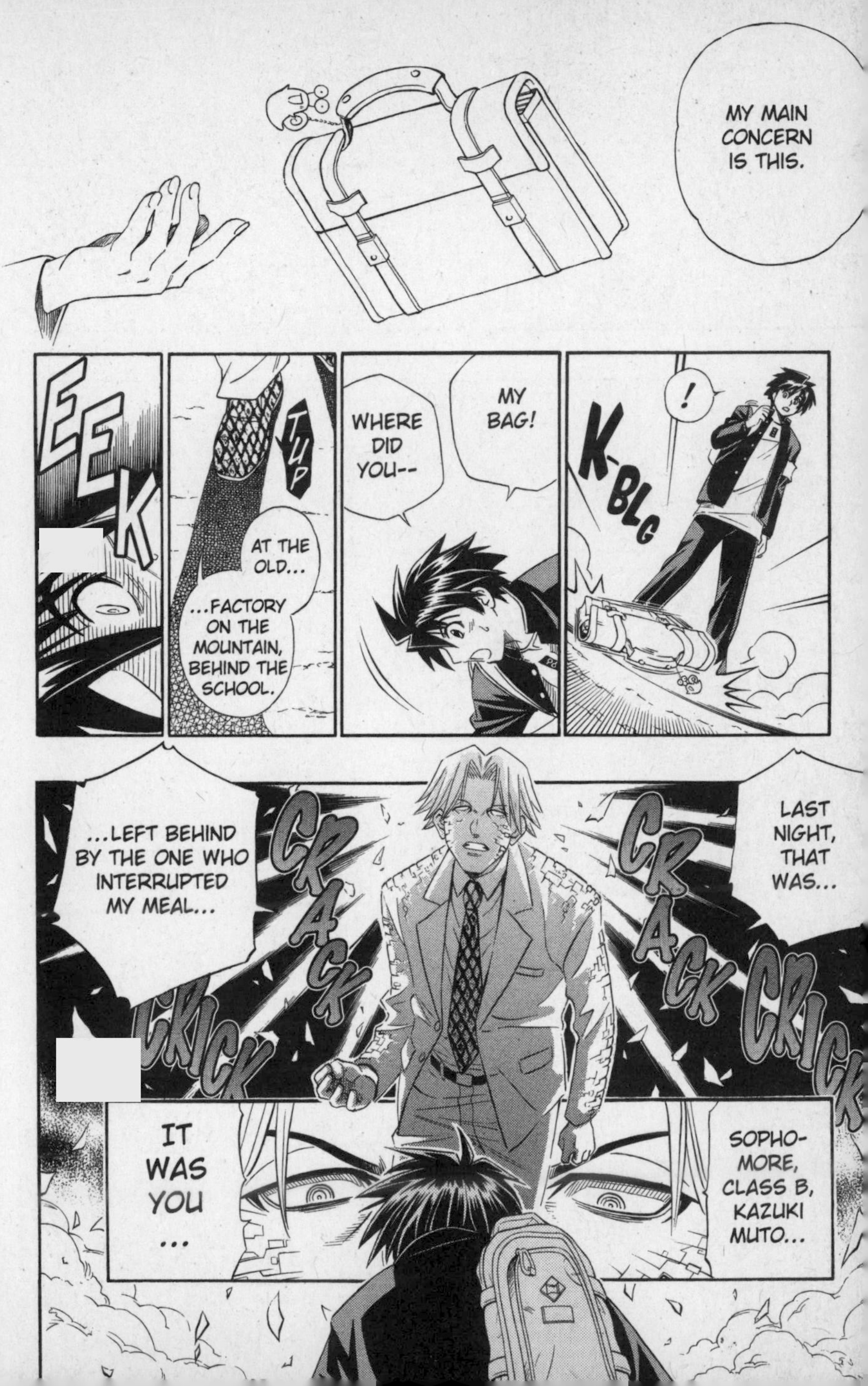
MY MAIN CONCERN IS THIS.
!
K-BLG
MY BAG!
WHERE DID YOU--
TUP
AT THE OLD...
...FACTORY ON THE MOUNTAIN, BEHIND THE SCHOOL.
EEK
LAST NIGHT, THAT WAS...
...LEFT BEHIND BY THE ONE WHO INTERRUPTED MY MEAL...
CRACK
CRACK
CRICK
CRICK
SOPHOMORE, CLASS B, KAZUKI MUTO...
IT WAS YOU ...

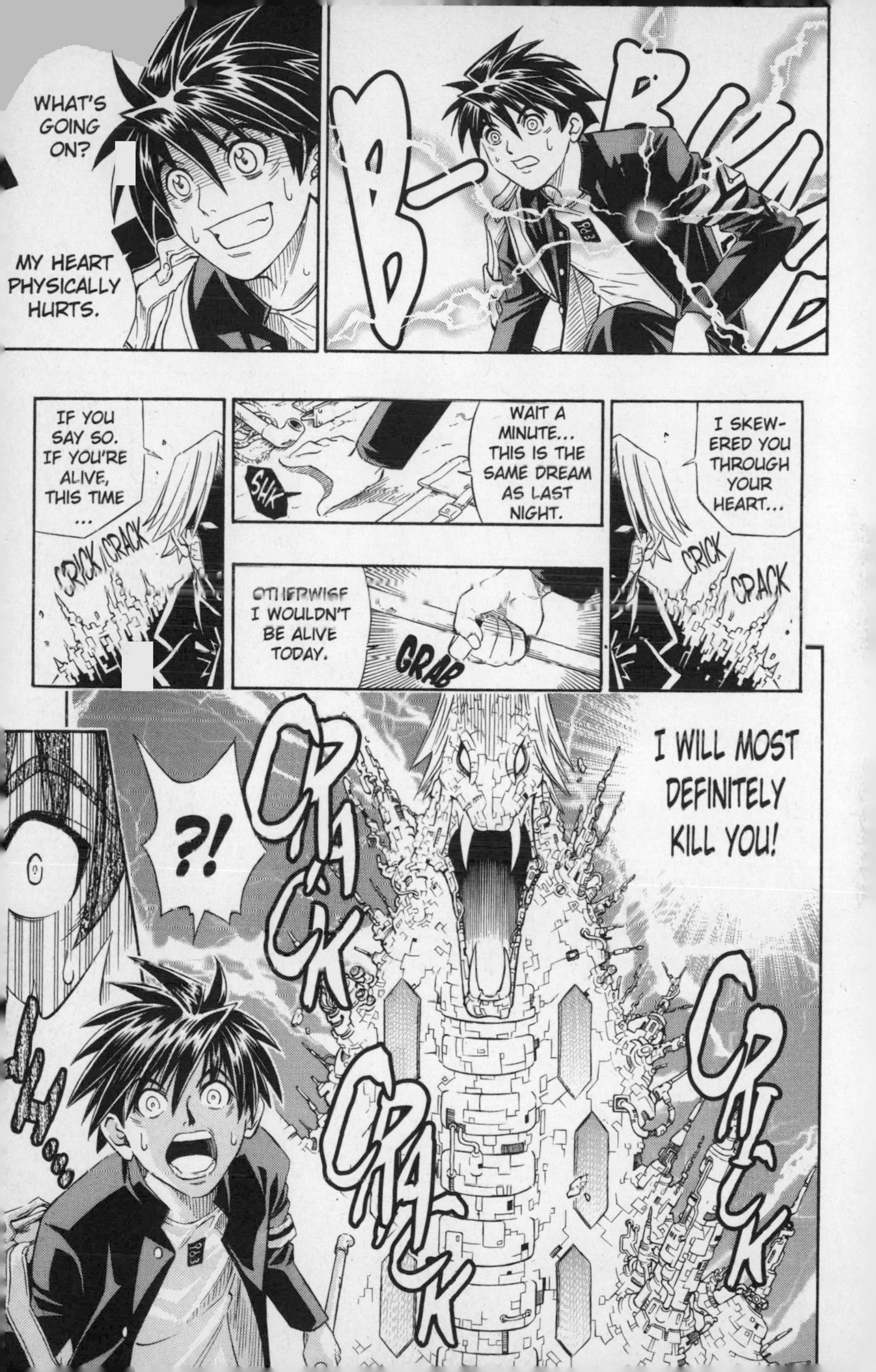
WHAT'S GOING ON?
MY HEART PHYSICALLY HURTS.
I SKEW-ERED YOU THROUGH YOUR HEART...
CRICK
CRACK
WAIT A MINUTE... THIS IS THE SAME DREAM AS LAST NIGHT.
SHK
OTHERWISE I WOULDN'T BE ALIVE TODAY.
GRAB
IF YOU SAY SO. IF YOU'RE ALIVE, THIS TIME ...
CRICK CRACK
I WILL MOST DEFINITELY KILL YOU!
CRACK
?!
CRACK

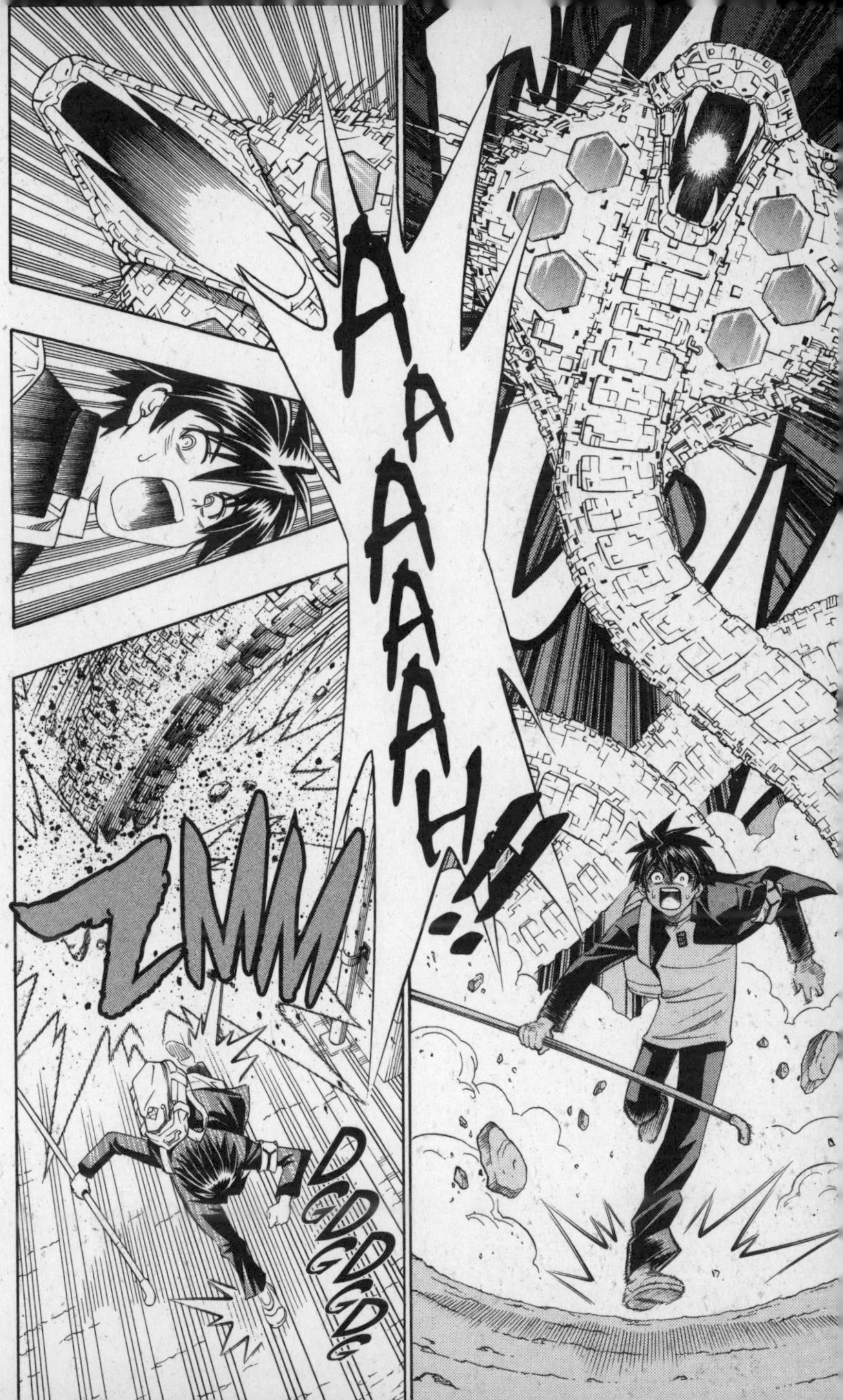
AAAAAH!!
ZMMM
DGDGDG

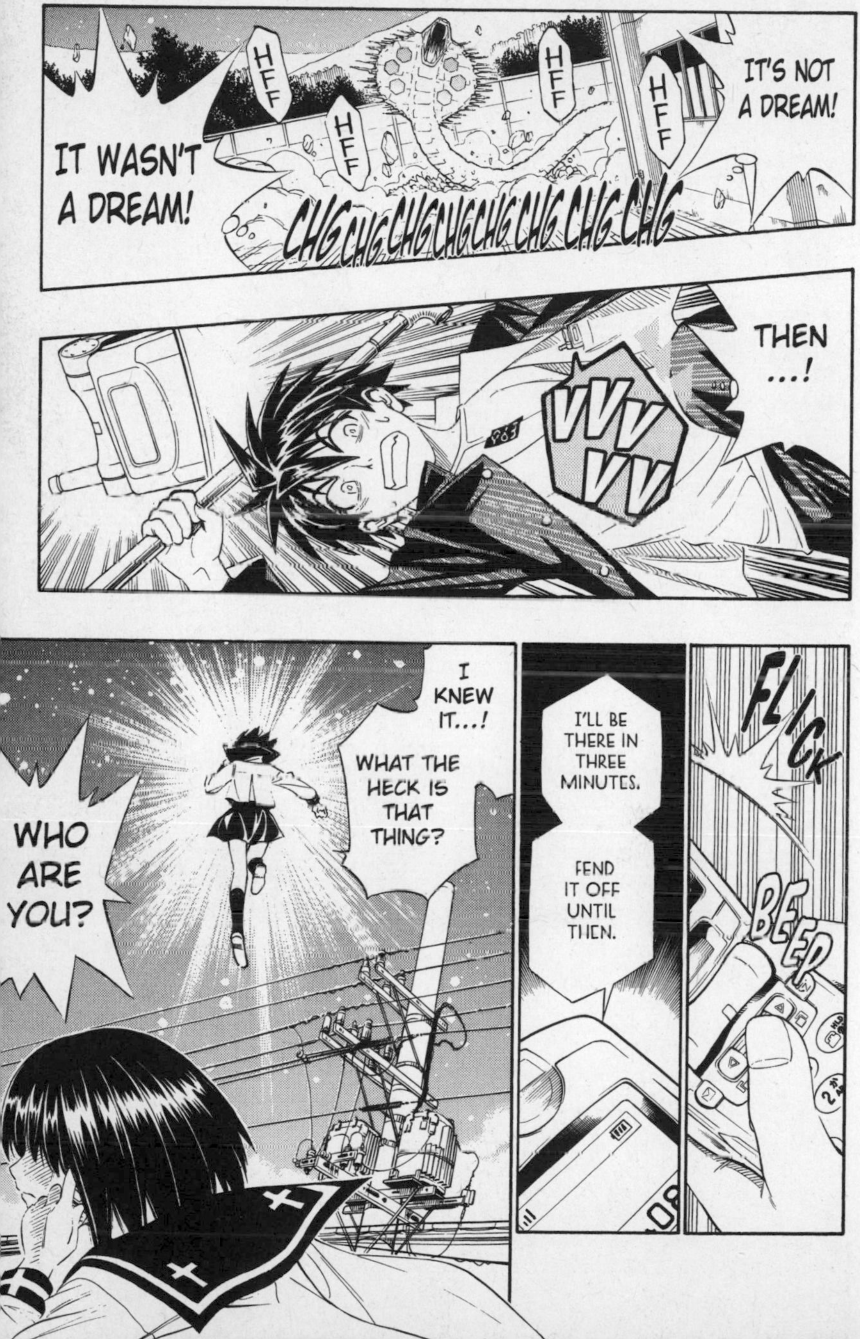
IT'S NOT A DREAM!
HFF
HFF
HFF
HFF
CHG CHG CHG CHG CHG CHG CHG CHG
IT WASN'T A DREAM!
THEN ...!
VVV VV
FLICK
BEEP
I'LL BE THERE IN THREE MINUTES.
FEND IT OFF UNTIL THEN.
I KNEW IT...!
WHAT THE HECK IS THAT THING?
WHO ARE YOU?

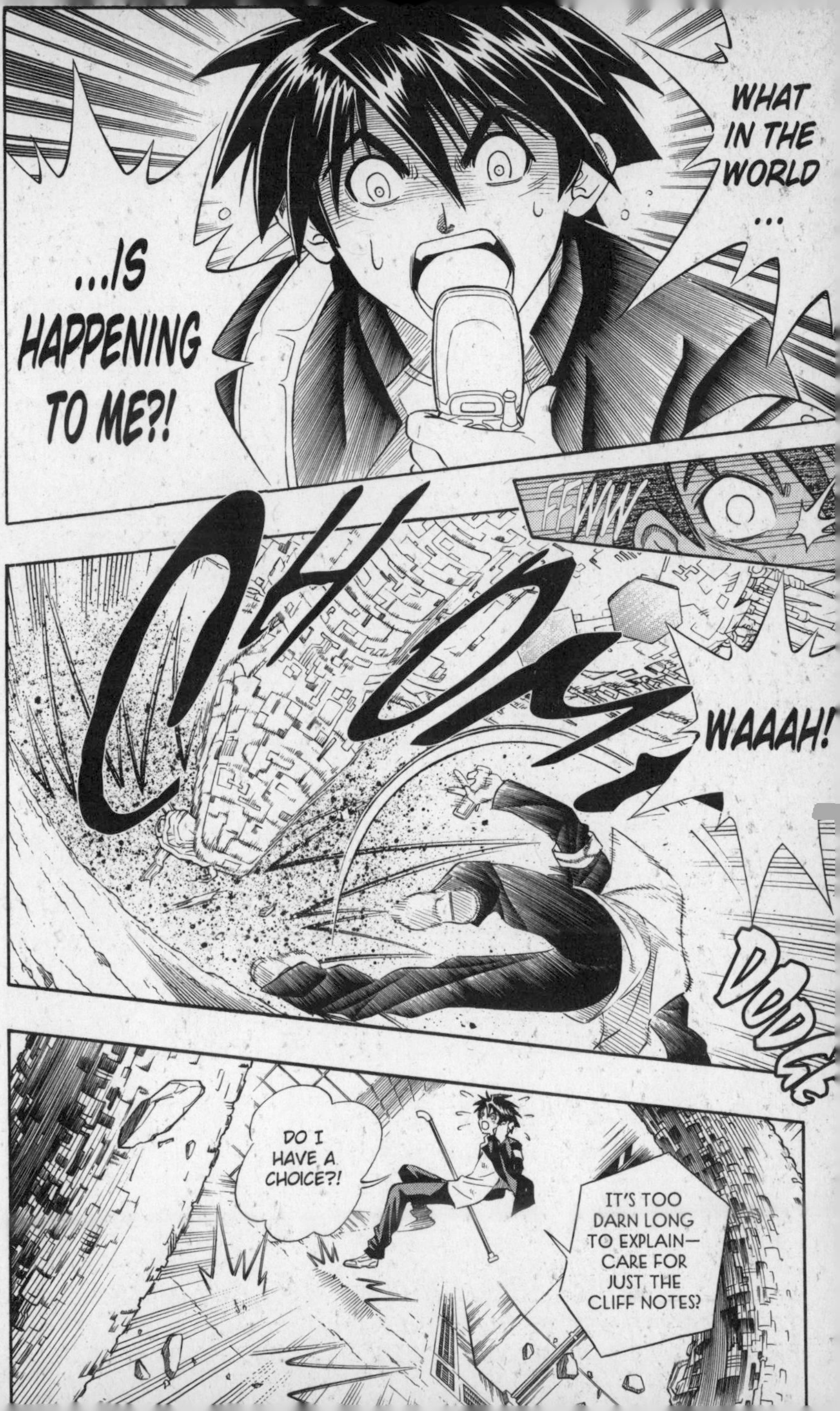
WHAT IN THE WORLD...
...IS HAPPENING TO ME?!
FFWW
WAAAH!
DODGE
IT'S TOO DARN LONG TO EXPLAIN—CARE FOR JUST THE CLIFF NOTES?
DO I HAVE A CHOICE?!

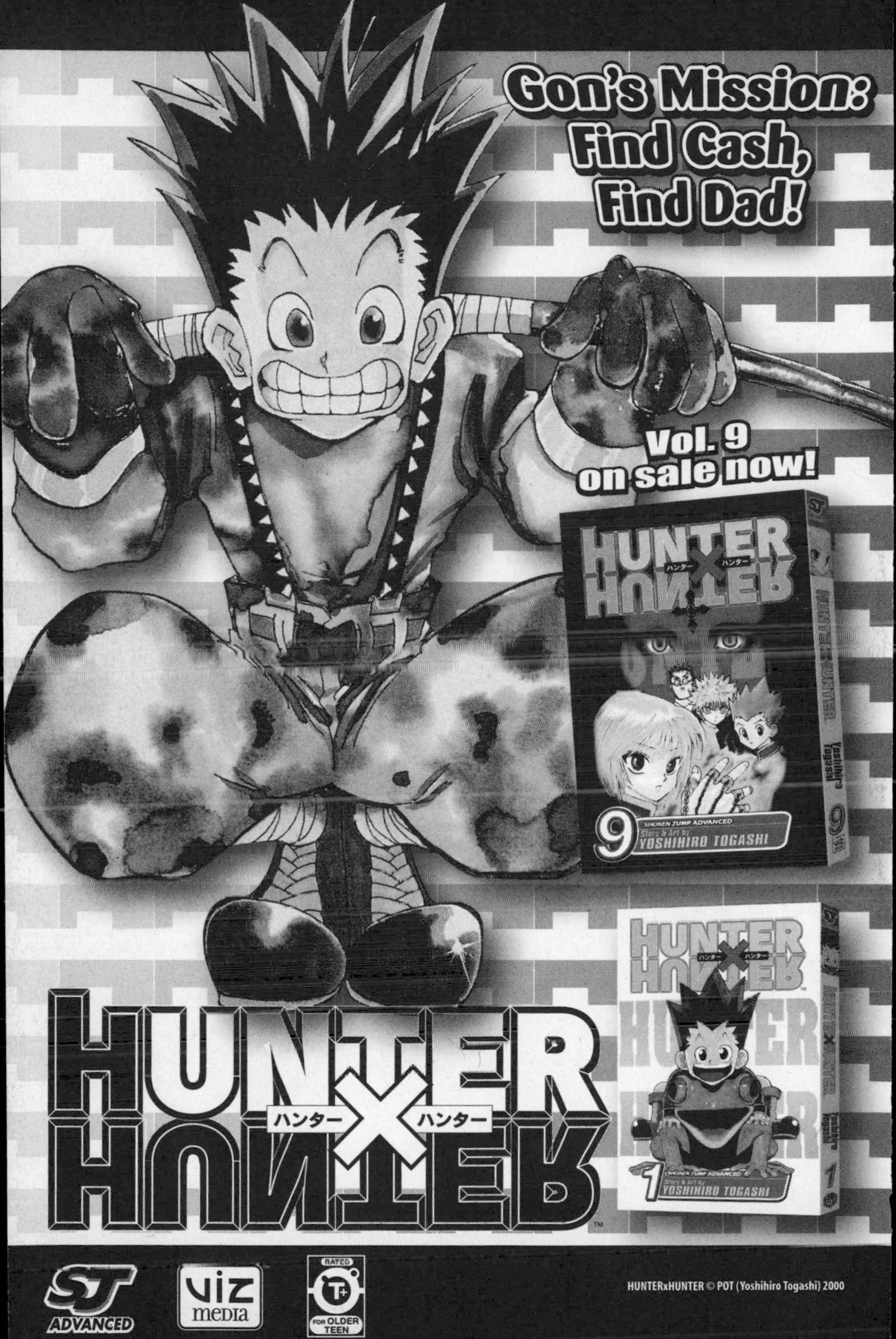

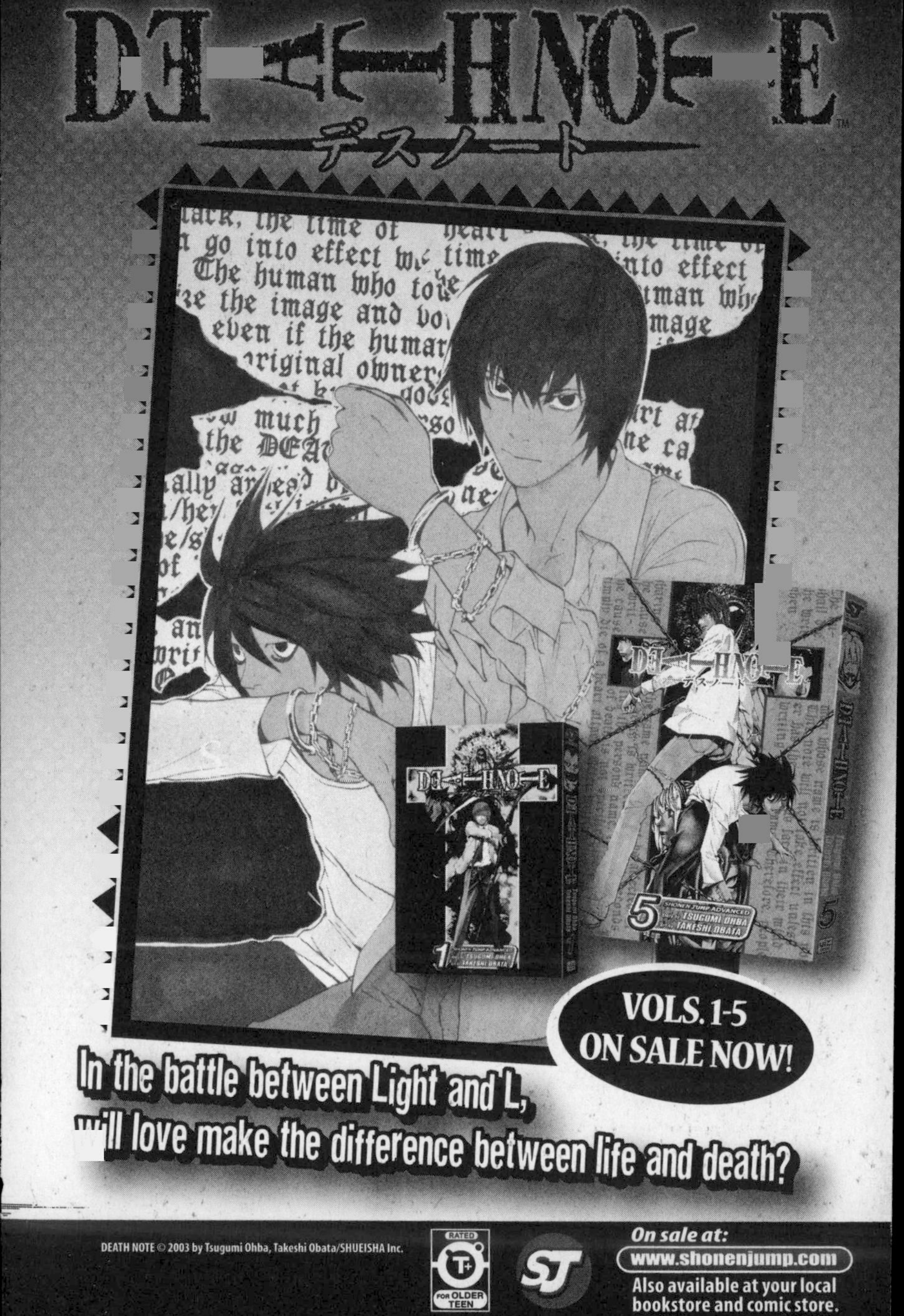

DEATH NOTE™
デスノート
VOLS. 1-5 ON SALE NOW!
In the battle between Light and L,
will love make the difference between life and death?
DEATH NOTE © 2003 by Tsugumi Ohba, Takeshi Obata/SHUEISHA Inc.
RATED T+ FOR OLDER TEEN
SJ
On sale at:
www.shonenjump.com
Also available at your local bookstore and comic store.

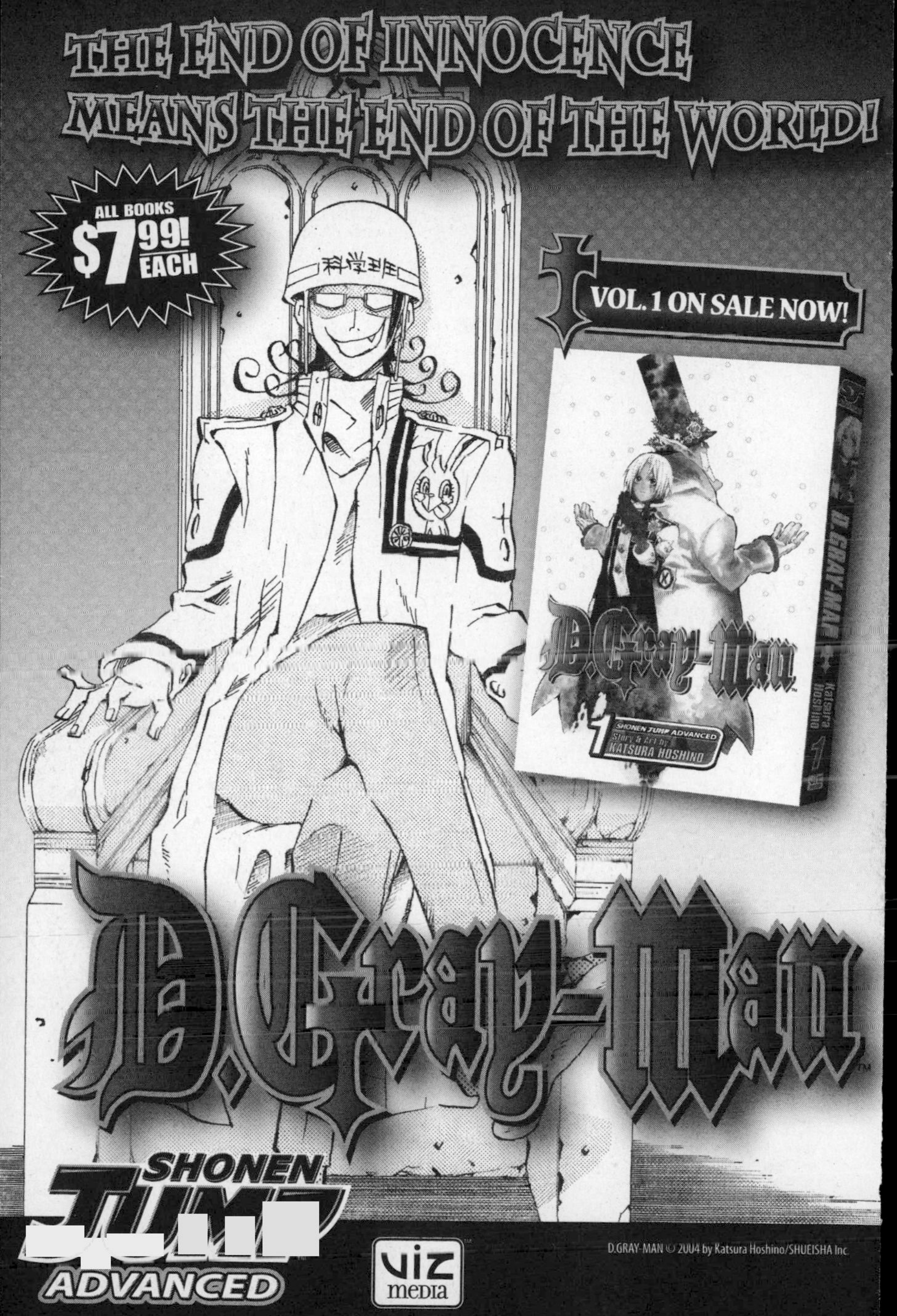
THE END OF INNOCENCE
MEANS THE END OF THE WORLD!
ALL BOOKS
$7.99! EACH
VOL. 1 ON SALE NOW!
D.Gray-man
SHONEN JUMP ADVANCED
Story & Art by
KATSURA HOSHINO
D.GRAY-MAN
Katsura Hoshino
D.Gray-man™
SHONEN
ADVANCED
viz media
D.GRAY-MAN © 2004 by Katsura Hoshino/SHUEISHA Inc.

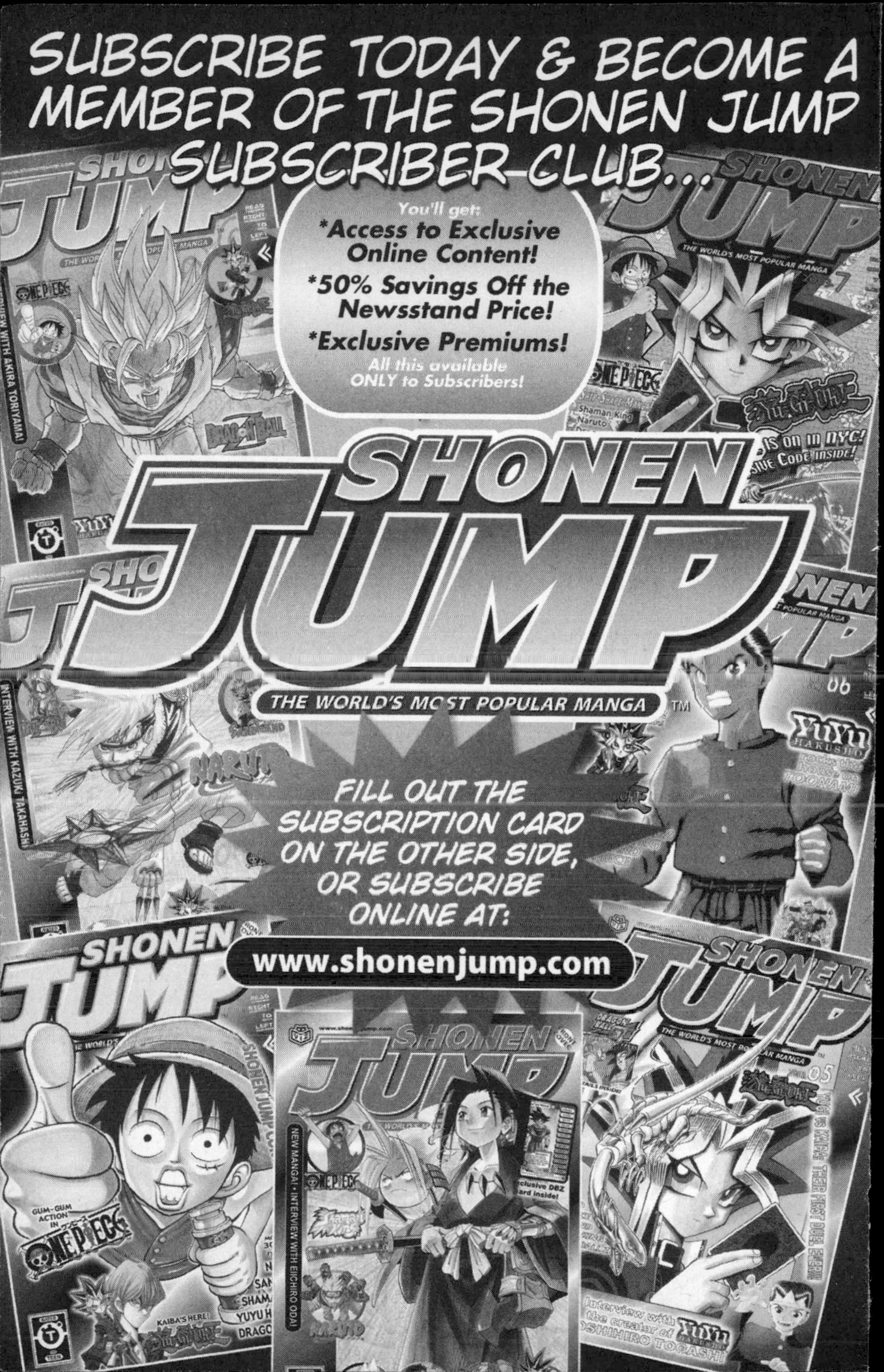
SUBSCRIBE TODAY & BECOME A MEMBER OF THE SHONEN JUMP SUBSCRIBER CLUB...
You'll get:
*Access to Exclusive Online Content!
*50% Savings Off the Newsstand Price!
*Exclusive Premiums!
All this available ONLY to Subscribers!
SHONEN JUMP
THE WORLD'S MOST POPULAR MANGA™
FILL OUT THE SUBSCRIPTION CARD ON THE OTHER SIDE, OR SUBSCRIBE ONLINE AT:
www.shonenjump.com

Save 50% off the newsstand price!

THE WORLD'S MOST POPULAR MANGA

SUBSCRIBE TODAY and SAVE 50% OFF the cover price PLUS enjoy all the benefits of the SHONEN JUMP SUBSCRIBER CLUB, exclusive online content & special gifts ONLY AVAILABLE to SUBSCRIBERS!

☑ **YES!** Please enter my 1 year subscription (12 issues) to *SHONEN JUMP* at the INCREDIBLY LOW SUBSCRIPTION RATE of $29.95 and sign me up for the SHONEN JUMP Subscriber Club!

Only $29⁹⁵!

NAME

ADDRESS

CITY   STATE   ZIP

E-MAIL ADDRESS

☐ MY CHECK IS ENCLOSED   ☐ BILL ME LATER

CREDIT CARD: ☐ VISA   ☐ MASTERCARD

ACCOUNT #   EXP. DATE

SIGNATURE

CLIP AND MAIL TO ➤ SHONEN JUMP
Subscriptions Service Dept.
P.O. Box 515
Mount Morris, IL 61054-0515

Make checks payable to: **SHONEN JUMP.**
Canada add US $12. No foreign orders. Allow 6-8 weeks for delivery.

P6SJGN   YU-GI-OH! © 1996 by Kazuki Takahashi / SHUEISHA Inc.